Government and Rural Development in East Africa:
essays on political penetration

INSTITUTE OF SOCIAL STUDIES

SERIES ON THE DEVELOPMENT
OF SOCIETIES

VOLUME II

INTERNATIONAAL INSTITUUT
VOOR SOCIALE STUDIËN - 'S GRAVENHAGE

GOVERNMENT AND RURAL DEVELOPMENT IN EAST AFRICA

Essays on Political Penetration

Edited by

L. CLIFFE
J.S. COLEMAN
M.R. DOORNBOS

MARTINUS NIJHOFF / THE HAGUE / 1977

ISBN 90 247 1884 8 mb

PRINTED IN BELGIUM

CONTRIBUTORS

CHAMBERS, ROBERT
Fellow of the Institute of Development Studies at the University of Sussex, specializing in rural development. Experience includes the management of rural development projects, lecturing in public administration, rural research in East Africa, Sri Lanka and India, and rural consultancies in Ghana, Kenya, Burundi and Botswana. Until 1977 was Evaluation Officer with the UN High Commissioner for Refugees.

CLIFFE, LIONEL
Worked for ten years in East Africa; at one time as Research Fellow at Makerere University, then at Dar es Salaam University, finishing up as Director of Development Studies. Until 1976 Reader in Politics at the University of Zambia. At present lectures on problems of underdevelopment at the University of Durham.

COLEMAN, JAMES
Formerly Professor of Political Science at the University of California, Los Angeles, and currently with the Education for Development Programme of the Rockefeller Foundation at the National University of Zaire.

DOORNBOS, MARTIN
Research Fellow, Makerere Institute of Social Sciences 1965-67; now teaches political science at the Institute of Social Studies, The Hague and at Leiden University.

HARRIS, BELLE
Tutor in politics at Kivukoni College, Dar es Salaam 1964-68; lecturer on Local Government at the Institute of Administration, Ahmadu Bello University 1970-73, on secondment from the Institute of Local Government Studies, University of Birmingham 1973-75. Currently Tutor in Public Administration at the North East London Polytechnic.

HYDEN, GORAN
Has spent the last twelve years in East Africa teaching at the universities in Kampala, Nairobi and most recently in Dar es Salaam as Professor of Political Science. Has done research on rural development and administration, and management of public institutions in East Africa.

HELLEINER, GERALD
Has been Assistant Professor, Yale University; Research Fellow, Nigerian Institute of Social & Economic Research; Director, Economic Research Bureau, Dar es Salaam; Visiting Fellow, Institute of Development Studies, Sussex; currently Professor, Department of Political Economy, University of Toronto.

LAMB, GEOFF
Studied at the Universities of Witwatersrand and Sussex; has done research in East Africa, the Caribbean, and on British administration. Currently Fellow and Deputy Director of the Institute of Development Studies, University of Sussex.

LEONARD, DAVID
Has done teaching and research at the University of Nairobi 1969-73, and at the University of Dar es Salaam 1974-76. Currently Assistant Professor of Political Science at the University of California, Berkeley.

MAFEJE, ARCHIE
Former Head of the Department of Sociology, Dar es Salaam University and Visiting Professor of Social Anthropology and Sociology of Development, Institute of Social Studies, The Hague. Did field work in Uganda in 1966-67 while working as Research Fellow at the Centre of African Studies, Cambridge.

MUTISO, GIDEON
Associate Professor, Department of Government, University of Nairobi. Studied and taught in the USA 1960-70.

RIGBY, PETER
Professor of Sociology, Makerere University 1968-74; Visiting Professor, New York University 1967-68; Foreign Visiting Fellow, Churchill College, Cambridge 1973-74; Visiting Professor, Princeton University 1974. Currently Professor of Sociology, University of Dar es Salaam.

SHARMAN, ANNE
Associate of the Makerere Institute of Social Research 1965-67. Since 1969 lecturer in Sociology at the University of East Anglia.

SWARTZ, MARC
Professor of Anthropology at the University of California, San Diego. Worked among the Bena in Western Tanzania in 1962-63 and in 1967; is at present completing a study among the Swahili of Mombasa.

THODEN VAN VELZEN, H.U.E.
Professor of Cultural Anthropology at the University of Utrecht. Research Fellow of the Afrika-Studiecentrum, University of Leiden 1966-71.

VINCENT, JOAN
Professor of Anthropology at Barnard College, Columbia University since 1975. Visiting lecturer in Political Science, Makerere University College 1966-67; Fellow, East African Institute of Social Research 1966-67; Burgess Fellow, Columbia University 1967-68; John Simon Guggenheim Fellow 1973-74; Institute of Development Studies, University of Sussex 1976.

CONTENTS

Contributors   V

Preface   XI

I. INTRODUCTION
'PENETRATION' AND THE EAST AFRICAN CONTEXT

James Coleman, *The Concept of Political Penetration*   3

Lionel Cliffe, *'Penetration' and Rural Development in the East African
Context*   19

II. THE COLONIAL LEGACY AND THE DYNAMICS OF
POLITICAL CONTROL

Joan Vincent, *Teso in Transformation: colonial penetration in Teso
District, Eastern Uganda, and its contemporary significance*   53

Peter Rigby, *Local Participation in National Politics: Ugogo, Tanzania*   81

Archie Mafeje, *The Legitimacy of the Uganda Government in Buganda*   99

III. INSTITUTIONS AND STRATEGIES FOR RURAL DEVELOPMENT

Robert Chambers, *Creating and Expanding Organizations for Rural
Development*   119

Gerald Helleiner, *Economics, Incentives and Development Penetration*   139

Belle Harris, *Leadership and Institutions for Rural Development: a case
study of Nzega District*   151

IV. DISTRICT POLITICS AND RURAL TRANSFORMATION

Geoff Lamb, *Promoting Agrarian Change: penetration and response in Murang'a, Kenya*　171

Goran Hyden, *Political Engineering and Social Change: a case study of Bukoba District, Tanzania*　183

Ann Sharman, *Improving Nutrition in Bukedi District, Uganda*　201

V. THE DYNAMICS OF RURAL SOCIETIES

H.U.E. Thoden van Velzen, *Staff, Kulaks and Peasants: a study of a political field*　223

David Leonard, *The Social Structure of the Agricultural Extension Services in the Western Province of Kenya*　251

Marc Swartz, *Legitimacy and Coercion in Bena Politics and Development*　273

Gideon Mutiso, *A Low Status Group in Centre-Periphery Relations: Mbai Sya Eitu*　293

VI. CONCLUSION

Martin Doornbos, *Recurring Penetration Strategies in East Africa*　317

PREFACE

The gestation period of this collection has been lengthy even by academic standards. Some of our long-suffering contributors prepared their original drafts for a workshop held in Nairobi in 1967, and although they have all up-dated their contributions they are still essentially reporting on research conducted in the late 1960s. However, we feel that their various findings and analyses of the issues they respectively treat have a continuing validity in our comprehension of the problem of rural development. Other contributions reporting on more recent work have been incorporated at different times since, most of them not commissioned especially for this symposium but all adding something to our understanding of the problem.

The slow accumulation of material which makes up this final collection parallels an evolution in our own collective thinking, if indeed not that of most students of 'development' over the past decade. The progression has not been towards final clarification of the complex and changing East African realities, nor towards formulation of an accepted model for their analysis; rather, it has been marked by the questioning of the initial, somewhat simplistic assumptions with which some of us started out and a continuing debate and widening polarization of views about the significance of that process of government 'penetration' of the rural areas which is our focus, about the positive or negative value of 'development' policies in East Africa and, indeed, about the appropriate theoretical approaches to the study of 'development' in general.

When this project was first conceived in 1967 the editors were all members of a political science research unit in the Institute of Social Research at Makerere University College in Uganda. The term 'penetration' then seemed to offer a possible rubric under which to group much research, typical of the period, on which they and several others were engaged. There had been in the mid-1960s a shift in scholarly attention away from the overarching studies of national political systems to more detailed explorations of more specific fields. Many of these focussed on local politics or central-local relations, on the politics of a particular institution or of some social or economic programme, and inevitably the structures and processes involved were for the most part concerned with rural development. Many of the researchers shared a perspective that welcomed the recent achievement of independence and sympathised with the new national states and their aspirations — although in retrospect that translated perhaps too readily into support for the new national power-holders.

In these circumstances it was not surprising that the general research climate was characterized by the hope that investigations might make some 'practical' contributions to 'development' — in a socio-economic sense by indicating how official bodies could implement and replicate programmes more 'effectively'; such improvements in the 'capacity' of institutions in running their administrations or handling populations were in turn seen as contributive to a process of 'political development'.

Given such a perspective the new theoretical tools of American political science which attempted to isolate the conditions and components of this process of 'political development' were assured of a sympathetic initial reception. But while some of our colleagues used a methodology based on this functionalist approach and have continued to uphold it, others have favoured a different perspective. Indeed, the present volume benefits considerably from the fruits of analyses by sociologists, social anthropologists and others who by-passed rather than confronted the functionalist models. However, even in the early stages of this enterprise various participants were stimulatingly sceptical not so much of the concept of 'penetration', but of an approach which tended to see problems from the perspective of the 'elite', the 'modernisers'. In fact, it was evident that the model that derives most directly from that view, i.e. which conceptualizes the penetration process as simply a relationship between a 'centre' and the citizenry at the 'periphery', was no adequate base on which to organize our case studies. Thus the very ordering of the essays has recognized the need to understand relations between at least three different levels: from the face-to-face contacts within a local community through various strata of sub-national political organization to the national level and beyond. And far from seeing power as residing merely at the centre, analyses have to see power-holders as operating at each of these levels, and view them as representing groups and interests within the society rather than as elements withdrawn from, or situated above, it.

Beyond the negative conclusion that rejects an elite-mass view of politics as simplistic, no new consensus is represented here. The actual post-independence trends in East Africa have prompted various contributors to make more fundamental and controversial departures from the 'orthodoxy' of the 1960s. They have pointed to the privileged, class character of the elites who have come to power, and to the exploitation and inequality resulting from a pattern of economic growth which they prefer to term 'underdevelopment'. Indeed, most of the assessments of rural development programmes contained in the later essays clearly document the inequalities that are generated, even if they disagree about the causes and prescriptions for these tendencies. For these authors, the key questions are not concerned with the capabilities of the state to achieve *any* objective but *who* is doing the penetrating and for what *purposes*. These two issues have been given further significance within East Africa ever since Tanzania began to set itself apart from its neighbours and to attempt a very different development path, one that seeks to promote equality through a nationally integrated economy and which relegates the 'elite' to being a central part of the *problem* and not the solution. Not surprisingly, with a socialist alternative at least on the agenda, in assessing these different development experiences and the conditions which gave rise to them, some analysts have been influenced by the methods of historical materialism rather than those of comparative history.

In addition to the separate substantive themes dealt with in the various contributions, some clusters of papers, if read together, reflect some of the dialectic noted above. Thus, the two papers in the Introductory section provide some background, one theoretical, the other of the actual East African context, but they also represent two different approaches to the analysis of politics and development. Then follow three case studies, each concerned with the imposition of new types of institutional arrangements in different localities. In discussing the Teso experience Vincent stresses the economic concomitants of colonial administration and the changing social structure. Rigby and Mafeje explore the reactions to external initiatives of particular societies with different social structures: Rigby discusses what he sees as the comparatively homogeneous, *cultural* response of the Ugogo of Tanzania, whereas Mafeje illustrates the differential *socio-economic* responses among the Baganda due to the divergent interests in their highly articulated class structure.

The two following essays are concerned with the effectiveness of selected structures and mechanisms at a national level in stimulating rural development. Chambers argues for the utility of an 'institutional conservatism' while Helleiner advocates utilization of market rather than administrative mechanisms, even in Tanzania during the early stages of its transition to socialism. Harris then discusses the attempts in Tanzania to develop alternative structures to those inherited from colonialism and their appropriateness for a transition to socialism.

The focus in the next set is on the district level, that critical nexus where agents of central authorities, government or party, confront leaders or other actors thrown up by local socio-political forces. Lamb, Hyden and Sharman all examine the nature of the relationships and of the respective actors in this confrontation. Their foci and emphases differ, but all suggest that those relationships, and particularly the problem of 'resistance' to central government programmes, are determined more significantly by the status or class interests of the actors — both bureaucratic agents of the centre and the local political activists with whom they interact — than by any 'traditional' 'cultural' traits characteristic of a particular 'tribe'.

In the last four contributions, this examination of the relative significance of cultural factors versus socio-economic status of the actors is pursued further at the grassroots level. Thoden van Velzen and Leonard reach similar conclusions, based on totally different kinds of evidence, regarding the uneven distribution of the benefits of government agricultural services; however, their analyses of the reasons for such an unevenness differ significantly. Swartz and Mutiso, on the other hand, are both concerned with the determinative importance of the cultural characteristics of their communities, but both show that these can be seen as facilitating rather than necessarily constraining or obstructing certain kinds of rural development. Finally, the concluding essay pulls together some of the main lines of analysis, pointing to a sobering reassessment of the role and structural position of the bureaucracy in East African rural development.

It is our hope that readers may get as much out of the presentation of these controversies as did the participants in these academic debates over development theory, development strategy and the politics of rural development during a period when East Africa provided a remarkable stimulus for creative research.

Lionel Cliffe
James Coleman
Martin Doornbos

I

INTRODUCTION:
'PENETRATION' AND THE EAST AFRICAN CONTEXT

JAMES S. COLEMAN

THE CONCEPT OF POLITICAL PENETRATION

Political penetration is a broad organizing rubric subsuming processes associated with the formation of new post-colonial states.[1] It is an heuristic concept aggregating that ensemble of processes by which the political-administrative-juridical centre of a new state (1) establishes an effective and authoritative central presence throughout its geographical and sectoral peripheries, and (2) acquires a capacity for the extraction and mobilization of resources to implement its policies and pursue its goals, however these may be determined. In both historical and comparative perspective these processes are an integral part of the more all-embracing concept of 'state-formation'.[2] The latter, however, includes all of those processes by which both *external* sovereignty (i.e. independence vis-à-vis the new state's international environment) is maximized and internal sovereignty (i.e. supremacy vis-à-vis its internal environment) is established. Although the two dimensions are empirically inseparable, due to the interpenetration of external and internal forces and influences, the emphasis in this volume is upon the creation of 'internal' sovereignty in new states, with reference where appropriate to how the prevailing international system may condition or inhibit that process.

THE NATURE OF THE CONCEPT

As an aggregative concept, political penetration serves as 'an umbrella for a number of subconcepts which do share something in common.'[3] The main subconcepts are:
(1) centre-formation, consolidation and coordination;[4]
(2) structural integration of the centre and its peripheries;
(3) coordination of outreach structures of the centre at the peripheries, and their articulation and integration with local structures at the peripheries;
(4) legitimation of the structural arrangements in (1) through (3).
Two subconcepts — one ('extraction') is implicit and the other ('legitimation') is explicit — in the foregoing formulation are in different but interrelated ways a measure of effectiveness of penetration. The object of penetration is not only to extract the requisite resources to maintain the centre's presence but

also to pursue other national (particularly developmental) goals. The structural arrangements for such extraction are as integral a part of the overall pattern of penetrative structure as are those concerned with regulation.[5] However, the effectiveness of the structures of regulation and extraction is significantly determined by the extent to which they have become legitimated, i.e. institutionalized. Although conceptually separable, both extraction and legitimation are manifestly critical dimensions of the concept of political penetration.

The twin processes of extension of central power and the institutionalization of central structures are directed towards the progressive establishment of the central presence throughout the peripheries; yet more is demanded and required of the centres of new states of this epoch. Initially at least, and possibly for the predictable future, they are, by default or by assertion, the locus of initiative, planning, resource extraction, mobilization and allocation, for the proto-national societies of which they are the political and administrative centres. As a UN report summarized:

... the central government of a developing country must initiate and, at least in the early stages, carry out most of the things that must be done to accelerate social and economic development ... the distinguishing feature of developing countries — and indeed a measure of their underdevelopment — is the degree of reliance upon the central government and more particularly upon decisions in the national capital for public services carried out locally. In countries in the earliest stages of development, the conduct of all but the most traditional affairs may be centred in the nation's capital.[6]

Political penetration is not only conceptualized as a process; it is also concerned specifically with structure. It is here that the conceptual distinction between *state*-building and *nation*-building is analytically useful, indeed essential. As Nettl argues 'If the entry of the third world onto the stage of modern socioscientific consciousness has had one immediate result (or should have had), it is the snapping of the link between state and nation. What were awkward exceptions before (Switzerland, the Soviet Union, empires generally, and so on) have now become almost a rule of nonnation-states.'[7] Once this conceptual distinction is made between the essentially structural (i.e. organizational) character of *state*-building, and the essentially cultural (i.e. inculcation of values, attitudes, orientations, beliefs and feelings) nature of *nation*-building,[8] the interdependence of these two processes, or at least their overlap, must be recognized. Indeed, one dimension of the history of the modern epoch is that of self-conscious nations (i.e. groups of people whose members feel themselves to constitute a single and distinctive terminal community) seeking to establish their own states (i.e. a sovereign single-centred ensemble of authoritative structures embracing their 'national' territory) under the principle of national self-determination (i.e. the ethical imperative that every nation should have its own state) *or* by the wielders of power in non-national states seeking to weld together into one nation, coterminus with the boundaries of that state, the diverse nationalities over which they exercise power, whether inherited or asserted. Ex-colonial new states of this epoch, like those emerging from empires in other periods in the modern era, are engaged in the second of these two major historical processes.

The conceptual distinction between state building and nation building is blurred somewhat by the concept of legitimacy. The structural arrangements which coercively bind a group of people together in one state, in a world of sovereign states, and through which decisions are made from an ultimate single territorial centre affecting all of the peripheries, cannot and will not become stabilized, nor endure, unless for the majority of the people — or at least for the majority of the politically conscious strata and groups — those structures are felt and believed to be necessary and right. It is in this sense that the historic concept of nation, and the more recent social scientific concept of 'political community' — the objects respectively of nation-building and state-building — become both logically and empirically linked. However, Callaghy is undoubtedly correct in his assertion that 'Despite assertions of much of the academic literature and of African leaders themselves, state formation, not nation-building, is the primary focus of political action and of ruling elites in Africa today.'[9]

All concepts, conceptual schemes and models have their weaknesses, but the concept of penetration seems to be particularly vulnerable and to have more than its fair share of impedimenta. These weaknesses and vulnerabilities must be squarely faced. First, like all such global aggregative concepts, it cannot be operationalized or used in theoretical models designed for the purpose of testing propositions; such concepts are weak in 'explanatory power' and their indiscriminate use tends to degenerate into neo-scholasticism.[10] However, operational purists have noted that despite their theoretical limitations or uselessness such concepts can serve a useful pedagogical and heuristic function, evidence of which is their continued prominence in all of the social science disciplines.[11] Stein Rokkan, a scholar long concerned with the macro-micro gap, has suggested that through the development of time series data and composite indicators such summative concepts have considerable potential utility in the comparative analysis of the state-and-nation-building processes. In any event, the use of a summative concept here is based not on any scientific pretentiousness but on its assumed heuristic and organizing utility in conceptualizing a broad historical process.

The second vulnerability of the concept 'political penetration' is specific to it, namely, the way it has been used by one school of analysis has given it a manipulative, authoritarian, unidirectional, conservative and elite-centric bias, or at least imagery, which has led to a positive valuation of anything an all-powerful centre (and particularly the incumbent power elite) does to penetrate its peripheries. Richard Sandbrook has illuminated this particular vulnerability with great force, noting that some users of the penetration concept subtly shift from making the *empirical* point that governments seek to penetrate and control their peripheries to the imperative that the incumbent elites *should* do so.

... the interest in order of those at the top is given logical precedence over the interest in social justice of those below... If a central government is committed to rural development, its lack of an effective presence in the countryside will impede the implementation of progressive policies designed to ameliorate the lot of the people. But note the conditional nature of this reformulation. Penetration, the problem of central control, is not treated as a problem in its own right, but one which is dependent upon the actual commitments and performance of a regime. If political scientists are not to be simply technicians available to whoever is in power, they need to pose a prior question: penetration for what? Penetration, after all, historically has often meant greater oppression of the underprivileged strata. [12]

Kesselman asserts that the imperative of penetration as propounded by some analysts tends to a fusion of the perspectives of powerholder and scholar: 'my objection is not to describing how authorities attempt to maintain dominance, but rather to the implicit espousal of their cause.'[13] The presumably analytically objective 'centre', it is suggested, easily becomes not only the 'governing power elite', but the *incumbent* elite; the developmental imperative of effective penetration thereby becomes a justification for the preservation of the status quo.[14] Sandbrook's conditional reformulation of the way in which the penetration concept can be employed is a useful precaution.

A third vulnerability of the penetration concept arises from focussing singularly upon it as an organizing rubric; the consequence is that because one of the principal objectives of penetration is to establish political order, the latter value *ipso facto* acquires primacy. Several political developmentalists, of course, have explicitly stressed the priority and primacy of order in new states, e.g.:

Given the extreme weakness of national political centres in Africa, the greatest priority from the point of view of political development may entail the reinforcement of the centres themselves... The rapid extension of participation can indeed create more problems than it solves by jeopardizing the very existence of the centres (Zolberg). [15]

... the primary problem is not liberty but the creation of a legitimate public order. Men may, of course, have order without liberty, but they cannot have liberty without order. Authority has to exist before it can be limited... (Huntington). [16]

To this genre of argument Kesselman has introduced a vigorous dissent:

... political values do not exist in isolation from one another. The achievement of one value may facilitate or impede the achievement of others... Even if one grants that order *logically* precedes liberty, this need not dictate that order *chronologically* should precede liberty... Granted, political order is less secure in changing societies than in modern societies; yet so too are liberty, freedom, and other core values. A predominant concern for political order would be warranted only if it could be shown...that, compared to other values, it was *disproportionately* endangered.[17]

Suffice it here to disclaim that in focussing singularly upon penetration in new states no emphatic primacy or priority to the value of political order is intended.

A fourth weakness in the penetration concept, common to many concepts and models in the social sciences, is the neglect or exclusion of the international environment as a major variable in the formation and evolution of new states. In his comprehensive survey of recent literature on development as it relates to state formation Charles Tilly laments the general tendency to ignore international variables:

The extreme concentration on the individual nation, political system, society, *or* state has drawn attention away from the international structures of power within which 'development' takes place... I have encountered impressively little discussion of the way the structure of world markets, the operation of economic imperialism, and the characteristics of the international state system affect the patterns of political change within countries in different parts of the world.[18]

In focussing upon the processes of establishment and consolidation of internal sovereignty within new states as a working conception of 'political penetration' there is an even greater danger of being intra-system-centric, of ignoring or being insensitive to international penetration as a variable. According to the theory of dependency and underdevelopment the state is 'the instrument of a national oligarchy whose position depends on control of local land and capital – a control bolstered by the state's repressive apparatus, but exercised within stringent limits set by the outside powers to which the national economy is subordinate.'[19] By the measure that such international penetration is empirically operative in a new state its intra-state penetrative processes will obviously be affected.

Despite the foregoing vulnerabilities of the concept of 'political penetration', there remains a need for an organizing concept to delimit a range of empirical processes associated with the formation and consolidation of the central authority of new states. If all of the dangers of bias and potential ideological use and usefulness are made explicit, penetration still remains a useful summative rubric, and usefulness is the only real test of a concept. Many of the most commonplace concepts in social science analysis – whether used by bourgeois developmentalists or the radical underdevelopmentalists – would have to be discarded if their vulnerability to valuative or ideological biases were the test of their utility.[20] Moreover, unless one is a doctrinaire philosophical anarchist, it hardly seems necessary yet once again to argue for the logical necessity and the empirical reality of a centre in any form of organized human existence. The prime requisite of the existence of a political system is that there be a centre where there is a 'last word', whether it be that of an individual, a constitution, a legislature, or an institutionalized process for authoritative decision making for the whole. The centre is wherever this 'last word' is situated. Without this there logically and empirically could be no political system.[21] And if there is a centre there is a periphery, and between them there characteristically is some sort of structured relationship.

THE NATURE OF THE 'CENTRE' IN NEW STATES

To be useful, the concept 'centre' must be disaggregated and placed within a working conceptual framework. For present purposes, stated rather starkly, the 'centre' in a new state is the locus of 'state power', exercised through the 'state apparatus' by a 'state bureaucracy' ultimately controlled and directed by a 'ruling group'. Thus, political penetration is that process by which the most influential and powerful actors – the penetrators – in the ruling group and state bureaucracy use state power and the state apparatus both to maximize state sovereignty and to pursue the ideal and material interests both of themselves and ideally of the society over which they exercise control.

Jackson has argued that most post-colonial African societies are 'one-class societies':

This is the political-administrative class comprising all those persons who hold public and parastatal posts which confer upon occupants a measure of authority or discretion. Included among this stratum would be national politicians and party officials, police officials and military officers..., civil servants and parastatal officials above clerical ranks, university professors..., and generally all other persons who enjoy public employment involving some exercise of authority, actual or potential.[22]

Others have found it useful – as I have done above – to distinguish within this stratum at least two main categories:
(1) the ruling group, or 'political class' more narrowly defined (i.e. as John Saul puts it: 'those who staff the state *at the most overtly political level* – including, most obviously, the President/Prime Minister, his cabinet and immediate circle of advisors, senior officials of the ruling part...');[23] and
(2) the 'state bureaucracy' viewed broadly, to include sub-categories of (a) career bureaucrats, (b) managers of state enterprises, and (c) officers of the armed forces and police. These latter distinctions can be important both in terms of role function, differing institutional interests, ideological orientation and political competition within the state apparatus.[24]

There is a lively debate on the extent to which, following Jackson, the ensemble of all of these various categories constitutes a class. The consensus appears to be that it is only a class in formation, a 'protoclass', fragmented into competing factions, presenting to the analyst the task of trying, as Roger Murray put it, 'to comprehend the contradictions inherent in the accession to *state power* of unformed classes.'[25] This same quality of fractionalization by crosscutting tendencies characterizes all other social formations (peasantry, entrepreneurs, urban labour, etc) which at this stage remain only classes in formation in terms of any disposition for meaningful political action or class conflict. Thus, in most new states, given the brevity of their existence, neither 'centres' nor their 'peripheries' are empirically composed of stable and coherent entities.

Once this inchoateness in the formation of self-consciousness among different categories of presumptive classes is noted, there can be little doubt that the centre is perceived by its peripheries as dominated by a contrastively distinctive stratum, largely due to the colonial legacy. In observing the elements of continuity in fundamental perceptions between the 'colonial conquest state' and its post-colonial successor, Callaghy observes:

During the period of colonial rule, the administrative stratum was the one stratum recognized by all African groups as being a class apart. With independence, an African inheritance elite took over these positions and has used them to consolidate the emerging class interest. The political aristocracy is now the only group recognized by all Africans as a separate and dominant stratum. The members of this stratum also recognize this fact.[26]

The same point has been made even more pungently eloquent by Amilcar Cabral:

Some independent African states preserved the structures of the colonial state. In some countries they only replaced a white man with a black man, but for the people it is the same. You have to realize that it is very difficult for the people to make a distinction between one...white...administrator and one black administrator. For the people it is the administrator that is fundamental. And the principle — if this administrator, a black one, is living in the same house, with the same gestures, with the same car, or sometimes a better one, what is the difference? ... The problem of the nature of the state created after independence is perhaps the secret of the failure of African independence.[27]

Thus, although the centre may be the arena for the struggle for status among various differentiable competing protoclasses and factions, it tends to be perceived by much of the rest of society as a single dominant stratum.

STRUCTURES AND PATTERNS OF PENETRATION

State power penetrates, or seeks to penetrate, a society through a variety of structures[28] which schematically would include the following.
(1) Governmental structures, which are formal, presumptively authoritative, usually constitutionally prescribed, and territory-wide in purview, namely: executives, bureaucracies, armies, courts, police, parastatal agencies, public enterprises, etc — the ensemble of which constitutes the state apparatus through which the centre endeavours to establish and maintain its presence,

exact compliance, extract resources, and evoke a supportive response. The ensemble also includes:

(a) structures of territorial (regional, provincial, district, village, etc) administration, which are the outreaches of the state apparatus (including, of course, sectoral ministries) to the peripheries, some of which may historically have varying degrees of limited autonomy, depending upon the penetrative capacity, the centralizing will or the permissiveness of the centre;

(b) presumptively participant structures, which can be either formal bodies (legislatures, councils, etc) or associations, either officially created and sanctioned or tolerated by the state, and used, or not, as channels of participation (i.e. upward penetration) at best, or at least for communication or for their symbolic value;

(c) process structures for

   (i) resource extraction (systems of taxation, levies, conscription, etc),
   (ii) economic control and direction (pricing and marketing mechanisms, subsidies, land registration, etc),
   (iii) patronage (patron-client systems), rewards, inducements,
   (iv) manipulated elections,
   (v) intimidation, punishment, coercion and repression.

(2) Associational structures, which are groups formed, independently or by state direction, presumptively representing the interests of a definable group, aggregate or protoclass (labour unions, farmer cooperatives, traders' associations, ethnic associations, etc) or, in one-party systems, the entire society.

(3) Structures of education, communication and mass media.

(4) Residual traditional structures of authority or symbolism.

The foregoing central structures of penetration can be and are selectively perceived by those affected either as meaningful and legitimate channels of regulation and extraction, or as illegitimate sources of direction and coercion to be avoided or resisted. They may impinge only intermittently or indirectly, or not at all, as Zolberg has argued in his conception of 'residual space'[29] (i.e. significant areas and activities within new states regarding which there effectively is no central penetration). The really effective structures of penetration, as perceived by and as affecting behavior at the periphery, may be partially or totally discontinuous with any centre nexus, even in the most ostensibly monolithic and declaredly penetrative regimes, as Bienen has shown.[30] The range and depth of the potential penetrative power of the full panoply of structural linkages between a people and the state apparatus in a new state is overpowering; the functioning actuality in most instances is at most only an uneasy, fragile and intermittent penetration of the strategic sectors, due mainly to the frailties of their inheritances and the special character of the dominating international environment into which they are born.

Among the several patterns of penetration which have characterized the process of state formation in post-colonial African new states, three are of particular interest, namely (1) *departicipation*, (2) *ethnic management*, and (3) *socialist transformation*. In his very insightful analysis of penetrative processes in new states, under the organizing rubric of 'departicipation', Nelson Kasfir argues that 'Forcing people out of politics is a strategy available to the leadership in many countries for enhancing its capacity to rule and making its tenure secure.'[31] Certainly the dominant political feature of the terminal colonial period in most former colonies was a vast expansion in popular participation and consciousness, and a belated effort by the departing colonial powers to erect central, regional and local participatory structures of a presumptively democratic character. Since independence the general pattern throughout the continent has been characterized by systematic efforts to contain and to reduce participation as a means of enhancing the power of the centre in general and of the existing regimes in particular:

Departicipation is the most striking feature of postindependence political change in black Africa... political structures which markedly increased participation were hastily installed in the last hectic years of colonial rule. Since independence they have been unceremoniously dismantled with the same alacrity....[32]

The main features of this continental (indeed, global) syndrome of new state formation have been covered extensively in the literature and following Kasfir's analysis need only be summarized briefly here.

(1) Dismantling of federal structures (e.g. Uganda and Kenya) which were part of the independence compromise and the diminution or extinction of powers of traditional authorities, middle men,[33] local government bodies[34] (*corps intermédiaires*) as part of an inexorable process of progressive concentration and monopolization of power at the centre.

(2) Progressive strengthening of executive power (e.g. Zolberg: 'a steady drive to achieve greater centralization of authority in the hands of a very small number of men who occupy top offices in the party and the government, and even more in the hands of a single man at the apex of both institutions'[35]), a process of 'monocentralization' leading in most instances to what Apter has termed 'presidential monarchs.' The many dimensions of this process are also familiar, including progressive diminution of the powers of legislative bodies, the vast expansion in the powers of provincial and district commissioners accountable directly to presidents, and the assumption by the latter of discretionary powers of detention without trial and restrictions on movement, assembly and the press.[36]

(3) The harrassment and ultimate banning of opposition parties and the steady move towards the consolidation of one-party systems;[37] the interpenetration and, in many instances, the fusion of structures of government and the party; and a terminal trend towards what Wallerstein aptly termed 'inanition' and the 'no-party state.'[38]

(4) The assertion of state control over all interest associations, particularly

labour organizations and agricultural cooperatives, and their attempted conversion into 'transmission belts.'

(5) The foregoing first-phase processes of political and administrative centralization, monocratization and other dimensions of new state formation and consolidation reach their culmination in the establishment of military regimes, which Kasfir notes, have become the 'modal form of government in black Africa.'[39] Only those civilian regimes still controlled by remaining 'founding fathers' (e.g. Kenyatta, Nyerere, Kaunda, Houphuet-Boigny, etc) have been spared; but all odds are on the military becoming their successors.

The explanations advanced for this general post-independence syndrome of centralization, departiciption, monocracy and ultimate consolidation under authoritarian bureaucratic-military regimes in new states have been extensively analyzed elsewhere and certainly do not need, yet once again, repetition here.[40] The explanations include the destabilizing conditions (particularly the politicization of ethnicity) which new governments faced in the years immediately prior to and after independence, supportive or predisposing elements in traditional society, various aspects of the colonial legacy, the statist ethos and assumptions undergirding the political culture of the new governing groups, with special emphasis upon the priority of order — all being reinforced and facilitated by the intrusion of external influences and by the fairly pervasive passivity and manipulability of the peasantry, the mass of the population. The end result everywhere is the preeminence of state bureaucracies, aptly summarized by one central Minister of Internal Affairs:

Thus, one paradoxically comes back again to the administrative structures existing before June 30, 1960, that is, a central and strong authority basing itself on decentralized provincial administrations which realize through district commissioners and territorial administrators all the options of economic and social progress.[41]

The prominence, indeed in most instances the overriding determinative importance, of ethnicity as a force in African politics and in the processes of state formation — or in politics anywhere in the contemporary world — would hardly by now be disputed by any analyst.[42] There is, however, a vigorous division in interpretation between so-called 'modernization' analysts and class analysts regarding the subjective or objective basis of the phenomenon. As Kasfir has summarized the division:

Radical analysts tend to see ethnicity as a subjective, rather than an objective phenomenon. Since classes are based on objective economic relations, acting on the basis of ethnic loyalties can only be subjective...ethnicity must be understood in terms of the elite (or bourgeoisie), not the masses...a tool used by the elite to consolidate its class position... [whereas] modernization analysts...argue that ethnicity has to be understood as an objective phenomenon, characterizing the masses at the level of fundamental values...[43]

Despite this difference of view among analysts as to whether the ultimate basis of political action is class or ethnicity, the fact is that throughout Africa ethnic divisions have been and are the primary bases for the activation and escalation of the ethnic consciousness of peoples by elites competing for power at the centre irrespective of their own sense of class identity. The nationalist movements which struggled for and won independence, and the nationalist elites which sought and achieved consolidation of their power after independence were mainly based on *ethnic manipulation*. Ethnic identification was and remains at once the most secure base and ethnic manipulation (including 'ethnic arithmetic') both the easiest and the most powerful penetrative tactic and strategy available to any politician or coalition of politicians struggling to reach, remain in or dominate the centre. And, as in Kenya, where ethnic hegemony has been achieved, it remains the ultimate weapon, as Leys has argued:

> The Kikuyu bourgeoisie were well aware that many of their special advantages depended on their political dominance within the state apparatus. So long as enough of the Kikuyu masses believed that this was also of prime importance to them, appeals to tribal solidarity would serve the double purpose of reinforcing the Kikuyu leadership's position at the centre, and repelling challenges based on class antagonism within Kikuyu society.[44]

Among all new states in independent Africa Tanzania stands out in so many respects as exceptional in how it has endeavoured both to institute new modes and structures of participation replacing those inherited at independence and to minimize and constrain ethnic manipulation as a penetrative instrument. It had certain inherited advantages at birth, as Cliffe has shown, but the critical variable has been a leadership which has been both rhetorically and genuinely deeply committed to values of participation and ethnic irrelevance.[45] But even more striking has been its uniqueness in seriously pursuing a path of socialist transformation, a model, as some would argue, of a socialist strategy of penetration for national development. However, even among its most sympathetic analysts, whether conventional or radical, there are serious reservations whether this virtually unique experiment will succeed, mainly, but not entirely, for reasons beyond its control.[46]

State building — internally the penetration by the centres of state power to their peripheries — everywhere and throughout history has involved varying degrees and modes of coercion.[47] The more transformative and radical the structural changes being attempted the more overt and direct must be the coercion.[48] In historical perspective one of the most distinctive features of contemporary state-formation in Africa is that it is being attempted in an epoch in which coercion — although in variant forms omnipresent — is at least repugnant to dominant ethical ideals, and in a situation in which the coercive capacity of state power at the centres is relatively weak and tenuous in comparison with the functions they must perform and the goals they seek.[49] The second distinctive feature is that it is taking place or being attempted in an international environment, and a situation of all-embracing dependence on that environment, which is unique in history. As Sandbrook observes, 'Perhaps the main element which is unique in the contemporary situation of the underdeveloped countries as compared to Euro-America a century or so ago is the importance of the *transnational* influences upon political and economic development.'[50] These unique aspects of state-formation in our epoch clearly limit the value of historical analogies and make all the more interesting studies which reveal how penetration is being attempted and occurring, or not, in the new states with which this volume is concerned.

NOTES

1. The adjective 'political' as the modifier of 'penetration' is used in its most general sense, embracing all analytical aspects of 'political organization' as defined by M.G. Smith: 'Political organization consists in the combination and interplay of relations of authority and power in the regulation of public affairs. Briefly, the political organization is the set of arrangements by which a public regulates its common affairs. Such regulation always integrates two modes of public action, the *administrative*, which consists in the authoritative conduct of public affairs, and the *political*, which consists in the exercise and competitions of power to influence or control the course of these affairs.' *International Encyclopedia of the Social Sciences*, 12, 194 (italics added). Adopting this wider concept of 'political' obviates the need for the more cumbersome phrase 'political-administrative penetration'.

2. The concept of 'state' is here used interchangeably with that of 'political system', it being understood that the latter refers to a unit which is member of the international states system. Charles Tilly has perceptively observed that political scientists, perhaps too precipitately, 'lost interest in talking about the state as such twenty or thirty years ago', partly, as Almond argued, to 'separate out analytically the structures which perform political functions in all societies regardless of scale, degree of differentiations, and culture', and partly 'to extend the analytical scope of political analysis to include political culture, political socialization and similar phenomena relevant to government but outside the formal structure of government.' This introduced a fluidity and problem of comparability in the political units of reference. Charles Tilly (ed), *The Formation of National States in Western Europe* (Princeton University Press, 1975), 617-618. But, as J.P. Nettl has convincingly argued regarding the 'state', '... the thing exists and no amount of conceptual restructuring can dissolve it'. 'The State as a Conceptual Variable', *World Politics*, 20, 4 (1968), 559.

3. Samuel P. Huntington, 'The Change to Change: Modernization, Development, and Politics', *Comparative Politics*, 3, 3 (April 1971), 303.

4. Stein Rokkan, 'Centre Formation, Nation-Building and Cultural Diversity: Report on a symposium organized by UNESCO', *Social Science Information*, VIII (February 1969), 89.

5. Robert H. Jackson, 'The Crises of Penetration and Extraction' (Unpublished ms), p. 2.

6. United Nations, *Decentralization for National and Local Development* (New York, UN, 1962), 5-6.

7. Nettl, 'The State as a Conceptual Variable', 560.

8. Almond and Powell make this distinction: 'we might view the problem of state building...as essentially a structural problem. That is to say, what is involved is primarily a matter of the differentiation of new roles, structures, and subsystems which penetrate the countryside. Nation building, on the other hand, emphasizes the cultural aspects of

political development. It refers to the process whereby people transfer their commitment and loyalty from smaller tribes, villages, or petty principalities to the larger central political system.' Gabriel A.Almond and G. Bingham Powell Jr, *Comparative Politics: A Development Approach* (Boston, Little, Brown, 1966), 36.

9. Thomas M. Callaghy, 'Implementation of Socialist Strategies of Development in Africa: State Power, Conflict and Uncertainty' (Unpublished ms), p. 28.

10. Social science concepts of the summative type, such as political penetration, state-formation, and nation-building, are only useful if, as Huntington suggests, '... they help to separate out two or more forms of something which would otherwise be thought of as undifferentiated.' 'The Change to Change', 303. Cf. Joseph LaPalombara's trenchant self-criticism of the innovations in macro-conceptual nomenclature: '[We are] armed to be sure with new terminology, but not any more successful than were the ancients in narrowing the gap between abstract formulations and theoretical realities.... Concept-refining very quickly degenerates into the scholastic game...' 'Macrotheories and Microapplications in Comparative Politics: A Widening Chasm', *Comparative Politics*, I, 1 (1968-69), 54-55.

11. 'What, if anything, can be done with summative units when they are employed in theory building? ... May we then employ such units in our theories with any profit or utility? My answer is no. Such units are useless in theories and theoretical models that are designed for the purpose of the testing propositions. Summative units have their function in a scientific discipline, but not in relation to theoretical models.' Robert Dublin, *Theory Building* (New York, The Free Press, 1970), 62-63.

12. Richard Sandbrook, 'The "Crisis" in Political Development Theory', *The Journal of Development Studies*, 12, 2 (January 1976), 180-181. Sandbrook cites Donal Cruise O'Brien's insightful revelation of the authoritarian bias in much of the political analysis of developing countries during the 1960s: '... there does emerge one major common prescriptive assumption, that the new institutional order should be the work of political elites, able and willing to impose new structures on the masses from above.' 'Modernization, Order, and the Erosion of a Democratic Ideal: American Political Science 1960-70', *The Journal of Development Studies*, 8, 4 (1972), 362. This same point has been made by several others, particularly Raymond F. Hopkins, 'Securing Authority: The View from the Top', *World Politics*, XXIV, 2 (January 1972), 271-292, and Mark Kesselman, 'Order or Movement? The Literature of Political Development as Ideology', *World Politics*, XXVI, 1 (1973), 139-154. The empirical reality of oppression historically being associated with penetration is illuminated in the study of Western state-making by Charles Tilly and his colleagues: 'The European experience...does not show us modernizing elites articulating the demand and needs of the masses, and fighting off traditional holders of power in order to meet those needs and demands. Far from it. We discover a world in which small groups of power-hungry men fought off numerous rivals and great popular resistance in the pursuit of their own ends...' *The Formation of National States in Western Europe*, 635.

13. Kesselman, 'Order or Movement?', 144.

14. '...supposedly value-neutral models of political development possess ideological use to the extent that these reinforce or challenge...the...*status quo*.' Sandbrook, 'The "Crisis" in Political Development Theory', 181.

15. Aristide R. Zolberg, 'Political Development in Tropical Africa: Center and Periphery' (Unpublished ms). It should be stressed that Zolberg does not advocate 'monolithic penetration'; on the contrary, he very emphatically rejects authoritarian measures as necessary 'to maintain order and to bring about modernization in the political, the economic, and other spheres' not only because the costs would be extremely great and incompatible with African values, but also because it would probably be unsuccessful. See his *Creating Political Order* (Chicago, Rand McNally, 1966), 158-161, where he recommends the political machine as possibly the most effective mode of penetration in new African states.

16. Samuel P. Huntington, *Political Order in Changing Societies* (New Haven, Yale University Press, 1968), 7-8.

17. 'Order or Movement?', 146-147.

18. Tilly, *Formation of National States*, 620.

19. Ibidem, 628. See also Sandbrook, 181.

20. 'Nation-building', another summative concept, in Third World rhetoric is probably

one of the most unchallengeable and highly valued concepts, but it was not so long ago that nationalism and nationhood (following the Nazi-Fascist extravagances) were regarded as pathologies by many who believed in world peace and the basic unity of mankind. From this perspective 'nation-building', or indeed the concept of 'nation-state', was viewed as retrograde. And its utility to handle emerging phenomena is not unquestioned. See Nathan Glazer and Daniel P. Moynihan (eds), *Ethnicity: Theory and Experience* (Cambridge, Harvard University Press, 1975).

21. The exceptions would be the so-called stateless political systems and the international political system. Our concern here is with (national) political systems of this epoch for which the statement holds true. See David Easton, *A Systems Analysis of Political Life* (New York, John Wiley & Sons, 1965), 282-285; and Roger D. Masters, 'World Politics as a Primitive Political System', *World Politics* XVI, 4 (July 1964), 595-619.

22. Quoted in Callaghy, 'Implementation of Socialist Strategies of Development in Africa', 22. The reference is taken from Robert H. Jackson, 'Political Stratification in Tropical Africa', *Canadian Journal of African Studies*, 7, 3 (1973), 381-400. Callaghy adds that 'The Road to status, power, and wealth in African states is clearly through entering this official realm, through acquiring political or administrative office. This class is created and defined by its direct and close relationship with the state. The state creates the class, and it in turn controls the state. Linkages between the ruling class and other groups in the stratification structure are primarily through the state via patron-client ties that are often ethnically based' (p. 22).

23. John S. Saul, 'The Unsteady State: Uganda, Obote and General Amin', *Review of African Political Economy*, 5 (1976), 18.

Although Callaghy himself fuses the two at one point in the broad term political aristocracy, elsewhere he makes the crucial distinction: '... state formation can be viewed as a three-way struggle between a ruling group, the official/administrative apparatus, and the various internal and external competing groups and organizations, each with their own ideal and material interests... The dominant coalition of the state attempts to use its administrative staff to lessen or manage its dependence on groups in its environment. Paradoxically, however, the dominant coalition must also reduce its dependence on this administrative staff. This is the search for sovereignty and the three-way struggle of state formation.' 'Implementation of Socialist Strategies', 3.

24. Colin Leys argues that at least in the Tanzanian one-party case it is useful to distinguish a fourth component, namely 'the party-recruited element' bought into the state apparatus, which has 'political links with workers and peasants' and which thereby 'may be significant for understanding the origins and course of the struggles that do occur inside the state apparatus.' Regarding ideological orientation he notes that the 'officials entering the "state enterprise" branch are especially exposed to the bourgeois values embodied in the technology, management practices, "efficiency" ideology, etc. of the firms they take over...'. 'The "Overdeveloped" Post Colonial State: A Re-evaluation', *Review of African Political Economy*, 5 (1976), 44.

25. Quoted by Saul, in Ibid., p. 16. Saul stresses the ambiguity and incoherence in the process of the bureaucratic fraction of what he calls the 'petty bourgeoisie' crystallizing into a class. However, Callaghy is more certain: '...this political aristocracy is also consolidating itself as a class. It does so primarily by establishing patron-client ties and alliances within the class. The political aristocracy is a class in reality, and it is becoming increasingly conscious of its existence as a class'. 'Implementation of Socialist Strategies', 22.

26. Ibidem, 23.

27. Quoted in Editorial, *Review of African Political Economy*, 5 (1976), 1.

28. The concept 'structure' is used here in its most aggregative and global sense, to include concrete membership structures (clusters and complexes of roles) such as parties, pressure groups, armies, courts, bureaucracies, etc; analytical process structures (i.e. the structure of patterned action), such as the 'structure of law enforcement', the 'structure of patronage', the 'structure of rewards and punishments', the 'structure of ideological diffusion', etc; and analytical holistic structure (patterning and interrelation of parts as dominated by the general character of the whole of reference) such as the 'economic structure', the 'structure of communications', etc.

29. Zolberg, *Creating Political Order*, 133 ff.
30. 'What Does Political Development Mean in Africa?', *World Politics*, 20, 1 (1967), 132.
31. Nelson Kasfir, *The Shrinking Political Arena* (Berkeley/Los Angeles, University of California Press, 1976), 14. Kasfir argues, convincingly that 'Because it is a continuous variable not necessarily related to a specified institutional complex, participation/departicipation is a more discriminating concept than the democracy/authoritarian dichotomy.'
32. Ibidem, 14.
33. 'There seems to be little interest in the establishment of intermediate institutions, political, economic, or social. In this sense, post-colonialism has failed to transcend the "dual" political structure of colonial society. Indeed, it is arguable that the periods of decolonisation and early independence have seen a consolidation of the "bureaucratic policy-implementing structures", and a steady atrophy of those structures which briefly promised some widening of popular representation and control.' Martin Staniland, 'The Rhetoric of Centre-Periphery Relations', *The Journal of Modern African Studies*, 8, 4 (1970), 617-636.
34. Colin Leys stressed the strength of local government in Uganda in the immediate post-independence period: 'local government in Uganda was unusually strong, both constitutionally and psychologically...[and]...is not likely to disappear completely at once.' *Politicians and Policies: An Essay on Politics in Acholi, Uganda 1962-65* (Nairobi, East African Publishing House, 1967), 9. This was written just before the radical centralization measures of the Obote regime followed by the total extinction of local government by the Amin regime.
35. Zolberg, *Creating Political Order*, 135.
36. Kasfir, *The Shrinking Political Arena*, 232.
37. Kasfir notes that as of 1976, 'To the fourteen single-party states that had banned opposition parties by 1963 can be added the formerly multiparty states of Uganda, Kenya, Tanzania, Sudan and Zambia.' Ibidem, 241.
38. Immanuel Wallerstein, 'The Decline of the Party in Single-Party African States', in Joseph LaPalombara and Myron Weiner (eds), *Political Parties and Political Development* (Princeton University Press, 1966), 208.
39. Kasfir, *Shrinking Political Arena*, 324.
40. James S. Coleman and Carl G. Rosberg Jr, *Political Parties and National Integration in Tropical Africa* (Berkeley, University of California Press, 1966), 655-674; Zolberg, *Creating Political Order* (entire) and 'The Structure of Political Conflict in the New States of Tropical Africa', *The American Political Science Review*, 62, 1 (March 1968); and particularly Kasfir, *Shrinking Political Arena*, 227-290.
41. Quoted in Kasfir, ibidem, 236.
42. Glazer and Moynihan have forcefully argued that in fact ethnic conflicts almost everywhere appear to have become the primary form in which interest conflicts between and within states are pursued for two related reasons: (1) 'the strategic efficacy of ethnicity in making legitimate claims on the resources of the modern state,' and (2) the 'nature of inequality... Men are not equal; neither are ethnic groups.' *Ethnicity: Theory and Experience*, 11.
43. Kasfir, *Shrinking Political Arena*, 68. Those emphasizing the subjective basis of ethnicity include Sklar 'tribal movements may be created and instigated to action by the new men of power in furtherance of their own special interests which are, time and again, the constitutive interests of emerging social classes. Tribalism then becomes a mask for class privilege,' and Mafeje ('If anything,...[tribalism]...is a mark of *false consciousness*...On the part of the new African elite, it is a ploy or distortion they use to conceal their exploitative role'), quoted in Kasfir, ibidem, 68. John Saul notes that there are manifestly cultural differences among African peoples, as well as uneven development between regions that do provide an objective basis for activation and escalation of ethnicity for elite selfserving goals: '...it is relatively easy to induce the lower strata of any given ethnic group to interpret the essence of their backwardness as being the result of a zero-sum game over the distribution of scarce resources played out between tribes rather than being primarily a result of class division, world-wide and local.' 'The Unsteady State', 20.

44.   Colin Leys, *Underdevelopment in Kenya: The Political Economy of Neo-Colonialism 1964-1971* (London, Heinemann, 1975), 205.
45.   Lionel Cliffe, *One Party Democracy* (Nairobi, East African Publishing House, 1966), John S. Saul, 'African Socialism in One Country: Tanzania', in Giovanni Arrighi and John S. Saul, *Essays on the Political Economy of Africa* (New York, Monthly Review Press, 1973), 237-335; and, most recently and succinctly, Kasfir, *Shrinking Political Arena*, 251-262.
46.   One of the most penetrating critiques of the Tanzanian experiment of socialist transformation as a penetrative strategy is Michael F. Lofchie, 'Agrarian Socialism in the Third World: The Tanzanian Case', *Comparative Politics*, 8, 3 (April 1976), 479-499.
47.   Tilly, *The Formation of National States*, 636.
48.   There tends to be a curious avoidance of the coercive implications or requisites for socialist transformation in much of the advocacy of and commentary on strategies for radical socialist transformation in African states. Callaghy notes, for example, that Arrighi and Saul argue for the creation of 'a state power dedicated to the task' but 'proceed to discuss state power as if coercive capacity was not a crucial or even important element of that power.' 'Implementation of Socialist Strategies', 6. Similarly, great emphasis has been made by many analysts regarding Nyerere's refusal to use force (e.g. Lofchie, 'Agrarian Socialism in the Third World', 488), but Leys notes a fine distinction between an 'ujamaa', a 'socialist', and a 'development' village: '[Nyerere's] 1968 statement was that no-one could be forced into an ujamaa village — it could not be a *socialist* village if force was used. The villages into which people have since been forced are actually termed "development villages". While the President was obviously very reluctant to use force, for any purpose, he seems to have concluded that it was justified in order to improve the ability of the government to direct an increase in agricultural production.' 'The "Overdeveloped" Post Colonial State: A Re-evaluation', 47.
49.   Referring to Tanzania, but of equal applicability to other new states, Nellis notes that contemporary regimes possess 'no reliable coercive means of significance, no financial means of substance, and no ruthlessly efficient administrative-organizational mechanisms.' John R. Nellis, *A Theory of Ideology: The Tanzanian Example* (Nairobi, OUP, 1972), 193. In analyzing the Ugandan case, Saul notes that the frailties in the system are such as not to provide sufficient state power '...even to guarantee that minimum degree of stability necessary for the consolidation of a smoothly functioning neo-colonial system'. 'The Unsteady State', 21.
50.   'The "Crisis" in Political Development Theory', 177. He correctly argues that such transnational dimensions 'must be systematically incorporated into models of development if these are to advance understanding of the contemporary situation in the Third World.' Ibidem, 177.

LIONEL CLIFFE

'PENETRATION' AND RURAL DEVELOPMENT IN THE EAST AFRICAN CONTEXT

The task of this second introductory essay is to provide an overview both of the penetrative efforts being made by the East African governments and of the societies that they aim to change. Analytically two kinds of penetration can be recognized: attempts to institutionalize a viable presence, and those which seek to use that presence to promote some social or economic change. The main emphasis in this paper, and in the volume as a whole, is on the latter, and specifically on policies for rural development. In practice, however, there is an important overlap between the two: the kinds of efforts to establish, restructure or reinforce central control that are described in some of the early essays usually have some broader economic purpose behind them, or at least have some basic societal consequences. In the first of these case studies, Vincent neatly summarizes the historical interconnection between the political and the socio-economic processes at work on the rural populations of East Africa: they were 'transformed into the administered, cash-crop growing, taxed and locally-represented public of the colonial era'. This analysis of the connection between the colonial administrative presence and the onset of the cash economy provides a useful starting point for the *evaluation* of post-colonial penetration in the East African context attempted in this paper, particularly in assessing to what ends policies for control and for change have interacted with rural society in that latter period.

First, however, we must make clear the basis for such evaluation. The modernization theorists offer one simple answer. Penetration is defined as one of the component elements in 'political development'. Penetrative efforts are then assessed on pragmatic grounds. If it works, if the penetration is 'effective' in an operational sense, then by definition modernization is enhanced. Yet this apparently objective basis for evaluation hides crucial value judgements: it is really saying 'we establish the ground rules and then judge the performance'.[1] Moreover, as several commentators have pointed out,[2] the concern with 'institutional' capabilities creates a bias towards stability and order that gets written into the ground rules. Bias is admittedly not inherent in the concept of

penetration, but it is inherent in the assumption that its achievement necessarily connotes 'modernization'. Nor is this begging of the question merely a
minor logical flaw of only academic significance, for the tacit equation of
penetration and order maintenance with 'development' leads some theorists to
mouth pseudo-scientific justifications for the most blatant and barbarous acts
of US imperialism. Lucien Pye's textbook can coolly treat 'counter-insurgency'
as one of the 'Aspects of Political Development'; while Samuel Huntington,
Ithiel de Sola Pool and others completely destroy any 'analytical utility' they
seek in terms such as 'nation-building' and 'modernization' by using them to
describe, and justify, American destruction of the Indochinese people and
countryside.[3]

A less simplistic, though still definitional reason for the positive evaluation
of effective penetration is that 'it is a prerequisite of the modern state' — and,
therefore of economic and social development. But to accept this as a necessary condition is not to admit that it is automatically sufficient. Historically as
well as logically there is an invalid assumption, for the model of development
that it implies does not fit the circumstances of contemporary underdevelopment. Penetration is presented in this sense as a component of a 'process
model'[4] — one where state power, in the hands of a 'modernizing elite', is used
to generate transformation of a still largely 'traditional' economy and society.
If it has any referent, this corresponds broadly to Japanese experience. But as
Barrington Moore[5] and others, as well as history, have pointed out, that
pattern of autonomous, state capitalist development has not been repeated in
this century. It is an option no longer available to late 20th century would-be
developers, for even in Africa 'the modern world [has] penetrated into the
furthest corners of the bush',[6] although 'the social scientists from the invading
metropolis seem unable to see how efficiently this penetration integrated these
societies into the dominant world system and how universally the latter imposed its social organization and alienation on the people whom Frantz Fanon
has called the damned of the earth.'[7]

Once this penetration and integration is recognized, however, the replica-
bility of the Japanese model must also be precluded by the resulting international and internal conditions. It is no longer the national society, even if
one exists, but the international capitalist economy on which one must focus
in order 'to study the system whose characteristics are the determinant ones
for development and underdevelopment'.[8] And this system is in turn repro-
ducing the *internal* conditions of this *under*development in most parts of the
Third World, and in particular inhibits the emergence of a national bourgeoisie
with the size, capital, power or interests to use the state to entrepreneur
separate industrialization. This recognition of the inapplicability of a model of
autonomous national development through state capitalism thus exposes modernization theory as 'not much more than thinly-veiled bourgeois ideology',[9]

to quote one of its leading practitioners. The required role of the modern state in development becomes one of facilitating the penetration of *international* capital, or as Pye euphemistically put it, 'the progressively deeper involvement of representatives of the international system in the domestic modernization process'.[10]

If we refer back to the historical origins of the modern state and its penetration into the rural areas of East Africa, we see that they were in fact colonial phenomena. Contrary to the modernization school which views colonialism as 'one of the stages in the process of modernization',[11] this paper will argue that the result of the interaction of the colonial state with the societies it penetrated was to promote the latter's underdevelopment and dependence.[12] Moreover, this reference back to the basic political economy of colonialism is a useful basis for evaluating the state in post-colonial societies and its strategic role in determining development prospects. The concurrence between analysts of left and right regarding the central role of the state is in fact nothing more than an agreement about 'the weakness of the bourgeoisie'.[13] The vacuum of local capital and power is vastly more marked in view of their great external structural dependence; for this is an era in which the power of international capital is now inestimably greater than when the Japanese embarked on their development. There is even less possibility of a reformed landed class and an incipient bourgeoisie controlling a strong, authoritarian state in order to promote such a path. Thus, there are logically only two alternatives facing the managers of the new states at the time of independence: one is to use the state to win a degree of political and economic independence and to mobilize the society for nationally integrated development which can transform its dependent, capitalist structure; the other is to continue to operate the state as a vehicle for penetration by *international* capital which at best might promote 'growth without development'.

This clearing of the methodological ground is necessary to establish a basis for evaluating the rural penetration occurring in East Africa. But it also involves the analyst in making a parallel choice. The two alternative perspectives on the study of penetration in general are graphically brought out in Gramsci's statement as to what constitutes the 'elements of politics':

In the formation of leaders, one premiss is fundamental: is the intention that there should always be rulers and ruled, or is the objective to create the conditions in which this division is no longer necessary? In other words, is the initial premiss the perpetual division of the human race, or the belief that this division is only an historical fact, corresponding to certain conditions?[14]

In the specific context of Africa, after more than ten years of independence, this choice is the one between complete liberation and continued dependence, between development and underdevelopment.

The 1970s offer a different perspective from that when much of the research reported here was begun; one which leaves 'independent Africa far from the political promise of independence, let alone from social change'.[15] Economic backwardness is as great as before and much of the continent is even more in pawn to foreign capital; with few exceptions, 'those who came to power mouthing the rhetoric of change faced the critical poverty of their countries with frivolity and fecklessness'.[16] The fearful predictions of Fanon that without fundamental social change independence would be a charade or a fancy dress parade, or, in Nyerere's equally striking phrase, merely 'flag independence', have been fulfilled in much of Africa. In such circumstances Africa truly 'needs a pitiless look at herself'.[17] Hopefully the generation of African scholars who are now taking over from the foreign researchers will face up to this responsibility. Meanwhile, as they depart from their interim role it would seem incumbent on the first, largely expatriate generation of students of post-independence Africa to explore pitilessly why development, viable nationhood and real independence have not been forthcoming, rather than to be apologists for the frivolous and feckless elites who have 'held African development to ransom',[18] and who 'organize the loot of whatever national resources exist'.[19]

In the brief pan-East African survey which follows we shall attempt to offer such a summary assessment of the relationship between the process of penetration in new states and the prospects for broad-based self-sustaining development. It will first provide some outline of the structures of the societies, not as some 'traditional' givens but as they have evolved due to the colonial situation.[20] This will establish the basis for an examination of the internal social character of the post-independence states and the external involvement in them in order to see how far they represent interests and pursue objectives different from those of the colonial period.

SOCIETIES AND STATES OF EAST AFRICA

The basic social structure of East African societies can be analyzed from two different but interrelated perspectives. Its *ethnic* diversity has been shaped by the differing environments and the resulting distribution of peoples within the present state boundaries and by the patterns of uneven development associated with colonialism. The underdeveloped nature of the society and its particular *class* character is in turn a resultant of the articulation of the colonial system with the varied pre-colonial social formations.

One key feature of the East African environment is the absence of a hinterland. Apart from a very thin coastal belt (and the islands of Zanzibar) which spawned a quite different, cosmopolitan 'Swahili' people with a distinctive, pan-tribal and predominantly Moslem culture,[21] much of the population is found far inland away from the coastal lowlands and the dry and barren plateau which covers much of the interior. In fact, well over a third of the 33 million people that the area supported in 1970 could be found in the well-watered areas around Lake Victoria. A significant proportion of the rest, perhaps another quarter, could be found in fertile, mountainous areas (in southern and western Uganda, in the central highlands of Kenya, and in various islands of fertility in Tanzania, most of them scattered round its borders). These two kinds of areas — the lakes and the mountains — capable of sustaining a dense, settled agricultural population free from the ravages of tsetse, provided the conditions for more complex societies and ultimately of larger and more hierarchical political units. The most significant state systems to emerge in the precolonial period were mainly in the northwestern part of the East African area. Away from the lakes and mountains, sparse populations depending largely on livestock and more marginal, shifting agriculture did not allow for complex social organization and the people were more widely scattered and culturally diffuse.

This particular historical pattern was further shaped by the colonial presence. The western kingdoms proved the chief initial attraction to European interests. The Protectorate of Uganda that was built up as the colonialists moved out from the largest indigenous state, Buganda, progressively incorporated other groups with similar hierarchical political forms, and elsewhere attempted to reproduce them or to promote some other more centralized system. Much of the land was fertile but already occupied by a settled African farming population. The colonial pattern that emerged was one where the primary economic emphasis was on peasant cash crop specialization (in coffee and cotton);[22] politically, a system of 'indirect rule' was developed mainly based on the pre-existing units and preserving something of their form. Conversely in Kenya, the opening-up by the Uganda railway of only partially-occupied highlands reminiscent of Europe attracted settler farmers as the standard-bearers of a different form of capitalism.[23] Their need to control land and labour together with the absence for the most part of any indigenous date systems led to a colonial administration which in its practice as well as its legal form was of a more 'direct' kind.

As nationalist politics emerged, their character differed markedly in the two countries. In Uganda they were more muted and local in focus, ultimately characterized by a struggle among changing alliances of local educated élites (some having a 'traditional' base) regarding both their own relative position and power and the status of their home areas within an African-run state. This pattern only partially mobilized the peasant mass of the population and then only behind their local, tribal or religious, political boss.[24] The elites in Kenya had first to assert themselves vis-à-vis the settler class. The latter had dominated the colonial state since the beginning of the century, its privileged and exploitative position being maintained at the expense of the landless, the labourers and poorer peasants in the areas most affected by settlement, all of whom became increasingly impoverished by denial of access to land, cash crops or other opportunities. The decolonization 'deal' was one that was initially forced to some extent on the settlers by other commercial and industrial interests able to persuade a British Conservative government of the advantages of accommodation with a new African élite and of concessions about the growing of cash crops and about land distribution.[25]

The history of the colonial impact on rural Tanganyika was not so clear-cut. The prior existence of a few state systems based on the exploitation of peasants by a non-producing class, coupled with conditions for profitable peasant agriculture in the northwest and in a few other highland pockets, was just one of the pre-colonial patterns. Elsewhere, smaller chiefdom units were based on a limited gathering of tribute from less intensive economies combining livestock with agriculture, while in the remainder of the country many very small segmented communities founded on domestic production were dispersed through very marginal environments.[26] A system of colonial administration, although formally labelled 'Indirect Rule', meant many different patterns in practice[27] and did not lead, as in Uganda, to notable cases where the existence and privileged position of some separate states was preserved to complicate the definition of nationhood and the form of the independent State. Equally, despite a German policy (prior to 1914) of encouraging settlers and its periodical re-emergence thereafter, their presence did not lead as in Kenya either to their domination of the political life of the territory or to the subservience of peasant economy to their interests.[28] At the same time, the greater size and more dispersed population of Tanzania coupled with the greater heterogeneity of its traditional political and economic forms minimized ethnicity as a divisive factor and encouraged the development of Swahili as a means of communication for administrative and other purposes and as a cultural and political cement allowing for more social and political cohesion in the urban areas.

Whatever the different territorial patterns of economic exploitation or forms of administration, within each of the three territories there was a great unevenness in their impact, which in turn accentuated differences between areas and affected their interrelationships. Thus, the southern districts of Uganda, primarily those that already saw themselves as retaining a separate political structure, enjoyed the benefits of rapidly expanding production of cotton and later coffee, as well as the secondary economic opportunities and educational and other social services that thereby became possible. Moreover, the demand for more labour on the part of emerging large farmers called forth a migration from less fertile areas in the north or more overcrowded areas like Kigezi. For a time these latter areas were officially prevented from growing cash crops, but after these restrictions could no longer be maintained politically, labour was brought in from Rwanda and even north-west Tanzania. In the latter country, the major peasant-produced cash crops (cotton and coffee) were limited in practice to a dozen or so of the sixty mainland districts — while a few districts which had become the 'traditional' labour-supply areas for the plantation/settler sector were deliberately underdeveloped in a manner similar to the general strategy that prevailed in Kenya.[29]

A very limited and somewhat arbitrary expansion of education and other social services, much of it in the hands of missionaries, was skewed in favour of the more pleasant and fertile climes and served to heighten intra-territorial regional inequalities. In addition to disparities in income and living standards among areas, the differential provision of education had significant effects on the regional and ethnic composition of the new non-rural social classes that began to emerge with the expansion of administration, commerce and services. Although these latter developments were limited to those essential for the continuation of the extractive agricultural economy, they did give rise to growing numbers of a commercial and petty bourgeoisie of traders, shopkeepers and a few larger businessmen and even some manufacturers, and also to a class in urban wage employment. In Kenya, with its settler agriculture and related business and later a growing local industry, the local bourgeoisie included many Europeans, while overseas companies were involved in the commercial networks in all three countries. A larger number of Asians were also found among the commercial and petty bourgeoisie and in the salariat of government and corporations. There were also significant numbers of Africans, drawn preponderantly from the more prosperous areas, occupying the lower levels of petty trading and of the wage and salary earners. Those selling their labour make up only a small proportion of the labour force — 5% in Tanzania and Uganda by the 1960s, 12% in Kenya with its semi-industrialization. With some national variation, these wage earners are more or less divided equally between agricultural (estate) labour, public sector employment, and private industrial and other urban jobs. The agricultural labour is still often migrant and tends to be drawn from the less privileged peasant families in areas of land shortage or from very marginal agricultural areas with limited cash crop opportunities. Official figures do not give much idea of the growing categories of landless, and of poor peasants who are dependent on selling their labour — as migrants or as neighbours to rich peasants in the favourable areas.

Some measure of how varying local conditions have differently affected the ethnic composition of the bourgeoisie and petty bourgeoisie, and urban worker classes, can be gleaned from the make-up of the urban populations, especially those of the capital cities, which contain over a third of the total urban populations and between 2-5% of the total population. Kampala (and Entebbe, the *administrative* capital of Uganda) and Nairobi both contain very large minorities drawn from the largest and most prosperous (and most centrally situated) tribe — the Ganda and Kikuyu respectively; Nairobi has also very substantial minorities from the three other large ethnic groups who also occupy favourable areas. Likewise, organized politics — the bureaucracies, the national political parties, trade unions and other interest groups — tend to be the preserve of these urban classes and to be the scene of rivalries between a few groups of élites each with allies drawn from an ethnic basis — and recruitment patterns tend to reinforce this pattern. Tanzania is not without such jockeying alliances for power, status and jobs but the combination of Swahili and the much more mixed composition of urban populations prevents vertical factions on an ethnic basis being the only or typical mode of politicking.

The uneven impact of colonial economic forces had consequences for the political involvement of the different local peasantries and of the various strata among them. An extreme case was that of Central Kenya where the desperation of the small peasant majority who were denied cash crops and access to more land and more particularly of the landless who were finally pushed back to overcrowded reserves in the early 1950s, led to their armed resistance to the settler-colonial authorities and to the 'landed gentry' in their own areas.[30] At this time there was some rural protest elsewhere in Kenya by emerging élites and by other peasant communities excluded from land and crop opportunities and hounded by conservation enforcement; outside these populated settlements in the West and Centre, an undifferentiated peasantry was not yet sufficiently disturbed to be involved. The 'peasant revolt' was regionally isolated and the partial satisfaction of peasant demands for cash cropping opportunities and land rights succeeded in buying-off all strata apart from the landless minority. In Uganda less dramatic outbreaks of resistance by peasants in Buganda to landlord and chiefly elements and to expropriation through the colonial marketing system occurred in the late 1940s.[31] This was also a time of peasant political activity in various areas of Tanzania. More often this was a general resistance by all the embryonic strata to pressures of colonial agricultural policy rather than an expression of any emerging classes within local society, although there was some opposition to chiefs.[32]

Rural protest took different forms, however. It could be confined to élite protest in backward areas or involve broad demands of an undifferentiated peasantry, but in a few areas it did represent a form of class struggle. It had, in Fanon's phrase, a different 'dialectic' from the urban protest; it was restricted to certain areas, and peasant demands were confined by the colonial authorities or met with partial concessions. In Kenya and Uganda where the separation of rural and urban politics and the regional differences were sharper, it was in the final stage possible for the colonial interests to negotiate a deal for decolonization with small groups of more educated, urban political activists of the major nationalist parties.

The party leaders did have supporters at a sub-national though hardly grassroots level, usually among traders, large farmers, sometimes chiefs, teachers and other 'notables' — people who had moved socially out of the purely peasant class and geographically out of the local community milieu to play roles as 'brokers' or 'middlemen' vis-à-vis the broader political and economic systems.[33] (Examples of such centre-local political links are provided by the contributions of Harris, Lamb and Hyden.) These locals were able to mobilize at least ritual affirmation for the party and the leaders in the immediate post-Independence period, and periodically more concrete support in elections (although none have been held in Uganda since 1963). Beyond this, the 'party' offered very little real opportunity for non-élites to wield political influence — and anyway, in all three countries observers are agreed on the preeminence of bureaucratic structures, even in Tanzania with its uncontested, apparently broadly-based national movement.[34]

Thus, apart from a few national party figures, state power is in the virtually unchallenged hands of the bureaucracy for which it is useful to distinguish two levels: (i) the central government ministries, some of which have a hierarchy of technical staff reaching out into the country; and (ii) the local administration and local authorities. Some of the latter have been landowners or others with 'traditional' economic status in many parts of Uganda and a few areas of Tanzania. With the latter exceptions, the members of the bureaucracy at all levels have been recruited principally on the basis of education — although their recruitment to one agency rather than another and their promotion and other opportunities may depend on ethnic alliances and loyalties or nepotism. Although not exclusively drawn from one class or area, its membership is shaped by the history of educational expansion and in turn by the unevenness of colonial development. Inevitably the more prosperous areas are overrepresented;[35] and it is generally the better-off families in these (and other) areas whose sons get the educational opportunities for civil service preferment. To that extent, bureaucrats will have important links with privileged rural or trading classes. The over-representation of officials from certain tribes also intensifies ethnic nepotism and alliances and conflicts for jobs. Indeed, promotions and influence on an ethnic basis are particularly pronounced in the bureaucracies. This is the case in appointments to, and the working of, public institutions in Tanzania even though such conflicts are largely absent in other arenas. But despite certain ethnic and class biases in the composition of the bureaucracy, it is education rather than class origin that is still the major key to entry. This gives education itself an elite flavour, reinforced of course by the typically élitist content of that education, thus creating the problem of alienation and privilege[36] which Tanzania alone of the three countries has sought to tackle.

The decision-making power is in the hands of a bureaucratic meritocracy, not drawn from or *obviously* subservient to any particular class; but that does not imply that it corresponds to a disinterested, modernizing élite selflessly neutral in the running of the state. Indeed, one must ask whose interests these bureaucracies are serving. One answer is they serve their own. The trends in post-independence Africa generally reflect efforts made by a politico-administrative élite using their new positions of power to achieve and preserve for themselves economic and social privileges. The inherited higher civil service

salary scales were essentially those of a European economy and place the incumbents in an enormously elevated position in the local economy. This pattern has been preserved and in Kenya even increased.[37] In all three countries
there was a tendency for political leaders and officials to use their income,
political influence and status to move into property and business undertakings
— and again in the Kenya case various credit and other provisions were available to them.[38] In Uganda, the accusation that 'most Ministers own fleets of
cars and houses and many businesses'[39] was given as a justification for the
army coup in 1971 and as evidence of the falseness of the claim that the members of the previous government had the common man's interests at heart.
Under Amin, it was members of the army and civil service hierarchies who had
first access to the businesses taken over from Asians. There is understandably
little systematic data as to how far civil servants were and still are benefitting
(not necessarily illegally) from such extra-curricular activities, but even in
Tanzania where it is less marked, this tendency for political leaders and officials 'to get into the practices of capitalism and landlordism' was noted by
Nyerere in 1967.[40] But despite an overall policy there which attacks this
pursuit of privilege there have been tendencies for bureaucrats to try to get
better terms for their own stratum by administrative action.[41]

There is then a very real prospect of bureaucrats and politicians using their
élite political position in order to become a property-owning 'class'. However,
even then they become not a truly 'national bourgeoisie' but only a dependent,
petty-bourgeois class, for very few of these bureaucrats are involved in entre-
preneuring the production of new wealth. As Fanon has observed, they do not
perform that developmental role of a 'classical bourgeoisie', but rather use their
influence to buy into existing opportunities — to 'be part of the racket'.[42]
Thus in Kenya and Uganda the most obvious instances of officials gearing
public resources to their interests are the political measures to help aspirant
Africans to replace Asians in trading, and in Kenya for them to buy into the
settler class.[43]

If we now try to summarize the structures of the emerging post-colonial
society and the purchase which different segments of the national society have
over the independent state, the answer to our queries as to whose interests it
represents will still not be unambiguously clear. Despite the different mixes of
size and form of the pre-colonial societies within the territories which now
form the three states, and the different economic policies and political structures used in the colonial period, there is still a basic similarity in their economic and social structures, as the figures below indicate. In each country the
peasantry, variously differentiated, constitutes the large majority of the population and when combined with those landless and other labourers working in
the rural sector account for between 80 and 90% of the population. Most of
this part of the population has benefitted little from growth either before or
after Independence and has no direct influence in political life, except for some

of the richer peasants and other local notables. These excepted categories, operating through a system of patronage, have some leverage upon political influentials at regional or even national level and on this basis maintain their own local position.[44] Beyond this local, rural setting the small urban population is predominantly made up of a group of employed workers whose number has scarcely increased in the last 20 years, plus a rapidly increasing number of school leavers and landless seeking permanent jobs. These latter categories of proletarianized or semi-proletarianized workers and 'marginal' groups have only a limited political voice — through industrial unions largely concerned with narrowly economic matters and through their involvement on the periphery of the political parties. At the national level, the indigenous petty bourgeoisie drawn differentially from more prosperous ethnic groups, who overlap with both the tiny group of politicians and the bureaucracy, have the most immediate connection with, and derive the greatest benefit from, the activities of the state. Moreover, the position of both political leaders and of senior government officials depends on a patronage pattern which provides a link between their ambitions, and in turn their ability to deflect resources 'back home', and the

The Composition of the East African Population by Source of Income

	Tanzania (1967)	Kenya (1968)	Uganda (1966)
Total Labour Force	5,525,000	4,300,000	4,000,000**
Employers	28,000	10,000*	n.a.
Employed on own account			
— urban (traders etc.)	52,000	120,000	n.a.
— rural (peasants)	4,100,000	3,120,000	3,000,000**
Family workers	900,000		
Employed workers			
— estate agriculture	90,000	150,000	55,000
— peasant agriculture	250,000	360,000	300,000
— urban	140,000	500,000	190,000

* Includes only firms and employers of more than 14 persons
** Author's estimate

Source: IMF, *Surveys of African Economies*, II (Washington DC, 1969).

aspirations of the local notables on whose organized support they partially depend. In brief, then, some tiny minorities of the indigenous population — large farmers, small traders and the bureaucrats — gain access to, and on the basis of ethnic groups compete for, state-controlled resources. And yet each of these is too small and politically too weak to be considered as in undisputed control of the state, and economically they are totally incapable of using their own meagre capital or even state resources to promote development. To further explore the real basis of state power and the roots wherein the prospects for development lie, we must then turn to an examination of the international influence at work on the state and society.

INTERNATIONAL PENETRATION

The continuing control that interests in the international capitalist system are able to exert in the new post-colonial states is due to the persistence of negative constraints limiting the freedom of action of these states to redefine policy and to the existence of positive channels for interference or influence. The major constraints are imposed by the nature of East Africa's integration in the world economy — the legacy of colonialism. The terms and extent of this involvement are indicated by the direction and central importance of foreign trade, the dependence of this trade on overseas markets for a few crops, and by the reliance on foreign capital investments in past and current plans.[45] The influence of these links on policy choices derives in the first instance from a concern not to jeopardize the short-run wellbeing of the economy. But more fundamental is the determinant effect they have had on the structure of the internal economy and the social structure and thus, in turn, on the political forces likely to be operative. Such economic dependence imposes severe limits on the policies that can be pursued not only to reshape the *internal* society and economy but also to pursue an independent foreign policy.

In addition to these broad constraints deriving from the underlying economic realities, a number of institutional arrangements provide specific instruments for ensuring continued dominance. These range from some of the provisions that were entrenched in Independence constitutions (like the land and anti-expropriation clauses in Kenya)[46] to the requirements of international agencies. The latter include, for example, the 'open-economy' condition imposed by the International Monetary Fund[47] and the subtle but profound inflection of the development path implicit in the granting or withholding of the stamp of approval of the World Bank or other agencies.[48] Post-Independence decisions not to disturb this basic relationship with the international capitalist economy, and to opt for major reliance on foreign private investment in development strategies naturally reinforced the imperative for conformity with foreign norms. All three East African states passed legislation 'voluntarily' denying themselves freedom of action in relation to foreign capital, and property relations generally, in an effort to solicit investment.[49] Particularly in Kenya the oft-reiterated public appeals for 'political stability' are always made in the name of providing — 'the key to development'[50] — a climate attractive to foreign investors (and also increasingly to tourists).

Dependence of a military rather than economic sort has also left East African countries open to foreign manipulation. The small national armies that originated in colonial days retained British officers for some time after Independence, and the countries looked to the West for equipment and training. And yet the security of the three states was not seriously threatened from the outside. The internal threat was, however, brought home most forcefully when an infectious wave of mutinies affected the three armies in January 1964: it was the British army that had to step in to 'restore order'; in other words, to guarantee the regime.[51] After that Tanzania and Uganda tried to diversify their reliance on overseas arms and trainers,[52] but Kenya has continued this alliance with Britain through a number of military agreements and the retention of British personnel in her armed forces, while also obtaining public security and counter-insurgency assistance from both the US and UK.[53] But even in the former countries the potential significance and scale of this continued presence was not always realized.[54] Under Amin, the dependence on arms suppliers has become vital to the military regime, and their desperation to guarantee deliveries is at the heart of many foreign policy shifts.

These external dependency connections and the military and political weaknesses of the regimes — both relatively in the international arena and domestically vis-à-vis their own societies — obviously render the new states more vulnerable to direct leverage by external agencies. There have been many instances where donor governments have linked the granting and withdrawing of aid to political conditions. In 1966, President Julius Nyerere noted twelve instances where Tanzania had refused to alter her own policy stance and had had to forego assistance.[55] Since then, the British have cancelled or frozen loans already agreed on several occasions, and even vetoed a World Bank loan on grounds that inadequate compensation had been given for expropriated property.[56] Britain, too, froze a loan of £10 million to Uganda, after the government's decision to expel Asians who were British citizens.[57] The solidly racist basis for Amin's decision does not make Britain's ability to influence any the less. Whatever the specific impact of such incidents, they act as permanent general markers indicating to the new states just how far their actions are circumscribed whenever they rely on this assistance.

Intervention by agencies of foreign governments no doubt occurs on a regular basis through a variety of diplomatic and political as well as economic channels, even though only occasional tips of this iceberg are susceptible to scholarly perusal. In Kenya especially, there has been a long tradition of external financing of political groups and individuals, which has occasionally been indicated publicly.[58] That more clandestine acts of interference occur cannot be fully documented but can be surmised by the world-wide scale of operation of such imperialist instruments as the Central Intelligence Agency,[59] and by occasional clues which enter the public record, such as the disclosures of a former US Ambassador to Kenya or the use of foreign jets to drop anti-TANU propaganda.[60]

Perhaps the most salient influence is not that transmitted through official agencies of foreign governments but that arising from the thorough penetration of the economy by overseas capital, which provides a whole array of institutional mechanisms for direct control of areas of economic and political life. First, their general importance in the economy ensures that 'although they do not have access to the tools of coercion, foreign business interests could "buy" it in a situation of crisis,' as one Kenya commentator puts it.[61] The kinds of calculations that are made and the pressures (both negative sanctions and economic rewards) are illustrated by certain dimensions of the coup in Uganda in January 1971. The British Government gave almost immediate recognition to Amin's Government, and in applauding this *The Times* pointed to numerous shortcomings of Obote's regime, but their first charge was that it was 'hostile to British interests.'[62] It was not surprising then that plans were soon announced that the new Government of Uganda would restore a controlling interest in the banks and other foreign-owned businesses partially nationalized in 1970,[63] or that this announcement was followed by accommodating loans and other assistance being extended to the Government.[64] Despite his excesses, Amin was only belatedly considered to be inadequate to the task of safeguarding capitalist interests, and at that point the British Government made no secret of its intention to bring about a change of regime, through a set of economic pressures orchestrated with the Kenyan Government.

Less dramatic but more pervasive are a number of regular levers that such interests can apply. Individual decisions to invest or not, to expand or contract, to hire more labour or introduce more capital-intensive machinery, when aggregated have a largely determining effect on the wellbeing of large numbers of people, and on the character of the actual development path — and even of the emerging social structure. This influence continues to be predominant in the 'modern' sector wherever private investment is relied upon for the promotion of industrialization and in the absence of any independently worked-out industrial strategy. Even Tanzania's efforts at 'self-reliant' development are in fact severely limited because these circumstances persist even under a nationalized industrial corporation, as Packard and others have shown.[65] Another success in foreign capital's ability not merely to shape projects but to define the whole context within which certain activities are carried out has been charted by a study of industrial relations in Kenya,[66] which shows that international corporations working through an Employers' Federation were able to dictate 'the personality of the trade union movement', the wage structure and the character of much of the labour force, and also to ensure that conflicts between labour and capital are fought out 'on ground chosen by management: within the business rather than the political arena.' The same defining intervention has been experienced in the rural sector. The Tanzania strategy of concentrating on a costly 'transformation' pattern of new capital-intensive settlement which was defined in the final colonial period, was thereafter promoted and given the stamp of approval by the World Bank, and thus was continued for five years after Independence.[67] An even more decisive impact was behind the combined agrarian policies of phased and partial Africanization of the settler sector (maintaining exports and land values) and the introduction of individualistic landholding in the former 'reserves', started in the terminal colonial period and still pursued by the Kenya Government today.[68] Some of the fundamental consequences of these rural policies for defining the social structure will be indicated in a subsequent section.

Development strategy in all areas is also subject to external influence due to the degree of initiative that is allowed (partly by the absence of alternative plans) prospective investors and foreign public assistance providers, and this influence is augmented when, to fill some of the gaps in local planning, 'experts' are provided often to assist in such areas as 'project preparation'.[69] A related influence must be mentioned here, support for and involvement in education programmes. Although the three countries have fairly rapidly taken over full responsibility for primary education, there continues to be a concentration of foreign resources in technical education and in such fields as public administration and the social sciences generally by Western governments and foundations[70] which have a determining impact on future development paths through dictating the personnel, the kind of technology and even the theoretical models on which future development is based.

Some final points must be made in discussing the mechanisms used for the continued involvement of international capital in East Africa. First, it should be stressed that the main purpose of this brief survey is to illustrate not occasional instances of pressure or influence over some particular project or policy, but rather to indicate a fundamentally neo-colonial pattern where much of the detail of administration and implementation is left in the hands of the local state managers (at least as long as they can be trusted). Nevertheless, those few key areas of decision making which have defining influence over future development trajectories and thus over the structural arrangements of the internal society and its external links are subjected to almost decisive control by foreign interests.

The least obvious but most persistent institutional means for foreign penetration has been, of course, the mechanism of the market. Indeed, to the extent that governments leave market forces unregulated and increasingly open up their societies to trade and investment, more vigorous and overt day-to-day control is no longer as necessary as it was in the early colonial period. The major instances of direct political intervention are in fact occasioned by threats to the 'free' market entry of foreign goods and capital.

The continuation of both direct political and indirect market penetration is in fact facilitated by the political weakness and the limited experience, size and capacities of indigenous ruling élites. But it is also encouraged by the privileged but dependent class position of these élites. The extent of domination was gradually realized and challenged by the leadership in Tanzania which proclaimed a policy of 'Socialism and Self-reliance' in 1967,[71] and in a more tentative fashion by Obote in Uganda in 1969 and 1970.[72] What was also partially realized was the connection between external capital and the class interests of the incumbents. In Tanzania the self-reliance policy was accompanied by measures — constraints on business interests of political actors, broader demo-

cratic control and political education — designed to reduce the equation between political power and economic privilege.[73] The reaction of those whose
interests were threatened was essentially the stumbling block on which Obote's
efforts in the same direction foundered.[74]

In Kenya the congruence of interests between international capital and
those that are being acquired by the new élite of politicians and bureaucrats is
most evident. This congruity is reflected in their shared concern to preserve the
structural status quo — the same pattern of imports, of tax and income structure, of encouragement of private business and protection for property — and
is reinforced by the (western) educational basis for élite recruitment, and by
cultural intrusion and assimilation. This pattern also involves a division of
labour whereby foreign capital controls the major productive undertakings and
the national élite maintains the requisite conditions for them, administers and
shares in the benefits without risk. Moreover, this élite is drawn initially from
the top levels of politics and the bureaucracy, but its economic interests are
confined to the lower end of the business spectrum. There are thus no aspiring
national industrialists likely to be in conflict with the large foreign corpora-
ations and, as yet, there is not even much competition between settler and
indigenous large farmers in Kenya. However, there are great pressures, essentially from the political élites themselves, to allow greater entry into trade and
smaller commercial ventures — and it is these conflicts in aspirations which are
behind various measures directed against the petty bourgeois element among
the Asian communities.[75] In more substantial business activities there are
usually alliances between African businessmen (many of whom are actively
engaged in politics)[76] and foreign companies, through partnerships, special
financing, supply of goods, and similar arrangements.[77]

A more problematic question is whether this congruity is likely to persist.
One possible contradiction, to which we shall return, is that even now apparent
between the more farsighted of the overseas interests and local political managers (who stress the need to maintain the political conditions for the basic
neo-colonial pattern and urge reformist measures to ease unemployment,
satisfy some landless, and limit the grosser inequalities) and those newly 'part
of the racket' who are not prepared to lose their short-run benefits.[78]

STATE POWER AND NATION BUILDING

This portrayal of the character of the independent states of East Africa in the
context of the international political economy hopefully illuminates the case
studies which follow by providing some definition of the nature of that 'centre'
whose efforts at penetration form their subject matter. It also provides a framework for some preliminary evaluation of those efforts. This section will further
examine the first of the two dimensions of penetration: what is often seen as

the basic 'crisis' that new states face in their attempts to survive and to control and administer the societies. But, consistent with the aim of this paper, these nation and state building initiatives will be assessed not just by the yardstick of 'capacity to rule' but by their development implications. Are the attempts to build legitimate institutions and to make policy measures stick only a means of mystification and repression or the real prelude to improving conditions of life?

Posing the issue in such a way allows one to go beyond the popular discussion of the crisis of penetration, which typically poses it in terms of the difficulties that face the centre in handling the ethnic and other factions which seek greater autonomy from government control. Certainly ethnicity has been a real factor in the politics of East Africa as well as the one most often discussed. The conflicts that have beset the Uganda Government in accommodating Buganda are discussed by Mafeje.[79] Kenya gained Independence amid speculation that there would be Congo-like destruction, and at subsequent stages of her post-Independence first the Kalenjin and coastal peoples, then the Luo and to some extent the Kamba have been viewed as being alienated from the centre.[80] Even in Tanzania, noted for the general absence of fissiparous tendencies, such factors have come into play. These have typically occurred in areas like Ugogo, discussed by Rigby, where the absence of indigenous middlemen and of development programme alike tended to make people consider the whole institutional apparatus as alien.

In exploring the significance of ethnicity we should first heed the caution that incorporation is not the only or easiest solution. In some situations there may be other possible forms of 'linkage' to the centre than assimilation or subservience. The strategies of regional and ethnic groups (insofar as they can be considered as single actors) is often to seek not autonomy but alliance with the centre, especially when provision of services is at stake. Secondly, the centre is clearly not neutral or homogeneous in ethnic terms. Efforts to exclude representatives from an area or cut off resources to it and reactions to these measures will be influenced by the ethnic make-up of the centre. In Tanzania, for instance, the home origins of Nyerere and most of his fellow leaders give the central authorities a national colour and thus make possible a number of initiatives which were not possible to Obote or even to the Kenyatta Government. And yet the two latter regimes differed from each other in ethnic composition: the largest group in the former sought autonomy from the centre, in the latter hegemony over it.

Initiatives from the centre are, frequently and understandably, interpreted and reacted to by different parts of the population as steps which promote the control or influence of one ethnic group over another. Such reactions occur even though the initiatives are justified as attempts at genuine state or nation building.

Thus efforts to consolidate central state power in, say, Uganda in the 1960s have been interpreted as aimed at bringing Buganda 'into line', or as a device for establishing the hegemony of the northern leaders over the Bantu people of the South, or even of Protestants over Catholics. Were similar jockeyings and enforcements in Kenya the efforts of a neutral, state-building centre to combat regionalism, or part of a design to give preference to the larger tribes or just to the Kikuyu, or even simply a Kiambu District establishment? Or were these centralizing tendencies in both countries but the consolidation of a ruling clique's monopoly of the spoils of independence? As several writers have reminded us,[81] both attempts to promote 'integration' as well as the manipulation of an ethnic, clientelist pattern of symbolic participation may only serve to cloud the fact of continued extraction of the national surplus by the state power holders and to inhibit an awareness of where the interests of the non-privileged classes lie.

That political initiatives by the centre against one region and the responses to them are essentially matters of intra-élite conflict is suggested by some of the more dramatic episodes in recent East African history. In Kenya switches in the calculations of provincial leaders (in the case of the coast and Rift Valley people in 1964) and the sudden emergence of an alternative group of Luo leaders in 1970, both brought temporarily alienated areas back into acceptance of the centre,[82] seemingly without demur from the ordinary population. Mafeje's study of Uganda also shows that separatist resistance of Buganda to central control was a response of the local ruling group and not a single homogeneous reaction by a united 'tribe'. The responses of other sections of the population of Buganda varied according to the interests of different classes. Where there is a relative absence of such opportunities to manipulate parochial support and to mystify different local publics into accepting that the answer to their poverty lies in ethnic competition, as in Tanzania, an opening to the left can be possible. A degree of class rather than ethnic consciousness there has made possible effective imposition of some curbs on élite privileges and a redistribution of resources for development purposes.

Given the high degree of internal social stratification it might well have been possible for the Obote central government to penetrate Buganda more effectively and to mobilize support from other strata of the society against the Ganda ruling class had it used a differentiated approach. In fact, Obote did proclaim a policy after the 1966 intervention to 'punish the top and serve the masses in Buganda'.[83] However, the opportunity for doing so – for instance by reallocation of sinecures and land – was missed, partly because of the conservatism of some members of the central élite as well as of the influence of Buganda bureaucrats, both through their prominence in the civil services and their patronage over the rural population of Buganda. A similar blunting effect of privileged strata on more egalitarian policies is found in Tanzania where the better-off professional traders and large farmers, acting as 'middlemen' in dealings with the centre, were thus able to inhibit and divert central efforts to change the rural social structure of Tanzania.[84]

A comprehensive analysis of the capacity of local socio-economic structures to influence the national political institutions and their policies, including those aimed at social transformation, is beyond the scope of this essay. It would entail a specification of the different strata and classes within each area (or ethnic group), indicating for each not just the generalized links with the centre but those differential connections and orientations maintained by the separate horizontal strata. However, this differentiated perspective of the linkages along two dimensions is stressed in several of the studies contained in this collection particularly those of Mafeje, Lamb, Vincent, Hyden and Harris.

One common feature in the patterns of linkage between the centre and the differing strata of several varied peripheries is their mediation through a many-tiered structure of ethnic patronage. Leys has drawn 'a speculative parallel' between on the one hand, this

'pyramidal' character of clientelist political structures, which consist essentially of unequal exchange relationships produced again and again at each level from the village up to the national party leaders and their lieutenants, and between the latter and the various kinds of power holders in developed countries; and on the other the structure of exploitative relationships portrayed by Frank between centre and periphery, from the metropolitan power down through the neo-colonial capitals to the rural townships and finally into the fields.[85]

Seen in this light such an internal 'clientelist' hierarchy parallels and supports the continuing external dependence and resulting underdevelopment; moreover, it also serves to sustain a myth of 'participation' which still leaves unchallenged the status quo of élite privilege and international penetration.

The general applicability of this pattern should not obscure for the observer, as it often does for those clients in the system, the basic underlying reliance of the inherited system not on a limited and manipulated ethnic participation but on relationships of power and exploitation. The colonial administrations were essentially based on force not authority, and had as prime functions the preservation of law and order and the collection of taxes. That these are the continuing preoccupations of the contemporary administration and their use of similar methods are illuminated in a survey by Brokensha and Nellis of what Kenyan officials actually do.[86] Elsewhere it has been argued that in Kenya, partly as a result of calculations about 'national integration', 'public order had to be stressed at the expense of human rights, and once the new Government had made the same choice as the old and departing administration, the legal and administrative systems were ready to hand to implement it.' And that, whether or not this choice *had* to be made (and it will be argued below that it derives as much from the choice of a particular, neo-colonial development strategy), it has resulted in a continuing 'increase in the powers of the Executive'.[87] To the panoply of repressive measures inherited from the colonial government (including administrative supervision of almost all political activities) the powers of detention, control of specified tribes and other measures were added as 'emergency' powers of the President and then were made routine under the Preservation of Public Security Act.[88] Similar powers although not so widespread or so often invoked were introduced in the other two countries.

Among the many consequences of this kind of tight administrative 'penetration' for the prospects for development, two contradictions should be noted. Firstly, the resulting relationships between people and administrators inevitably preclude the possibility of government's being able to promote development in the sense of development of the people's own capabilities.

As the studies by Brokensha and Nellis and that by Harris in this volume make clear, at a purely operational level a bureaucracy charged with preserving order which spends much of its time chivying people for taxes will have neither the inclination, the time nor the trust to mobilize popular energies. Not only do the powers inherited from the colonial administrations inhibit the development efforts of the people but so do their very authoritarian styles. In Kenya the officials of the Provincial Administration issue their stern warnings from beneath pith helmets.[89] In Tanzania in 1971 TANU endeavoured to reverse the tendency towards 'commandism' in an effort to get genuine mobilization, but the interests of the bureaucrats and the methods of work to which they have become accustomed made this reversal very difficult.[90]

A second consequence of this tight central control is that it leads to increased resources being diverted from potentially developmental purposes. In Kenya, the salaries of a growing bureaucracy are taking up an increasing share of government revenue and in that country and Uganda expenditure on internal security has been growing rapidly.[91] This tendency has become so marked under the military regime in Uganda that a recent government statement that more military equipment was on its way had to be accompanied by an announcement that eleven new rural hospitals would not be able to open their doors due to the unavailability of funds for their upkeep.[92]

STRATEGIES FOR RURAL DEVELOPMENT

The establishment of a central presence is not sought as an end in itself — not even by the colonial regimes — but to effect certain policies. It has been argued that in fact the historical purpose of the state and its control in East Africa was to integrate the countries effectively into the international capitalist system, a process resulting in 'underdevelopment'. The whole set of post-independence policies for change, whether they can be conceived as a coherent development strategy (at least by anyone other than the World Bank teams who laid them down) or merely as an aggregation of separate initiatives, reflected considerable continuity with that colonial pattern. There was a change of emphasis and pace — each of the countries aiming to widen their range of export crops, to promote some import-substituting light industry, and to expand education more rapidly — but there was no serious effort in the immediate post-Independence period to change the colonial economic patterns of dependence or the internal socio-economic structure.

In Kenya, some change in the racial exclusiveness of the economic structure had been initiated during the terminal period of colonial rule. African peasant producers were granted the right to grow coffee and other cash crops, new farming techniques were promoted, and a legal reform was carried out in the pattern of land tenure, individual freehold titles being granted to confirm the increasingly individual practice in production, thereby also confirming the position of the various rural classes and giving the middle peasants (but not the landless and poor) a stake in the status quo. Likewise a significant area of European farms was divided up and distributed to individual Africans, initially many of the landless and then subsequently to those who could afford the deposits for larger plots. But in both the 'Peasant' and 'Large Farm' (as the former White Highlands were thereafter termed) Sectors of Kenya agriculture, the basic intent of the reform was simply to modify and hence stabilize the existing patterns: the land issue was defused; and the prospects of the large remaining settler area were preserved.[93]

In the two other countries with already established peasant cash-crop producing areas, agrarian policies aimed at diversifying from reliance on cotton and coffee, and thus at expanding cash-cropping into new areas — through a slightly less authoritarian, more 'community development' system of agricultural extension advisory service for individual peasant producers. Instead of enacting formal changes in land rights as in Kenya, both Uganda and Tanzania governments allowed an evolutionary transition towards individualism, commercialization and stratification to continue. Some costly 'schemes' which created new structural arrangements in a few limited areas were part of the rural strategies in these two countries. Uganda sought to promote mechanization especially of cotton growing in 'group farms',[94] while Tanzania continued its transformation policy of village settlement. Both of these kinds of schemes were discontinued in the latter 1960s, proving too costly and capital-intensive but also suffering from failures of their administrations to involve the 'members' effectively and productively.

Various problems of 'reaching the peasant' in both these new, organized schemes and in a peasant context are dealt with in the case studies in this collection. Chambers surveys some of the institutional arrangements that were set up, as do the district and divisional surveys of Kenya (by Mutiso) and Tanzania (by Harris and Rigby). The complementary pair of studies by Van Velzen and Leonard on agriculture and Sharman's study on nutrition raise key issues about the working of extension services. These studies — as well as a considerable volume of other findings from East Africa and elsewhere[95] — clearly suggest that the 'problem' of penetration is scarcely ever to be sought in the resistant cultural stance of the peasant. They thus give the lie to the elitist assumptions, like that of LaPalombara,[96] that 'the most widespread and fundamental form of penetration crisis', the peasants 'fiercest opposition to center-determined programmes designed to improve their lot', stems from the 'obstinate refusal of the peasantry to have its material condition improved'. Rather the body of evidence from East Africa indicates that the origin of the 'problem of communication' has to be sought in the organizational inadequacies and the alien and authoritarian style plus the privileged social character and milieu of the rural bureaucracies and their personnel. Further, our case studies of development programmes in harsh environments like those of Ugogo as well as other programmes such as the Bukedi nutrition programme (again supported by an accumulation of other evidence)[97] indicate that plans conceived by the centre cannot always be assumed to bring actual benefit to the 'target' population. Another striking conclusion which also casts doubt on the notion of inherent peasant conservatism is suggested by figures of cash-crop producers among local peasantries given by Lamb and Leonard which show that even such simple 'normal' benefits as a regular source of cash income or some simple improved crop variety are often available only to a minority of peasants. Leonard's further evidence about the counter-productive concentration of agricultural services, together with the general tendency for complex mechanized schemes to fail, suggests the general conclusion that rural development strategies have benefitted only a portion of peasants without transforming the agrarian systems socially or technically — there has been 'growth' (within the limits of falling export prices and quotas) enjoyed by some which has increased stratification, but no development of the peasantry as a whole.

continued crop exporting as the basis for a few foreign-owned industries coupled with rural development strategies of individual peasant improvement) in countering dependence and underdevelopment and their class forming tendencies were realized in Tanzania after 1967. The Arusha Declaration policies of nationalization and self-reliant industrial development, of educational reorientation and the move toward mass politics, and their intensification in the 'TANU Guidelines' of 1971, marked a clear departure from élite-initiated plans supported and dictated by foreign capital. The rural policy of *ujamaa* sought to initiate a structural transformation of peasant life through cooperatives as a means for promoting broad-based development without class formation. These changes in strategy have been dealt with in some detail elsewhere,[98] although the contributions of Harris and Hyden deal with some elements of this socialist strategy. The basic conclusion from the evaluation of this alternative development experience reveals the limited capacity of the new political élites (given their existing values and interests) to implement policies with a socialist content. Other work on Tanzania underlines a further consequence of the ideological inadequacy of the bureaucratic stratum: that in this situation foreign capital is free to determine, in its own interests, the development path of even nationalized undertakings.[99]

Another component of strategy in addition to the policy objectives which must be briefly examined, is the deployment of the various media and institutions. Although the central organs of the colonial state and the provincial administrations were basically similar in the three countries, some significant institutional differences occurred at the sub-district level because the direct form of administration was more pervasive in Kenya compared with the efforts to work through (modified) indigenous structures in many parts of Uganda and Tanzania. Beyond this, it is also relevant to an assessment of the centre's development role to note that state institutions took on a wider range of activities in East Africa than was generally the case in British West African colonies. Settlerdom in Kenya, and its influence on its neighbours through the East African common market, dictated the proliferation of state involvement in areas of the economy, especially crop marketing and other aspects of agriculture that were elsewhere in the hands of market forces or international monopolies.[100]

Generally there has been a marked continuity in the framework of institutions and their roles — the penetrative core of a provincial administration survived, with modifications in Tanzania and Uganda and with increased power in Kenya: and the state role in marketing, servicing of agriculture and the provision of economic infrastructure has remained central. The partial industrialization has often depended on an extension of the state's role — the guarantee of monopolist conditions. One pattern of change that has been a feature of institutional developments in all three countries is the multiplication of new structures whose questionable benefits are examined by Chambers. In that context it is worth noting how far the interests of bureaucrats *qua* bureaucrats seem to dictate calculations about expansion and deployment. The potential distorting effect of such tendencies on the implementation of more egalitarian and progressive policies is documented in Tanzania by Packard[101] and, at grassroots level, by Van Velzen.

Again though, some major departures from inherited patterns can be observed in Tanzania. One dimension of the changed deployment is the role given to participatory agencies. The nationalist party has continued to play a significant role in both decision-making and implementation of policies and attempts have been made to broaden its base — whereas in the two neighbouring countries, as virtually everywhere on the continent, the parties have ceased to exist except for some periodic symbolic or manipulative function. Educational channels to politicize both incumbent and next generation 'élites' and the worker and peasant masses have been used in an effort to change the pattern of élite-dominated politics.[102] And more recently some first steps were taken to shift power away from the privileged bureaucrats and from the intervention of agents of international capital by a new Declaration which included the formation of a people's militia, a call to end commandism, greater party control over state agencies, coupled with renewed political education about the

relation between imperialist underdevelopment and the socialist alternative.[103] There has also been a major attempt at decentralization of government
development agencies and their fusion with local representative bodies.[104] But
the general pattern emerging in Tanzania is that the intentions of the leadership
have not been realized. The ujamaa programme has in practice become a
bureaucratic exercise in relocation, villagization; decentralization has led to
more local projects but power has passed to the more numerous officials in the
regions not to the people; the nationalized economic institutions are still
operating according to capitalist norms and under the direction of international
agencies.

CONCLUSIONS

In this introduction to the East African context it has been possible only to
raise some general issues about 'penetration' and development rather than offer
definitive conclusions. It has in particular tried to push two matters to the
centre of the discussion: the question of the historical roots of the problem of
East Africa's underdevelopment and, hence, the direction wherein development
prospects are to be found; and secondly, whether patterns of penetrative activities have in fact contributed to development or underdevelopment. Posing such
questions explicitly must inevitably reject the approach of most western
models of 'modernization' which beg them by their definition of 'development'
as evolutionary and western (thus assuming away the most debatable proposition) and by evaluating any form of penetration for whatever ends as a contribution to 'political development'. Alternatively, answers to these two issues
have been sought by an examination of the origins of underdevelopment in
colonialism and of the international character of the penetrative efforts of the
colonial state. The historical base was used to explore the social character of
the independent state and to assess whether the control and extractive mobilization dimensions of recent penetration marked a departure from a neo-
colonial continuation of the underdeveloping of East Africa societies through
the penetration of international capital. The individual case studies can help
to further illuminate some specific aspects of these issues, and in turn can, if
read in this broad context, shed light on the theoretical problem of identifying
the prospects for development, both the social and economic opportunities
and the appropriate political measures.

By and large the pattern that is suggested by this short survey, by the cases
here and much other work since this volume was put together, is that the East
African states represent a range of experiences, but all within that continuum
that can be labelled neo-colonial. Those who have occupied state power in
Kenya have willingly lent themselves to institutionalizing a structure suited to
the needs of a new generation of foreign investments and in the course of it

have been themselves among the foremost in the breeding of a greedily acquisitive petty and commercial bourgeoisie. They have done so with only a minimum of organized political opposition which they have so far contained by ethnic manipulations and by some limited reforms in the agricultural sector. Tanzania is a different and interesting case for us to consider as the leaders have attempted to a degree to use state power to penetrate the society for a different purpose, to reverse some of the inherited patterns and reduce dependence and to foster some kind of 'domestic socialism'. In particular they have set out with a quite different strategy to 'transform' rural society, but these efforts have in fact founded on the rocks of bureaucratic control and conservatism, and of the interests of kulaks, traders and other petty bourgeois elements within the society and those of foreign capital in all its institutional guises. Uganda represents an intermediate case, where some internal political shifts were used as the basis for a limited programme of economic nationalism, but resistance to this effort allowed the emergence of an arbitrary and repressive military regime very much more immediately geared to its short-run personal interests and power rather than to those of a broader indigenous class and thus ultimately put international capital in jeopardy.

NOTES

1. The quotation is from E. Friedman & M. Selden (eds), *America's Asia; Dissenting Essays on Asian-American Relations* (New York, Pantheon Books, 1971, vii), but a number of critics note this concern of the 'modernizationists' with global typologies and categories, even more sympathetic commentators including W. Illich and N. Uphoff, *The Political Economy of Change* (University of California Press, 1969).

2. R.I. Rhodes, 'The Disguised Conservatism in Evolutionary Development Theory', *Science & Society*, 32, 4 (1968) and D. Cruise O'Brien, 'Modernization, Order and the Erosion of a Democratic Ideal: American Political Science, 1960-1970', *Journal of Development Studies*, 8, 4 (July 1972).

3. Pye's book: *Aspects of Political Development* (Boston, Little, Brown, 1966) has a chapter entitled 'Insurgency and the Suppression of Rebellions'. Huntington and de Sola Pool were among the more well-known academics who participated as planners and advisers in the Vietnam war; the former offers an astounding example of cynical barbarity when he heralds US success in 'stumbling upon the answer to "wars of national liberation" – forced draft urbanization and modernization' ('The Bases of Accommodation', *Foreign Affairs*, 46, 4, 1968) – a euphemism for the systematic terror bombing of the rural population! The general manner in which many of those who have made the running with modernization theory have prostituted themselves as apologists for American imperialist expansion is documented in N. Chomsky, *American Power and The New Mandarins* (New York, Pantheon Books, 1967); in J. Coburn, 'Asian Scholars and Government – The Chrysanthemum and The Sword' in Friedman & Selden, *America's Asia*, and in C. Cruise O'Brien and W. Dean Nanech (eds), *Power and Consciousness* (University of London Press, 1969).

4. The phrase is used by R.P. Dore, 'On the Possibility and Desirability of a Theory of Modernization' (Institute of Development Studies, Sussex, Communications Series 38, October 1969) in arguing that modernization theorists have concentrated on defining the *nature* of the transition rather than the method or cause. The simplistic and paternalist view of the possible means which does occasionally emerge is exemplified by the way Pye

sets up the problem of penetration: to bridge 'the gap between the world of the ruling elite and that of the masses of the people who are still oriented toward their parochial ways'. *Aspects of Political Development*, 64.

5. Interest in the Japanese process as a model of 'Non-Western modernization' is seen for instance in the volume by R.E. Ward and D.A. Rustow, *Political Modernization in Japan and Turkey*, in the prestigious Princeton University Press series on Political Development. Barrington Moore's analysis in *Social Origins of Dictatorship and Democracy: Lord and Peasant in the Making of the Modern World* (Harmondsworth, Penguin, 1969) stresses the unique circumstances of that experience — as well as its authoritarian consequences.

6. F. Fanon, *The Wretched of the Earth* (Harmondsworth, Penguin, 1967), 58. This assertion is at the heart of the literature on the 'development of underdevelopment', and is documented for Africa by W. Rodney, *How Europe Underdeveloped Africa* (Dar es Salaam, Tanzania Publishing House, 1972) and in several of the works of Samir Amin.

7. A. Gunder Frank, 'Sociology of Development and Underdevelopment of Sociology' in J.D. Cockcroft, A. Gunder Frank & D.L. Johnson, *Dependence and Underdevelopment, Latin America's Economy* (New York, Anchor Books, 1972), 334.

8. Ibidem, 339.

9. J. LaPalombara (editor among other works of *Bureaucracy and Political Development* [1964] in the Princeton series), 'Decline of Ideology: A Dissent and an Interpretation', *American Political Science Review*, LX (1966), 14-15. The manner in which this ideology is used to serve imperial purposes is illustrated by the following, from the US Dept. of Navy, Information Program for Foreign Military Trainees, 14 December 1966, quoted by M.D. Wolpin, *Military Aid and Counterrevolution in the Third World* (Lexington, Heath, 1973): '... if military trainees are subjected to systematic political propaganda and organization, and return home with explicit theories as to how their countries' political structure should be changed, it is quite conceivable that such politically oriented training would improve the chances that the donor country retain influence over their trainees.'

10. Pye, *Aspects of Political Development*, 14. A number of similar quotes, calling for 'deliberate political and economic intervention', 'more extensive American involvement', from the works of such academics as Black, Deutsch, Emerson, Huntington and Pye are cited in A.R. Dennon, 'Political Science and Political Development', *Science and Society*, 33, 3 (1969) and D.L. Johnson & J. Ocampo, 'The Concept of Political Development', in Cockcroft, Frank & Johnson, *Dependence and Underdevelopment*.

11. Again Pye provides a forthright example: 'the spread of imperialism and colonialism and the resurgence of nationalism stand out as phases of broad cultural contact in the world-wide process of modernization.' C.E. Black, *The Dynamics of Modernization* (New York, Harper & Row, 1966), gives it as his assessment of colonialism that 'it served to diffuse the benefit of modernization at a cost that is, relatively speaking, modest', p. 131.

12. For discussion of *structural* underdevelopment see, among others, P. Baran, *The Political Economy of Growth* (New York, Monthly Review Press, 1956); T. Szentes, *The Political Economy of Underdevelopment* (Budapest, Akademiai Kiado, 1971), and S. Amin, *L'Accumulation à l'échelle mondiale* (Paris, Anthropos, 1971).

13. J. Peck, 'The Roots of Rhetoric — The Professional Ideology of America's China Watchers', in Friedman & Selden, *America's Asia*, 57.

14. A. Gramsci, *Selections from the Prison Notebook* (London, Lawrence & Wishart, 1971), 144.

15. R. First, *The Barrel of a Gun, Political Power in Africa and the Coup d'etat* (Harmondsworth, Penguin, 1972), 8 and 9.

16. Ibidem.

17. Ibidem.

18. Ibidem.

19. Fanon, *The Wretched of the Earth*, 37.

20. G. Balandier defines 'The Colonial Situation' in I. Wallerstein (ed), *Social Change, The Colonial Situation* (New York, Wiley, 1966) not merely as the colonial state or its policies but as the synthesis of the dialectic between them and the colonized society.

21. For more information on the 'Swahili' impact on politics, see the articles by Lonsdale and Abdulaziz in L. Cliffe & J.S. Saul (eds), *Socialism in Tanzania, An Interdisciplinary*

Reader, Vol. I, Politics (Nairobi, East African Publishing House, 1972), and W. Whiteley, *Swahili* (London, Methuen, 1969).

22. For the economic history of colonialism in Uganda, C. Wrigley, *Crops and Wealth in Uganda* (Kampala, East African Institute for Social Research, Makerere, 1959), and W. Elkan, *Migrants and Proletarians, Urban Labour in the Economic Development of Uganda* (Kampala, East African Institute for Social Research, Makerere, 1960). An interesting recent re-analysis in class terms of the Ugandan colonial and independence experience is contained in M. Mamdani, *Class Struggles in Uganda* (London, Heinemann, 1976).

23. On the settler impact on Kenya see M.P.K. Sorrenson, *European Settlement in Kenya* (Nairobi, Oxford University Press, 1965); C.G. Rosberg & J. Nottingham, *The Myth of Mau Mau* (London, Pall Mall, 1966), and the Introduction in D. Barnett & K. Njama, *Mau Mau from Within* (New York, Monthly Review Press, 1966).

24. For details of the origins of organized politics in Uganda see D.A. Low, *Political Parties in Uganda 1949-62* (London, Institute of Commonwealth Studies, 1962) and for an interesting case study of this patronage politics, C. Leys, *Politicians and Policies, An Essay on Politics in Acholi, Uganda, 1962-65* (Nairobi, East African Publishing House, 1967).

25. In addition to Rosberg & Nottingham, *The Myth of Mau Mau*, and Barnett & Njama, *Mau Mau from Within*, see M.P.K. Sorrenson, *Land Reform in the Kikuyu Country* (Nairobi, Oxford University Press, 1966) and for an insider's view, M. Blundell, *So Rough a Wind, The Kenya Memoirs of Sir Michael Blundell* (London, Wiedenfeld & Nicolson, 1964): 'the only possible policy was a liberal one which attracted the best of the new African thought which was now coming to the fore, allied with measures which created a wider economic sphere for the African generally', p. 263.

26. General surveys of some of the societies in the immediate pre-colonial period are contained in A. Roberts (ed), *Tanzania Since 1800* (Nairobi, East African Publishing House, 1969); the inherited patterns are summarized in H. Glickman, 'Traditional Pluralism and Democratic Processes in Mainland Tanzania', in Cliffe & Saul, *Socialism in Tanzania*, Vol. I.

27. As an example of what it meant in practice, see R. Austen, *North-West Tanzania Under German and British Rule, Colonial Policy and Tribal Politics, 1884-1939* (New Haven, Yale University Press, 1968).

28. J. Iliffe, *Agricultural Change in Modern Tanganyika* (Nairobi, published for Historical Association of Tanzania by EAPH, 1972).

29. See Iliffe, *Agricultural Change* and J. Wayne, 'The Development of Backwardness in Kigoma Region', in Rural Development Research Committee (ed), *Rural Cooperation in Tanzania* (Dar es Salaam, Tanzania Publishing House, 1974).

30. Sorrenson, *Land Reform in the Kikuyu Country*, and his paper 'Counter Revolution to Mau Mau' (East African Institute of Social Research, June 1963), as well as Barnett & Njama, *Mau Mau from Within*. All document this class dimension of 'Mau Mau'.

31. A number of incidents are referred to in Mamdani, *Class Struggles in Uganda*.

32. L. Cliffe, 'Nationalism and the Opposition to Agricultural Enforcement in Tanganyika during the Colonial Period', in Cliffe & Saul, *Socialism in Tanzania*, Vol. I.

33. These terms and the local patron-client pattern of politics to which they are related are discussed in the work of F.G. Bailey and others; see especially his *Stratagems and Spoils: a Social Anthropology of Politics* (Oxford University Press, 1969), and a discussion of these approaches in relation to African 'penetration' in M. Staniland, 'The Rhetoric of Centre-Periphery Relations', *Journal of Modern African Studies*, 8, 4 (1970). Saul in 'Class and Penetration', Cliffe & Saul, Vol. I, uses the term 'activist' in this connection.

34. On the position of the bureaucracy in Kenya see C.J. Gertzel, *The Politics of Independent Kenya, 1963-68* (Nairobi, EAPH, 1970) esp. Chs. 1 & 2; and G. Hyden, R. Jackson and U. Okumu (eds), *Development Administration: The Kenyan Experience* (Nairobi, Oxford University Press, 1970). On Tanzania see H. Bienen, *Tanzania, Party Transformation and Economic Development* (Princeton University Press, 1967), and L. Shivji, 'Tanzania, The Silent Class Struggle' in Cliffe and Saul, Vol. II.

35. This is so even in Tanzania whose population is not dominated by any large groups. R. Hopkins in his *Political Roles in a New State* (New Haven, Yale University Press, 1971) indicates, for instance, that about 50% of those whom he describes as 'elites' are drawn

from four tribes (Haya, Chagga, Nyakyusa and Nyasa) who make up only about 10% of the total population.

36. See Nyerere's 'Education for Self-Reliance' and for some scholarly confirmation, I. Resnick (ed), *Revolution by Education* (Nairobi, Longman, 1968) and the essays by G. Von der Muhll and Cliffe in K. Prewitt (ed), *Education and Political Values, an East African Case Study* (Nairobi, East African Publishing House, 1971).

37. There have in fact been three commissions to review salary scales of the public service in Kenya since Independence, all of which have led to rises in salary scales (although the first two mainly in the lower ranges).

38. For instance, loans for purchase of large (former settler) farms are available to them (and anyone else with a deposit and regular income) through the Agricultural Finance Corporation and the Agricultural Development Corporation; from 1964 the special 'Z-plots', larger acreages incorporating the former settler's house, were made available to civil servants, MPs, and other 'leaders of the community'. Kenya Government, Department of Settlement, *Annual Report 1963-64* (Nairobi).

39. Broadcast after the army takeover, January 25, 1971.

40. J.K. Nyerere, 'Socialism is not Racialism', in *Freedom and Socialism, Uhuru na Ujamaa* (Nairobi, Oxford University Press, 1968), 259.

41. For instance, Karadha, the state hire purchase company, granted loans to civil servants to purchase cars, but this practice was criticized and later reversed by TANU. See J. Loxley, 'Financial Planning and Control in Tanzania', in Uchumi Editorial Board, *Towards Socialist Planning* (Tanzania Studies No. 1, Dar es Salaam, Tanzania Publishing House, 1972).

42. Fanon, 120.

43. For discussion of Government pressure and protection on behalf of African businessmen see P. Morris & A. Somerset, *African Businessmen: A Study of Entrepreneurship and Development in Kenya* (London, Routledge & Kegan Paul, 1971), 170-172 and C. Leys, 'The Limits of African Capitalism: the Function of the Monopolistic Petit-Bourgeoisie in Kenya', *Development Trends in Kenya* (Edinburgh, Centre of African Studies, 1972) as well as note 38 above.

44. See references in note 33 above, and also the contributions by Vincent, Thoden van Velzen, and especially Lamb in this volume.

45. Foreign trade was a very high percentage of Gross National Product in 1970: Kenya 47% (1964 50%), Tanzania 53% (1962 62%) and Uganda 40% (1962 67%). UK, USA and the EEC countries together took almost two-thirds of this trade. The first post-Independence Development Plans of the three countries relied heavily on foreign financing for public investment – Kenya 90%, Uganda 56%, Tanzania 80% (although these proportions have been reduced in later Plans) – and on foreign private investment.

46. Republic of Kenya, *The Constitution of Kenya* (Kenya Gazette Supplement 27 [Acts No. 3] 10th April 1969), 36-38; in this connection see also Y.P. Ghai & J.P.W.B. McAuslan, *Public Law and Political Change in Kenya, A Study of the Legal Framework of Government from Colonial Times to the Present* (Nairobi, Oxford University Press, 1970), 201-202. A similar provision was made in Article 31 of the Uganda Constitution.

47. These conditions are documented in T. Hayter, *Aid as Imperialism* (Harmondsworth, Penguin Books, 1971).

48. The East African strategies pursued in the immediate post-independence period were in fact virtually what was suggested by the various World Bank reports on *Economic Development in Tanzania* (1961), in Uganda (1962), in Kenya (1963) (published by Johns Hopkins University Press, Baltimore).

49. Thus Uganda had a Foreign Investment Protection Act and has bilateral investment guarantee treaties with USA and West Germany; Kenya had an Act (No. 35 of 1964) of the same name. The similar Act in Tanzania was slightly amended in 1967.

50. Thus President Kenyatta in a typical off-the-cuff speech in Swahili to a crowd on October 20, 1967: 'So my countrymen, we want PEACE in our country, because we want prosperity, and that comes through capital', in Jomo Kenyatta, *Suffering Without Bitterness, The Founding of the Kenya Nation* (Nairobi, East African Publishing House, 1968), 344. The importance of foreign investment to Kenyan industry is indicated by the fact

that it accounts for almost half of the equity capital in manufacturing. But the questionable benefits are also indicated by the fact that only in 1968 did Kenya achieve a net inflow over and above repayments. See R. Lacey, 'Foreign Resources and Development', in G. Hyden, R. Jackson & J. Okumu (eds), *Development Administration: the Kenyan Experience* (Nairobi, Oxford University Press, 1970), and also the very interesting report by the Christian Council of Kenya, *Who Controls Industry in Kenya?* (Nairobi, East African Publishing House, 1967).

51. For a fuller discussion of these events, see H. Bienen, 'National Security in Tanganyika after the Mutiny', *Transition*, 6, 21 (1965) reprinted in Cliffe & Saul, Vol. I, and A. Mazrui & D. Rothchild, 'The Soldier and the State in East Africa; Some Theoretical Conclusions on the Army Mutinies of 1964', *Western Political Quarterly* (March 1967), 82-96.

52. Tanzania received training and other military assistance from Nigeria, West Germany, Canada and China; Uganda from Israel, India, Czechoslovakia, USA; for some summary (not very accurate) information see R.C. Seller, *Armed Forces of the World, A Reference Handbook* (New York, Praeger, 1971).

53. Kenya concluded a military agreement with Britain in 1964, which provided for British troops to visit and train in Kenya — and on each occasion such visits seem to be associated in certain eyes with internal political events; see for instance questions asked in Parliament reported in *East African Standard* (Nairobi, 27 November 1971 and also in January 1971).

54. General Amin, for instance, is quoted as expressing surprise on discovering that there were 700 Israelis working in Uganda in 1972, *Uganda Argus* (Kampala, 31 March 1973).

55. J.K. Nyerere, *Principles and Development* (Dar es Salaam, 1966).

56. Attempts were made by Britain to veto a loan of T.Sh. 83/- million because of claims by British citizens about the compensation they received for property under the Acquisitions of Buildings Act, 1971. The objections were temporarily dropped after Tanzania took a 'conciliatory attitude'. *East African Standard* (Nairobi, 25 February 1972).

57. *The Times* (London, 30 August 1972), 1.

58. Thus Vice-President Moi alleged that some £400,000 of foreign funds passed to Kenya politicians in the 18 months up to the end of 1965. For similar patterns during the 1970 elections see G. Hyden & C. Leys, 'Elections and Studies in Single Party Systems — the Case of Kenya and Tanzania', *British Journal of Political Science* (1972).

59. See Africa Research Group, 'CIA Intervention in Africa', in *Intelligence and Foreign Policy, CIA's Global Strategy* (Cambridge, Mass., n.d.), and more generally, R. Barnett, *Intervention and Revolution* (London, Paladin, 1970).

60. W. Attwood, *The Reds and the Blacks; a Personal Adventure* (New York, Harper & Row, 1967) in his memoirs as Kenya Ambassador 1963-65 says the 'CIA is and will be an essential instrument of our foreign policy' and that the (Kenya) 'government appreciated the leads we were able to furnish them on certain strangers in town', pp. 315 and 250. This revealing book was banned in Kenya. See also reports in the *Daily Telegraph* (supplement; series on the CIA, January 1972). It is also interesting to note that the Kenya student airlift of the early 1960s was stage-managed by the Institute for International Education later identified as a conduit for CIA funds.

61. S.E. Migot-Adholla, 'Ideology and National Development — The Case of Kenya', *Ufahamu* (Los Angeles), II, 1 (Spring 1971). An illuminating example of the weight of international corporations is offered in *Newsweek* (September 1972): 'The President of Firestone International Co. arrived in Nairobi on a trouble-shooting mission and the Kenya Government promised the company a more sustained effort to curb tyre imports', p. 65.

62. *The Times* (27 January 1971).

63. The general formula adopted was to give back a controlling interest of those companies in which government had compulsorily purchased a 60% share in equity in 1970, government providing its own risk capital to the extent of 49%. In 1972 the unpredictable Amin announced plans for a complete takeover of British interests, but the reaction of *The Times* (London, 28 August 1972) was to coolly suggest that this statement would in practice only impair British interests to the same minimal extent as Obote's partially implemented measures.

64. Thus National & Grindlays Bank announced a loan of £2 million to the Bank of Uganda, *Uganda Argus* (10 January 1972); this was followed by an announcement on 23

February 1972 that National & Grindlays would be allowed 51%, as opposed to only 40%, interest in the bank.

65. P. Packard, 'Management and Control of Parastatal Organizations', *Development and Change*, III, 3 (1972). For further discussion of the continuing influence of foreign capital see I. Shivji, 'Tanzania, the Silent Class Struggle'; B. Van Arkadie, 'The Role of the State Sector in the Context of Economic Dependence', *Institute of Development Studies Bulletin*, III, 4 (August 1971); and Justinian Rweyemamu, *Underdevelopment and Industrialization in Tanzania* (Nairobi, Oxford University Press, 1973).

66. A.H. Amsden, *International Firms and Labour in Kenya, 1945-70* (London, Frank Cass, 1971) and R. Sandbrook, 'The State and Development of Trade Unionism', in Hyden, Jackson & Okumu, *Development Administration: the Kenyan Experience*.

67. See L. Cliffe & G. Cunningham, 'Ideology, Organization and the Settlement Experience', in Cliffe & Saul, Vol. II, and Chambers' essay in this volume.

68. For the origin of this policy see Sorrenson, *Land Reform in the Kikuyu County*, and Kenya Government, *Report of the Mission on Land Consolidation and Legislation 1965-66* (Nairobi, 1966).

69. For a discussion of the consequences of, and alternatives to, the activities of foreign 'experts' see J. Loxley, 'Technical Assistance, High Level Manpower Training and Ideology in Tanzania', *Conference on Comparative Administration in East Africa* (Arusha, 1971).

70. The weight given to this mechanism for indirect control by the imperialist powers is indicated by the first substantive point in the Statement of Policy approved by the Nixon Administration on 26 March 1970, *The United States and Africa in the 1970s*: 'Africans have taken much of their political inspiration from the United States. Their thousands of students in the United States today – and the many Americans studying and teaching in Africa – continue the tradition of this exchange. More than a few Africans who studied in America became leaders of independence of their countries'. Reproduced in I. Brownlie (ed), *Basic Documents on African Affairs* (Oxford University Press, 1971). In this context it is illuminating to note the complete dominance of the US Rockefeller and Ford Foundations in the fields of economic and development research, and in political science and public administration through financial support, American secondments, and recruitment and training of African scholars throughout the Universities of East Africa. See Loxley, 'Technical Assistance ... in Tanzania'.

71. 'The Arusha Declaration and TANU's Policy on Socialism and Self-Reliance' and other key documents of Tanzania's reconsidered policy are collected in Nyerere, *Freedom and Socialism – Uhuru na Ujamaa. TANU Guidelines 1971* (Dar es Salaam, 1971) pursue this logic further.

72. 'The Common Man's Charter' was published by President Obote in late 1969, having been promised at the beginning of that year, and was followed by partial nationalization on 1 May 1970.

73. 'Leadership conditions' were imposed by TANU and the Interim Constitution of Tanzania (Amendment) Act (No. 2) 1967 gave effect to them; see also in this connection L. Cliffe, 'Personal or Class Interest? Tanzania's Leadership Conditions', Cliffe and Saul, Vol. I. For information about political education and participation, see Cliffe, 'Tanzania – Socialist Transformation and Party Development', Ibidem.

74. For an assessment of the background to the coup see Mamdani, *Class Struggles in Uganda*, and H. Maya, 'The Imperialist Threat to Africa – 1. Uganda', *African Communist*, 65 (2nd Quarter 1971).

75. In Kenya, these were the Trade Licencing Act of 1967 and other legislative and administrative measures together with assistance to African businessmen through the Industrial Commercial Development Corporation and other programmes.

76. Leading politicians like the late Josiah Mwangi Kariuki, see 'My Journey Down the Avenue to Success', *Sunday Nation* (Nairobi, 22 June 1969), and Charles Rubia, are well-known as substantial businessmen. A forthright example of the strategy of transnational corporations in this regard is offered by the strategy of Lonrho, as stated by its Chairman. 'We work through personal contacts and heads of states', *Newsweek* (20 January 1969). The companies' Managing Director in Kenya is Kenyatta's son-in-law. For the business adventures of the 'royal family' as a whole see articles in *Sunday Times* (London), 10, 17 & 24 August 1975).

77. See Leys, 'The Limits of African Capitalism'.
78. Thus there have been numerous official discussions of the possibility of reformist measures such as ceilings on landholdings, more income redistribution, more settlement schemes for landless, measures to tackle unemployment. Kenya Government Sessional Paper No. 10, 'African Socialism and its Application to Planning in Kenya' (Nairobi, 1965) and also *Report of the Select Committee on Unemployment* (National Assembly, Nairobi, 3 December 1970) advocate some of these measures, but apart from anti-unemployment measures no action has so far been agreed.
79. Also on these ethnic dimensions of Uganda's recent history, see the following articles in *East Africa Journal* (Nairobi); A. Nsibambi, 'Federation: its Rise and Fall in Uganda' (December 1966); E. Bundy, 'Uganda's New Constitution' (July 1966); A.C.C. Gingyera-Pincywa, 'Prospects of a One Party System in Uganda' (October 1968).
80. See C.J. Gertzel, *The Politics of Independent Kenya, 1963-68*, for further details of these ethnic conflicts.
81. See Saul on 'Class and Penetration'; also Staniland, 'Centre-Periphery'; and R. Sklar, 'Political Development and National Integration', *Journal of Modern African Studies*, 5, 1 (1967).
82. The point here is illustrated by the switch of the support of former KADU leaders to the government in 1964 without consultation with their constituents. Similarly, newly elected Luo Leaders after the 1969 elections were able quickly to give government support despite the earlier dramatic conflicts between Luo and the authorities; in this latter connection see Hyden & Leys, 'Elections and Studies in Single Party Systems'.
83. *Uganda Argus* (11 June 1966).
84. See L. Cliffe, 'The Policy of Ujamaa Vijijini and the Class Struggle in Tanzania' in Cliffe & Saul, Vol. II.
85. C. Leys, 'Politics in Kenya: the Development of Peasant Society', *British Journal of Political Science*, 1, 333-334. His reference is to A. Gunder Frank, *Capitalism and Underdevelopment in Latin America* (New York, Monthly Review Press, 1967).
86. D. Brokensha and J. Nellis, 'Administration in Mbire: Portrait of a Rural Kenyan Division (Institute for Development Studies, University of Nairobi, Discussion Paper 114, August 1971).
87. Ghai & McAuslan, *Public Law and Political Change in Kenya*, 455.
88. This Act was introduced to expand special powers, previously available under the Constitution, on the Declaration of a State of Emergency, and to change the conditions in which they could be assumed. It was brought into action soon after its enactment in 1966 and has continued in force ever since.
89. The flavour of the Kenya style of administration can be gauged by the following newspaper quotes all gleaned from items appearing in one 'average' week in September 1967 (italics added):
The President 'issued a stern *warning* to anyone intending to demonstrate against the visit of the Malawi President'. Provincial Commissioner Nyanza '*warned* those farmers who did not develop their farms that they should be prepared for eviction'.
P.C. Western '*warned* that unless people worked hard in their areas to uplift their standard of living they would not benefit from Independence'; also '*warned* against excessive drinking and laziness'.
District KANU Chairman Nyeri ,*warned* people who took the law into their own hands'.
'Minister *warns*: Don't encourage Squatters'.
District Agricultural Officer, Kisumu, 'issued a stern *warning* to Asian sugar canegrowers'.
90. These new policies calling for an end to administration 'through directives' were outlined in *TANU Guidelines 1971*. When several groups of factory workers took the Guidelines literally they were several times accused of 'misinterpreting TANU policies to suit non-productivity', *Daily News* (Dar es Salaam, 2 September 1972).
91. Figures quoted in Hyden, Jackson & Okumu, *Development Administration: the Kenyan Experience*, pp. 9-10, show that not only has the number of posts in the Kenya civil service increased but the *proportion* of the recurrent budget spent on emoluments rose to reach 50% in the estimates covering 1968-70. Also the expenditure on the Provincial Administration and its local police increased by 50% between 1967-68 and 1970-71.

92. *The Standard* (Dar es Salaam, 14 March 1972).

93. For a very illuminating summary of the various changes and their net effect see C. Leys, 'Politics in Kenya: the Development of Peasant Society'.

94. M. Hall, 'Agricultural Mechanization in Uganda' in G.K. Helleiner (ed), *Agricultural Planning in East Africa* (Nairobi, East African Publishing House, 1968).

95. See in this connection Cliffe & Saul, 'The District Development Front', in Cliffe & Saul, Vol. I. For other discussions of the shortcomings of rural administrators and their plans rather than peasant conservatism, see F.G. Bailey, 'The Peasant View of the Bad Life', *The Advancement of Science*, 23, 114 (December 1966) and R. Apthorpe (ed), *People, Planning and Development Studies* (London, Frank Cass, 1970); in the East African context, L. Cliffe, 'Nationalism and the Reaction to Agricultural Enforcement in the Colonial Period in Tanganyika', in Cliffe & Saul, Vol. I.

96. J. LaPalombara, 'Penetration: Crisis of Governmental Capacity', in L. Binder et al, *Crises and Sequences in Political Development* (Princeton University Press, 1971).

97. See 95 above for references.

98. See in particular, Cliffe & Saul, Vol. II.

99. See references in footnote 65.

100. For the more laissez-faire role of the state in the Gold Coast see, for instance, R. Fitch & M. Oppenheimer, *Ghana — The End of an Illusion* (New York, Monthly Review Press, 1968).

101. Packard, 'Management and Control of Parastatal Organizations'.

102. See Cliffe & Saul, Vol. II.

103. See *TANU Guidelines 1971*.

104. J.K. Nyerere, *Decentralization* (Dar es Salaam, Government Printer, 1972).

II

THE COLONIAL LEGACY AND THE DYNAMICS OF POLITICAL CONTROL

JOAN VINCENT

TESO IN TRANSFORMATION

COLONIAL PENETRATION IN TESO DISTRICT, EASTERN UGANDA,
AND ITS CONTEMPORARY SIGNIFICANCE

The crisis of penetration is largely seen today as one facing the new nations of
the Third World. Yet, taking a deeper historical and a broader sociological perspective, it is apparent that such a crisis faces any group that seeks to rule another and is, indeed, characteristic of that eventful phase in which a political
group external to a society or a newly formed group within it, seeks to extend
its power, initiating change. The representatives of the government at the local
level with which this paper deals were expatriate British colonial officers and
African 'client chiefs'.[1] For both, political and administrative penetration entailed, in sequence, strategies of access, neutralization, legitimation and mobilization.[2] These strategies were, to an extent, conditioned by factors arising out
of interaction between groups within the society to be penetrated – Teso District in eastern Uganda. The argument to be presented here has, therefore, two
facets. On the one hand, we consider the immediate and subjective form that
the 'problem' or 'crisis' of penetration took for British administrators in Teso
in their efforts to establish and maintain relations with peripheral groups. On
the other hand, an attempt is made to delineate the extent to which interaction
and conflict among the leading elements of Teso society conditioned the
nature and success of the penetration process.[3]

This is, then, a case study of colonial administration in one district of Uganda from 1898 to 1934. A group of appointed client-chiefs was brought into being and maintained within a local political environment in which neither traditional rulers nor the principle of hereditary succession to political office was
recognized. Growing bureaucratic and authoritarian aspects of client-chiefship
are traced, along with changes in the relations of the chiefs with the colonial
regime and with the people over whom they ruled. In time, their increasing
powers of coercion and accumulative control of patronage led to the emergence of a group interest in maintaining a conservative stance within a colonial
administration that was gearing itself to considerable economic and social

change. This paradox of penetration in Teso was reflected until well after Independence in the embourgeoisement of these former colonial client-chiefs
who were able to maintain their local power bases in an increasingly class-
conscious nation state, which at times leaned toward radical policies. Hence the
contemporary significance of this early period of colonial penetration. Not
only does it seem intrinsically worthwhile to present from archival and oral
sources the early modern history of Teso district in as much detail as possible
(as I have begun to do here) but it is hoped that comparisons may be made
with other colonial societies at the turn of the century. The concluding date
marks a watershed in the political history of Africa when metropolitan policies
advocating popular representation began to take effect within local political
arenas. The era of populism that followed — emerging in direct contradiction
to the period with which we deal here — merits equally detailed treatment on
its own account.[4]

The first part of this essay provides a brief historical overview of the establishment of colonial administration in Teso District showing how Baganda conquest followed by British consolidation undermined the diffuse power structure of a localized Iteso gerontocracy. I describe the way in which the boundaries of the district were drawn and the political composition of the Teso
'public' contained within them. In the second part of the essay attention is
turned to the chiefs appointed by the British to act as their intermediaries
within this newly-created political arena. Two major cleavages grew up within
the society at this time: a gulf between chief and peasant, and a rift between
north and south. Much of the political action of these early years can be understood in terms of these oppositions which, moreover, established the patterning
of confrontation in the years that followed.

AN HISTORICAL OVERVIEW: TESO 1898-1962

Although culturally and historically the affiliations of the Iteso people lay with
other eastern Nilotes — Karamojong, Jie, Turkana, Dodoth and Toposa — at no
time was there a sense of political community among them.[5] At the end of the
19th century the region of eastern Uganda known as 'Bukedi' was inhabited by
peoples whom Arab and European travellers called el-Kony (peoples of Mount
Masaba), related to the Masai. Administration of Teso from Kampala was inaugurated in 1899 by the British appointment of Semei Kakunguru, a Muganda
general engaged in building up a small personal satrapy in the east, as Native
Assistant in charge of Bukedi at a salary of two hundred pounds per annum.
Three years later the administration of the area was placed under the direct
control of the Mbale Collector. In 1909 a separate Collectorate was established
to the north, in Kumi, which over a few years extended its boundaries and consolidated an increasingly large number of Iteso, Lango and Kumam peoples. In
1912 this administrative unit was re-named Teso District.

For the first decade Baganda Agents were retained, originally as chiefs and then as advisers to Iteso chiefs. The five divisions of Teso at this time (Figure 1) were compartmentally administered until 1918 when a district-wide system was established in which a hierarchy of county, sub-county, parish and village chiefs was set up along with councils of local notables at each level. Council members were at first appointed, later elected, to office. Both chiefly and representative officials were responsible to the District Commissioner whose position between the central government and the locality provided a linchpin in the political and economic development of the district. By 1919 Teso District had taken on very much its present administrative form.[6]

Native Councils were introduced in 1924 largely to increase peasant, as opposed to chiefly, representation and, by 1937, the Teso District Council, which headed this branch of government, had grown from a body dominated by ex-officio members into a predominantly elected representative body in which the exercise of power by chiefs could only be covert. In its move towards representative local government, Teso was twelve years in advance of any other district in Uganda.

Teso was also among the first districts to adopt the District Council Ordinance of 1955 — but three years later disputes between northern and southern factions (the roots of which will be uncovered in this essay) led to the suspension of the Council. Up until this time, Teso had been considered one of the most 'progressive' districts in Uganda; indeed, the early flowering of this factionalism reflected the rapidity of its economic advance. When we observe that the crux of the dispute between north and south lay in the control of an elected committee to select and appoint county, sub-county and parish chiefs, we are seeing one result of the emergence of class privilege that is the subject of this essay. Even in 1955, after thirty years of popular representation, bureaucratic office ensured the most rewarding political spoils in Teso District.

Nationalist politics entered the district in 1951 in the guise of the Uganda Farmers Union (a forerunner of the Uganda National Congress). Thereafter, in the national arena, Teso electoral support was divided fairly equally between the Uganda Peoples Congress (UPC) and the Democratic Party (DP). The local distribution of support was significant and the grounds for this, too, will be covered in the period under present survey. The southern counties of Teso returned two DP candidates in 1962, the northern counties three UPC candidates. One DP member subsequently crossed the floor. At the time of my first fieldwork in Teso (1966-1967) the Democratic Party provided a small, powerless, but bitterly vocal, opposition in the Teso District Council.

Between 1898 and 1934 the amorphous population of Teso was transformed into a closely-administered, cash-crop growing, taxed and locally-represented peasantry. Although the nature and course of political penetration was shaped to some extent by a pattern of conquest, bureaucratic administration and electoral politics, it was also shaped by the patterning of conflict which ensued as different elements within Teso society jockeyed for positions in the political arena. In order to perceive the political process by which Teso client chiefs became sufficiently established to affect the trend of social and economic development, we must inquire into the politicization of various groups as they sought access to the 'power house' of Teso politics.[7]

The definition of the Teso political community, and the manner in which it was constructed, shaped the forms that confrontation took. The initial actions of the administrative secretariat and departmental officers controlled the very arena in which political conflict took place. It was they who, to a great extent, not only held the ropes but laid down the rules of the game. As a small, closely interacting group of individuals, these officers were distinguished firstly by their transient roles as individuals on the Teso political stage and secondly, by their orientation towards a wider political arena than the district. These structural characteristics distinguished district officers from chiefs as bureaucrats. Client chiefs in Teso District were bureaucrats and politicians both, and it was their skillful manipulation of office and role that led to the emergence of a privileged chiefly elite.

BAGANDA PENETRATION AND BIG MAN POLITICS: THE ACCESS PHASE

Teso prior to the advent of the Baganda was populated predominantly by Nilotic peoples, although communities of Bantu speakers were to be found in the south and west.[8] These were mainly Banyoro, Bakenyi, Swahili-speaking Arabs and Nubians engaged in trade or fishing, located in the Serere peninsula and along the trade route from Karamoja to the slopes of Mount Masaba. Relations with these minority groups were by and large friendly, almost symbiotic in nature, social intercourse and intermarriage making for fluid group boundaries. Iteso relations with their fellow Nilotes, on the other hand — with Lango, Kumam and Karamojong — were frequently hostile, dominated by cattle raiding. (Changes in the ethnic composition of the district, related to political and economic development, are shown in Table 1.)[9]

Indigenous political leadership was gerontocratic, there was no institutionalization of hierarchical office or ranking of groups — apart from that found in all small-scale societies where elders, youths and womenfolk are set apart by the specialization of their labour and their opportunities for social power. The Iteso age organization that mobilized the young men of the communities was apparently locally coordinate like that of the Karamojong, linking only neighbouring homesteads.[10] It did not provide the basis for large-scale resistance against the Baganda, nor for the mobilization of labour in the years that followed.[11] Decision making was in the hands of local Big Men, and only on the basis of kin and community recognition could such men cooperate and muster groups of any size in the face of external threats.[12]

LANGO

KARAMOJA

AMURIA

NORTHERN   DIVISION

Orungo

USUKU

SOROTI
DIVISION

KABERAMAIDO

Toroma

Soroti

Tira

Bugondo

CENTRAL

NORTH
SOUTH

SERERE

Serere

DIVISION

Ngora   Kumi

DIVISION

BUKEDEA
DIVISION

BUGISHU

NORTH
SOUTH   BUSOGA

BUKEDI

District Boundary
County Boundary

0   10   20 MILES

Table 1. *Ethnic Composition of Teso District (African Population) 1911-31*

	Central Division (Kumi)			Bukede Divison			Soroti Division			Northern Division			Serere Division		
	1911	1921	1931	1911	1921	1931	1911	1921	1931	1911	1921	1931	1911	1921	1931
Teso	78,501	77,627	95,337	19,360	32,276	43,471	42,526	44,002	78,605	48,502	64,699	41,380	54,073	30,811	39,269
Bakenyi	1,330	1,014	1,679			31	506	383	955	460		551	2,097	1,380	2,662
Bagwere		21	170	3,258	735	598		1	43			1			84
Banyoro		4	64		30	3		260	259			10			
Basoga		1,211	358		203	351		94	267		22	4		1,516	1,814
Baganda		291	403		340	509		555	558		32	63		1,524	1,731
Bagisu		16	11		18	1,643		6	52			6		1,215	619
Other Bantu		2	12			51		2	3						70
Sebei, Kumam, Karamajong		2						15	172						307
Northern peoples (Lango, Acholi, Alur, Lugbara)			11			7		27	1,099		5,664	10			118
Non-Ugandans		39	310		27	339		37	342			27		8	78

Such a form of horizontally articulated political organization checked any deep or rapid military penetration by Kakunguru's forces in the early years and prevented the easy consolidation of administrative units in the period that followed. Garrisons could be established only within the homesteads of Iteso collaborators and only under such protection could aliens, Baganda and European, officials, catechists and traders, operate. Beyond these isolated strongholds, the countryside was passive or hostile according to the measures taken by the garrison to live off the land and the direction their forays took. Kitching, a contemporary, assessed Kakunguru's achievement in Teso thus: 'The way in which he handled the country is a good illustration of the rare capacity of the Baganda for organization and government, and also of rapacity and over-bearing towards all whom they consider beneath them. Order was indeed established but rather after the method of making desolation and calling it peace.'[13] That a pacification programme may destroy a country's people in order to 'save' them is not an unknown occurrence; within a few years the Teso administrative system was regarded as a model for eastern and northern Uganda, where similar diffuse political authorities were encountered. Later it was to be esteemed for having involved a parochial peasantry in the wider political process. Perhaps its historical contribution was the creation of a cash economy which engendered rural inequalities far greater than any known in the indigenous Iteso political system.

Different patterns of rural inequality arose as Big Men in different parts of the region responded differently to penetration. Those in the west tended to welcome Baganda support against Lango attacks; those who encountered the Baganda as they moved northwards and eastwards, met them with armed resistance, bringing forth the scorched-earth policy described by Kitching. For the Baganda, any advantage gained by winning over or eliminating a local leader was measured by the extent of his influence over neighbouring areas. In most cases this seems to have covered at the most an *etem*, an area of between fifty and a hundred square miles, roughly equivalent to a modern sub-county.

The subsequent usefulness of a Big Man to the Baganda administration would depend more upon those who considered it worth their while to come within his orbit (in order to further their own interests) than upon the number over whom he already had influence. Operating from their local garrisons, Baganda Agents, appointed by Kakunguru, recruited fellow Bantu-speakers (Banyoro and Bakenyi) to their service, first as interpreters, intermediaries and scouts and later as clerks and catechists. Further, they backed their petty local chiefs as they coerced the population into building forts and roads, caravan porterage and later, into the erection of administration houses, bomas and schools.

Kakunguru's conquest established a hierarchical administration in which Baganda chiefs and their hirelings dominated, along with a few favoured Iteso gerontocrats whose skill in the 'politics of survival'[14] surpassed that of their fellows. On the whole, Baganda penetration in its access phase changed the patterning of groups within Teso society by establishing some Big Men as chiefs at the expense of others and by backing them with armed force so that their relations with their erstwhile followers changed markedly in calibre.

The overall effect of penetration was to destroy the one institution of Iteso society that reached beyond the localized community, the age-set organization; to render Iteso communities more dependent upon political leaders unchecked by traditional mechanisms and, moreover, backed by the armed force of aliens; to provide a hierarchical structure of administrative chiefs within which individuals of all groups (save women) might advance, provided they acquired Luganda and accepted Baganda patronage; and, finally, to secure the entry of two new groups — Europeans and Asians — into the region. Baganda rule in Teso, although historically short, was radical in its impact.

Yet the indigenous Iteso political institution of Big Manship persisted. With the appointment of client chiefs its locus of operation shifted from control over men, women and cattle to privileged access to guns, labour and the money economy. The reinvestment of the old political facilities in the domain of the new provided capital for the rapid rise to social, political and economic power of the Teso client chief. The networks of influence and patronage which engendered Iteso Bigmanship provided the New Men of Teso politics with the makings of a political machine that went virtually unrecognized by the British until it was eventually used against them. Bigmanship proved not only resilient, but extraordinarily adaptive to the exogenous changes brought about by colonial rule.

BRITISH PENETRATION AND THE POLITICAL COMMUNITY: THE NEUTRALIZATION PHASE

In 1902, the British took over the political structure created by Kakunguru and set about using it to develop the country in their own interests. Whereas Baganda interests had been in loot and the acquisition of estates, those of the British were more managerial. To adopt an analogy of the times, Teso became yet another corner in the colonial estates of the British Crown and the task of the administration was to see that its potential was realized. Where the fabric of Teso society was most ruptured by Baganda mercenaries (the southeast), development proceeded most rapidly; where the incursions of the Baganda had been more conciliatory (as in the southwest) obstacles to change arose; where the Baganda failed to penetrate (the north) the involvement of the Iteso within the developing society was slowest.

The first task of the administration was to establish boundaries around a political community. If we choose to see the British administration holding the ropes, as it were, around an arena in which local combatants fought out a struggle for local power, we become aware of the topological characteristics of such an arena, pulled as it is first in one direction and then in another, first including then excluding different groups and sub-groups from the Teso scene. At moments of interregnum, such as 1902 when the British took over from the Baganda, or in 1962 when the independent nation was established, such political elasticity becomes most apparent.

British assumption of authority over Teso had preceded their physical presence by eight years. A northern limit to the Uganda Protectorate had been established with a line of treaties obtained by Captain A.R. Macdonald of the Nile Expeditionary Force in 1897. This delineation of an area of some three and a half thousand square miles for possible inclusion in Uganda provided full scope for the district officers of Teso to carve out a colonial estate of some magnitude. Although there was an element of individual empire building by pioneer administrators, including Iteso,[15] the exact location of boundaries was also a response to the societal forces that penetration encountered. For the first twelve years, until the last military expedition was dispatched against Ojotum in Usuku, the shifting boundaries of Teso District ebbed and flowed as Big Men — whose communities were being raided from the north — tried to come under the protection of the British while rebel leaders in the east tried to challenge their authority.

Now, if government is taken to be the regulation of public affairs, and the critical element in government is seen to be its public character, the first goal of penetration is clearly the consolidation of a public of some kind, 'an enduring, presumably perpetual group with determined boundaries and membership, having an internal organization and a unitary set of external relations, an exclusive body of common affairs, and autonomy and procedures adequate to regulate them.'[16] The need to establish such a public in Teso was critical. Earlier experiences in Buganda and the western kingdoms had in no way prepared the administration for an amorphous mass of peoples among whom no State had previously been consolidated. It was therefore necessary first to establish boundaries around a 'public', the nature of which must in some way be defined, and then to consolidate the shifting population contained within these boundaries. And this in the face of the differing interests of the groups encountered in the process.

The boundaries of Teso District were determined by cultural criteria, the non-Ateso speaking Lango of Omoro and the Kumam of Kaberamaido being excluded.[17] In 1925 Ateso was adopted for instruction in all schools in the district. Boundary decisions involving Kaberamaido reflected the elasticity of the Teso political arena at the height of the initial and terminal stages of colonial penetration, and proved most important in the administration's efforts to homogenize its 'public'. In 1907 Kaberamaido was not part of Teso District, although competition between Kumam and Ateso-speaking groups remained a feature of the local power struggle. For the era of colonial penetration with which this essay is concerned, the Kumam problem as such was defined out of existence for Teso administrators. In western Soroti and Serere counties, heavily populated with the clansmen of the Kaberamaido Kumam, political involvement passed unrecognized by the administration of that time, causing a minor crisis in 1953 when Kaberamaido was again restored to Teso District. When the question of district boundaries came up before a meeting with the Provincial Commissioner in 1920, the Teso District Commissioner reported that 'a distinction, although not very marked, [must be recognized] between the population of the western and middle and eastern parts. There is practically a dividing line Orungo-Soroti-Tira-Serere, to the west of which are Kokolimo speaking people, who are apparently regarded as an inferior type of Kumam.'[18]

Realignments such as these of Kumam, Lango and Iteso by the early district administrators served three specific purposes. Firstly, they countered the growth of peripheral ethnic particularisms; secondly, they facilitated administration by making possible the use of one indigenous African language, Ateso; and thirdly, they served to create a political identity on a district-wide basis which legitimized both the administrative boundaries of the new political unit and the office of District Commissioner as the representative of the 'people of Teso' in his relations with sub-groups within the society, with other districts and with provincial and central government.

In response to this administrative search for political identity, ethnic competition took the place of such symbiosis as had existed between Iteso pastoralists and the Bantu-speakers who filled the interstitial economic niches of fishing, communications and trade. Under the Baganda regime, bureaucracy and mission-fostered education, although not excluding the sons of Iteso Big Men from opportunities of political advancement, had nevertheless favoured Bantu-speakers, Banyoro, Baganda and Bakenyi — who, at that time, formed small minorities within the southern and western counties. British efforts to create a homogenous district within the Protectorate subsequently led to the status reversal of Bantu speakers, and within the district structure, to a denial of legitimacy to minority ethnic groups as such. The 1911 census categorized the population of the district in ethnic terms but the classification adopted by the administration relates ethnicity to political identity within the newly-established Kumi Collectorate.[19] A distinction was made between 'natives' on the one hand and 'resident' and 'floating aliens' on the other. 'Resident aliens' — Bakenyi, Banyoro and Basoga — paid taxes to their own sub-chiefs who were obliged to tour the district to collect them. Iteso 'natives' paid tax to parish chiefs, while 'floating aliens' were presumed to pay taxes in their home districts. All Baganda were included in this last category. Although these distinctions were abolished in 1925 when every adult male in Teso paid tax as a resident parishioner regardless of ethnicity, a mere twelve years later, when local representative government was introduced, ethnic consideration became critical again.

If the first problems of penetration involve defining the criteria on which membership in a political community is based and fixing its boundaries, the next task facing the administration is to pin down its inhabitants and, having done so, to control their movements thereafter. Nominally, as we have seen, administrators could define certain problems of control out of existence as far as their jurisdiction was concerned and this, in effect, was what was done in recognizing the category of 'floating aliens'. But the reality of the situation took the form of extensive social networks linking 'natives', 'floating' and 'resident aliens' which crossed administrative boundaries. This meant that not only did political actors pass unrecognized in the Teso arena but also that administrative problems of neutralization, mobilization and politicization were not so easily defined away. I have illustrated the process by which an individual, whether 'native' or 'alien', could operate in several arenas in a study of the micropolitics of a small township in Teso[20] and the same principles were applied in disregard of constraining District boundaries.

Although administrative authority was firmly established within a bounded area by 1923, the inhabitants of this area — whether categorically defined as natives or floating or resident aliens — were at liberty to move away. They could opt out of the Teso administrative system by choosing to reside beyond its borders and, because taxes in Teso were higher than in the neighbouring districts, this many of them chose to do. As we have seen, early penetration met both with requests for protection and with resistance but, when taxation was introduced and cotton cultivation enforced — as they were by 1907 — the administrative problem became not one of penetrating the public but of consolidating it. Very early, mechanisms were introduced to prevent what was termed 'border-hovering' by members of the Teso 'public'.

By virtue of their primary occupations, many in Teso society were already extremely mobile. Pastoralism, trading, fishing and — to a lesser extent — bush cultivation all required a certain amount of individual mobility. Bakenyi fishmen, for example, maintained networks of kin and affinal ties which extended around the eastern shores of Lake Kyoga and crossed numerous administrative boundaries. Banyoro and Basoga similarly came and went between western Teso and their homelands, while Iteso pastoralism and land inheritance patterns called for the exchange of cattle and individuals over wide areas. Movements to avoid taxation and enforced cash crop cultivation were thus readily articulated with existing patterns of migration, so that for certain periods of the year or in places where there was heavy labour recruitment, the young men of a parish might visit kin elsewhere for extended periods of time, returning months later when the tax hue and cry was over, the work on the roads or the clearing of the sudd completed. All this an administration had cause but not power to prevent. Such individuation[21] was extensive enough to affect the administration's development plans and its concern over migration may be illustrated from early county touring books. Characteristic entries read:

A Musoga headman has been found in the district, collecting tax from Basoga removed from his country into this district. The removals are not of recent date and the practice is an objectionable one ...[22]

Some of the removals to Busoga have been traced by DC Busoga. 97 removed, of whom 24 were Ganda and Soga. The County agent for Serere who is concerned with the collection of tax for non-natives of the district has been instructed to report and discourage immigration of Basoga.[23]

Provincial Commissioner on tour to District Commissioners, Teso and Lango: '(a) it is the duty of District Officers to discourage migrations ... (d) A Chief who encourages migrations is not fit for his post and will not long retain it after such conduct has come to the notice of this office ...'[24]

May 1913. ADC Lango and DC Kumi agreed that chiefs should come to locate their men. The Kenyi emigrants in the Kelle region planted cotton so as not to be returned to Teso.[25]

Between May and October, 1916, correspondence passed between the District Commissioners of Busoga and Teso about 57 Bakenyi and 42 'Teso' emigrants pursued by their chiefs (12 bore Ateso names; 30 appear to have been Basoga and Banyoro). The Teso DC attributed his problems to the extreme effectiveness of his administration, observing that 'Border-hovering continues to be a fairly popular pastime with the people and but little abatement can be looked for until administration on both sides of the boundary is approximately identical. Each year shows some improvement in this direction.'[26] By October 1916, he thought he was beginning to see the end of the road: 'I hope that the fact that the Bakenyi are now being drawn for labour from all the four districts of the Province will be of great assistance in checking any further tendency to emigrate.'[27] Not until the administration of Lango, northern Busoga and eastern Bunyoro was as effective as that of Teso could a concerted effort be made to prevent mobile individuals migrating from a Teso parish where high taxes were paid to a neighbouring district where taxes were lower and administrative intervention in daily affairs less. For the most part, such emigrants were young men whose labour services the Teso administration most valued, and the problem was aggravated by the fact that the neighbouring regions where they settled were mostly areas of marginal administrative returns. Realistically, no prompt action by Lango and Busoga district officers could be expected. Yet, by 1921, the stabilization of Teso's tax-paying population had been achieved, largely through the coercive efforts of local chiefs and the heavy penalties they were empowered to inflict. To see how the process of penetration was, at this stage, moved into higher gear, we must turn our attention from the populace to their rulers.

By 1921 the early strategies of access, neutralization, and legitimation had produced a political community founded on law and order within the administrative district of Teso. In the fourth phase of political penetration, that of mobilization, the intercalary positions of client chiefs within the administrative structure were most critical to the economic development of the district and the mobilization of its peasantry within the cash economy of Uganda.

DEVELOPMENT ADMINISTRATION: THE MOBILIZATION PHASE

British administrators in Teso, at this time, appear to have been operating with an evolutionary model of society. In 1917, the Provincial Commissioner for the Eastern Province suggested that 'Instead of alluding to the general progress in Native Affairs as in former reports, it is now more correct to consider this matter from the point of view of two main stages of progress. The first stage being along the line from utter chaos to law and order and the second, and more dangerous stage, being along the line created by the counter current related to economic development.'[28]

In the first stage the Teso chiefs were ascribed an important role in countering economic individualism in a people moving much more rapidly into the second stage than the administration was prepared to countenance. Their less conspicuous and self-chosen role in economic advancement was realised somewhat belatedly by the British administration. In 1917, the Provincial directive went out thus:

The natives are but children and require for many years to come firm and sympathetic guidance. They are quite unfitted for a policy of individualism; feudal and communal systems should be supported in every way. The peasant must in no way be encouraged to break from the restraining influence of his chief who, in turn, must be under the guiding influence of the District Officers... The premature introduction of a general system of individualism would be disastrous.[29]

The effect of this policy was to entrench the chiefs at the expense of the peasants who could no longer 'vote with their feet' as they had in earlier times. Political participation in Teso thus involved either submitting to chiefly demands or departing from the district altogether and this, as we have seen, was no longer advantageous. The political arena within which administrators were operating had been effectively stretched to one coterminous with the Province, a widening of operations that had brought their actions into alignment with the patterning of social relations of most of the erstwhile peripheral groups. The 'crisis' of penetration had thus been solved not just by the imposition of new regulations on the public, nor by any specific adjustment on the part of either public or district officers, but by the district itself being gradually absorbed within a more extensive political arena.

Let us examine, then, the newly emergent framework of development administration that the Provincial Commissioner considered 'the second and more dangerous stage'. Colonial rule brought into existence in Teso a peasantry whose productivity was geared to the demands of a centralizing power, yet, apparently, a local commitment to the development of such a peasantry was contrary to the directives of both the Provincial Commissioner and the Director of Agriculture.[30] Those pioneer administrators who deliberately turned blind eyes to orders which forbade the extension of the district's boundaries northwards,

Table 2. *Measurement of Development 1911-1920*

		Population		Poll Tax	Cotton	Bicycles
		1915	1920	1920	Production	
South	Kumi	93,432	79,534	19,701	1,400	118
	Bukedea	35,226	30,477			54
West	Serere	49,552	36,659	10,622	600	93
North	Soroti	49,557	50,726	12,561	450	62
	Usuku	47,770	45,674	9,316	350	35
Totals		275,537	243,070	52,200	2,800	362

Table 3. *Distribution of luwalo (Compulsory Unpaid Labour for Local Chiefs) 1935*

	Total Luwalo Labour	Paid Labour	Population Not In Labour Force	Total Population
Kumi	13,426	3,047	3,258	19,731
Serere	3,733	4,928	339	9,000
Amuria	13,004	2,427	1,936	17,367
Soroti	7,657	3,378	2,020	13,055
Kasilo	3,452	2,812	118	6,382
Ngora	6,804	2,593	–*	9,397*
Usuku	9,266	961	1,508	11,735
Total	57,342	20,146	9,179	86,667

* Not known

Table 4. *Poll tax and cotton revenue 1910-1929*

Year	Poll tax in rupees & shillings	Chiefs' percentage	Cotton production (in tons)	Average price in shillings (per 1,000 lbs.)
1910	R 62,949	6	500	
1911	R 138,189	6	1,100	
1912	R 163,086	6	2,800	9/4
1913	R 195,834	6	3,000	
1914	R 227,490	6	8,836	
1915	R 358,564	6	5,739	
1916	Shs 345,485	10	5,529	11/-
1917	350,560	10	6,658	
1918	351,200	10	2,340	13/4
1919	344,340	10	3,100	14/-
1920	502,332	15	5,813	20/-
1921			8,750	
1922	733,338	15	2,420	16/-
1923	872,637	15	11,357	18/-
1924	938,819	15	9,384	28/-
1925	985,384	15	14,000	20/-
1926	990,629	15	12,053	
1927	1,267,417	21	7,795	14/-
1928	1,410,306	21	8,719	18/-
1929	1,440,284	21	12,959	9/-

also sponsored the introduction of cotton as a cash crop, regardless of the fact that other, and preferred, plants were under trial at Entebbe. Both innovations were 'adventures' of local administrative officers[31] and we must examine the local situation for the forces at work at that time. Regional divisions within Teso District are again relevant. Just as it was necessary to consider the west, south and north separately with respect to Baganda and British penetration and consolidation, so it is necessary now to distinguish different patterns of economic development in each sector (Table 2).[32]

Cotton seed was apparently first imported into Teso District by the Church Missionary Society and by 1907 cotton was being grown throughout southern and western Teso, its distributional climax lying along the line between Kumi and Ngora, but reaching as far as Kadungulu in western Serere. The pattern of its early distribution was due to the location of administrative and missionary headquarters at Kumi and Ngora and the development of Bugondo as a port on Lake Kyoga from which cotton was shipped south. Increases in the crop brought about an expansion in communications, and attempts to clear a canal linking Lake Kyoga with Lake Bisina continued until 1918. Population density in the southern counties seems to have increased considerably at this time, aggravated by consolidation within the district's southern boundary. Missionary endeavours became more intensive and schools and hospitals, cotton ginneries and trading posts became so concentrated in this area that when, in 1919, it was decided that chiefs should be appointed outside of their own counties, 'most of the talent at that time was to be found in Kumi'.[33] The District Commissioner noted that, 'Kumi on account of its supremacy in intellect produced by the two Ngora schools has been for some time the exemplary county of the district. During the last few months many changes have been made throughout the district in respect of sub-county chiefdoms, and Kumi has been extensively drawn from to fill vacancies.'[34]

Following upon the introduction of cotton and the expansion of a cash economy, new regional distinctions began to emerge. Administrators started to rank the counties according to their development and a county chief's advancement could be measured by his transfer from Serere to Soroti to Kumi, just as his fall from grace was manifest in a posting to underdeveloped Usuku. Yet, within the counties, not all groups were equally able to take advantage of the new economic opportunities. In Ngora, Kumi, Serere and southern Soroti county, cotton seed was distributed by the Administration in 1909 and the crop was bought up quickly by agents of Allidina Visram, the British East Africa Company, Arab middlemen from Pallisa, Asians from Mbale and Europeans in Serere and Bugondo. When necessary, the Administration stepped in to keep prices high.[35] Although cash was paid to whoever brought in the cotton, seed was distributed only to Agents and chiefs. Thus office not only allowed them to divert labour and porterage to their own ends, but also gained them control over the even scarcer resource, cotton seed. This they employed both to increase the profits from their own estates and in patronage over peasants under their jurisdiction.

From the outset, complaints of extortionate labour demands filtered into District headquarters. Baganda Agents received labourers from sub-county chiefs for work on their own cotton and food gardens; chiefs diverted corvée (*luwalo*) labour intended for road making and public works to employment on their own lands. The manipulation of a work force quickly became one of the most visible sources of power and prestige. Some indication of the size of the labour force at the disposal of chiefs is given in Table 3.

As the counties developed economically, so opportunities for chiefly aggrandizement increased. By 1926 concern was being expressed at the extent to which Teso chiefs were hiring out labour for cash to the Indians resident in their areas.[36] Administrative officers in Teso meticulously measured the district's economic progress by the increase in its cotton cultivation, but the political dimensions of this achievement were unappreciated and its social costs ignored. The colonial vision that, as in feudal Europe, economic development would be gradual, a squirearchy emerging to lead the mass of the people paternally into the modern era, was not shattered in Teso until the mid-1920s.

It is necessary at this point to look more closely into this group of client chiefs whom the Baganda had appointed and whose retention the British administration was beginning to question. Basically they were of two kinds: first, those Big Men of the indigenous system who had received recognition after their cooperation with the Baganda and, second, lesser men who, by virtue of armed force, had been able to set themselves up as clients of the conquerors.

Clearly those who benefited most in these competitive years were men who had acquired chieftainships under the Baganda and retained them under the British. Yet, to perceive only those who had their authority legitimized by British recognition as forces in the chiefly political arena, is to under-estimate the networks of patronage and power that existed. Shortly after 1912, strategies of consolidation called for the amalgamation of many localities upon the deaths of their petty chiefs. In many cases, their administrations had been inefficient and for several reasons. First, the imposition of alien rule had been, as we have seen, by the selective use of force. When this force was withdrawn from those who were not Big Men in their own right, their power and authority was liable to crumble. Rations of guns and the employment of mercenaries were effective only in the short run. In other cases, chiefs might themselves have selectively utilized the armed force of their patrons without necessarily accepting all that went with it. When, as administration developed, such client chiefs were called upon to change their roles from being administratively-backed local leaders to being agents of government, some were able to make the transition while others were not.

It was at this time that the Administration began to appoint minor chiefs from Kumi and school leavers who had gone through a clerical apprenticeship

within the office staffs of successive District Commissioners as chiefs in the
other four counties. The precedent was established as early as August 1913
when there was transferred into Serere county 'where there are no men of
ability fit for selection as sub-county chiefs, able men from the advanced
counties of Kumi and Bukedea who can hardly hope for the promotion they
deserve in their own counties.'[37] That such appointments were resented by
chiefs in other counties was clear but in 1920 the administration thought that
envy could be turned to advantage. Noting that 'the whole of the administration of Teso seems to pivot on Kumi,' the District Commissioner reported
that, 'the County Chief Institution has already started the right sort of competition among counties, generally with a view to bettering Kumi.'[38]

Yet a loss of office for local Big Men did not necessarily mean a loss of political prowess. Deposed chiefs continued to operate behind the scenes for many
years after they had been discharged from office and were to be found, serially
incumbent as chief, parish councillor, 'clan elder', district councillor and party
patron, through the pages of Teso's political record. Much of their power derived from personal networks of patronage established at the beginning of their
political careers, and these they operated regardless of shifts in administrative
recognition. Even as late as 1927, men such as these were causing the administration so much trouble, fomenting rural unrest, that a new regulation had to
be introduced whereby 'Chiefs, when dismissed ... must remove from the
gombolola [sub-county] of which they were lately in charge. They should not
be able to return within six months at least. This is designed to prevent the
constant cases of intrigue in which dismissed chiefs endeavour to make the
work and position of their successors as difficult as possible.'[39]

The ease with which it was possible to stir up peasants against chiefs in 1927
permits us to gauge the extent to which the chiefs were emerging as a class. In
response to new economic opportunities, and especially by mobilizing their
peasant followers, chiefs had been able to corner much of the African share of
the new wealth of the district. They were also able to ensure its future control
by their kinsmen and clients. Their early advantages in acquiring education for
their sons and for those whom they chose to send to the mission schools, in
disposing of labour and in acquiring land were consolidated by strategic mar-
riages with those whom they recognized as members of their privileged cohort.
By the mid-1920s these chiefs comprised a formidable group whose political
achievement could be measured not only by the growing gulf between them
and the peasantry, but also by the resentment that was beginning to be expressed by northern chiefs who were later entering the administrative arena.

CLEAVAGES AND FACTIONS: THE CHALLENGE TO COMMUNITY

The gap that had grown up between chief and commoner can perhaps best be
suggested by reviewing first their respective cash incomes and then the sanc-

tions that enabled a chief to exploit and widen the gap between 1907 and 1927. A full series of statistics is not available, but we are able to construct an approximation of political reality.

The salary scales of chiefs in 1929 range from Shs. 560/- a year for a newly appointed (Grade 9) sub-county chief to Shs. 22,000/- a year for the highest grade County Chief. Those of village and parish chiefs (between Shs. 80/- and Shs. 560/-) are at the level of skilled peasant employees, and it is in the range of sub-county chiefs' remunerations that vast differences of wealth begin to become apparent.[40] At this time, the two sources of cash income available to the majority of peasants were the sale of cotton and the sale of labour. The price of the former varied between Shs. 9/40 to Shs. 20/- per 100 lbs. between 1912 and 1924[41] and we may estimate that from an average yearly production of about 248 lbs. (one acre), a peasant would receive an average cash income of about Shs. 38/-. For voluntary unskilled labour, the highest wage paid during these years was Shs. 5/- a month, without food.[42] If such work were available throughout the year (and it rarely was), an unskilled labourer might expect a cash income then of Shs. 60/- per annum — an income, that is, 25 percent lower than that of the lowest-grade village chief.

In estimating relative costs for chiefs and commoners, it is useful only to take into account that which demands payment in cash — school fees, taxes and fines account in large part for cash expenditure in a peasant economy.

In 1927 the education of one child at the only High School in the district cost its parent Shs. 60/- per annum, the total year's cash income, as we have seen, of the unskilled labourer or 1/69th of the annual income of a Grade 5 County Chief. At the Teso central schools, school fees for the year were Shs. 24/-.[43]

Poll tax, which was imposed upon all adult males, increased throughout this period — from Shs. 6/- (1907-14) to Shs. 10/- (1915-18) to Shs. 15/- (1919-26) to Shs. 21/- (1927-30).[44] Not only did many chiefs neglect to pay their own poll tax, but they also received rebates of between 5-10 percent on tax collected up until 1911, and 10 percent on tax collected thereafter. Even as early as 1910, chiefs shared among their number 39.8 percent (Rupees 34, 725) of the total cash revenue (Rupees 138,198) of the district. The rise in poll tax revenue in the district at large is shown in Table 4. Ten percent of this revenue was shared among the chiefs.

Imposed fines suggest how far the sanctions of the chiefs reached down into the security of the peasants. In 1927, for example, for drunkenness, a man might be fined Shs. 30/- at the discretion of the chief; for smoking bhang, a first offender would be subject to a Shs. 20/- fine or twelve lashes at the discretion of the chief; for moving cattle without permission, a first offender would be liable to a Shs. 50/- fine, as well as six months' imprisonment and 12 lashes. Labour defaulters were fined Shs. 5/- for each day's absence — and of this, Shs. 3/- went to the chief, Shs. 2/- to the Native Administration. A peasant wishing to commute his compulsory labour obligation to chiefs was called upon to pay Shs. 10/- for each 24 days he did not wish to work.[45] Each homestead head was responsible for the strip of road near his homestead and could be fined if he failed to keep it cleared to the satisfaction of his chief.[46] By the Courts Ordinance of 1911, which was proclaimed in Teso August 1917, a chief — along with two of his officials or elders — was given powers to hear all civil cases (up to Rs. 100/-), and all criminal cases except those involving death or deportation.[47]

One might have expected an expansion in the realms of economic opportunity to bring with it a greater openness in the Teso chiefly oligarchy, but this does not appear to have been the case. The large bulk of the Teso peasantry was not in a position to gain access to the administratively-controlled political ring of these early years. A wider range of economic opportunity was certainly opened up to those who lived near missions, schools, markets and administrative centres, but this did not necessarily entail entry to the political elite.

Although individuals gained materially during this period, prestige could not be extended beyond kinship groups and neighbours without converting economic wealth into the currency of political office. This they might try to do by attaching themselves as clients to administrative chiefs, missionaries or Asians and Europeans of the commercial class — but even so, skills acquired in this way could not be transferred to the political arena while the chiefly class controlled access to it.[48] Thus the initial burst of economic activity which built up an external trade in cotton and a contribution to the Protectorate's economy upon which the district administration prided itself, served, within Teso, merely to sustain a conservative leadership determined to maintain the *status quo*.

Although the predominant cleavage in Teso society between 1907 and 1927 was that between chief and peasantry, a lesser cleavage developed between the chiefs themselves as a result of their differential economic opportunities — a cleavage between north and south. It was this that was to bring Teso politics momentarily to a standstill in 1955, when the game had still to be played according to the rules of the colonial bureaucracy. Penetration, consolidation and economic development had, as we have seen, been divisive, in west, south and north, but the political events that were set in motion in 1920 with the appointment of the first Iteso County Chiefs brought the centralization process to a new threshold at which, for the first time, Iteso were being given access to the outer corridors of power. The centralization of the polity was accompanied by a heightening of its vulnerability,[49] as competition between north and south, between the haves and have-nots of the earlier establishment became increasingly vehement.

There had clearly emerged in Teso a powerful, salaried, nominally Christian, group of southern chiefs whose growing corporate interests brought into being an opposition composed of those who had not been able to enter the political arena until later, when much of the southern power had not only been consolidated but spread. Since the logistics of mission penetration into southern Teso from Busoga had encouraged a working alliance between the administration and the Protestant missions, northern leaders seeking European patrons to intercede on their behalf, saw as their best political ploy the engagement of the support and encouragement of the Roman Catholic Church. The Catholic missionaries, having long chafed at the over-representation of the Protestant establishment among the chiefs, appear to have lent their active support.[50]

The specific event which provoked the mobilization of the northerners and Catholics was the appointment of Iteso as county chiefs in 1920. Fearing that northern demands for parity would be given a hearing, the southern chiefs launched a concerted challenge to the District Office. Mustering their grassroots support, reluctant and indebted as it may well have been, they confronted the colonial officers with a show of strength in the one area of strategic resource over which they had the closest access and the closest control: the sale of the peasants' cotton crop.

The appointment in June 1920 of Nasanairi Ipokiret from among the cohort of New Men was heralded as 'perhaps the most significant event in the History of Teso indicating that the local native is now considered to have reached the stage beyond the necessity of outside tuition and help in his internal affairs.'[51] Much of the conflict between chiefs and British administrators in the years that followed related to their different perceptions of what constituted 'outside' help. To the British, the 'outside tuition and help' that was to be withdrawn was that of the Baganda Agents who had acted as their intermediaries in governing Teso since 1899. The new Iteso county chiefs, on the other hand, interpreted their *rites de passage* as a charter to develop the district and deal with the people without any outside help, including — and perhaps especially — that of the British.

Their first show of concerted strength occurred in 1921. Prices for cotton that season were extraordinarily low, and County and sub-County chiefs throughout the district countermanded the instructions of the 'government' persuading the growers to withold their cotton from the market. Only after the District Commissioner had addressed a gathering of all County and sub-County chiefs assembled at Toroma, following upon the intervention of the District Superintendent of Police who threatened all present with criminal prosecution, was the matter settled. 'The chiefs were controlling the situation, the Bakopi [peasants] with few exceptions, were taking their lead from the chiefs.'[52] The District Commissioner was obliged to negotiate at lengthy late-night sessions with their spokesman Enosi Epaku, county chief of Soroti, and it was with him that a settlement was finally reached. As a result, Epaku issued a letter authorizing the settlement and pledging that there would be no further delay in cotton reaching the market. It would appear that, at this moment, Epaku had temporarily at least usurped the actual, if not the nominal, power of the Dis-

trict Commissioner and it is not surprising that Emwanu, writing of resistance
to alien rule in Teso, singles out the administrative career of Enosi Epaku for
special attention.[53]

By 1923 a political machine was in the making. In its first appointments of
county chiefs, the District Office had hoped to form an administrative arm
with which, with 'young chiefs to provide the initiative and necessary impetus
and a percentage of elders to maintain the ballast',[54] a steady course of political development could be pursued. They had underestimated the corporate political interests of the New Men and the covert political interests of the missions, let alone the extent to which the skills of both groups could be brought
to bear upon the stabilizing ballast. Thus in 1923, for example, Ecodu, the one
County Chief of the old school, and a northerner, asked to be transferred from
Serere where he could no longer 'get on with' his young, progressive sub-chiefs.
That he was transferred to Usuku, economically the most backward county in
the district, and retired there shortly afterwards, suggests the District Commissioner's inability to maintain the ballast and keep the political vessel on the
steady but slow course envisaged for it. Ecodu's place was taken by Opit,
'young, clever and progressive but not altogether an ideal chief' in the eyes of
one administrator.[55] Shortly afterwards, Opit put himself forward for appointment to Kumi in agreement with Epaku of Soroti, who was running his
'brother' Oiko for office in Serere county. As if coincidentally in March 1925,
Isaka Onaba, Chief of Kumi, resigned, expressing his 'inability' to cope with
the forces of change.[56]

Already by 1924 the chiefs considered themselves to be a privileged class.
Their demands for a Chief's Ward at Soroti Hospital and for special privileges at
local dispensaries were acceded to by the District Officer.[57] In that same year
African Local Government was introduced in Teso, largely so that elected representatives might to some extent offset the powers currently held by Teso
chiefs, but two years later, in 1926, the chiefs in the Teso Native Council
(which headed the local government system) openly challenged the authority
of the District Commissioner by voting a resolution to the effect that they disapproved of the Commissioner intervening in matters raised by subordinate
councils without these matters having been brought to them. Politically sensitive to their strategic position controlling access to the peasantry, the chiefs
were aware that they were increasingly likely to be bypassed by the British
officers who clearly had less reason to rely on them than previously.

The ultimate threat to the administrators came from two directions — spear-
headed by Epaku, County Chief of Soroti, and the Mill Hill Mission. It was
averted by dismissals and deportations of chiefs and priests alike. These affairs
are politically controversial still, and the remaining records throw little light on
the finer issues, yet apparently the political methods for containing the conflict
were still those of the authoritarian era. A political issue within the local arena
was settled by recourse to the larger Provincial power base; those who mobilized around the issue were removed from the district.

In June 1927 the Provincial Commissioner (Eastern Province) addressed a large public baraza at Soroti and, after a lengthy speech attacking the corruption and self-interest of the chiefs, publicly dismissed from office Epaku, County Chief of Soroti, and Opit, County Chief of Serere.[58] He drew attention to the seditious activities of other chiefs, threatening that they too would be dismissed if they did not disengage themselves from certain unnamed political organizations. His allusion was presumably to 'The League for the obtaining for Roman Catholics of a greater share in the Administration of the country', founded by Father Kiggen of the Mill Hill Mission. The Commissioner reminded the assembled chiefs of their client positions: 'The Teso individuals whom the government permitted to hold the responsible positions of County Chiefs have exploited the peasantry and made themselves rich by the sweat of *their* brow and at their expense.' He spoke of excessive attention being paid to fashionable clothing and motor cars, and more pointedly, of nepotism, bribery and cliques in power. In emphasizing the individuals, he was attacking a class. 'The machinations of a few', he suggested, 'have meantime produced maladministration and unrest' and again reminded those who would be powerful that their strength depended upon their British patrons: 'It was the Government who introduced the position of County Chiefs into Teso where it never existed before'. As if to demonstrate the power of the patrons, Baganda Agents were recalled to duty as County Chiefs.[59]

Two fighting issues may be distinguished, one made explicit by the Commissioner, the exploitation of the peasantry, and the other, nowhere explicit, the challenge by indigenous leaders to the authority of the Teso District Officers. The manipulation of a political machine by the southern County Chiefs had become increasingly apparent between 1920 and 1927, but competition for the spoils of office was restricted in its effects to the elite — just as, later, factionalism between north and south in the District Council represented the ambitions of competing councillors for patronage powers rather than a grass roots movement. In 1927, the challenge was to the British establishment, the southern chiefs providing the cutting edge for Iteso demands.

The Provincial Commissioner spoke as if he believed there was a conspiracy afoot and, whatever the truth of the matter, the newly appointed County Chiefs had clearly been too ambitious in their political goals for the established administration they now confronted. That their goals were set to benefit the peasantry, rather than to profit the chiefly class, seems unlikely.[60] Since the British administrators also claimed to have acted to protect the peasantry against their chiefly exploiters, it is in the state of the peasantry that the case must finally rest.

A continuity of experience rare in colonial administration led a newly appointed Provincial Commissioner in 1929 to recall the days when he had served as a District Officer in Teso and to assess the progress made by the peasantry in the intervening fifteen years. 'While there has been great advance in material prosperity', he remarked, 'and considerable superficial advance in Native Administration, the fundamental progress of the people themselves has been negligible.'[61] Measuring the 'progress' of the peasants by any increase in their access to such strategic resources as salaried employment or educational advancement such an assessment would seem to be valid. Certainly a greater sense of relative deprivation, *vis-à-vis* their chiefs, had developed among the peasantry.

Although peasants' ability to appeal against the privileges of chiefs and their abuse of power was severely limited, by the mid-1920s this, too, was changing. In the early days, when communication was largely through a language not spoken by administrative officers or Agents, the chiefs were strategically placed to control both the access of the District Office to the peasants and that of the peasants to their administrators. By the mid-1920s, however, streams of complaints, written in English, began to flow into the District Office at Soroti. Mostly these were petitions from aggrieved parishioners, usually anonymous — presumably for fear of reprisals — and a fair number were also received from members of minority ethnic groups.[62] From these there emerged a picture of oppression and injustice that could not be ignored. It was confirmed when district officers began to tour the district more frequently. The following extract from a report on Kateta sub-county was by no means typical of the district at the time:

Large numbers of appeals in *Lukiko* [court]. Grounds of complaint:
(1) appellants refused permission to appeal to county court
(2) excessive beating out of court and then punishment again in *Lukiko*
(3) complaints against sub-chiefs refused a hearing
(4) sub-county chiefs frequently embroiled in fights with *bakopi* [peasants].[63]

Further evidence of peasant unrest lies in the records of arson, and even murder, of chiefs that occurred during the later 1920s.

CONCLUSION

The exploitative nature of the chiefly class that grew up in Teso between 1898 and 1934 is a matter of record. Regardless of whether the chiefs were indeed a class in their own right, in the eyes of the peasantry they were oppressors against whom there was little appeal. This should not be a matter for surprise since, as we have seen, client chiefs were obliged to be responsible to the demands of office as defined by their colonial rulers. In their unrest at exploitation by their chiefs, the Teso peasants at that time were expressing dissatisfaction with an oppressive system. However, it is also a matter of record that, perceiving the problem somewhat differently, the British administration began the third decade of the 20th century as they had begun the first — searching for Iteso leaders who might be promoted to positions of authority as the 'true representatives' of the Teso people. Thus, a small but significant act on the part of an incoming District Commissioner in 1934 marks the terminal situation in this sequence of events. In a report to the Provincial Commissioner on the proposed establishment of a conciliar system and the nomination to office of parish chiefs, the customary heading of 'Native Administration' which had appeared in every report since 1907 was replaced by one that read 'Administrative and Political'.[64] The drama that was the political transformation of Teso District was moving into its second act.

NOTES

1. 'Client chief' refers to 'civil service' chiefs created by the British administration. Since their positions are not hereditary they cannot be said to be 'traditional' and they are immune to many of the checks upon the abuse of political power seen to operate within the traditional context (See J.H.M. Beattie, 'Checks on the Abuse of Political Power in some African States', *Sociologies*, IX (1959), 97-115.) The term client chief seems to have been introduced by Lloyd A. Fallers in *Bantu Bureaucracy* (East African Institute of Social Research Publications, 1956). See also L.P. Mair, 'Clientship in East Africa', *Cahiers d'études Africaines* (1961), 315-325; and J. Goody, *Technology, Tradition and the State in Africa* (Oxford University Press, 1971), 7-8. For Teso client chiefs see J. Vincent, *African Elite: The Big Men of a Small Town* (Columbia University Press, 1971). The two aspects of the office especially relevant here are (a) their personal attachment to and dependence on persons in authority above them, i.e. the client chief to the administrator as contrasted with chiefs who might rely on the support of their people, and (b) their position as territorial subordinates.

2. The terminology is that of P. Selznick, *The Organizational Weapon: A Study of Bolshevik Strategy and Tactics* (1952), 4-12.

3. Fieldwork in Teso District was carried out as a Research Fellow of the East African Institute of Social Research from 1966-67, and financed by a grant from the Ministry of Overseas Development of the United Kingdom. A return visit in 1970 was made possible by a grant from Barnard College. A condensed version of part of this essay appears as 'Colonial Chiefs and the making of class: a case study from Teso, Eastern Uganda', *Africa* (forthcoming).

4. See P. Worsley, *The Third World* (University of Chicago Press, 1964) and G. Ionescu and E. Gellner (eds), *Populism: Its Meaning and National Characteristic* (Weidenfeld and Nicholson, 1970).

5. The substantive historical data in this essay are drawn from J. Gray, 'Kakunguru in Bukedi', *Uganda Journal*, 27 (1963); R. Robinson and J. Gallagher, *Africa and the Victorians* (1959); H.G. Jones, *Uganda in Transformation 1876-1926* (1926); A.T. Matson, 'Uganda's Old Eastern Province and East Africa's Federal Capital', *Uganda Journal*, 22 (1958); A. Roberts, 'The Evolution of the Uganda Protectorate', *Uganda Journal*, 27 (1963); H.B. Thomas, 'Capax Imperii – The Story of Semei Kakunguru', *Uganda Journal*, 6 (1939), and A.D. Roberts, 'The Sub-imperialism of the Baganda', *Journal of African History*, 3 (1962).
Extensive use was also made of the Teso District Archives (TDA) located at Soroti. *An index list to the archives at the office of the District Commissioner, Teso District* was compiled in 1960 and may be found in the library of the Makerere Institute for Social Research, Makerere University College, Kampala.

6. J.C.D. Lawrence provides a very useful actor's model of Teso political development, *The Iteso* (1957). See also F. Burke, *Local Government and Politics in Uganda* (Syracuse University Press, 1964).

7. B. de Jouvenal, *On Sovereignty* (1952). Notions of politics as competition for access to 'strategic resources' are to be found in the work of Morton H. Fried, most recently in

his *The Evolution of Political Society* (Random House, 1967), and bear a relation to David Easton's definition of the role of government as 'the authoritative allocation of values', *A Systems Analysis of Political Life* (Wiley, 1965). While the colonial British must be seen as a ruling class, it is useful to recognize those who compete for administrative office within its political system as a ruling elite. In this I follow the anthropological usage of A. Southall, 'The Concept of Elites and their Formation in Uganda', in P.C. Lloyd (ed), *The New Elites of Tropical Africa* (Oxford, 1966) where an elite is defined as 'the growing edge of social activity ... that which at any time is not yet institutionalized (although it inevitably will be if successful)', p. 344. This is different from the usage of the term by many political scientists (although it has its roots in Pareto). An elite may be contrasted with an 'establishment'. Originally coined to describe the British oligarchy, this term is valuable in comparative studies for its class connotations. Cf. J. Vincent, 'Anthropology and Political Development' in C. Leys (ed), *Politics and Change in Developing Countries* (Cambridge, 1969), 57-59.

8.   R.T. Kirkpatrick's description of Serere, for example, gives clear indication of the presence of Bantu settlers: 'Lake Choga and Surrounding Countryside', *Geographical Journal*, XIII, 4 (April 1899).

9.   Table 1 is adapted from the Census of the African Population of the Uganda Protectorate for the years 1911, 1921 and 1931. Although the figures are probably far from reliable, they nevertheless give an indication of the Bakenyi, Baganda and Banyoro presence throughout the district and the greater ethnic heterogeneity of Kumi, Serere and (later) Soroti counties.

10.   N. Dyson-Hudson, *Karimojong Politics* (Oxford, 1967).

11.   In 1966 the Teso District Council introduced a bylaw whereby youths could be mobilized, according to age set organizational principles, for compulsory labour. A copy of this was shown to me in the field in January 1967. As far as I know, nothing came of the proposal.

12.   The type of political leadership to which the term Big Man is given in the ethnographic literature is commonly to be found in acephelous societies and peasant societies which are not feudal. Relevant discussions are to be found in P. Worsley, 'The Kinship System of the Tallensi: A reevaluation', *Journal of the Royal Anthropological Society*, 89 (1956); J. Barnes, 'African Models in the New Guinea Highlands', *Man*, 62 (1962); and A. Strathern, 'Despots and Directors in the New Guinea Highlands', *Man*, N.S.1 (1966). A developmental relationship exists between the Big Men of acephelous societies and the patrons and political brokers in the contemporary local scene.

13.   A. Kitching, *On the Backwaters of the Nile* (1912), 31.

14.   J.E. de Ajaye, 'The Continuity of African Institutions under Colonialism', in T. Ranger (ed), *Emerging Themes of African History* (Dar es Salaam, 1968), 197-200. For the range of policy alternatives in the colonial situation, see J. Gus Liebenow, 'Legitimacy of Alien Relationship: The Nyaturu of Tanganyika', *The Western Political Quarterly*, 14 (1961).

15.   See also footnote 31. G. Emwanu, 'The Reception of Alien Rule in Teso 1896-1927', *Uganda Journal*, 31 (1967), refers to 'Enoka Epaku who early in his career as a public servant led a spectacular expedition which marked the boundaries of the district, covering an area much wider than either his fellow chiefs or the British administrators ever thought likely,' p. 178.

16.   M.G. Smith, 'A Structural Approach to Comparative Politics', in D. Easton (ed), *Varieties of Political Theory* (Prentice-Hall, 1966), 115-116.

17.   The language of administration shifted from Luganda to Swahili to Ateso to English. Not only did this reflect, and help determine, the changing ethnic composition of the secretariat, but the difficulty of acquiring Ateso was one of the key factors permitting the growth of an indigenous elite after 1920. With the exception of J.C.D. Lawrence, no British District Officer acquired fluency in the tongue.

18.   *TDA*, VADM/5 (1920).

19.   *TDA*, 1911 District Census (Kumi).

20.   Joan Vincent, *African Elite: the Big Men of a Small Town*, 77-78.

21.   R. Dore, *City Life in Japan* (Routledge and Kegan Paul, 1958), suggests that 'indi-

viduation' be used rather than 'individualism' in such a context so that there are no connotations of 'a consciously held politico-economic philosophy', p. 387. As will be seen,
the administration was greatly concerned over the individualism of the Iteso

22. *TDA*, XADM/6. 14 (1913).
23. Ibidem.
24. *TDA*, XNAF/3.21 (1913).
25. *TDA*, XNAF/3.21/13 (1913).
26. *TDA*, XADM/5.98 (1916).
27. *TDA*, XNAF/3.3/10 (1917).
28. *TDA*, XADM/5.85 (1917).
29. *TDA*, XADM/5.127-9 (1917).
30. Since it is the political dimensions of the peasantry that concern us, Eric Wolf's definition is most apt since it focuses upon 'social relations which are not symmetrical, but are
based, in some form, upon the exercise of power ... where someone exercises an effective
superior power, or domain, over a cultivator, the cultivator must produce a fund of rent
which critically distinguishes the peasant from the cultivator', *Peasants* (Prentice-Hall,
1966), 9-10. See also R. Firth, *Malay Fishermen: Their Peasant Economy* (1946); 'The
Peasantry of Southeast Asia', *International Affairs*, 26 (1950), 503-512; and Eric Wolf,
Peasant Society (1967), for this inclusive use of 'peasants'.
31. J.C.D. Lawrence, *The Iteso*, 36; J.R.P. Postlethwaite, *I Look Back* (1947), writes:
'Both my predecessors and myself were very much struck by the vagueness of the boundary set to the active administration of this district in the north, a boundary which was in
no sense tribal and a constant source of petty irritation, and we accordingly pushed out
and further afield, determined to embrace at any rate the whole of the Teso tribe ... I must
record that our policy of penetration was officially anything but popular, though not for-
bidden in such definite terms as to preclude our going on with it. I was subsequently told
that my Provincial Commissioner had coined the phrase, 'The poisonous Postlethwaite
policy', to indicate our humble efforts.' (pp. 44-45). 'It was in the years 1911 and 1912
that the start of cotton production as a real industry was being made in Uganda territory.
An initial experience of mine, when taking over charge of Kumi District ... was an evening
when the first Uganda Director of Agriculture told us that he doubted the success of
cotton growing, and we also read a letter received from our Provincial Commissioner, who
had just returned from leave, deprecating cotton production in view of lack of transport.
However, we decided — insubordinately if you will — to persist ...'
32. Four measures of development are shown in Table 2. The population figures reflect,
to some extent, an ability to support local population and attract incomers; the poll tax
collected indicates not only population size but the efficiency of chiefs; cotton production
figures and the number of bicycles serve as indicators of the relative wealth of each
county.
33. *Teso District Annual Report* (1920).
34. Ibidem.
35. *TDA*, VADM/3/1 (1910).
36. *TDA*, XADM/2 106 (1926-27).
37. *TDA*, XADM/6. 14 (1913).
38. *TDA*, VADM/8.1 (1920).
39. *TDA*, VADM/5.2 (1927).
40. *TDA*, VADM/5.2 (1929).
41. *TDA*, XADM/5.41.
42. *TDA*, XADM/5.2.
43. *TDA*, XADM/5.2.
44. *TDA*, VADM/5.2; *TDA*, XADM/5.41.
45. *TDA*, VADM/5/2.
46. *TDA*, VADM/5/3. No. D 32 of 1927.
47. *TDA*, XADM/9.
48. African opportunities may be measured by the expansion of Asian traders to some
extent. In 1908 there were Asian shops at Bululu, Serere, Ngora, Kumi, Mukura, Kapiri
and Soroti, according to the Uganda Protectorate *Intelligence Report* (1908). The develop-

ment of Usuku, Amuria and Northern Soroti was much slower. For the Asian role as patron and economic broker for the non-Bantu peasants of Teso and Lango, see *African Elite*, 181-184.

49. M.G. Smith, 'A Structural Approach to Comparative Politics', 121.

50. I base this statement on fragments appearing in miscellaneous files and correspondence between the District Commissioner, Teso and the Provincial Commissioner. Letter books (TDA, VADM/8/1.2) are sketchy, but correspondence between 1912 and 1922 suggests, in the form of address, the tone of the correspondence, etc., that Administration's relations with the Catholic Missions — having at first been amicable and cooperative (cf. Postlethwaite, *I Look Back*, p. 30), later became extremely tense, reaching a low point in 1927. A passage in the *District Report* for that year reads: 'Disloyalty was fostered by a Catholic Mission Priest who had to be deported from the District in June. It is still being fanned by a fanatical and anti-Government Sein Finn lawyer who desires the Catholic Church to have temporal and spiritual power in Teso' (*TDA*, XADM/9.15). I have not yet been able to look at the records of the Mill Hill Mission of this period and would not want to develop this argument further without having done so.

51. *TDA*, XADM/6.11 (1920).

52. *TDA*, VADM 8/1; *TDA*, XADM/7.4.21.

53. Emwanu, 'The Reception of Alien Rule in Teso 1896-1927'.

54. *TDA*, XADM/9.29 (1920).

55. *TDA*, XADM/6.4.3-5 (1923).

56. *TDA*, XADM/6.40.5 (1925).

57. *TDA*, XADM/9. A.R.

58. *TDA*, ADM/17 (1927).

59. Ibidem. The tone of the District Commissioner's comment upon this move is significant: 'This may appear paradoxical to our Western ideas of self-determination and democracy. In Teso, thank goodness, we are not yet troubled by either of these false premises. The peasantry has suffered so heavily from the contempt and exploitation by their black coated compatriots that they frankly welcome a protective shock-absorber above them' (*TDA*, XADM/106/105).

60. Emwanu suggests that Epaku, for example, was discharged because of the 'immense popularity which he enjoyed among his own people, a fact which was well known to the administration. He was especially concerned with the welfare of the people of Teso as a whole.' 'Reception of Alien Rule', 179. I explore this issue more fully in 'Colonial Chiefs and the Making of Class' (forthcoming).

61. *TDA*, XADM/9 (1929).

62. *TDA*, XMIS/1. The file bears the title 'Miscellaneous' (22 files).

63. *TDA*, VADM/IJ, 3.

64. *TDA*, VADM/5/6.

PETER RIGBY

LOCAL PARTICIPATION IN NATIONAL POLITICS, UGOGO, TANZANIA

As an anthropologist, my intention in this paper is to present an analysis of recent political processes and events in Gogo society as it exists today. Many of these political processes and events emanate from sources in the national governmental structure of Tanzania and the national party organization, the Tanganyika African National Union (TANU). To analyse the political structure of Ugogo today without reference to the wider political context would be indefensible.

One way of handling the problem would be to consider these wider political processes merely as part of the 'environment' of the Gogo political system, that is, as a set of external 'forces' impinging upon an internally coherent system. I have presented such an analysis of Gogo political development elsewhere,[1] and I summarize this study later in the present paper. To some extent, one cannot escape this kind of approach, nor is it desirable to do so. But one can, I think, adopt an alternative analytical standpoint which is not based upon the central concept of 'the Gogo political system', but which postulates a 'field' of political action in which various individuals and categories of the Gogo population are involved.[2] Such an analysis, however, can only be attempted after the Gogo political system viewed as a set of distinctive structures, is understood.

A political field contains several 'structures', often cross-cutting and contradictory. There are 'systematic' elements which can be discerned in all aspects of this field, but only one of them is delimited by what we may call the 'traditional' political structures and orientations of Gogo society. Clearly, it has been extremely rewarding to compare 'total systems' in terms of their response to political change and modernization.[3] But, for example, the classic distinction between 'centralized' and 'non-centralized' polities[4] is no longer an adequate analytical tool in explaining different responses to external political forces and values.[5] Neither are more sophisticated categorizations of total systems, such as on the basis of Apter's pyramidal/hierarchical/segmental and consummatory/instrumental continua,[6] sufficient for understanding in depth, simply because they classify total systems and thereby obscure crucial variables.

But we do not have to abandon sociological differences in the processes of 'internalizing political values',[7] however valid this type of explanation is upon one level. We must instead find new analytical frameworks with which we can better explain the new data available to us. My suggestion here is that one possible solution lies in viewing political action as constituting 'sets of partial systems', rather than easily categorized 'total systems', and in trying to apply to politics what Leach has suggested for the study of kinship.[8] This, however, is not a theoretical treatise and it leaves entirely open a discussion of the objections Southall[9] raises to this kind of procedure. I attempt merely to examine some political processes in Ugogo in terms of analytical ideas different from those I originally brought to bear upon similar data.[10]

Two complementary principles operate in the traditional political system of the Gogo.[11] The formal organization of the politico-jural domain is based primarily upon religious authority and ritual differentiation related to clanship. Most secular authority is, on the other hand, vested in the 'elders' (wanyamphala or wawaha), acting both as homestead-heads and as members of ad hoc local courts. As the Gogo political system is still largely intact, these principles are still operative in the Gogo political field today.

The traditional politico-religious structure of Gogo society can be characterised as highly egalitarian, with ascriptive roles predominating in the ritual sphere and 'achievement' roles, influenced by age-status, predominating in the sphere of secular influence and authority.[12] Any 'normal' man with average abilities and luck can hope to achieve a position of status and secular influence during the course of his life. Owing to the exigencies of a marginal economic environment and a commitment to pastoralism (although the Gogo subsist primarily upon cereal agriculture, they have large herds),[13] homestead-groups are spatially mobile. A man can therefore exercise his secular influence and authority in whatever area he happens to be residing. Ritual authority is tied to areas and, although related to clanship, it does not provide the basis for corporate group formation. Gogo political structures, therefore, cannot be characterized as segmentary or centralised; neither does it fall within the category of systems in which age-organization provides the primary basis for political action.

Gogo country lies across what used to be one of the major routes of foreign penetration in East Africa. Arab, and later European, travellers' caravans plying between Bagamoyo on the coast and Uganda and the Congo, regularly passed through Ugogo from Mpwapwa (Mhamvwa) in the east to Kilimatinde (Cilimanhinde) in the west. Most of these caravans travelled in the extended dry season when food and water resources in Ugogo are extremely scarce. The travellers often dangerously depleted Gogo resources. In some areas, Gogo organized the extraction of taxes in each ritual area, and the small size of these countries is attested to by the wrath of many early travellers who had to pay what they considered exorbitant sums in cloth and other goods to travel only a few miles. The behaviour of many early European travellers towards the Gogo was extremely aggressive and did not augur well for good 'external relations'.[14] These early contacts and organization for the extraction of taxes may have given some ritual leaders military and political power they did not possess previously, but Gogo political structure remained essentially the same until the arrival of the Germans.

The early German base at Mpwapwa (1887) was destroyed by the Gogo, and it was not until German influence was consolidated in about 1890 that colonial 'administration' began. At this stage, it was concerned primarily with the collection of taxes and the protection of travellers from attack. The German administrative post (*boma*) at Kilimatinde was established by Tom Von Prince in 1895, but the first 'effective' German administrator in Ugogo was Von Sperling, who was initially based at Mpwapwa.

The administrative system used by the Germans was based upon appointed *majumbe* and *maakida*, who were mostly non-Gogo, many being Muslim Africans or Arabs from the coast. This was in a sense an extension of the previous Arab technique of using *maakida*, African or Arab assistants, along the various trading routes.[15] Mnyampala refers to *maakida* as 'tax clerks', which was probably their primary function. Under the Germans the authority of these assistants was, in the words of a later British administrator, one of 'rough invective and rude homilies'.

In such a situation, and after several experiences in which Gogo who had put themselves forward as leaders of their communities had been executed, Gogo ritual leaders stayed largely in the background. A few of the Gogo who were appointed to official positions by the Germans were members of the clans with ritual control in their areas, but more often their 'slaves' (*wawanda*) were put forward for the job. Hence, although a new 'field' of political relations was established at the imposition of colonial control, the Gogo response was to involve marginal categories of persons in the new structural positions; or at the very least, an attempt was made to conceal the real nature of their own political institutions from the colonial authority. The impact of colonial authority therefore 'extended' the field of political action in Ugogo, but only on the basis of accommodating two political structures which the Gogo attempted to keep distinct. The colonial authority was concerned primarily with administration; Gogo political action remained predominantly inward-directed in terms of the traditional pattern, while some attempt was made to mediate 'external' relations with as little disruption as possible. This pattern, in modified form, continued through the later period of British colonial administration.

The German system did not last long enough to succeed in gaining any legitimacy in Gogo terms. The Anglo-German war severely affected the Gogo area, causing considerable social disruption and contributing to the worst famine in Gogo living memory: that of Muyunya in 1918-1919.[16] A British military administration was established in 1916 and lasted until 1920, when civil administration began. The early British administrators based their system explicitly upon the German one. They were concerned largely with settling claims for loss of relatives during the war, and with trying to reunite lost persons with their families. But in 1925, the 'theory' of indirect rule became the basis of administrative policy in Tanzania, and a major effort was made to change the structure of local government. I have described this period in some detail elsewhere[17] and do not go into it in detail here. Because the traditional political units (the ritual areas in Ugogo) were so small, a process of 'amalgamation' took place before 'chiefdoms' and 'sub-chiefdoms' could be created. The British found Ugogo difficult to administer, and changes constantly took place in local government during the period of their control until 1961, when Tanzania became independent. But on the whole, the pattern they created was one of larger 'chiefdoms', in which the previous ritual areas became 'sub-chiefdoms' headed by 'sub-chiefs' who were called *wapembamoto*. The term *mutemi* was adopted for 'government chief', necessitating the Gogo distinction between *mutemi we ligoda* ('the chief of the stool', or ritual leader) and *mutemi we serikali* ('government chief').

Some Gogo ritual leaders became government chiefs or sub-chiefs, but this was not the general pattern. The two roles remained essentially separate, and this was of advantage to both the Gogo and the colonial administration. Gogo ritual leaders did not wish to expose themselves to the colonial 'public eye', and the administration did not want to be tied to a strict rule of succession which governed recruitment to the Gogo ritual office. But during the British period, most of the government chiefs and sub-chiefs did belong to the clans with ritual leadership in their areas, and they were frequently close kinsmen of the ritual leaders.[18] This fact assisted in the accommodation of the Gogo political process to the new office of government chief.

Government chiefs, if they were to be effective, depended primarily upon 'external' sanctions and 'alien' institutions for their power and recruitment. Some Gogo government chiefs were prepared for office at the old 'school for chiefs' at Tabora, and they had new sources of prestige and wealth. But most of them were said to have witchcraft and sorcery power, and many consciously tried to attain ritual authority for themselves to make their new roles legitimate in Gogo values. This usurpation of ritual influence itself was quite 'legitimate', as it was quite common throughout Gogo political history. Some government chiefs were therefore able to establish a *modus operandi* during the period when the system functioned with a modicum of efficiency, from about 1935 until 1962. The offices of government chief, sub-chief, and village headman had attained some legitimacy in Gogo terms, although they remained largely dependent upon 'externally' based authoritarianism for their ultimate sanctions. Over this period also, courts, councils, magistrates and, later, village committees, were set up to make the system of local government somewhat more 'democratic'.

When political chiefship was abolished in Ugogo in 1962, together with the sub-chiefs and village headmen, their secular functions were transferred to the new village executive officers, divisional executive officers, village development committees, and related offices. But the ritual leaders were still there, free to perform their traditional duties, which are still far from disappearing.

Prior to the abolition of the chiefships and village headmanships, village councils had been set up to assist in administration and community development matters such as adult literacy classes. The village development committees superseded these earlier councils, and their size, functions, and recruitment have varied somewhat since their inception. However, basically village committees are elected by several 'villages' in combination, and function within an area approximating to the old sub-chiefdoms. A chairman is elected, but it is not a paid position. A village executive officer is appointed by the district council, and this is the lowest paid position in the hierarchy. The wider units, the old chiefdoms, have been re-named divisions, with some boundary changes here and there. The divisional executive officers and TANU chairmen at both levels play an important part in instituting changes at the village level. I discuss the operation of these new structures and recruitment to the new roles in some detail below.

In 1964, a new system of a representative for every ten homesteads (*nyumba kumi kumi*) was instituted, and applies equally to urban and rural areas. The *kumi kumi* representative is a party member. The elective office (unpaid) is one of liaison between members of the ten homesteads and party and local government officials. This is essentially an element of party organization and is *formally* distinct from the village development committees, although in parts of Ugogo (and elsewhere in Tanzania) there is some confusion of functions, and I refer to this again later. But we may note here that the Second Vice President, Mr. Kawawa, addressing a meeting of TANU cell leaders, said that they all should be members of the village development committees '...so as to enable them to fulfil effectively their duties in nation building as a whole'.[19] He also told them that the party cell system was established to consolidate TANU leadership in the villages and so that people would be able to air their views, opinions and grievances more easily.[20] Although village development committees were supposed to be made up entirely of cell leaders, there was considerable variation in practice throughout Tanzania and within Ugogo.

Village development committees participate in the day-to-day administration of affairs which in the past were performed by village headmen, sub-chiefs, and their assistants, with the exception of tax collection and the settlement of disputes.[21] The former should be controlled by the village executive officer, the latter by local magistrates. In fact, many disputes never reach the official courts at all[22] and, as I show later, in some places even tax collection breaks down. But the village committees have new functions which, ideally, are the more important ones: those of creating new settlement patterns, and thus new kinds of community, and the implementing of development and nation-building projects. They are designed to provide avenues for the development of new kinds of political leadership at the local level, and I return to an examination of this aspect later.

However, we can say that new structures have entered the field of political relations in Ugogo since independence in 1961, in which the accommodations achieved during the colonial period of government chiefship have no formal validity. This state of affairs is not determined by political action in Ugogo, but by national political decisions. From the national point of view, unless the new structures and offices are effective, the implementation of even such basic administrative functions as tax collection becomes impossible. But of course, contrary to the aims of the colonial government, the TANU national government in Tanzania is not merely interested in accomplishing administrative tasks. It is also interested in mobilizing political action and leadership, so that decisions about development and change can be taken and implemented at the grass roots level, albeit as a part of a nationally coordinated plan. TANU is only ideally a monolithic organization. It is in actuality fraught with contradictions and discontinuities, like most structures of social action.[23]

Many of the ideological and administrative problems besetting both party and government in independent Tanzania concern the failure in 'getting to the villages'. Discontinuities appear between districts, regions, and Dar es Salaam. I show later how true this is for Ugogo. Yet it is between the villages and the district and regional organizations that the greatest gulf in communication and cooperation lies.

Since independence in 1962, the Tanzanian government and TANU have attempted to solve the problems of 'penetration' on levels of both administration and communication. Both government and party, closely allied to effect change, are involved in these efforts. Apart from such activities as recruiting drives for party membership, the principal political changes and events affecting the Gogo have been (a) the policy of self-help schemes and 'villagization', (b) the 1962 presidential elections, (c) the abolition of chiefs and the creation of village development committees, (d) the creation of TANU cell organization, and (e) the 1965 parliamentary and presidential elections.

I have stated that the 'traditional' Gogo political and religious system is still functioning, although reduced in relative importance.[24] It is possible that the categories of persons involved in that aspect of the political field still 'occupied' by the traditional political structures may also be involved in the new structures of the present field. In examining the processes and events just outlined, it is therefore necessary to keep in mind all the categories of persons who may be involved in varying degrees. These categories may be listed as follows.

1. Traditional ritual leaders and diviners.
2. 'Elders'.

3. Ex-chiefs, who participated in the system of colonial administration.
4. 'Warriors', or young men still largely committed to Gogo society and its values, who are also still the majority of the young population.[25]
5. Young people, both men and women, who have had some modern education, which usually implies that they are Christians. This category is known as *wasomaji* (Kiswahili: 'the read') by the Gogo.
6. Members of category (5) who have moved to the towns, taken up jobs, and virtually left Gogo society. Numerically very small.
7. Gogo women as a category, opposed to men.
8. 'Non-Gogo' 'townsmen' who have lived in the towns of Dodoma, Mpwapwa, and Manyoni, and smaller divisional trading centres. The older members of this category have a predominantly 'Kiswahili', Muslim culture and orientation; the younger may be either Christians or Muslims.[26]

Some of these categories are not, of course, mutually exclusive. None of them are irrelevant for our present purposes. 'Elders' and 'warriors' are not formally involved in political activities and offices outside those which are strictly 'traditional', but they can and do influence such modern processes and events which impinge upon them. The varying participation of these categories in modern politics will emerge in the following analysis.

The policies of 'self-help' and 'villagization' were closely related, although chronologically the former preceded the latter. The self-help schemes were put into operation before independence by the Ministry of Community Development, with the aid of TANU local bodies. This was TANU's first real attempt, having organized brilliantly and achieved the road to independence, to encourage participation at the 'village' level in both decision-making and the implementation of development policies. But the real impetus came in 1962, when the People's Plan for village development was launched by the then Prime Minister, Rashidi Kawawa:

This plan was based on autonomous development committees at village level, whose task was to plan individual development schemes....Community development workers were to bring new awareness to the leaders and the people at village, district, and regional levels... and leaders told TANU regional, district, and local officials that they ought to be, in effect, community development officers.[27]

I have presented the evidence elsewhere[28] and only draw the conclusion here that, as far as Ugogo was concerned, the remarkable success of the self-help schemes in 1962 was mainly due to the fact that the chiefs and village headmen, not yet removed, were still in charge. The young people elected to the village councils were almost totally unable to mobilize any support. The chiefs and headmen, however, who had sometimes made strenuous efforts to identify themselves with TANU before independence, relied upon their authority derived from their status under the colonial government (*vide supra*). During 1961 and 1962, the chiefs were also able to threaten recalcitrant self-help workers with the withdrawal of famine relief maize, as Ugogo had suffered a severe famine in 1961 and another milder one in 1962.

Hence, at this stage, TANU's efforts to involve more people at the village level in making decisions about social change and development did not work out the way it was intended in Ugogo. Most of the young people elected onto the village committees had some modern education, and they fall within the category *wasomaji*. Although Gogo, they have none of the qualities which fitted a man for leadership in Gogo society, nor do they have access to the basis of authority set up under the colonial system. Nevertheless, it is important to note that a new 'arena' for political competition was created with the institution of the village committees. They still exist and provide the most important of the new political structures in Ugogo. I return to a detailed examination of them later. But at this early stage, the actual tasks of administration were carried out by the old government chiefs and village headmen, a category of persons who were already participants in a wider political field than that of traditional Gogo society. And this category of persons was not open to everyone, least of all to the younger Christians and Muslims with some schooling but no traditional stature, or wealth, traditional or modern. When the chiefs were deposed at the end of 1962, the mobilization of labour for the self-help schemes dropped radically in Ugogo.

By this time, TANU and government policy was moving from the policy of independent self-help schemes at local level to an overall concept which came to be called 'villagization'. The idea of villagization did not, however, come up from the village development committees. It stemmed from central government policy as a result of discussion with Israeli and other experts, including those involved in channelling foreign aid to Tanzania. From the national point of view:

The villagization program was designed to group a scattered population into villages in order to husband scarce resources — tractors, managerial personnel — and facilitate the provision of social services and the mechanization of agriculture. Grouping people into compact villages would make central direction of agricultural development easier. At the same time, TANU leaders believed that stronger local political organizations could be built in such villages. The idea of villagization was tied up with voluntary labour schemes to build the villages, and such self-help programs were to provide the focus for strengthening TANU at the local levels.[29]

From the Gogo point of view, villagization was an ecological, economic, and social impossibility. Apart from two or three settlement schemes (the villagization policy itself later became concerned almost solely with settlement schemes), on which tenants are bound by contract to obey certain rules, it could be said that, as of 1968, the villagization policy has had no impact whatsoever upon Gogo society in general. But as a political issue, it comes up again in a discussion of the village committees (see below), and it is likely to remain such. The basic principles of villagization are reiterated in Mwalimu Nyerere's 1967 paper[30] on *Socialism and Rural Development*.

The committees set up while the headmen were still in office were primarily concerned with matters affecting the adult literacy campaign and other community development matters, instituted before independence by the Community Development Department. The new committees are distinguished from them in form and function. In Ugogo, the new committees were originally referred to as 'committee of twenty' (*halmashauri ya makumi myejete*). But it appears that the new committees are recruited in rural Ugogo from the same categories of persons who had belonged to the now superseded adult literacy councils, although other categories may try to influence the process of recruitment. I describe here the election of two of the three village development committees set up in the area in which I was working in 1963, and the simultaneous selection of village executive officers in this area.

A local government officer from the district headquarters at Dodoma first addressed a meeting in the area. He explained the new government offices which were to be set up and the division of functions relating to them. At this meeting, the new 'village' areas were defined and the boundaries pointed out, not without considerable opposition from the local populace, as will become apparent. Subsequent meetings were arranged and the villagers were told by the divisional executive officer to elect, at their own meetings, twenty men as committee members from each of the newly-defined areas, together with two or three women. They were also told to select candidates for chairman of each committee (unpaid) and for the village executive officers (paid).[31] Those selected were then to attend a smaller meeting of themselves, the divisional executive officer and a clerk, in order to confirm the selections and appoint the village executive officers. They were also to allocate tasks and priorities for schemes such as road building, agricultural development, and the construction of schools and clinics. I participated in these meetings and activities in one area only, but I heard that much the same was going on throughout Ugogo.

After the first meeting, the election of village committee members was carried out fairly quickly, most of those who had been on the previous adult literacy committees being re-elected. Four Gogo neighbourhoods,[32] which I shall for present purposes call 'villages', were grouped into pairs with a village development committee of 22 members each. At a later meeting with the divisional executive officer, there were many objections raised to this grouping which had been administratively decided. In fact, two villages which were closely linked ritual areas (they had separate sets of rainstones but the ritual leader of one was the full brother of the other, and both had been within one sub-chiefdom in the past) were placed under separate committees. Neither the divisional executive officer, who was from Uhehe, nor the TANU secretary, a Mugogo from another part of Ugogo, knew or got to know of this. The objections were raised by the village committee members on the grounds of distance.

Members from village A, who were on the same committee as those from B and required to attend meetings at the latter place (which was on the main road), said they could not walk twenty miles to each meeting through thick bush. They would rather go to C (to which their area was ritually linked), a distance of some 14 miles. These objections were overruled by the divisional executive officer, who said that the decisions were made and that the people of A might be required to move their village anyway (a reference to the possible application of a future 'villagization' scheme in this area). To this a committee member replied that, if they had any choice, they would move to C, 'where our relatives are', and not to B.

The meeting at which this took place was held at B and attended by members of both committees, representing A/B and C/D, the four linked villages. These committees will be referred to as the 'B' and 'C' committees respectively. Thirteen members of the B committee were present, and seven members of the C committee, which had previously been split into several factions over the choice of a village executive officer, as we shall see. Members of these committees represented the younger age categories of men between 20 and 40 years of age. Ideally, all committee members should be literate; but in this case, some were not. This prompted the divisional executive officer to urge them to set an example in attending adult literacy classes. All the literate committee members were Christians; others followed traditional Gogo religion. None of the village headmen or sub-chiefs who had been in authority a short while before were represented on this group (they were all non-literate in this area). The sole exception was one Baraguyu elder who had previously been a paid assistant 'village headman', and who helped in the collection of taxes from the substantial Baraguyu minority and represented them to the administration. He was asked to continue in this role in an unpaid capacity, but he refused. He remained on the village committee, however.

The divisional executive officer, himself a Muhehe who had been a town clerk for many years in Ugogo and spoke good Cigogo, emphasized that the village committee members should be representative of 'all groups' (Cigogo, we zimbavu zose, 'from both sides'). This was taken to mean: the Christian denominations (there are village school teachers employed by the churches), other religious groups (the Muslim Welfare Association was mentioned), government servants (such as PWD workers, although there are very few permanently resident government employees outside the division headquarters), and so on. Conspicuously lacking in the list put forward were any categories of persons traditionally important in the politico-religious system: 'elders', diviners, and ritual leaders.

Of those on committee C, one Christian, whom we shall call Daudi, was trying to gain for himself the position of village executive officer. He was the classificatory 'son', that is, not 'actual son' but one called such in terms of lineal descent, of the ritual leader of the area in which C lies. He was given the job of recording the proceedings of the meeting for C committee. Another Christian member of the committee was a man of about 30 years of age. His father, who had been a 'slave dependent' (*muwanda*) of one of the members of the ritual leader's clan, had been *jumbe* under the Germans.[33] His descendant had not held any authority positions since then. None of the members of this committee had the status of associations linked with leadership, either in terms of the Gogo politico-religious system or in terms of that operated by the colonial administration.

At this meeting, a chairman of the B committee was elected, by show of hands, from among three candidates. The main criterion was literacy and therefore the ability to keep records of committee meetings and send in reports to the divisional and district executive officers. The chairman for C had already been selected by the C committee. He was the local adult literacy teacher and a CMS trainee.[34] He was very reluctant to accept the position and had not come to the meeting in question, but the divisional executive officer thought that he could be persuaded to accept.

The meeting now turned to the selection of the two village executive officers for B and C, to which A and D neighbourhoods had been respectively affiliated. It was clear that this was where conflict over political interests in the new structures was going to occur, and this it did. I have already mentioned that, owing to this conflict, some of the C committee members had not attended this meeting. First, applicants for the B executive officer post were requested to write their applications on paper. There were four contestants, including the local Muhehe storekeeper at whose shop the meeting was being held. These four were then asked to move some distance away and their applications were read out to the meeting by the divisional executive officer, with comments upon their abilities as writers of Kiswahili. By show of hands, the Muhehe storekeeper was elected without argument.

Gogo committee members from C later alleged that this election had been 'arranged' previously by the Muhehe storekeeper who, they said, had bribed all the committee members to vote for him. They implied that the divisional executive officer, also a Muhehe, had known this all along. The idea of bribery as an instrument of power in politics and the settlement of disputes has been firmly held by Gogo since the period of government chiefs under the British colonial administration. The chiefs used it as a means of gaining wealth, which in turn was used to 'legitimate' their alien-imposed offices.

However, the selection of the executive officer for C was the arena for a considerable struggle for power. An examination of this struggle provides an insight into the kind of adjustment which is being made by Gogo to the new structures in the field of political action.

There were four contestants for the office. Let us call them Calo, Matonya, Daudi, and Zakariya. Daudi was the classificatory 'son' of the ritual leader already mentioned. He had taken the action of sending his application for the

post of village executive officer to the district office in Dodoma. This infuri-
ated the divisional executive officer, who said that his position in the hierarchy
had been ignored and that Daudi had 'gone over his head' to higher authority.
It earned Daudi a good half-hour lecture full of scorn and anger, and he was declared an 'upstart'. Later action (see below) by the faction of committee members who were against him ensured the continuation of the rift between him
and the divisional executive officer. This effectively eliminated him from the
running.

Calo had already been tentatively selected by one faction of the committee,
but he was not at this meeting. He is literate, about 34 years of age, but has
little wealth or status based upon any criteria. He is of mixed Baraguyu and
Gogo parentage and is the younger half-brother of the Baraguyu elder mentioned above, who is also a member of the committee. The latter was totally
against the appointment of Calo as village executive officer. It was suggested
at this meeting that Calo had, with meat and beer, 'bribed' the faction which
supported him. Thus his tentative election was considered an imposition by
other committee members.

Zakariya was another literate Christian who had little support from anyone.
In the face of this, he nominated James, a young man of about 18 who had
also been to church school. The divisional executive officer rejected this nomination on the grounds that James was much too young to handle the duties of
executive officer.

The fourth candidate was Matonya. He was working in Dodoma in a comparatively well-paid messenger's job (Dodoma being some 60 miles away). He is
literate, and thought well-versed in dealing with outsiders and government
agents. He was being sponsored primarily, but of course unofficially, by the
ritual leader at C. Matonya is the classificatory 'father' (*sogwe*) of the ritual
leader and is therefore a member of his clan, although he is much younger than
the latter. Matonya made several visits to C at his own expense during this
struggle for power. However, no decision could be reached at the meeting in
question, since there were so few representatives from C/D. The divisional
executive officer told the committee members who were there that he would
come to C after a month to see if the conflict had been settled, and that he
would address a meeting then. This he did, but the conflict continued on
several fronts, one of which was a case concerning Daudi.

The actual offence of which he was accused was of minor importance as far
as the committee members were concerned. The real motivation behind the action of the *halmashauri* was a political one: to ensure that Daudi was dis-
credited and therefore disqualified as a candidate.

Later, when the divisional executive officer arrived to conduct his meeting,
together with the local TANU chairman, they stayed two days at Calo's homestead and Calo slaughtered a young ox (*nzeku*) for them. He also supplied the
party with beer. This action would normally have been construed as Gogo hos-

pitality, but most elders considered it was another example and clear confirmation of the fact that Calo was intent upon securing the post of village executive officer by bribery (*kufupa*). It was commonly believed by people in area C that the salary of village executive officer would be in the region of Shs.150/- a month. This is relatively high, but the general opinion was that the incentives to power and influence in the new structures of political action outweighed any purely cash considerations. Matonya, the messenger working in Dodoma, told me that he was getting a salary of Shs.250/- a month, but still thought it worthwhile to secure the village executive officer's position if he could.[35]

As a result of this conflict, the TANU secretary at the public meeting at C warned the elders that they should keep an eye open for disruptive struggles between the *halmashauri*, and that they should report any attempts to discredit others.

I have dwelt at some length on the election and composition of the new village committees and the emerging role of village executive officer, the latter primarily in terms of its recruitment rather than its operation, a point I return to later. The picture is by no means clear, but does illustrate some of the processes taking place at the local level as a result of the radical change in local government structures brought about in conformity with national policy. It is clear, however, that the persons involved in these processes and as potential leaders in new political roles have few qualities legitimating their political and administrative authority. They specifically cannot share those qualities of 'chiefly' authority which emerged during the period of colonial government and 'indirect' rule. Those individuals who controlled the old hierarchy at the local level can hope only to influence the recruitment and operation of the new structures indirectly. An example of this is the effort made by the ritual leader and ex-sub-chief to back Matonya for the position of executive officer. The ritual leader, however, did not attend any of the meetings concerned, nor did the ex-village headman.

But what of the operation of the new structures and those who are prepared to get involved in them? Calo was eventually selected village executive officer for C/D and his appointment confirmed. In 1964, just a year later, he had been removed from office, partly because of his excessive drinking habits and consequently bad relations with his neighbours. But also, I learned, because Zakariya, who had also been a candidate for the post in 1963, had been working consistently for Calo's downfall. Zakariya is one of the most educated homestead-heads in the area. He is also, as we have seen, a Christian.

Zakariya reported Calo's difficult relations with other people at 'village' C and the police came to investigate. They spent the night at Zakariya's homestead, where they feasted upon one of his goats. As soon as the police left, Zakariya began spreading the story that Calo was finished as village executive officer, and implying that he was going to take over. But Zakariya also immediately took a case to the local magistrate's court implicating the police and

Calo for forcibly taking one of his goats and eating it. This was probably an attempt by Zakariya to clear rumours that he had been trying to 'bribe' the police to take action against Calo. One of the constables concerned was arrested, and the case came to court. The policeman agreed in evidence that he and his companions had eaten the goat at Zakariya's, but maintained that Zakariya himself had 'cooked it for them' (*yawavujira mweneco*), that no force had been used.

Giving evidence, Zakariya eventually admitted that he had given the goat voluntarily to the policemen, and the case was abandoned. But through it, Zakariya had destroyed any chances he may have had of taking over the role of village executive officer. The Area Commissioner called him to Dodoma and told him (in the words of one informant from village C):

This kind of behaviour is that of a fool, and I do not want to hear of this sort of thing coming up again. If you come to the courts or to me with nonsense, I will have you removed from the village in which you live.

Nevertheless, Calo's behaviour had been exposed, and he was removed from the position of village executive officer. As there was no suitable (or willing) candidate to take over his office for village C/D, the two areas were transferred to the village executive officer at B, the Muhehe storekeeper who had been elected in 1963. The storekeeper became executive officer for all four neighbourhoods, A, B, C and D.

However, this was purely a formal arrangement and did not function for very long. At a meeting held at C in September 1965 to explain the presidential election and voting procedure,[36] the new village executive officer did not come.[37] Present at the meeting were the local TANU chairman, the tax clerk, several members of the village development committee, and the ex-village headman, now also a *kumi kumi* cell leader. The non-appearance of the village executive officer, an occurrence which had been going on for some time, was explained to me as follows:

He is afraid of coming to C, because the people of C refuse to be under him and would assault him. You may think that the 'representative' of ten houses, the ex-village headman, was chosen by the people of C. In fact it was the Muhehe executive officer [from B] who chose him. As he is afraid to come here himself, he thought that the ex-village headman of the old chief could handle things as he used to in the past. But the people of C don't want the ex-village headman at all. When he says anything they don't even listen to him. He particularly had trouble with two village committee members. When the ex-village headman brings instructions from the village executive officer, telling them to do this and that, they just refuse and say, 'Do it yourself.' Do you think we are still under the colonial government [that we listen to village headman]?

The pattern of factions established in 1963 clearly continues. In 1965, there was almost an administrative hiatus which certainly affected the elections in this area.[38] In November 1965, many Gogo in the same area refused to pay cattle tax. Their Member of Parliament had to hold several meetings to persuade them to do so. In April 1966, several rich men had still not paid.

It is clear from these struggles for power and influence that some kind of adjustment is being made in terms of the new structures and values, but that an important element in this adjustment is the traditional Gogo penchant for egalitarianism and argument. The influence of the more traditionally based categories of persons with influence and authority is stronger now than when the new structures were established, but this influence is indirect. Those prepared to compete for positions in the new structures remain marginal categories as far as most Gogo are concerned.

We may conclude that the Gogo are quite prepared to express their views in a national political arena upon how national political events and processes impinge upon their own society. In order to do this, they are also prepared to participate in large numbers in such activities as voting in national and local elections. But the opinions they express are still largely fashioned by the values of traditional Gogo society. This in itself can be considered an achievement from the point of view of national party and governmental organization. It may be taken as an index of success as far as one form of political penetration is concerned. The electoral process had gained a form of legitimacy which may satisfy both party and governmental aims as well as the Gogo penchant for expressing opinion upon an egalitarian basis. The electoral system is therefore an extension of the field of political action which presents no real conflict of values to the Gogo, and participation is relatively strong.

However, as far as some of the other structures in the new political field are concerned, there is a certain withdrawal and aloofness. The material presented in this paper on the village development committees and associated roles and offices indicates that the categories of persons, Gogo and non-Gogo, who are involved in the new structures of political action are 'resented' for one reason or another. Yet most Gogo are very concerned about the recruitment and functioning of such offices, although most are not prepared to consider themselves as possible candidates for them. Thus, paradoxically, the majority of Gogo may be prepared to 'expand' the field of political action in terms of participation in the electoral process; only a very small minority, often of what some Gogo consider 'marginal categories', will at the moment participate in the governmental and party structures which communicate national policy to them, and through which they are supposed to express their views to the 'centre' upon everyday issues.

But the paradox is lessened if we conclude from the material presented in this paper that the two kinds of structure, the 'electoral' and the 'administrative', have very different kinds of legitimacy attached to them from the Gogo point of view. Expressing an opinion in the national political arena is legitimate as an 'extension' of Gogo political values. Getting involved in structures of authority and decision making based upon criteria alien to Gogo political values is left to categories of persons who stand essentially 'outside' Gogo society. But at the same time, those with authority, religious or political, in the traditional political system (elders, ritual leaders) attempt to influence the recruitment to, and hence the functioning of, these new structures and roles. In this way, the new structures are accommodated in the total political field, however conflicting they may at times appear to be.

TANU and governmental agencies are fully aware of the problems posed by lack of participation and legitimacy, viewing them as problems of penetration and communication. On the one hand some attempt is made in part of Ugogo to utilize the lingering authority of pre-independence local government figures, such as village headmen and chiefs, to accomplish certain administrative tasks. On the other hand, and more importantly, TANU is prepared to introduce radical organizational innovations and new policies to 'reach the villages'. It is too early to assess the impact of the policies and ideals expressed in the Arusha Declaration and *Socialism and Rural Development*. However, in them may lie the appeal necessary to involve such peoples as the Gogo in the vanguard of political change and rural development.[39]

In this paper I have attempted merely to view the various political structures and processes of change in Ugogo as constituting a common field of political action. That aspect of the field constituted by the 'traditional' political system of the Gogo is, at the moment, the only one which satisfies the values and orientations of the majority of Gogo. But certain categories of people, including Gogo, are prepared to participate in the operation of the new structures, in varying degrees of involvement. To this extent, such events as the national elections have been most successful in mobilizing the Gogo population. But this participation still remains to be translated into full acceptance of the new structures designed at the national level to achieve local democracy and development.

NOTES

1. P.J. Rigby, 'Politics and Modern Leadership Roles in Ugogo', in V. Turner (ed), *Colonialism in Africa 1870-1960, Profiles of Change*, Vol. 3 (Cambridge University Press, Cambridge, 1971), 393-438.
2. M.J. Swartz, V.W. Turner and A. Tuden (eds), *Political Anthropology* (Aldine, Chicago, 1966), 27, note that the primary implication of the term 'field' is that of an indeterminacy of boundaries and a flexibility which other terms such as 'system' do not have. Related to the concept of political field is that of 'political arena'. F.G. Bailey, *Tribe, Caste and Nation* (Manchester University Press, Manchester, 1960) 243-8. This concept need not detain us except to note that competition (and resulting conflict) for access to the means of policy making, what R.W. Nicholas calls 'public power' ('Segmentary Factional Political Systems', in Swartz, Turner and Tuden, *Political Anthropology*), takes place in what may conveniently be termed an 'arena'. Two other familiar concepts will be frequently used, 'legitimacy' and 'support'. 'Support' means 'anything that contributes to the formulation and/or implementation of political ends', and includes force which, however, cannot for long be the only means of support for political action. Swartz, Turner and

Tuden, 'Introduction', 10. 'Legitimacy', on the other hand 'is a type of support that derives not from force or its threat but from the values held by the individuals formulating, influencing, and being affected by political ends' (Ibidem). For present purposes it is sufficient to note that different kinds of legitimacy may operate simultaneously within a political field.

3. E.g. L. Fallers, *Bantu Bureaucracy* (Heffer, Cambridge, 1956); but cf. R. Apthorpe, 'The Introduction of Bureaucracy into African Politics', *Journal of African Administration*, 12 (1960), 125-134, and 'Political Change, Centralisation and Role Differentiation', *Civilisations*, 10 (1960), 217-223; and P. Rigby, 'Political Change in Busoga: A Note', *Uganda Journal*, 30 (1966), 223-225.

4. M. Fortes and E.E. Evans-Pritchard (eds), *African Political Systems* (Oxford University Press, London, for International African Institute, 1940).

5. A.W. Southall, *Alur Society* (Heffer, Cambridge, for EAISR 1956), and 'A Critique of the Typology of States and Political Systems', in Michael Banton (ed), *Political Systems and The Distribution of Power* (ASA Monograph 2; Tavistock, London, 1965).

6. David E. Apter, 'The Role of Traditionalism in the Political Modernization of Ghana and Uganda', *World Politics*, 13 (1960), 45-68; and *The Politics of Modernization* (University of Chicago Press, Chicago and London, 1965), 81-122 *et passim*.

7. R. Levine, 'The Internationalization of Political Values in Stateless Societies', *Human Organisation* 19 (1960), 51-58.

8. E.R. Leach, *Rethinking Anthropology* (London School of Economics Monographs on Social Anthropology 2; Athlone Press, London, 1961); but cf Southall, 'A Critique of the Typology of States'.

9. Southall, ibidem.

10. P.J. Rigby, 'Politics and Modern Leadership Roles in Ugogo'.

11. Aspects of Gogo social structure, religion, and cosmology are described in various papers by the author. I therefore present only a brief outline here. Ugogo is the country of the Wagogo people (sing. Mugogo), and Cigogo is their language and custom.

12. P.J. Rigby, *Cattle and Kinship* (Cornell University Press, Ithaca, 1970), Ch. 3; and Rigby 'Politics and Modern Leadership Roles'.

13. The size of herds varies considerably, from several hundred head to only a few; indeed, some 15 percent of the households in one study had no cattle at all (P.J. Rigby, *Cattle and Kinship*). As I shall indicate later, this was one factor influencing a person's standing in traditional politics.

14. See C. Peters, *New Light on Dark Africa* (Ward, London, 1871); H.M. Stanley, *How I Found Livingstone* (New York, Scribner, Armstrong and Co., 1872); J.H. Speke, *Journal of the Discovery of the Source of the Nile* (Blackwood, London, 1863); V.L. Cameron, *Across Africa* (Daldy, Isbister and Co., London, 1877); and R. Oliver and G. Mathew (eds), *History of East Africa*, Vol. 1 (Oxford University Press, London, 1963); but cf E.J. Southon, 'Notes on a Journey through Northern Ugogo in East Central Africa', *Proceedings of the Royal Geographical Society* (1881, 3), 547-553.

15. M. Bates, 'Tanganyika', in Gwendolen Carter (ed), *African One-Party States* (Cornell University Press, Ithaca, 1962); M.E. Mnyampala, *Historia Mila na Desturi za Wagogo wa Tanganyika* (The Eagle Press, Dar es Salaam, 1954), 11; P. Rigby, 'Politics and Modern Leadership Roles'.

16. C. Brooke, 'The Heritage of Famine in Central Tanzania', *Tanganyika Notes and Records* (66, 1967), 21, puts the date as 1916-18.

17. P.J. Rigby, 'Politics and Modern Leadership Roles'.

18. Ibidem.

19. This membership of TANU cell leaders in the village development Committees (VDCs) was in fact the system throughout Tanzania until 1969, when the VDCs were replaced by Ward Development Committees covering larger areas.

20. *The Nationalist* (Dar es Salaam), January 19, 1966; cf Henry Bienen, *Tanzania: Party Transformation and Economic Development* (Princeton University Press, Princeton NJ, 1967).

21. The local poll tax or rate was abolished throughout Tanzania at the end of 1969, thus removing one of the basic tasks from local administration.

22. See P.J. Rigby, 'Politics and Modern Leadership Roles'.

23. Cf Bienen, *Tanzania*.

24. P.J. Rigby, 'Politics and Modern Leadership Roles'.

25. This crucial fact is often ignored by administrators and those involved in development programmes in Ugogo, to their disadvantage. Instead of appealing to young people in this category, most efforts are directed towards the 'more visible' minority with some modern education.

26. P.J. Rigby, 'Sociological Factors in the Contact of the Gogo of Central Tanzania with Islam', in I.M. Lewis (ed), *Islam in Tropical Africa* (Oxford University Press, London, for International African Institute, 1966).

27. Bienen, *Tanzania*, 336.

28. P.J. Rigby, 'Politics and Modern Leadership Roles'.

29. Bienen, *Tanzania*, 337.

30. Apart from one or two new settlements, even the new policy scarcely applied at all to Ugogo until 1970, when local officials seized on a suggestion of the President and proclaimed that the whole 3/4 million population of Dodoma Region (including most of Ugogo) would be organized into ujamaa villages within some fourteen months. The setting up of villages proceeded apace, but some reports suggested that this ambitious target date might be beyond the present capabilities of local party and other organs. See, for instance, *The Standard* of 5 and 15 November 1970.

31. Village executive officers are actually supposed to be appointed by the district council (vide supra). However, in this case, the committees were directed to 'elect' a candidate who would be confirmed in office by the administration.

32. P.J. Rigby, 'Time and Structure in Gogo Kinship' *Cahiers d'études Africaines*, 28 (1967), 644-647.

33. In this case, as usual (vide supra), the ritual leader remained in the background and put forward as 'chief' one of the dependents of a close agnate, instead of the more usual pattern described above of advancing another member of the same clan. This first *jumbe* died, and the office was taken over by his brother-in-law (father of the present committee member) until the arrival of the British administration, which recognized another headman. The descendants of these dependents adopted the clan name and avoidance of their previous 'masters' when the status they occupied disappeared.

34. The Church Missionary Society, now the Diocese of Central Tanzania (DCT), had three large missions in or near Ugogo. They have been the foremost among denominations in this area in education and proselytization.

35. Matonya's comparatively high salary as a 'messenger' arose from the fact that his job required both literacy in English and a high degree of responsibility over money.

36. The post of divisional executive officer for the area was also vacant at this time. The previous divisional executive officer, who had participated in the meetings and elections prevented the cattle of the former government chief in the area (the most successful and powerful of Gogo chiefs) from watering at a certain well. The divisional executive officer was transferred to a division in western Ugogo, and Gogo interpreted this as a triumph of Gogo influence over the new system (see Rigby: 'Politics and Modern Leadership Roles').

37. P.J. Rigby, 'Changes in Local Government in Ugogo and the National Elections', in Lionel Cliffe (ed), *One Party Democracy* (East African Publishing House, Nairobi, 1967).

38. Ibidem.

39. P. Rigby, *Pastoralism and Prejudice* (Nkangi, Kampala, 1969).

A.B. MAFEJE

THE LEGITIMACY OF THE UGANDA GOVERNMENT IN BUGANDA

The story of Buganda is a long and involved one and has been told eloquently and sensitively by many writers, among whom may be mentioned Audrey Richards, Fallers, Low, Apter and Southwold. The accounts of these writers go up to the time of independence and shortly after. Since then a few scattered articles have appeared, recounting the continued struggle for power between Buganda and Uganda. Mine is also a limited addition to that trickle. In 1966, when the Uganda crisis exploded on the political scene, I was doing fieldwork among the coffee farmers in Buganda. During that period I could not help making certain observations about the way the people among whom I was working reacted to the situation. In the end curiosity got the better of me and I spent the months of June, July and part of August 1966, interviewing Buganda politicians at Mengo and elsewhere. I also kept my ears open so as to pick up reports about events in other parts of Uganda. These were supplemented by newspaper reports. It was nothing as intensive as the efforts of the traditional anthropological 'bird-watcher'. But who said that the traditional anthropological 'bird-watcher' has the monopoly of wisdom and truth?

BUGANDA-UGANDA RELATIONS SINCE INDEPENDENCE

Going back a little: the conference for independence in Uganda took place in 1961 in London. One of the most striking things about it was the fact that at the time most negotiating parties, with the main exception of Buganda, were in favour of a unitary constitution. Buganda wanted a federal constitution. That created tremendous problems because Uganda without Buganda was nothing as far as rudiments of a modern nation state and the necessary minimal infrastructure were concerned. Buganda held the balance of power and probably the key to independence. Fully aware of her strength and unique position, she pressed her claim and agreed to come into the union on condition she was granted a semi-autonomous status and certain substantial privileges, e.g. complete control over her finances, an independent police force and judiciary and an independent executive. When the independence constitution was finally accepted in 1962, Buganda was the only region in Uganda which enjoyed a full federal status. It was an elevated position, a state within a state, which was bound to excite jealousy of the other regions, particularly the other kingdoms which received a lowly status as semi-federal states and which afterwards resented being treated as 'third-class' federal states.

This was a premise of inequality which was never fully accepted by the other regions and which in the end became a *causa-belli*. It was seen by most as a perpetuation of Buganda's historical role of a 'conquering kingdom'. Those of the Uganda nationalists who were interested in establishing a united Uganda knew that it was in conflict with their projected goals, insofar as it was bound to create or intensify resentment and jealousy between regions. But because independence was their primary objective, they were prepared to compromise. The Uganda People's Congress (UPC) under the leadership of Milton Obote — a radical nationalist with no royalist background — though the strongest party in the country, surprised observers by inviting the royalist and neo-traditionalist Kabaka Yekka (KY) of Buganda to form an alliance with it for the elections of 1962. The alliance was not a concession to Buganda's chauvinism and conservatism, as has been supposed by some; it was rather a double strategy: (i) the UPC needed the support of Buganda to win the elections against the Democratic Party (DP), particularly in Buganda; (ii) it was a shrewd way of drawing Buganda into the centre of national politics, not as a dissenter but as a consenting and constructive party. From her point of view, Buganda saw this as an opportunity for gaining access to important offices in the national government, while maintaining solidly her neo-traditionalist base. It was a 'Trojan Horse' type of strategy. The 'unholy alliance', as it came to be called later, thus came into existence.

The UPC-KY alliance won the elections and independence in 1962 and Obote's party gave the Presidency of the new state to the Kabaka of Buganda. This was done in the face of strong opposition within the UPC; some members felt that it was 'too big a concession to be a sop'. Ripples began to appear on the horizon late in 1964 during the referendum on the 'lost Counties',[1] which had been provided for in the 1962 constitution. Buganda, quite unconstitutionally, was opposed to the return of the affected counties (Buyaga and Bugangazzi) to Bunyoro. There was no question of the central government giving in on the issue; it was important that it proved it had not 'sold out' to Buganda and was not going to sacrifice the interests of the other regions in order to placate Buganda. By this time the UPC had consolidated its position and a number of MPs — 15 from the DP and 10 from the KY — had joined its ranks, giving the Governments an absolute majority of 69 in a house of 92 members. In other words, Buganda's support had become dispensable. The most the Kabaka could do, as the Head of State and the ruler of his kingdom, was to refuse to sign the Bill legislating for the transfer of the counties and so refuse to preside at the opening session of Parliament in 1965. This brought to an end the days of the 'honeymoon' between the UPC and KY and inaugurated the beginning of a fierce struggle for dominance between the leaders of the two parties.

In the meantime a similar struggle was going on within the UPC. Two factions existed, one in favour of the Prime Minister and the leader of the party, Milton Obote, and the other in opposition to him. During the party's election in 1964 the anti-Obote faction made a successful bid for the post of Secretary-General. The successful candidate, Grace Ibingira from Ankole, was a member of the Cabinet and so were some of his lieutenants. Most of the support of the faction came from the 'Trojan Horse' infiltrators in the UPC and in Parliament. As would be expected, the anti-Obote faction was looked upon with favour by the Buganda politicians at Mengo and received ready support from them. Buganda became their base of operations. In early 1966, during the regional elections in Buganda, they gained control of all the important executive posts (Chairman, Secretary and Treasurer) in the UPC.

The way was open to more serious manoeuvres. Six leading members of the faction used to hold regular meetings near Mengo, discussing their strategy. They were also believed to be in constant communication with Mengo, the seat of the Buganda Government. This group had a more favourable attitude towards 'traditional leaders' (i.e. the monarchs and other traditional dignitaries) than their opponents. Their aim was to discredit Obote as a party leader and the head of the government, and have him thrown out of power by constitutional means.

THE CRISIS

Early in 1966 the anti-Obote faction mounted a powerful campaign against him, which culminated in very serious accusations of corruption in Parliament against the Prime Minister and some of his principal supporters, including his most high ranking supporter in the army, Colonel Amin.[2] The attempt largely misfired and amid mysterious army movements and rumours about a threatened coup by the anti-Obote faction, the Prime Minister, who had been away touring the Northern Region, returned only to start striking back at his opponents.

On February 22, 1966 Obote had the five Ministers, who were the leaders of the faction opposed to him,[3] arrested on the grounds that 'they had been conspiring to overthrow the Government by violent means'. Two days later he declared the constitution of the country suspended and announced the dismissal of the President and the Vice-President, the former for his role in 'the plot against the Government'. A new constitution was introduced and adopted on 15 April by 55-4 votes, despite strong protests from the DP and KY members who, all but one, staged a walk-out. Reception of the constitution outside Buganda was overwhelming; all the District Councils and other civic bodies sent their messages of acceptance and congratulated the President (as Obote was called after the new constitution) for his 'wisdom and unfailing guidance'. Naturally, a great deal of that was at the instigation of the government supporters.

Events were moving fast; the Obote faction was quickly closing up on the Mengo politicians by undermining their constitutional power. Realizing what was happening, the Mengo politicians were getting more and more desperate and cleavages within their camp were becoming more apparent. As a kind of 'last ditch stand', on May 20 they passed a resolution calling upon the Central Government 'to remove itself from Buganda soil by the 30th of May' (Entebbe and Kampala, Uganda's administrative and legislative capitals, are in Buganda). Though the Central Government knew that at the time Buganda was no military threat, it accepted her threat at its face value and ordered an attack on the palace of the Kabaka of Buganda, which was believed to be filled with Baganda ex-soldiers and illegal weapons. Whatever the details, 24 May, 1966 marked the end of an epoch in the history of Buganda. After a struggle of about twelve hours, the palace lay in ruin and ashes, the King of Buganda had been put to flight and his highly prized 'Kabaka's Government' had suffered complete collapse. What was the reaction of the Baganda to the destruction of the institution with which they were believed to identify to a man? What was their attitude likely to be towards those responsible? These were some of the questions which confronted policy-formulators in Uganda.

THE REACTION OF THE BAGANDA AT THE NATIONAL LEVEL

From the outset I wish to state that, contrary to popular belief at times reinforced by anthropological 'haloist' formulations, the general category of people called the Baganda do not necessarily form 'a society which is unusually single-minded about its values', nor can it be said that 'their Ganda-ness' makes their various leaders, *ipso facto*, 'members of a common elite'.[4] During the 1966 crisis reactions in Buganda were as varied, contradictory, and inconsistent as in any other society.

At the national level there were those Baganda leaders who supported Obote up to the hilt and accepted ministerial posts under the new constitution. There were no less than seven of them in a cabinet of 22 members. These were the men who were described, rather bitterly, by some fellow-Baganda as 'trying to be more non—Ganda than the non-Baganda themselves'. They were doing nothing of the sort; they *were* Baganda who happened to have made a different choice in accordance with their interests and motivations. In Parliament the same phenomenon was apparent. A fair number of Baganda, with varying degrees of consistency, voted with the Government and retained their membership in the UPC. This was notwithstanding the fact that some of them had been 'Trojan Horse carpet-crossers', as was shown for instance by the repeated demand by some UPC members for a more thorough screening of party members.

At the regional level the same differentiation was observable. The Baganda women UPC supporters, under the leadership of Mrs Nkata, gave unflinching support to Obote. Among the men the pro-Obote faction which, as early as July 1963, had passed a resolution calling for the dissolution of the UPC-KY alliance, were desperately trying to protect the party from infiltration by the Baganda militants, who described the UPC and the KY as 'twin brothers who could quarrel today and play the following day'. They rejected the new alliance which was being revived by the anti-Obote leadership as an 'unholy alliance' and in a public statement called upon 'all true UPC chairmen inside and outside Buganda to do everything in their power to resist the new move'. But their spokesmen had been suspended earlier from the party by the new national executive committee. When this was pointed out to them, their reply was:

The question of the problems facing Buganda is not subject to Mr. Ibingira's or the so-called Central Executive Committee's decisions. It is not up to Ibingira or the Executive to determine whether we should be in the UPC or not.[5]

The Baganda UPC youth-wingers expressed the same attitude in their public statements. We can, therefore, see that in this instance the Baganda, despite their 'Ganda-ness', were divided along party lines.

Another cleavage within Buganda which is worth mentioning, though it remained mostly latent throughout the crisis, is the cleavage between the DP and the KY which largely coincided with the now traditional division between the Catholics and the Protestants. The DP had always been opposed to the dominance in Buganda politics of the Kabaka and his chiefs, most of whom happened to be Protestants. It saw the establishment of more inclusive national institutions and increasing democratization of the regional institutions as an antidote to the oligarchical tendencies of the Buganda Government. It rejected the KY as 'parochial, old-fashioned and feudalistic'. It attracted some of the younger Baganda 'progressives' who held no important positions in the Buganda Government. These inferences came out clearly in a discussion of the 1966 crisis with one of the leading members of the DP, a Muganda himself. He said:

If the DP were in power, it would have done the same thing as Obote but in a different way. Putting aside the question of methods, we agree that it was improper for Mengo to have indirect representation in the National Assembly, an independent system of courts, a separate police force, and an executive monarch. The DP has always been opposed to the remnants of feudalism in Buganda. The policies pursued by the leaders at Mengo were destined to bring about disunity in the country. However, if we were in power, we would have spared the Government at Mengo but altered its powers. We reject the new constitution only because it was introduced in an undemocratic way.[6]

Then one understands the strong antipathy between the DP and the KY. At the local level it had some unpleasant effects, as is shown by the attitude expressed at the time by a housewife in Buddu County:

The past few months have been terrifying months but they have done us one good service, and that is they have freed us once and for all from constant persecution and arrogant behaviour by the members of the Kabaka Yekka. They are terrible people; I don't care what happens to them.

Even in the seemingly solidary oligarchy in Mengo factions existed. Ministers and permanent secretaries did not necessarily have the same political outlook as the Kabaka, the county chiefs, and other traditionalist elements. It is true that they were all part of the same machinery, but they were not all manipulating it with the same end in view. The county chiefs and their supporters saw the development of elective institutions and the growing influence of the nation state as a direct threat to their time-honoured dominance in the political affairs of Buganda. Apter observed the same reaction in 1961: 'The Kabaka's Government is a modernizing autocracy. It rightly foresees that in such a secular national state [Uganda] its own institutions can only be diminished and eroded.' At best the Kabaka, who had a broader outlook than most of his chiefs but whose position depended largely on tradition, saw himself as a 'modernizing autocrat', as Apter put it.[7] He was prepared to play along with the Uganda nationalists, provided they allowed him some eminence in the new national state (preferably something like the Emperor of Ethiopia), while keeping the kingdom of Buganda as his footstool. But emperorship with executive powers would have been seen by the Uganda nationalists and the other regions as a new form of Buganda's 'imperialism' and an undesirable revival of feudalism in the country. As has been mentioned already, opposition to feudalism is an attitude which was shared by the progressive elements in Buganda, e.g. the DP and some of the 'new men' in Mengo. The latter, while prepared to enjoy the exclusive privileges that attached to Buganda, were not prepared to subjugate themselves permanently to 'feudal' domination or forego completely their chance of sharing in the new forms of power and wealth in independent Uganda.

This is a contradiction, or opportunism, which the 'new men' in Mengo verbalized without any embarrassment. This is how one of the Permanent Secretaries described their position in a conversation:

It has been clear to us for some time now that from the point of view of sheer survival, a radical change had to be brought about in the whole governmental structure in Mengo. One of the ways of doing this was to recruit young and progressive graduates in ever-increasing numbers, while, on the other hand, retiring as many of the conservatives as was logically possible. The strangle-hold on the Mengo administration by the conservatives had to be broken by continual transfers and retirements where possible. Just to show you, in the past year we have managed to recruit no less than 40 young graduates, have retired no less than 50 old types, and have made no less than 200 transfers. Keep them moving, don't allow them to establish roots. Even now what has happened is a result of a constant failure by the Central Government to realise there is a group of progressives who are not much different in outlook from most of the people in the Central Government. These people realise that whatever contribution they make will benefit the country as a whole and are, therefore, prepared to cooperate fully with the Central Government, though without necessarily merging into a unitary structure. Even now, we have been saying to the Central Government 'Give us your new instructions and from our previous experience, we will know what to do.' But things are difficult, the whole structure has become so cumbersome and disrupted that it takes weeks or even months for instructions to come through. There has been a break in the line of command! Personally, I don't care who is in gaol and who is not. All I am interested in is to see the administrative machinery swing into action once more. [It was his reputed leaders who were in gaol.]

This might have been an individual expressing his own feelings about things, but it is important to note that all the upper administrative staff in Buganda, with only one exception,[8] filled in the forms for re-employment by the Central Government after the crisis. It is also worth noting that the Kabaka's Ministers were not with him when he was being attacked and hunted 'like big game'.[9] While the Buganda stalwarts had landed in gaol, five of the Buganda Ministers were cruising around Kampala in their black Mercedes Benz, as if nothing had happened. The most they did was to issue a joint statement on May 30, 1966 urging the people in Buganda 'to maintain peace and avoid any deed or words which would promote a threat to peace'. They appealed to the chiefs 'to ensure that the people in their areas obeyed orders and to inform the nearest police station of any people likely to cause trouble'.[10] Afterwards, four of the Ministers joined the UPC. Even in the case of the Katikkiro (Prime Minister) who fled with the Kabaka, there were some noteworthy inconsistencies in his behaviour. When the Lukiko passed that fatal resolution on May 20, 1966 he tried to resist it. Later in London he made a statement to the effect that 'he did not support secession by Buganda and that in the Lukiko he had tried to amend a motion calling upon the Central Government to remove itself from Buganda soil'. Finally, he said, 'I believe that a number of changes in the Buganda Government were essential, but they could have come by evolution rather than revolution.'[11]

In substance this is the same attitude as was expressed by a Muganda MP, Abu Mayanja, in April 1966 when he declared:

What we have been through is a great challenge, and I think the people of Buganda should rise to the occasion. The greatest thing at the moment surely is unity. The people of Buganda cannot afford to allow any consideration to stand in the way of playing their full part in Uganda's nationhood.[12]

Another Muganda MP, speaking in June, was even more blunt in his presentation: 'We nationalists in Buganda wholeheartedly support the current changes.' The point I am driving at here is that even in Buganda, apart from the neo-traditionalists, there does not seem to have been any group that was opposed to the principle of a Uganda National State or a Central Government established in accordance with the 1962 or, for that matter, the 1966 Constitution. The main objection was to the manner in which the changes had been brought about by the Obote Government. In the end unpleasant experiences suffered by individuals in Buganda got strongly associated with particular people in that Government, not so much with the institutions they were trying to create.

REACTION AT THE LOCAL LEVEL

The type of competition mentioned above usually occurs among the leaders themselves. But ultimately what matters from the point of view of policy implementation, is the support those in authority receive from the general mass of the population. This is what is fashionably referred to as 'grass-roots politics'. Buganda is famous for the vigour of its local politics. But this can only be understood against the background of the basic pattern of political and administrative organization in the region. Buganda was divided into 18 counties (*ssaza*), some 128 sub-counties (*gombolola*) and up to ten villages (*miruka*) per sub-county. At the head of each of these divisions were ssaza, gombolola, and miruka chiefs in their ranking order. All chiefs used to be responsible to the Kabaka and had traditionally depended on him for their land. In addition, for the management of the affairs of each country there were local councils — ssaza, gombolola and miruka. The councils were supposed to be representative bodies, but in practice were dominated by landlords.

During my stay in the villages in Buganda I found that in talking to the villagers, land and politics were the two subjects that preoccupied them. They talked about the local situation as well as the national leaders and their policies, and about the Kabaka's government at Mengo. This usually came out in the form of complaints about lack of any real benefits since independence, indifference of both the Uganda and the Buganda Governments to the fate of the rural poor, lack of facilities and aid and the problem of depressed cash-crop prices, for which the national government was held responsible. Their contact with the outside world was mainly through the radio and the vernacular newspapers — *Munno, Taifa Empya* and *Sekanyolya*, which all got banned at one time or another in 1966. During the Buganda crisis it was instructive to watch the men gather together in the village centre to hear the reports from the newspapers in the morning and from the radio at mid-day. It was also at these gatherings that news from the early morning bulletins were announced and discussed. The bigger farmers who, almost without exception, owned radio sets and who in some cases had a standing order for the newspaper, appeared only occasionally at these gatherings, mainly to check their information and current opinions.

It should not be assumed that this great interest in politics among Baganda villagers meant strong organization or unanimity among them. Politically, they were very loosely organized. Their allegiance to the two parties that were represented in the villages where I worked, viz. the DP and the KY, had largely become a matter of tradition among the Catholics (DP) and Protestants (KY). Active involvement had come to be regarded as a matter for professional politicians who, in this case, never visited the villages during the 15 months I was in Buganda. I suppose in the case of the KY the chiefs sufficed. This is not to say that the latent antagonism between Catholics and Protestants never came to the surface at the village level. But while Catholicism and Protestantism remained largely in abeyance during this period, other new and important identities asserted themselves and influenced opinions in different directions. Unlike the Buganda of 50-60 years ago which consisted of two main social categories: *Bakungu* (chiefs) and *Bakopi* (peasants), modern Buganda, which is anything but tribal, exhibits a high degree of social differentiation. There are:

(i) *Basajja banene* (big men) who are powerful landlords and represent a continuation of the traditional political elite. It is usually they who are appointed chiefs and it is also they who constituted the majority in the upper councils and the Buganda Lukiko (National Assembly). They are the *de facto* rulers in the villages in which they hold land and tenants. They were formerly the important link between the Kabaka's government and the peasants. They influenced policy both at the local and the higher administrative level. Understandably enough, it was these men who were very concerned and extremely worried about the events in 1966. Direct intervention in Buganda by the Central Government threatened their power. Despite all this, they realised that the odds were against them and decided to lie low.

(ii) In contrast to the men described above, there is a growing number of professional farmers in Buganda (*basajja bagaga*), who boast not chiefly of land-propertied backgrounds but who nonetheless have managed to accumulate enough wealth through farming (normally on purchased land). Their commercial interests and the modest amounts of land they own preclude them from taking on tenants and their lowly background is not a particularly good source of the prestige and the nuances that go to make a 'big man'. From the point of view of assimilation into the bureaucracy in Buganda, in all probability the Kabaka's Appointments Commissioner was not even aware of their existence. Furthermore, for their farming business (e.g. marketing, loans and licensing) they depended more on the Central Government agencies than on the Kabaka and his chiefs. Therefore, they stood to lose by getting too closely identified with the Buganda oligarchy. During the crisis most of them claimed neutrality and non-involvement. In public they supported neither of the two governments: 'Mengo had never done anything for us'; 'The Uganda Government was anti-Baganda'; 'But if it was willing to do something about the coffee prices, one would not mind so much', added one of them as an afterthought. Emotionally they were far from being indifferent, but the reality of their situation made them behave differently.

(iii) The most interesting category were the educated sons (secondary school boys and leavers) of both landlords and farmers. Unlike their fathers, they expressed strong nationalist sentiments. The idea of a Uganda nation state appealed to them more than a 'corrupt' feudalistic monarchy. They had some very sharp things to say about the Buganda system, the administration at Mengo and the Kabaka himself. In a conversation one of them shocked his elders by declaring that, given a chance, 'he would fight with the Uganda forces against Buganda'. One of the older men could not help remarking: 'This is a second Binaisa' (former Uganda Attorney-General and a Muganda who was largely responsible for drafting the various laws that did away with Buganda's special privileges). Nor is this just a matter of individuals. There are certain objective factors to remember. A high percentage of the civil servants employed by the Uganda Government are young Baganda; among the Security Forces which were active in Buganda during the crisis, there were several young Baganda officers; and finally, the UPC Youth Wing had an appreciable support among young Baganda in the Kampala area.

(iv) Below the various categories above are the ordinary villagers who, during the crisis, seemed extremely confused. They were very upset about the attack on the *Lubiri* (The Kabaka's palace), but did not know what to do. What was so confusing to them was the fact that their leaders, the chiefs and the landlords, could not give them any clear instructions. Although there was trench-digging and sporadic fighting in areas like Kyaggwe, Bugerere, Buddu and Ssingo, that represented no more than six sub-counties out of 128 sub-counties in Buganda. Organization was nil. I remember on one occasion when the people assembled in the village centre in the evening and waited for the chief to give them instructions. The Gombolola Chief appeared for a few seconds and said: 'Why are you looking at me, why don't you march to Kampala?' With that remark he disappeared very quickly, which was just as well: within minutes of his disappearance, a police van came and before it could even stop the peasants had vanished into the bush with all their sticks, pangas and other primitive weapons. It is not surprising that within days a pervasive sense of impotence ruled among them. With the chiefs and landlords immobilised, a power vacuum had been created in Buganda and nobody had come forward to fill it.

INTERPRETATION

Questions of 'democracy' and 'legitimacy' are hard to handle within the framework of a 'value-free' social science. It is for that reason that a 'value-free' social science has become a myth and a form of self-propaganda by those who pretend never to intervene in the affairs of man. The truth of the matter is that social scientists in their *social* role as advisers, consultants, lecturers and writers do influence public opinion and the direction of development of society. Like ordinary mortals, they are concerned with whys and wherefores and make choices according to their *value systems*. For instance, it is quite apparent that political scientists in East Africa give a positive evaluation to national unity and effective 'penetration' of the mass of the people by central governments and, hence, seem prepared to help find out how best this could be achieved. But in doing so, they run into another moral constraint, namely, their concern with democracy as a supreme moral principle in all political life. But Marxists and non-Marxists have different conceptions of democracy and focus on different aspects of political and economic organization. This again highlights the inevitability of values or normative predispositions as an important basis for selection of facts and their interpretation. Of course, this does not mean there could not be a common methodology in the social sciences for the processing of data and validation of general propositions, as is found for example in the other sciences. But it does show the primacy and immediacy of values in dealing with human affairs.

Without suggesting that we all become bad physicists in the human sciences, in interpreting the Buganda situation I am going to try and keep my logical schema (observer's normative system) separate from that of the actors, be they Uganda or Buganda Government adherents. But in either case I will make my ideological presuppositions explicit when necessary.

Political scientists distinguish between legitimacy of the political community, legitimacy of governmental forms and legitimacy of incumbents.[13] These are convenient distinctions between different levels of discourse, but it seems that they refer to different spheres of political organizations, namely, power relations and authority relations. Opposition to incumbents implies no more than competition and probably circulation of personnel, whereas opposition to authority structure and its ideological foundations means much more. It means diminution of the existing authority principle and the development of a revolutionary situation.

If this argument is valid, then the concept of 'legitimacy' is often used ambiguously by political scientists and is likely to confuse democracy with consent and the means for eliciting consent. The problem of analogues and homologues also asserts itself here. Competition at the level of incumbency does not necessarily affect the principle of democracy at the ideological level, in the same way as identification at the level of incumbency does not necessarily imply democracy in a wider context. In formally democratic structures people might enjoy less freedom than in what appears, formally, to be an undemocratic structure. A comparison between certain multi-party and one-party states in Africa brings this out clearly.

In Uganda it was striking that formal democracy for long prevailed,[14] despite the bitterness of the struggle at the incumbency level. Liberal democracy was an ideal which was adhered to by all the competing parties. This was evinced by the legalism and the 'violent constitutionalism' described by Engholm and Mazrui. To validate its claims, each party referred to the same constitutional principle. As far as governmental forms were concerned, the basic image of the Uganda state, as conceived in 1962, persisted even beyond the 1966 crisis. It is true that since July 1967 it became more unitary and the powers of the federal states were revoked. In reality it was only Buganda which suffered any significant losses. But she was meant to, as is shown by the recommendations of the Wild Commission (1959) and the Munster Commission (1961). The only difference was that, compared to other parties, Buganda was too powerful at the time and could have wrecked the whole arrangement. Not only was Buganda weaker than the Central Government in the period after 1966, but also the whittling down of her power did not mean any overall decline of the legitimacy of the Uganda Government in Buganda, as it did to the legitimacy of the Protectorate Government in 1953 when it sent the Kabaka into exile. Apart from the neo-traditionalist elite mentioned earlier, the Baganda leaders in the UPC and the DP, some former politicians and administrators in Mengo and some disgruntled individuals in Buganda accepted the idea of a Uganda nation state. Insofar as that is true, Obote can be said to have succeeded where Sir Andrew Cohen failed.

CONCLUSION

In the light of what has been described above, the only conclusion we can arrive at is that, to the extent that no new political principle and social organization was introduced in Uganda after 1966, there has been no revolution in that country.[15] Insofar as the Buganda Government in 1966 reacted against the authority of the Central Government *without* putting forward a new and competing political principle, it committed *rebellion*. It is a wellknown fact that the rebellious Buganda leadership was not interested in changing the basic structure either in Uganda or in Buganda. It was only interested in defending a privilege while it reserved its right to lord it over the mass of the people in Buganda. Secondly, as has already been shown, it was not necessarily representative of all political opinions in Buganda. Therefore, even its right to secession was in question.

At the same time, it must be stated that, although the idea of a Uganda nation state was generally sanctioned at the ideological and constitutional level, at the practical level the question of 'unity for what' was not fully answered. In Buganda, where people continued to nurse hurt feelings, scepticism remained widespread. The Obote Government had still to prove its good intentions. The concept of *bawejjere* (common man) had still to be given substance. But to do that successfully, the Government needed the cooperation of the people of Buganda. It has been indicated already that the civil servants in Buganda, i.e. administrators, teachers and extension personnel, were prepared to cooperate and accept the Uganda Government as a *fait accompli*. The educated youth in Buganda had shown themselves to be receptive to nationalistic ideas. The new commercial farmers were looking for opportunities for development and did not particularly mind who provided them. The Baganda peasants, whether that is a good thing or not, were used to being closely supervised. The administrative machinery in Buganda was as developed as anywhere else in Uganda. But it was effectively in the hands of the chiefs who, together with the landlords, controlled the peasantry.

The chiefs and the landlords were neo-traditionalists and, as such, the enemies of the Nationalist Government. They were experienced and shrewd politicians and given a chance, they could be the greatest single constraint on the Central Government reaching the people in Buganda. Lack of effective machinery on the part of the governing UPC party in the rural areas in Buganda made the position of the Obote Government even weaker. Even if they had had such machinery, it is still doubtful, short of a thorough-going revolution, whether the chiefs would have been easily displaceable. The only advantage the Government had over them was that, like all governments in underdeveloped countries, it was the biggest employer and the Buganda chiefs have been noted for their swift judgment in discovering which way the wind is blowing. This was already apparent in early 1967 when they were ordered by the Central Government to round up all tax defaulters in Buganda. They knew they were being tested and acquitted themselves brilliantly. Even so the question of incumbency was going to take a great deal of skill and manoeuvring to solve. One suspected that the Obote leadership had nearly over-spent one of its resources, viz. force. The prolonged state of emergency in Buganda, the detention technique, attempts on the President's life and that of his army officers, were unmistakable signs of an over-draft. Moving more left and trying to improve the living conditions of the mass of the people, which is what development is about, would have been one way of solving the problem and of finding a broader and more solid power base. But that would have certainly brought about a major confrontation at all levels and within the UPC itself. Then the imponderable question was whether the Uganda Government was ready ideologically and organizationally for a revolution — or was it condemned to a painful and brittle policy of containment?

POSTSCRIPT

The present paper has a limited scope both in time and in perspective. Its major focus is the Uganda crisis of 1966 and its aftermath in Buganda. Along with that, it attempts to evaluate the responsiveness or otherwise of the different sections of the population in Buganda to the integrating tendencies by the nationalist government of Obote up to 1969. Implicitly, it also tries to throw some light on the revolutionary potential of both the population in Buganda and its various leaderships and that of the national government itself.

As is often the case in Africa, since the writing of the original draft of the paper, a major change in government has occurred in Uganda. On January 25, 1971, General Amin, the man who was responsible for the attack on the Kabaka's Palace on May 24, 1966 under President Obote's orders, staged a military coup in his own right. In the circumstances it would have been normal to redraft at least parts of the paper, taking advantage of hindsight as far as possible. I have decided against this for two main reasons. Firstly, I do not believe that it would have made any difference to my analysis or conclusions. If anything, General Amin's takeover is a vindication of some of my hunches — stated or unstated in this particular paper. This will be demonstrated shortly by taking some of the major hypotheses and relating them to the post-Obote situation. Secondly, incorporation into the text of material from the Amin period would have involved me in unnecessary methodological problems, as I was not there to observe and check what had gone on in the same way as I did during the 1966 crisis. In summary form there are five main points made in the study.

(a) It is argued that, under the modern conditions of increased social and class differentiation among the Baganda, a *politically* 'solidary Buganda' is an unwarranted assumption. The failure of the Baganda to put up a united front during the 1966 crisis is used as evidence in favour of this contention.

(b) Consequent upon this observation, it is argued by implication that expressive behaviour, e.g. emotions and verbal affirmations at the heat of the moment are not a reliable index for checking individual or group interests. What people do in defence of their means of livelihood, e.g. (in the case of the Baganda) defence of chiefly perquisites and landed property, reluctance to give up salaried and privileged bureaucratic positions, concern with business interests in agriculture and in commerce, are better tests of individual commitment. They are a firmer ground for distinguishing between ideological mystification and the vested interests for which it is a rationalization than the usual ideational effusions.

(c) Most importantly, it is argued that in Uganda, irrespective of apparent cleavages between the national elites in the UPC, DP and KY, there was a prevailing belief in a liberal bourgeois democracy and a modern nation state, as is shown by the various constitutions and party programmes since 1962. But historically, as elsewhere, that has come into conflict with pre-existing social formations, e.g. autocratic traditional monarchs, land patronages and clientships and other pre-capitalist political hierarchies. It is, therefore, submitted that the major contradiction was not between Obote's government and the Buganda government but rather between forces of modern nationalism and those forces which sought to preserve the status quo in one form or another. Buganda became the centre of the storm only because it represented the best expression of the latter forces organisationally, politically and historically. Otherwise the inclusion of the other monarchies, when it came to it, remains inexplicable. But, again and unfortunately for Buganda, being the most advanced enclave in Uganda, she could not escape nationalist eruptions within her borders. This is exemplified by the unmistakable ideological concordance between the Uganda nationalists in the central government and the UPC, on the one hand, and the Baganda nationalists (oriented on Uganda) in the DP, and the 'new men' in the then Mengo administration and elsewhere, on the other. The regional competition between these Baganda nationalists and others would not have solved the contradiction between emergent nationalist and neo-traditionalist forces within Buganda, even if Buganda had succeeded in her secession.

(d) It is freely admitted in the paper that during Obote's government incumbency became a problem, not so much because of Buganda but primarily because of competition between elites from different regions or parties. Enlistment of the support of neo-traditionalists, particularly from Buganda, by Obote's party enemies, use of constitutional niceties and attempts to win the support of the army against the central government, only forced Obote's government, which had no organized party support, to use methods which became detrimental to its own cause in the end. The use of the army whose behaviour was not altogether exemplary in Buganda, prolonged use of the Emergency and Detention Regulations as a substitute for political support, and then *belated administrative* attempts at socialist transformation, were all bound to lead to a very serious problem of incumbency. By the end of 1969 when an attempt was made on Obote's life, it was apparent that the army and the police force held the balance of power in Uganda. Whether or not the Uganda army had the political acumen and the necessary sophistication to conduct a coup at this point in time, the subsequent power struggles within it which led to the assassination of at least one of the pro-Obote senior officers are an indication that the army was not unaware of its opportunities.

(e) The final hypothesis advanced is that, notwithstanding the political upheavals and constitutional changes during the critical years of Obote's rule, no revolution had occurred in Uganda beyond the nationalist bourgeois revolution that took place at Independence. All said and done, General Idi Amin's military takeover can be looked upon as a particular form of degeneration of bourgeois nationalist politics in Uganda, the counterpart of which, though more positive, was Obote's attempt to introduce socialism in Uganda more as a question of expediency than a principled ideological commitment. Administrative socialism, based on army and police support, with no particular backing from the general populace, is the surest way to political degeneration. Amin's coup, I believe, can be explained in exactly the same terms as the plots and counterplots described for the various factions of the national elite in the text.

REFLECTIONS

On points (a), (b) and (c): whereas Obote's overthrow and the return of the Kabaka's body from England drew an indubitable nationalist fervour among Baganda of all walks of life, it has not yet been demonstrated that beyond the visible emotional euphoria there was any coincidence of material interests or a common programme of demands among them. The refusal by Amin's regime to re-establish monarchism might have come as a heavy blow to the chiefs of Buganda, but not necessarily to those politicians, functionaries or bureaucrats who received attractive offers from Amin. Thus, it would be extremely rewarding to identify accurately the social categories from which such Baganda personnel came and to ascertain which categories were unacceptable even to Amin. In the meantime it can be inferred that if the wave of euphoria that was visible in Buganda after the takeover was representative of latent nationalist militancy, disillusionment would not have necessarily led to the evaporation of that militancy and to apparent resignation. I suppose, as a further inference, it can be concluded that, historically, the logic or dialectic of the bourgeois nationalist revolution precluded even an unpoliticised General such as Amin from committing the would-be fatal error of handing over executive power to antiquated monarchs.[16] Uganda is an emerging capitalist state with its own superstructural requirements. The composition of Amin's cabinet and the selection of his political advisers testify to this.

In reference to point (d): In denying the occurrence of any genuine revolutionary transformation in Uganda in the years subsequent to the 1966 crisis, we argued that the problem of Uganda at this time was primarily one of incumbency, a problem which could have confronted any of the nationalist leaders if they were willing to meet the historical requirements of nationalist ascendancy, as Obote felt obliged to, though in the process he incurred the wrath of the traditionalists in Buganda for perfectly clear reasons. The question to ask now is whether the problem of incumbency has necessarily been solved by Amin's military intervention. The indications are that, far from being eliminated, the problem has become more acute than ever before. According to reports, Obote has not given up his claim to the throne. Second, it is common knowledge that different sections of the army are vying with one another for power. Third, it is unclear yet how many of the Uganda liberal bourgeois nationalists are happy to be ruled by generals. It is apparent then that in practice Amin's intervention has neither satisfied the different sections of the army, the neo-traditionalists in and outside Buganda, the liberal nationalists, nor the would-be socialists. From that point of view Uganda politics in the next five years should prove a fascinating subject to the social scientist.

Coming to point (e): If it is true, as we argued, that the 1966 crisis in Uganda represented no revolutionary transformation, can it be concluded then that Amin's military takeover represented no counter-revolution? Or can it be argued that because of the fact that Amin's Government is within the perview of nationalist politics, then Amin's junta could not be accused of subversion of the nationalist revolution? Insofar as Obote's policies were calculated to do away with forces of conservatism in Uganda in the form of autocratic monarchs, insofar as they raised at all the question of the 'common man' and the possibility of socializing the means of production, and insofar as they tried to minimize foreign control over the national economy, they were *progressive*. In contrast, insofar as Amin's policies are aimed at reversing most of the progressive moves by the Obote government, they *are* counter-revolutionary. But insofar as Obote's methods of policy implementation depended on administrative manipulation and on the army and the police at the expense of popular mobilization and participation, they became counter-productive and largely indistinguishable from General Amin's methods. However, the latter point should not be over-stressed because, insofar as there has been a shift from a recognition of the necessity for organized party support and parliamentary backing during Obote's time to a greater emphasis on the army as a substitute for party politics and parliamentary democracy under the present regime, a distinction ought to be made between Obote's and Amin's regimes. Historical perspective obliges us to acknowledge the fact that, appearances apart, at this point in time there has been a noticeable degeneration in the political process in Uganda. This is a problem that Uganda shares with a number of other African countries and which deserves to be put into a firmer and more general historical context than has been the case hitherto.

NOTES

1.   These are the counties Bunyoro lost to Buganda towards the end of the 19th century.
2.   Now Field Marshal Amin and Head of State in Uganda.
3. They were the Honourable Members Lumu from Buganda, Magezi from Bunyoro, Kirya from Toro, Ibingira from Ankole and Ngobi from Busoga. Their regions are the five traditional kingdom-areas in Uganda.

4.   Cf. L.A. Fallers (ed), *The King's Men* (London, Oxford University Press, 1964), 191-206.

5.   Ibingira was Secretary-General of the UPC until his arrest. The discussion appeared in the press (*Uganda Argus* in particular) in mid-May 1966 as a series of accusations and counter-accusations.

6.   An attitude which is clearly reflected in some of the official statements issued by the DP, e.g. the statements of March 3, April 2 and May 5, 1966. DP Headquarters, Kampala.

7.   D. Apter, *The Political Kingdom in Uganda* (Princeton, University Press, 1961), 10.

8.   Kisosonkole, the Kabaka's father-in-law and the then Head of the Mukono Division.

9.   As the Kabaka referred to himself in an interview in London.

10.   *Uganda Argus*, May 30, 1966.

11.   Nkangi Mayanja himself was a Cabinet Minister in the National Government before he became Katikkiro in the Buganda Government.

12.   *Uganda Argus*, April 19, 1966. In 1969 Abu Mayanja, who at different times had served in both the Uganda and the Buganda governments, was detained by the Uganda Government ostensibly for violating Emergency Regulations. In fact, he had been long a political suspect, despite his affiliation to the UPC. He is now a Cabinet Minister in Amin's Government.

13.   D. Easton, *A Systems Analysis of Political Life* (New York, John Wiley & Sons, 1965), 286-288. It would not be unfair to political scientists to point out that this distinction is not their invention and that it has been in use for over 2000 years. Roman jurists under the pen of Cicero (106-43 BC) talked of *legitimum imperium, potestas legitima* versus *tyrannica usurpatio* and *iustus et legitimus hostis*. But, hopefully, we have moved on since Roman times.

14.   Cf. G.F. Engholm and A.A. Mazrui, 'Violent Constitutionalism in Uganda', *Government and Opposition*, 2, 4 (July-October 1967).

15.   It is not clear what the Uganda 'Common Man's Charter', announced by President Obote in October 1969, would have meant in practice.

16.   Cf. S.D. Ryan in *Mawazo*, 3, 1 (June 1971), 37-38.

III

INSTITUTIONS AND STRATEGIES FOR RURAL DEVELOPMENT

ROBERT J.H. CHAMBERS

CREATING AND EXPANDING ORGANIZATIONS
FOR RURAL DEVELOPMENT

A selective critique of departments for cooperative development, community development, settlement, and planning in East Africa.

Governments wishing to undertake new social and economic functions through direct intervention by organizations have four main choices: they can encourage or enable the private sector to perform them, whether through incentives or by means of contracts; they can add the new functions to the tasks of existing government organizations; they can create parastatal bodies; or they can set up new government departments. All four approaches have been used in East Africa, but where there has been an intention to penetrate and influence the rural areas in order to introduce a major change or carry out a major new activity, the fourth course has several times been followed. A new department or ministry has been created in the capital city, and a field staff installed in a descending territorial hierarchy in the provinces or regions and districts. The main argument of this chapter is that such new departmental organizations and their expansion have higher real costs than at first sight appear and have often been ineffective in achieving their objectives; and that these findings should affect future choices of strategy for rural development.

The creation of departments with field staff has followed a historical sequence. Before the second world war, the colonial governments set up a succession of agencies — the administration, the police, public works departments, and departments for agriculture, medical services, education, forestry, and other purposes — which were represented at field levels. In the new political situation after the second world war, the process continued and was, if anything, accentuated with the changes preceding and accompanying independence. During the past two and a half decades, four organizations in particular have been established in the three East African Governments; departments or ministries for cooperative development, community development, settlement and planning. These have typically come to comprise a central headquarters, a hierarchy of field staff, and field sub-organizations (cooperative societies, self-help committees and groups, settlement schemes, and development committees respectively). But there have been substantial differences between these four departments; planning in particular is somewhat divergent, having been less well established outside the capital and also being initially concerned mainly with influencing and controlling central ministries. But the four organizations have enough in common for some generalizations to be possible regarding their common characteristics as new or recently created government departments.

These four organizations — for cooperative development, community development, settlement and planning — have had varied origins. Departments of cooperation were set up after the second world war following despatches to the colonial governments from the Secretary of State for the Colonies:[1] the inspiration was largely that of a Labour government with a strong attachment to cooperation wishing to reform and develop part of the colonial economic system. Departments of community development were introduced under the influence of a movement which swept the developing world in the latter 1950s, and in Kenya as part of the official response to the Emergency and the strong political drive of the colonial government to create a 'stable and progressive' society in the Kikuyu Central Province. Settlement organizations were inspired by a more diverse collection of objectives. In Kenya, the African Settlement Board[2] set up in 1945 and its successors were intended to experiment with new forms of agricultural and social organization, including group farms; in the 1960s, the Department of Settlement was, more radically, intended to settle Africans on the extensive farms of the White Highlands previously farmed by Europeans, and thus to defuse an explosive political situation. In Uganda, the group farming movement, while not exclusively for settlement, was pursued and persisted with partly as a form of political patronage which made possible the introduction of tractors and agricultural services into some of the politically important but often economically less developed areas. And in Tanzania, the Village Settlement Agency had as one of its aims to pioneer the process of collecting people together into villages as a step towards achieving a more communal and modern way of life. Finally, planning organizations were set up in all East African Countries as new means for achieving the economic and political goals of independence.

Spanning the period of independence, these organizations were often expanded. There were many reasons why this should be so. Cooperatives were socialist in inspiration and directed towards developing new crops and ousting alien traders. Community development set a high value on self-help and assisting people to achieve for themselves the sort of society they wanted. Settlement seemed to offer an opportunity to create a new society in miniature and in the case of Kenya to right old wrongs as well as to move away from the soil conservation image of the old department of agriculture. Planning was necessary for the achievement of African socialism, and would demonstrate a more positive approach than that of the parsimonious and conservative colonial

Treasury. In addition, there were other forces encouraging a growth and pro-liferation of organizations. Foreign aid consultants tended to suggest new or-ganizations for new functions: for example the World Bank Mission to Tanzania which recommended the creation of the Village Settlement Agency to manage the new 'transformation' (as opposed to old conservative colonial 'improvement') approach to agriculture.[3] The new breed of foreign experts, most densely settled in planning organizations, were also often keen to associ-ate themselves with initiatives embodying radical innovation in line with national aspirations, not always with a very full appreciation of the effects that could be expected. Sometimes expatriate civil servants, after long and rather frustrating colonial service, saw in the more permissive atmosphere of indepen-dence an opportunity to push through ideas which they had long been nursing. Ministers and civil servants sought to increase their prestige and responsibility by expanding the size and functions of their ministries and departments. More-over, a new or expanded department presented a substantial opportunity for patronage through filling new posts and sometimes for securing political sup-port through providing services to particular constituencies. Above all, govern-ments wanted to introduce major changes in the style and activities of the bureaucracy in the rural areas and this seemed difficult with the larger, longer-established and supposedly conservative departments. For all these reasons, the early and mid-1960s saw a tendency for the four departments under review, and particularly those for cooperatives and settlement, to grow and proliferate rapidly.

THE COSTS OF NEW DEPARTMENTS

Any appraisal of the costs and benefits of government departments is full of difficulties and imponderables. The level of generalization is broad, and it could be argued that at the very least the universe of assessment should not be larger than one particular organization; and even within that organization, some sub-organizations will have better records of performance, by whatever criteria, than others. It is also true that costs and benefits are political and social as well as economic, and often not quantifiable. There is also consider-able variation between countries. For instance, Kenya's Department of Settle-ment has been more successful, by almost any standards, than either Uganda's group farm movement or Tanzania's pilot village settlements. There have also been variations over time: marketing cooperatives in the mid-1960s were gen-erally in a bad state in all three countries, but have somewhat improved since. Given these and other difficulties, the discussion which follows does not at-tempt an appraisal of individual departments but rather seeks to identify costs which apply to new government organizations in general and to these govern-ment departments in particular. The argument is that there are partially hidden costs entailed in creating new organizations such as these, making them less beneficial than they normally appear.

All four organizations can be described as marginal in the sense that the functions for which they were set up were already to a greater or lesser extent being performed by the private sector or by other government departments. Cooperatives often sought to take over marketing activities which were in the hands of small traders or of private or governmental buying agencies. Departments of community development struggled from their inception to show that they had different roles from the administration, the department of agriculture, and the health department, although working in fields which overlapped with all of these. Settlement organizations undertook activities previously performed by departments of agriculture. Planning organizations claimed tasks such as project appraisal previously within the ambit of treasuries and, in the field, coordination of development activities previously the prerogative of the administration.

There were, thus, alternatives to forming these new organizations. Cooperative marketing might have been left to the private sector or carried out by parastatals or by direct Government purchasing; community development might never have been started, or might have been the responsibility of the administration and the various specialized ministries; settlement might have been carried out by the existing ministries of agriculture; and planning might have remained under the wing of the treasury in the centre and of the administration in the field. In considering in retrospect the costs and benefits of these new departments, these alternatives should be borne in mind.

The most obvious and usual costs of a new organization are financial. Indeed, being quantified, these are often the only costs that are formally assessed. It may be noted here that the financial overheads in creating a new organization can be expected to be greater than in adapting or adding to an existing one. Whereas with an existing organization, much of the additional workload (for instance, accounting, secretarial work, and staff recruitment) can be spread with economies of scale among staff who are already employed, when a new organization is set up new posts have to be created for these functions. Moreover, capital charges have to be met for vehicles, office equipment and stores which might otherwise have been substantially reduced through sharing practices. In financial terms, thus, it normally costs more to set up a new organization than to expand an existing one.

Further, the prices of facilities required for a new organization may not reflect their true scarcity or opportunity costs. For example, in a country with a balance of payments problem and a quota system for Landrover imports, the marked-up cost to government of a Landrover for a community development programme may not represent its cost in terms of the benefits foregone from alternative uses of the Landrover or of the foreign exchange. Similarly, if office space in a capital city is scarce and especially if some government departments are having to hire offices, the true cost of the offices for a new department will be high although they may not be included in the accounted cost of the organization. Similar costs may arise with staff housing, whether in a capital city or in a field station.

Yet another partially hidden cost, applying in East Africa during the 1960s, was the opportunity cost of high and middle level manpower. Staff are normally assessed in terms of their salaries, allowances and other direct costs. Their true costs, however, include the benefits foregone from possible alternative employment. In the situation of critical staff shortages in the 1960s in East Africa, it may well be that if shadow prices reflecting opportunity costs could have been given to the staff required for the creation or expansion of the departments under review, any economic appraisal would have been much less favourable. For example, an agriculturalist in charge of a settlement scheme may have been much less productive than if he were working on agricultural extension in a district or on agricultural research; and community development officers and assistants might have generated greater benefits had they been trained in agriculture rather than community development.

Moreover, the creation or expansion of a department may sap and disrupt existing organizations through staff transfers and the chains of subsequent staff transfers which they provoke. There is, of course, a staff development aspect to transfers and promotions, and this may become more important in the 1970s with the promotion block which has developed at the top of government organizations; but in the 1960s the effects appeared mainly harmful. Departments of settlement poached staff from departments of agriculture at a time when the latter were seriously undermanned, giving rise to a danger of two anaemic departments instead of one more robust one. Indeed, any proliferation of government organizations can have a debilitating effect on the government machine by draining off high-level administrators or professional staff from vital posts. But such costs are rarely, if ever, taken into account.

At least as serious are the demands made by a new department on existing organizations. If it is a department within a ministry, it is an added burden to the permanent or principal secretary, and to the accounting, audit, establishment and administration sections. Financial and establishment negotiations will involve the ministry of finance and the central personnel organization. If technical assistance is required, complicated negotiations with donors may be involved, delaying the processing of other technical assistance applications. It is, of course, true, that these activities are partly what the other organizations exist for. But the bottlenecks which existed in central government in the three East African countries during the 1960s suggest that the imposition of such burdens had high costs.

At the field level, the effects may be less obvious but nonetheless important. Staff in new departments make demands on staff in existing departments. A community development officer may request the services of an engineer from a ministry of works to advise on the building of a well, or of an agriculturalist to recommend crops for a self-help group to grow, or of a surveyor to align a road. A regional planning officer may demand from a regional agricultural officer statistics which would take agricultural staff off productive work to become fact gatherers. Indeed, the planners, trained though they usually are in cost-benefit analysis, are sometimes prepared to cost anything except planning itself. Yet planning at a local level may have high costs. The cry of almost every report, a recommendation in the submission of almost every commission of enquiry, is for more coordination. But planning and the coordination which it requires, are far from costless: they may involve many staff in meetings to an extent which makes their departments less productive. It is arguable that there are circumstances in which coordination is strongly anti-developmental, for instance where road construction or the installation of water supplies may be delayed through the amount of staff time and energy taken up by meetings. The costs and benefits of a planned and coordinated approach to rural development have to be weighed against the costs and benefits of the alternative of less planned and less coordinated development;[4] and new departments are liable to increase the supposed and actual need for coordination and the amount of time staff in existing departments have to devote to it.

THE EFFECTIVENESS OF NEW DEPARTMENTS

The achievements of departments of cooperative development, community development, settlement and planning have often, though by no means always, been disappointing. In all three countries, the rapid expansion of cooperatives which took place in the mid-1960s led to widespread disillusion, the collapse of many cooperatives and in Tanzania a Presidential Special Committee of Enquiry.[5] Community development has sometimes suffered from the disability of seeking to encourage actions (self-help projects such as schools and dispensaries) which embarrass other ministries and which often cannot be staffed or supplied.[6] Settlement schemes have a mixed record, more successful by most criteria in Kenya, but very uneconomic, as well as of doubtful social and political value in the Pilot Village Settlements in Tanzania and in the quasi-settlement group farms in Uganda.[7] As for the attempts of ministries of planning to penetrate to provincial and regional level, these have taken a very long time. By 1971 Kenya had a Provincial Planning Officer in each province, but they were overworked for the wide range of functions expected of them, while the District Development Committees of which they were secretaries were only gradually developing as centres of district planning.[8] In Tanzania, attempts by the Ministry of Planning to penetrate the regions by posting out Regional Economic Secretaries had not been very successful.[9]

This negative assessment must be qualified in three respects. In the first place most innovations have chequered careers, and difficulties are part of a learning process which may lead to better performance in future. Second, negative assessments are sometimes made early in the life of an organization while it is still undergoing teething troubles. This has been particularly true of settlement schemes, which tend to attract the most attention at the time when they are most vulnerable to criticism, especially on short-term economic grounds. Third, some of these organizations, particularly for cooperative development in Tanzania and for settlement in Kenya, have at certain stages of their operation been impressively successful. Nevertheless, the generally poor record during the 1960s does require explanation. Four related factors appear to have been significant: staffing problems; difficulties over supervision and control; marginality; and the fight for survival. These will be discussed in turn.

In the first place, the staffing problem during the 1960s derived from the notorious shortage of trained manpower, particularly at the higher levels. This shortage was exacerbated by the proliferation of government and parastatal organizations, especially in Tanzania, and by the competition of the private sector in recruiting. At the time when many expatriates were leaving, independent governments were necessarily engaged in setting up foreign embassies. Africanizing the more sensitive posts in government, and establishing air forces and sometimes navies. During the same period national leaders were most anxious to take initiatives such as expanding cooperatives and launching settlement schemes in order to fuel and to demonstrate to the rural people that there had been a radical change from the colonial style of government. The strain can be indicated from the position of Uganda in 1964 when, of the established posts at the administrative, professional, technical and executive levels, only two-fifths were held by Ugandans, the remaining three-fifths being divided roughly equally between those held by expatriates and those vacant.[10] Although each East African country mounted numerous training programmes, adequate staffing with local personnel remained a problem throughout the 1960s, and the expansion of departments, particularly cooperatives, exacerbated the problems. The alternatives were to promote people who were not qualified, to retain expatriates who were already in post, or to recruit technical assistance personnel. All had their disadvantages: the recruitment of unsuitable settlement officers in Kenya led to cases of embezzlement which came before the courts;[11] the retention of expatriates could be seen as a political cost; and technical assistance personnel all too often found it difficult to be effective in a strange environment. The resulting rapid turnovers in staff, their occasional unsuitability for their work, the posts which were left vacant, and the overloads on other staff resulting from the vacancies, all contributed to the low effectiveness of the organizations concerned. Commonly, either expansion was slow and reasonably satisfactory as with the provincial planning organizations in Kenya, or rapid and often catastrophic, as with many marketing cooperatives in all three countries. Given the acute staff shortages generated by Africanization, de-Europeanization and the creation and expansion of organizations, it is not surprising that the 1960s were a period of generally disappointing performance with the newer departments for rural development.

This is, however, by no means the whole explanation. A second factor was the tendency with new and expanding departments for supervision and control to be weak. Auditors, already overworked, took some time to come round to examining the accounts of the latest organizations to be created or were unable to keep up with a rapid proliferation of sub-organizations. Senior staff were some times too busy recruiting other staff, working out routines and establishing the organization in its environment to be able to carry out the checks required to prevent abuses. Time also tended to be taken up sorting out problems which arose from imperfectly developed or understood procedures. The effect was that much staff time and effort were absorbed with internal and external management matters, reducing the staff resources available for the substantive tasks of the organization. Further, these were circumstances in which corruption could flourish. This did not conspicuously affect either community development or planning staff, but it did occur with some settlement schemes and many cooperatives.

A third factor, the marginality of the new departments and their sub-organizations, also limited their effectiveness. The very fact of being late on the scene and having to compete with those organizations or individuals who were already established tended to force them out into the less easy and less economic tasks. Marketing cooperatives often had to compete with or oust established traders, or alternatively to pioneer with a new crop or in a new geographical area which might not have proved economic to the private sector. Community development workers entered situations in which almost every activity which they could claim to perform was either already being carried out or within the prerogative of an existing government organization. Community development staff thus had either to take over or duplicate what was already being done or to try new activities, some of which, such as the promotion of sports, they might regard as a relatively low priority. Similarly, settlement schemes were frequently sited on marginal land which was not already occupied for some very good health, fertility or infrastructural reason, again placing a heavy burden on the department and reducing the chances of economic viability. Again, officers in ministries of planning often had difficulty establishing themselves initially because their activities and requirements — coordination and information, in particular — were regarded by other officers as a nuisance and of marginal or negative value.

A fourth and related limitation on the effectiveness of new departments is their need to fight to establish themselves and to survive once established. As we have seen, they may be launched into environments which are already occupied, and early in their lives they may have to struggle for their right to exist. Their rivals for roles, resources and power may prevent their coming to birth at all: in Kenya, for example, attempts made in 1956 and again in 1958 by the General Manager, Irrigation Development Projects, to secure acceptance for a statutory and semi-autonomous irrigation board were vetoed by the Provincial Administration which feared the creation of 'irrigated islands' separate from the normal administration of districts.[12] Or their rivals, already established, may greet them with hostility or indifference: marketing cooperatives cannot expect help from the private traders whom they seek to displace; community development workers often have difficulty gaining the cooperation of other government staff;[13] it is common for settlement schemes to be isolated from normal administration;[14] and planners like those at the regional level in Tanzania in the latter 1960s sometimes had difficulty extracting from departmental staff the information that was essential for their tasks as they saw them. Effectiveness is bound to be related to these problems. Those in the new organizations may respond vigorously, energetically attempting to overcome hostility or indifference; or they may respond with withdrawal and inactivity. In either case, in the short run at least, effectiveness in performing the substantive task of the organization is likely to suffer, and this probable shortcoming, like others, should be taken into account when deciding whether to set up a new organization in the first place.

THE REPERTOIRE FOR SURVIVAL

If it is typical for there to be a struggle over the creation of new government departments, it is also true that they quickly acquire an assured existence. In part this stability derives from inertia: vested interests develop; once staff are in post it is easier to allow them to remain than to close down the organization and have to dismiss them or resettle them elsewhere; recurrent budgets once established tend to be re-voted more or less automatically each year; and the organization becomes familiar as an accepted feature of the administrative scene. In part, too, this stability can be traced to the extensive defences which can be mustered to support continuation and indeed expansion. These include economic justifications; growth, proliferation and dispersal; alliances; subsidy and protection; and the manipulation of goals and ideology.

Economic justifications

Since the most stringent and damaging critics are usually economists, organizational survival can best be assured through demonstrable success in economic terms. With cooperatives, community development projects and settlement schemes, this has often not been possible. The experience with marketing cooperatives has been that they often have not made higher, prompter payments to producers than would have been available from private sector marketing.[15] Community development projects have all too commonly resulted in physical facilities which make demands on incomes (to subscribe to the school or health clinic or to keep them running) rather than directly augmenting incomes. Settlement schemes have frequently proved unsound economic investments compared with alternative uses of the same resources. This is not to deny that other benefits may derive from cooperatives, community development or settlement schemes, but merely to suggest that the possibility of satisfactory orthodox economic justifications has been the exception rather than the rule.

In this respect planning is perhaps in a position which is both protected and vulnerable: protected, first because planning departments are largely staffed by economists who are too busy applying their skills to the projects and programmes of other departments to have time for radical or self-annihilating introspection, and second, because the value of planning is almost an article of faith; and vulnerable because anti-planning heresies have tended to be underrepresented in East Africa and the weight of possible argument against planning has not yet been brought to bear. This has meant that establishing planning as a department has been comparatively easy although extending the controls it has sought over other ministries and departments has often been difficult.

Growth, Proliferation and Dispersal

Organizations also have improved chances of survival through growth, proliferation and dispersal. The larger an organization becomes, the harder it is to close it down. The more units it comprises and the more dispersed they are, the more difficult it becomes to make an evaluation, the harder it is for a critic to generalize his criticism, and the easier it is for visitors and observers to receive a misleadingly favourable impression of performance.

One interpretation of growth, proliferation and dispersal in a government department, though by no means the only one, is that they stem from drives within the organization to survive. In the case of the new departments for rural development being considered here, however, proliferation and dispersal are in the nature of the tasks and of the environment. Partly this is for the simple reason that rural areas are geographically extensive and deconcentrated administration is geographically scattered: district development committees, for instance, can scarcely but be based in districts. Partly, too, geographical dispersal is accentuated by functional marginality. Marketing cooperatives may find fewest rivals in distant places, poorly served by roads, where private sector marketing has not penetrated. Community developers may find undeveloped communities or communities with which other government departments have formed relatively weak contacts in areas with poor communications far from administrative centres. Settlement schemes tend to be remote and to have had communications because they are most readily established on unoccupied land.

In seeking territory and freedom from competition, these departments have quite often been forced out onto the physical margin. In these circumstances proliferation accentuates dispersal and both combine to improve the chances of survival. When there are many scattered settlement schemes in a country, or numerous dispersed cooperatives, or widely separated community development projects, or many regional or district development committees or plans, a rigorous and comprehensive appraisal becomes difficult. Weak projects and institutions are protected by dispersal, remoteness and poor communications.

Obversely, an organization which has proliferated and dispersed its units can usually develop and present a model project to show to visitors. Even if overall performance is poor, out of many cooperatives, some at least may be efficient; out of numerous self-help groups listed in a district, some will turn out regularly and predictably; out of many settlement schemes, some will have done well; and if there are development committees in all districts, it will be possible to identify some which have better records of effectiveness than others. A very few model projects or institutions are usually chosen, typically within a day's round trip from the capital city or convenient for the visitor to the district, and it is these which then provide much of the perception which dominates official thinking. To illustrate from Kenya, the special project is shown by the chief to the district officer, by the district officer to the district commissioner, by the district commissioner to the provincial commissioner and by the provincial commissioner to the minister, with a selective filter eliminating the less attractive projects at each level. The consequence is a self-reinforcing myth about the work of a department and about the rural situation generally, a perpetuation of a selective perception at the top of government about what is happening at the bottom. The biased impression of effectiveness then sustains and elevates the reputation and status of the department concerned.

Alliances

An obvious manner in which new departments can secure their positions is through developing cooperative relationships with existing organizations. The main strategies and relationships can be categorized as patron-client, cooptation and bargaining.

An insecure or weak organization often seeks protection of a patron. In Kenya in the 1950s both the relatively new African Land Development Organization and the Community Development Department sheltered closely under the wing of the Provincial Administration. In Tanzania, the Village Settlement Agency sought to maintain its independence of normal government administration through working direct to the ministerial Rural Settlement Commission. For some years the Community Development Department in Kenya sought to join a powerful ministry. Perhaps most obviously, though, there were debates in the mid-1950s about the best place to put planning, with some advocating its being lodged in the office of the Prime Minister or President.[16] Whatever the implicit or explicit reasons for seeking or welcoming a patron, the effect was liable to be to increase not just the power but also the security of the organization.

A second means which has been employed to achieve security is cooptation, defined by Selznick as 'the process of absorbing new elements into the leadership or policy-determining structure of an organization as a means of averting threats to its stability or existence'.[17] The advisory committees set up for isolated settlement schemes incorporate representatives of those organizations in the environment that are most likely to regard the schemes as alien intrusions. Similarly, provincial or regional and district development committees, meeting as in Kenya on the initiative of a representative of a planning ministry, can also be seen as means of cooptation, involving departmental officers in planning decisions, and thereby legitimating the planning process and the role of the planner.

A third defensive and adaptive relationship is through bargaining which leads to an exchange of resources or services. Irrigation and settlement schemes have been known unofficially to lend machines to neighbouring local councils, missions or government departments to do up their roads in exchange for goodwill and other services. A more formal example was the bargaining between the Mwea Irrigation Settlement in Kenya and the Embu African District Council in the later 1950s, as a result of which the levy of a Council cess on the scheme's rice was agreed in exchange for financial provision by the Council for the special scheme medical services for bilharzia and malaria.[18] As in this case, bargaining can, however, only be undertaken by organizations which have disposable resources and new departmental sub-organizations are typically weak in this respect.

Subsidy and Protection

Departmental activities and projects are protected and subsidised in many ways, and with varying degrees of visibility. The lack of concern with economic calculations common among civil servants makes it easy for this to occur. Thus settlement schemes in Ghana, Nigeria, the Sudan, Uganda, Tanzania, Zambia and Rhodesia have received direct government assistance which they are not expected to repay. Subsidies take the form of capital grants, recurrent expenditure on staff, free works and equipment which are not accounted to the scheme, and free food and services for settlers. Settlement schemes and cooperatives may also be protected by fiscal and legal measures which give them a competitive advantage over possible rivals. The Perkerra and Mwea Irrigation Schemes in Kenya, for example, have been protected by restrictions on the import of onions and rice respectively. Similarly, cooperatives are often sheltered from competition by the legal establishment of a monopoly buying position for a crop eliminating rivals regardless of whether they can give the producer a better service. Although the consumer may pay more for his onions and rice, or the producer may receive less from the cooperative than from private sector marketing, these costs are hidden and easily ignored. In addition, individual projects tend to be assessed on their own, and without the often considerable overheads of the parent department. Perhaps one of the most protective aspects of evaluation, however, is the tendency to examine *ex post* only what happened 'with' and not to try to assess what would have happened 'without'. With most settlement schemes, for instance, the land would have been cultivated anyway, and with some cooperatives at least the private sector would have marketed the produce. In both cases the economic activity would have occurred with negligible costs to government. One may also ask how many self-help projects claimed by community development departments would have been launched in any case through spontaneous local initiative. A department once created can protect itself both by adopting and claiming credit for offspring and by distracting attention from what would have happened without any official initiative.

Goals and Ideology

Given the common weakness of strictly economic justifications for cooperatives, community development and settlement schemes and perhaps for some aspects of planning, it is not surprising that the organizations concerned are often defended and justified on non-economic grounds. Goals for organizations are dynamic and adaptive variables which can be manipulated, whether consciously or unconsciously, to enhance the prospects of survival and growth for the organization.[19] The departments under review have as a major strength the multiple objectives which they are intended to achieve, and the opportunity to fall back upon the support of humanitarian, political or ideological goals when economic achievement is poor. In this respect all four organizations have been sensitive to their ideological environments, seeking to exploit them to establish and expand their activities. This is not to say that the creation of new organizations must not be related to long-term political perspectives; the point is that statements of goals and ideology can be used to justify organizational survival and expansion.

An illustration can be given for planning in Kenya. When the Ministry of Planning and Economic Development was attempting to establish planning units and controls in other ministries, it produced the manifesto *African Socialism and Its Application to Planning in Kenya*. While at one level this was a presentation of the Kenya Government's ideas on African socialism it can also be seen as a political document to be used by the planning ministry in establishing controls over other ministries, arguing for African socialism as a justification. Thus it states:

With planning, no ministry is free to act as an undisciplined, unrestricted entrepreneur promoting funds and projects to maximize the status of the ministry. Instead all must accept
the discipline of planning and join in maximizing the resources available for development,
determining the best use for these resources, and ensuring that resources are in fact used
as planned. If DISCIPLINE is rejected, so is planning and with it – African Socialism.[20]

In a similar fashion, goals of settlement, cooperatives, and community development have been associated with the stated aims of socialism in the three
countries. With settlement, non-economic goals were related usually not merely
to the ideological environment, which was different in each country despite the
common socialist label, but also to the political and humanitarian objectives
which were among the other purposes of settlement. Thus, economic evaluations might find settlement schemes poor investments, but the parent organizations could justify themselves in terms of relieving an explosive political
situation (Kenya) or achieving cooperative production (Tanzania). It is significant that the major settlement undertaking that was suspended during the
1960s – the Pilot Village Settlements in Tanzania – had been shown to be not
only poor investment but also dysfunctional ideologically, conflicting with the
Tanzanian policy of egalitarianism and self-reliance by creating a rural privileged elite with dependent attitudes. In these circumstances, the Tanzanian
settlements had no rationale to fall back on apart from their possible experimental value. The subsequent initiative in Tanzania – the *ujamaa* village movement – had such a high political priority, that by mid-1971 it had apparently
not been subjected to any economic analysis. Cooperatives and community
development have similarly sought and received support as being means towards socialism. It may be no coincidence that in Malawi, where there was no
such ideological support, cooperative marketing for agricultural produce was
abandoned in favour of direct purchase by an official buying organization,
whereas despite their many difficulties cooperatives have been consistently
supported in East Africa. Indeed, a nominally or actually socialist environment
sometimes allows inefficient departments to shield themselves from criticism.
There is some contrast here between Ghana before the first military coup,
where proliferation and corruption were rampant, and Tanzania since independence where the creation and expansion of, for instance, cooperatives and
parastatals has tended to be examined more critically although pursued far
more rapidly than could be justified on economic grounds. One is driven to
the conclusion that the creation, expansion and protection of inefficient or uneconomic Government organizations is a price that is liable to be paid for a
socialist rhetoric and policies, however desirable they may be on other grounds.

COMMITMENT AND RISK

The argument up to this point is that the costs of new departments for rural
development have been, and generally are, higher and their effectiveness lower

than might be anticipated at first sight. In the cases considered there have been organizations already in the environment which have claimed the right to perform the functions of the new departments. Time and energy have been taken up in establishing the departments and in struggles with rivals. The new departments have tended to be forced into activities or areas which are marginal. These factors must weaken the case for setting up any new government department for rural development in future. But in addition, the range and versatility of the repertoire an organization can muster for survival introduces a further consideration: the risk of irreversible commitment, the risk, that once created, an ineffective, uneconomic or inappropriate organization will, through growth, proliferation and dispersal, through alliances, through subsidy and protection, and through manipulation of goals and ideology, become irreversibly established although on economic and other grounds it is a poor national investment and should be closed down.

The degree of irreversibility of commitment to the sub-organizations of departments varies considerably. In Kenya, with the exception of Nyanza, the district development advisory committees launched with the Second Plan[21] were ineffective and rarely met. In the mid-1960s, in all three East African countries, numerous cooperatives quietly ceased to function, although official commitment to the larger ones was usually very strong. Most self-help projects can be adopted and abandoned by community development departments without difficulty partly because of their low cost and low visibility. With settlement schemes, however, commitment is much less reversible.[22] There are many examples of the tenacious stamina of such schemes even when uneconomic: the South Busoga settlement scheme in Uganda was abandoned and revived; the original intention with the Kenya Million-Acre Settlements, that special tutelage should be limited to two years, gave way to acceptance of a period of five years and speculation whether special treatment could ever be withdrawn. In Kenya, again, the Perkerra Irrigation Scheme, although grossly uneconomic since its inception in the mid-1950s, was consistently subsidized and sustained.[23] From the varying reversibility of these projects — marketing cooperatives, self-help projects, development committees and settlement schemes, it can be postulated that irreversibility varies directly with many factors, among them: the degree to which permanent physical works are involved; the level of expenditure; the gestation period of the project (the longer, the deeper the commitment); the extent to which departmental staff are committed full-time; whether departmental management is required after the development phase; and the extent to which there is a departmental responsibility for people's livelihood. On these scales, development committees rank very low, and settlement schemes rank high, with self-help projects and marketing cooperatives in intermediate positions.

The reversibility of the parent organizations depends partly on the reversibility of their sub-organizations: a community development department, for example, would be easier to disband than a settlement department. But all departments may be much harder to abolish than to create in the first instance. Personal and political vested interests have to be fought and a resettlement problem with refugees from the organization has to be faced. The organization may even have achieved a degree of indispensability, as in Ghana after the first military coup when buyers stated they were unable to re-enter the field for purchasing cocoa because when monopoly buying had earlier been instituted they had disbanded their organizations and disposed of their plant.[24] Perhaps the most powerful factor, however, is the dis-incentive for hatchet activities of this sort. It is easier for a civil servant to employ supportive non-economic arguments, to play for time, to maintain the *status quo*, and to wait until a transfer relieves him of responsibility, than it is for him to take personal risks by deciding to wind up a project or department.

The conclusion may, therefore, appear to be that a decision to launch a project or organization, and in particular to create a department for a rural development activity, should take into account irreversibility of commitment as a factor augmenting risks of failure. The real situation is, however, more complex. There is a place here for giving some weight to Hirschman's doctrine of the Hiding Hand in development. This is the idea that the difficulties that a project will encounter are habitually under-estimated, but that there is a habitual offsetting under-estimate of the creativity which can be brought to bear to overcome those difficulties.[25] Hirschman argues that industrial projects have an advantage over agricultural projects because of the greater degree of commitment to them, preventing abandonment and drawing out creativity. He argues that there is a danger of premature abandonment of agricultural projects. This illuminating set of insights is, however, only partly applicable in the context of this paper. In terms of prescriptions, Hirschman's concept is balanced by an opposite argument: that 'creativity' is not costless, for it implies the use of staff, finance, and sometimes subsidy, and the greater the creativity called forth, the greater too may be the cost. Creativity may mean saddling an economy with a dependent dwarf of a project, protected from competition, and paid for by the taxpayer and consumer. Moreover, government departments are not subject to the same economic criteria in appraisal as the world bank projects studied by Hirschman. They are much more likely to survive as a dead weight to be carried by the economy and to sustain uneconomic offspring. The implication remains, only slightly weakened by Hirschman's argument, that in *ex ante* appraisal of a proposal to set up a government organization or project, there is utility in thinking in terms of a coefficient of irreversibility which should be applied to the more obvious costs and risks of the organization.

CONCLUSIONS

The argument of this essay has been deliberately selective, examining similarities rather than differences, concentrating on costs and risks rather than benefits, and presenting reasons against rather than for the creation of government organizations, particularly new departments. The aim has been to moderate the unbalanced and uncritical view which seeks to set up new institutions whenever new tasks are to be performed. There are, however, contrary cases to put. Many of the differences between cooperative societies, self-help projects, settlement schemes and development committees are sharp and obvious; the benefits deriving from them have often been substantial, particularly if a long time horizon is taken; and the case for creating and expanding organizations, especially parastatals, can be strong, particularly when specialized services are required, as with major irrigation or smallholder tea, or when a pump-priming activity is required, for example introducing a market for livestock in a backward area not yet served by private sector purchasing. Moreover, the benefits deriving from the types of organization under review have often been substantial. The argument of this paper is not that these departments necessarily should not have been set up, nor is it that the outputs of these departments — cooperative societies, self-help groups, settlement schemes, and development committees and plans — are undesirable. The argument is, rather, that the creation and expansion of such organizations have high and often irreversible costs which are rarely fully taken into account.

These costs may be accentuated by the notorious tendency of bureaucracies to grow and by the reflex which automatically seeks to solve problems or perform new functions by setting up new institutions. None of the East African countries have approached the pathological condition of uncontrolled growth in Cuba where Castro in 1966 had reached the extremity of calling for the debureaucratization of the commissions set up to debureaucratize the bureaucracy.[26] In the early 1970s both Kenya and Uganda were proceeding cautiously. Zambia's experience with a Ministry of Rural Development had been disappointing, while Tanzania, more than any other East African country, had as part of the policy of socialism and self-reliance, created numerous new bodies including District Development Corporations and a large number of parastatals and their subsidiaries.[27] The example of Ghana under Nkrumah should be a warning. The risk is that creating organizations becomes addictive, a habitual response to problems or aspirations. Each new organization saps existing organizations of staff and thus multiplies the problems to be solved and the aspirations that are unfulfilled. As a government persistently tries to do too much and proliferates its organizations, whether departments or parastatals, the over-burdened, under-staffed and under-supervised machine becomes dysfunctional, demonstrating a spastic condition in which orders from the centre produce if anything unpredictable and often contrary twitchings in the extremities of the limbs. At the same time, the government bureaucracy continues to expand and lies as a deadening weight on the economy and the taxpayer. The terminal condition is a syndrome of bureaucratic elephantiasis, a stagnant or declining economy, a loss of political legitimacy for the regime, selective misperceptions in the centre about the condition of the rural periphery, and a reproduction of organizations which becomes pathological, leading lemming-like to self-induced annihilation (as was the fate of many of Nkrumah's corporations after the first military coup in Ghana). While this may be an extreme situation, the lesson should be clear: that governments should stringently control the sizes of their bureaucracies and that they should not try to do too much.

Indeed, government departments which maintain field staffs appear in East Africa to have reached a point of saturation in the sense that all the most obvious and important functions are covered. There may be a warning to be drawn from the fact that of the relatively recent newcomers both community development and planning have functions which they sometimes describe as coordination, although the provincial administration (by whatever name) already claims the right to coordinate in development matters. The marginal benefits of selective coordination may be high; but the marginal benefits of establishing any further organization with a coordination role would almost certainly be negative, generating as it would a need for coordination of the coordinators. Given the level of functional saturation already reached, there is a case for appraising the costs and benefits of the four departments discussed above, both at a national level and in terms of their geographical distribution. It might well emerge that in the more developed areas direct official support for community development, marketing cooperatives and settlement schemes should be phased out, combining this with launching the sub-organizations on a largely independent course; that further departmental effort and inputs in these fields should be concentrated on the less developed and poorer areas; and that decentralized planning should be evolved to serve all areas.

In terms of the direct activities of government organizations in rural areas, the opportunities of the 1970s seem to lie not so much in undertaking new tasks or making major structural changes as in selective expansion of activities which are already performed and in improving the operation of organizations which already exist. Where new or expanded tasks seem desirable there is a case for examining alternatives to direct departmental action, including the encouragement of the private sector and voluntary organizations, whether through commercial activity, subsidies, grants or contracts, the use of the parastatal sector, or the non-organizational alternatives of legislative and fiscal measures. There are, however, certain functions in rural development – family planning, improving nutrition, and decentralized planning among them – which have not previously been a major focus and which deserve development and promotion; and these might be achieved through adaptation and controlled expansion of departments which already have field staffs and on a geographically selective basis. The main opportunity of the 1970s in this context is, however, to mobilize more effectively the government personnel already in the rural areas. Departments of agriculture in particular carry large field staffs, the rather low effectiveness of which is a commonplace. They and the staff of other departments in the rural areas of East Africa can be regarded as major but expensive and under-utilized national resources. To create new government departments for rural development activities would now be largely to evade the problems and ignore the opportunities of exploiting those resources. For it is in the more difficult task of improving the management of existing organizations that the governments of East Africa face their main rural development challenge in the 1970s.

NOTES

I am grateful to Lionel Cliffe, Martin R. Doornbos, W.J.M. MacKenzie, J.R. Nellis, and K.E. Svendsen for comments on earlier versions. Responsibility for the views expressed is, however, entirely mine.

1. The Cooperative Movement in the Colonies, Despatches dated 20 March 1946 and 23 April 1946 from the Secretary of State for the Colonies to the Colonial Governments (Colonial No. 199, HMSO, London, 1946).

2. For this body and its successors see *African Land Development in Kenya 1946-1962* (Ministry of Agriculture, Animal Husbandry and Water Resources, Nairobi, 1962), 2-4.

3. The report was published as *The Economic Development of Tanganyika, Report of a Mission Organized by the International Bank for Reconstruction and Development* (The Johns Hopkins Press, Baltimore, 1961).

4. For an elaboration of this point, see Robert Chambers, 'Planning for Rural Areas in East Africa: Experience and Prescriptions' (Discussion Paper No. 119, Institute for Development Studies, Nairobi, 1971; mimeographed), 13-16.

5. *Report of the Presidential Special Committee of Enquiry Into Cooperative Movement and Marketing Boards* (Government Printer, Dar es Salaam, 1966). There is a substantial literature on cooperatives in East Africa, including Carl Gosta Widstrand (ed), *Cooperatives and Rural Development in East Africa* (The Scandinavian Institute of African Studies, Uppsala; Africana Publishing Corporation, New York, 1970), and Göran Hydén, *African Cooperatives: a Study of Organizational Management in Rural Kenya* (forthcoming).

6. For some of the problems of self-help see Frank Holmquist, 'Implementing Rural Development Projects', in Göran Hydén, Robert Jackson and John Okumu (eds), *Development Administration: the Kenyan Experience* (Oxford University Press, Nairobi, 1970); Philip Mbithi, 'Self-help as a Strategy for Rural Development: a Case Study' (paper to Universities of East Africa Social Science Conference, Dar es Salaam, December 1970, mimeographed); and John Anderson, 'Self-help and Independency: African Education in Kenya', *African Affairs*, 70, 278 (January 1971).

7. For a bibliography see Robert Chambers, *Settlement Schemes in Tropical Africa: a Study of Organizations and Development* (Routledge and Kegan Paul, London, 1969), 263-287.

8. For the early experience with these committees, see Cherry Gertzel, 'The Provincial Administration and Development in Kenya, 1965-68' (paper to Universities of East Africa Social Science Conference, Dar es Salaam, December 1970, mimeographed), 8-21.

9. For discussion of the experience with Regional Economic Secretaries in Tanzania see R.G. Saylor and Ian Livingstone, 'Regional Planning in Tanzania' (ERB Paper 69.25, Economic Research Bureau, University of Dar es Salaam, 1969, mimeographed); and James W. Tomecko and George Davies, 'Regional Planning: Planning for a Region in Tanzania' (paper to University of Nairobi/York University Seminar on Project Appraisal and Plan Implementation, Nairobi, 15-17 June 1971, mimeographed).

10. The exact figures for the end of September 1964 were:

Posts held by Ugandans	2,288
Posts held by expatriates	1,750
Posts vacant	1,669
Total	5,707

Source: B.L. Jacobs, 'The State of the Ugandan Civil Service Two Years after Independence' (East African Institute of Social Research Conference paper, December 1964, mimeographed).

11. See for example *East African Standard* (Nairobi), 20 July 1966.

12. Chambers, *Settlement Schemes in Tropical Africa*, 90-91.

13. See for example Violaine Junod, 'Problems of Integrating Rural Development at the Grass-Root Level: a study based on a Uganda Community Development Training Project run for University level Trainees' (paper to Africa Regional Conference on the Integrated Approach to Rural Development, Moshi, 13-24 October 1969, appendix B, mimeographed).

14. Chambers, *Settlement Schemes in Tropical Africa*, 190-193.

15. For example see O. Okereke, 'The Place of Marketing Cooperatives in the Economy of Uganda', in Carl Gosta Widstrand (ed), *Cooperatives and Rural Development in East Africa*, 167-168; and *Report of the Committee of Inquiry into the Coffee Industry 1967* (Government Printer, Entebbe, 1967), 21-22.

16. For an authoritative discussion with a comparative international perspective, see Albert Waterston, *Development Planning, Lessons of Experience* (The Johns Hopkins Press, Baltimore, 1965), 467-490.

17. Philip Selznick, *TVA and the Grass Roots, A Study in the Sociology of Formal Organization* (first published 1949 by University of California Press; Harper and Row, 1966), 13.

18. Chambers, *Settlement Schemes*, 102, 193.

19. See for instance David L. Sills, 'The Succession of Goals', and James D. Thompson and William J. McEwen, 'Organizational Goals and Environment', both in Amitai Etzioni (ed), *Complex Organizations, a Sociological Reader* (Holt, Rinehart and Winston, New York, 1962).

20. *African Socialism and Its Application to Planning in Kenya* (Sessional Paper No. 10, Government Printer, Nairobi, 1965), 50.

21. *Development Plan, 1966-1970* (Government Printer, Nairobi, 1966), 8.

22. For a discussion of this point, see Chambers, *Settlement Schemes*, 257-260.

23. For an account of the history of the scheme, see Robert Chambers, 'The Perkerra Irrigation Scheme: a Project in Search of an Economy', in E.A. Brett with D.G.R. Belshaw (eds), *Public Policy and Agricultural Development in East Africa* (East African Publishing House, Nairobi, forthcoming).

24. *Report of the Committee of Enquiry on the Local Purchasing of Cocoa* (Ministry of Information, Accra, 1967), appendices XVII-XXIII.

25. Albert Hirschman, *Development Projects Observed* (The Brookings Institution, Washington, D.C., 1967), 13 ff.

26. Quoted in *The Times*, London (12 December 1966). In a speech to a congress of the Federation of Cuban Women in Santa Clara, Dr Castro was reported to have said that some offices of the commissions for the struggle against bureaucracy had a staff of 100 when 20 would be enough.

27. The rapid increase in recurrent expenditure of the Tanzanian Government probably largely reflects the expansion of public sector organizations. Recurrent expenditure almost doubled in the five years 1965/1966 to 1970/1971, from 888 million shillings (actual) to 1,630 million shillings (estimated actual). Source: *The Annual Plan for 1971/1972* (Government Printer, Dar es Salaam, June 1971), 5.

G.K. HELLEINER

ECONOMICS, INCENTIVES AND DEVELOPMENT PENETRATION

It is usual in theoretical discussions of the penetration problem, much of which is known in the planners' profession as 'plan implementation', to postulate that the 'centre' has certain clear and coherent objectives (a welfare, utility preference or objective function in economic jargon) and an arsenal of weapons among which it may choose for their pursuit. It is then a matter of selecting the most efficient policy instruments with the constraint, in the more formalized models, that the number of targets does not exceed the number and/or capability of instruments. Of course, the world is rather more complex than this. Both the 'centrally-initiated' targets which are the whole object of the attempt to penetrate the periphery and the specific instruments chosen to attain them are themselves the outcome of a multidimensional and continuous bargaining and consultative process. This process has both a 'horizontal' dimension, involving discussions among the various Ministries or other agencies (not to speak of personalities), each of which has its own particular interests to promote or to protect, and a 'vertical' dimension involving those between the centre and the periphery. Among the factors influencing the ultimate policy outcome is the success with which various parts of the periphery have managed to 'reverse-penetrate' the centre. This outcome is likely already to be something of a compromise before it is even begun. There is frequently therefore a real question as to just who, on balance, is penetrating whom. In some instances much of the original developmental thrust may be coming from below; the periphery is not always passive and resistant to change. In others, the periphery may sensibly ignore or evade counter-developmental, centrally-initiated change.

At a more practical level, central government's efforts consciously to 'penetrate' may be classified broadly into projects and policies. Most discussion of centrally-initiated change in the development context is concerned with the preparation and evaluation of projects. It is obvious that care in the preparation of projects, both those which are directly productive and those which constitute social overheads, is crucially important not only to the overall development which the planners seek but also to the behavioural and attitudinal change with which those who speak of 'penetration' are more concerned. How the latter changes emanate from project experience is a matter about which we still know too little. Hirschman[1] suggests, for instance, that the emergence of unforeseen problems is an important means of developing managerial attitudes and talent, and that development would actually be hindered were the careful project analysts too well-informed as to the future difficulties! As far as behavioural and attitudinal change at the periphery is concerned, at least as important as the separable projects initiated by the central government are its general development policies as reflected in its laws, regulations, taxes, price controls, exhortation through the various media, and in the composition of some of its recurrent expenditures.

The instruments for this type of penetration of the periphery are many and varied. Some are blunt, some are quite fine; some are direct, some indirect. The most obviously direct and blunt instrument is the order or directive; sometimes it is incorporated in the form of legislation. Directness is not, however, necessarily related to effectiveness. The important question is whether these laws or orders are enforced or even whether they are enforceable. The limited skills in the administrative structure and the related relative weakness of official communication and control mechanisms set definite bounds to the possibilities under this heading in East Africa. The statute books are full of forgotten regulations, sometimes contradictory to one another, and the bureaucracy typically includes moribund or virtually non-existent bodies (commissions, standing committees, boards etc.) with long-forgotten responsibilities for their implementation. Frequently, only very few changes actually occur as a result of the centre's apparatus at the local level carrying out central directives (which are in turn themselves the product of the continual Ministerial, inter-Ministerial, Board, and Cabinet meetings at the centre), while the typically smaller changes resulting from the periphery's response to such orders are even more rare. There are simply too many fragile links in the official communications chain and too little involvement or identification on the part of the various segments of the periphery with the centre. Thus the original order or instruction often tends to be dissipated or distorted in its application as it moves outward from centre to periphery.

Education, persuasion and exhortation constitute another major set of direct instruments of penetration. These instruments are employed, perhaps even over-employed, by the political and administrative arm of the centre in all parts of East Africa. Many of the general messages, consisting of exhortations to work harder, drink less, save more, use improved techniques, pay taxes, cultivate loyalty to the nation, tend to be similar everywhere. The more specific ones, relating, for instance, to techniques of cultivation, crops to encourage, self-help schemes to support and so forth, are more area-specific and more likely to be transmitted by the technical-administrative representatives of the centre than by the government.

Experiences with these educative instruments have been a major preoccupation of the sociologist and the political scientist. In their analyses they emphasize the characteristics of the communications and their media, the social structure, customs and other attributes of the respondent, all having a bearing on the response behaviour of the population. Effective message communication, of course, is not the same as penetration in the full sense of inducing behaviour alteration. One encounters, for instance, quite frequent knowledge on the part of Tanzanian smallholders as to what constitutes the three enemies of progress ('poverty, ignorance and disease'), or farmers may even know of the existence and properties of fertilizers, accompanied by no observable behavioural reflection of this knowledge.[2]

Penetration instruments may also be indirect in their application. In their attempts to explain and control behaviour, economists have tended to focus primarily upon one set of indirect means: the structure of incentives – rewards and penalties, particularly though not exclusively material ones. Under appropriate assumptions as to the preference systems of the respondents, based on *a priori* reasoning or observation or both, any change in the incentive structure should induce behavioural change which is predictable at least in its direction. Conscious control of at least some of the incentives in the system can therefore also be an important instrument of penetration. An incentive structure always exists whether or not there has been any conscious attempt officially to manipulate it for the purpose of stimulating behaviour of a particular type. Failure to employ these policy instruments does not alter the fact of the existence of the incentive structure and is therefore also an implicit policy choice. It is therefore essential to know the pattern of incentives, when possible to measure them, if behaviour is to be understood. There are frequently substantial incentives built into the system which run contrary to the established objectives. For instance, insistence upon legal minimum wages, zero tariffs on imported machinery, an overvalued currency, and a cattle tax are together unlikely to stimulate the adoption of the intermediate ox-plough technology which it is, in Tanzania, government policy to encourage. These policy phenomena artificially inflate the costs of labour and livestock-holding while reducing those of purchasing and maintaining machinery, so that agricultural decision-makers will receive greater inducements to adopt labour-saving machinery instead of ox-ploughs, other things being equal, than if the Government had no policies whatsoever in these areas.

The selection of the appropriate policy instrument for the pursuit of a particular target is part of the art (not science) of political economy. Benefit/cost analysis can be applied to this choice as to any other. One of the principal advantages of incentives as instruments of penetration are their relatively low skilled manpower or other input requirements. Laws require enforcement officers; persuasion requires educators. In circumstances in which price controlling or influencing mechanisms already exist, as in East Africa, the marginal cost of their conscious use is close to zero.

This approach is based, in strict theory, upon the assumption that the individual (or collective) actor possesses a clear and specifiable welfare (or preference or objective) function; that he will respond in predictable fashion to changes in the variables, all of which are known, upon which his welfare is functionally dependent. Again, reality is not quite as simple. Human behaviour is rarely so rational and so consistent as to be capable of specification in a welfare function. Even if it were possible to list all the variables upon which behaviour of any particular type depends, which is itself doubtful, it would still be impossible to measure many or even most of them meaningfully, quite apart from the further difficulty of assigning coefficients to them. Even those which are measurable have relatively rarely been satisfactorily quantified and still more rarely have stable relationships been discovered. Nor can one assume that the actual values of these variables are in any case known, even in a probabilistic sense, to the actor in question. Further to complicate the picture, each individual's welfare function can be expected to differ from every other's welfare function; it is even possible that the sign of the coefficient attached to a particular variable can differ. The pursuit of centrally-initiated policy objectives through the manipulation of incentives should therefore, in principle, consider the characteristics of only the welfare functions of those whose behaviour is to be influenced. A not inconsiderable bundle of problems!

Is it arrogance or ignorance which permits the economist to make his usually fairly simple-minded policy recommendations in the sphere of incentive manipulation? The answer is probably a little bit of both. The 'arrogance' arises from the well-developed structure of the economic theory which purports to explain behaviour coupled with the rapidly mounting volume of supporting econometric evidence relating to peasant behaviour. Econometric techniques are suited to the testing of only the most simple-minded of behavioural propositions; they may not be the most important ones. Nevertheless the evidence is now persuasive that peasant farmers, generally speaking, respond positively to agricultural price changes as theory always assumed they did.[3] (Early observers often thought otherwise.) These positive supply responses are clearest with respect to the allocation of unchanged factor inputs − land, labour, capital − among various alternative uses; they are not so certain when it comes to the eliciting of increases in the total of these factor inputs in response to improved overall earning opportunity.

Econometric evidence of positive supply response by East African smallholders is not available in great quantity but includes some on Kenya coffee farmers[4] and some on the trade-off in Uganda between cotton and coffee.[5] In addition there abounds 'qualitative' evidence − the reported response in Dodoma and Songea Regions of Tanzania to the alteration in the relative prices of maize and tobacco;[6] the ingenious means smallholders are known to find to avoid selling their produce to the primary societies with the heaviest deductions (for credit repayment, central coffee pulperies or whatever), or to evade unremunerative compulsory marketing schemes, and so forth. The extraordinary rates of growth in smallholder cash crop production in recent years, particularly in Kenya and Tanzania where they have averaged nearly 5 percent compounded in recent years, are also *prima facie* evidence of positive responses to market incentives, in this case reflecting the (profitable) transfer from subsistence activities and/or leisure to cash cropping.

It is not necessary to have a *complete* understanding of the decision-making process for this proposition about price responsiveness to be employed. Its validity does not depend upon the actor being a *pure* economic man in the sense that he always maximizes material income to the exclusion of all other goals; it does not even depend upon his satisfactorily maximizing 'utility', which is supposed to incorporate his attitudes to risk and all other non-material aspects of his welfare. It only asserts that in whatever decision function he employs (and, of course, it need not be a smooth function), the coefficient attached to price carries a positive sign.

This simple proposition has great power for it enables one to predict that, through the combined effects of shifts in the composition of production of present producers and the appearance of new producers, a price increase will tend to call forth increased supplies; conversely, price reduction will tend to decrease them. Only when material incentive is the binding constraint upon the particular behavioural change sought will this instrument of price-incentive manipulation work. And complications quickly arise as soon as one considers the length of time necessary for the response to take place, the nature of the response function, etc. Still there is considerable relative strength in it if only because of the obvious facts that the would-be penetrator must confine the bulk of his attention to those instrumental variables which it is within his power to control, which are not unreasonably expensive to manipulate, and which produce reasonably certain effects. These latter criteria eliminate most of the variables upon which policy might otherwise operate with some hope of affecting behaviour.

The *pure* economist pretends nothing but ignorance as to the other components of the welfare function. It is not that they may not be more important; it is rather that there is not yet too much theory or much concrete evidence which predicts how various policy instruments will work upon them. The pure economist takes all these other factors as givens or as constraints and then seeks to achieve his objectives through the manipulation of those variables which are clearly subject to control and about which he knows something. There can be little doubt but that the changing of the givens and the loosening of these constraints, i.e. the alteration of the welfare function itself, through education, development of new modes of thought, social relations, land tenure, methods of production, etc. are ultimately far more important and must be the subject of all-out penetration efforts. As such efforts produce changing coefficients in the welfare functions, the fact of price-responsiveness, of course, remains; indeed the responsiveness is likely to increase.

To penetrate through manipulation of the incentive structure is thus not to penetrate radically. It is rather a means of doing what one can within the existing set of constraints and of providing the lubricating oil which is necessary for the more fundamental changes to occur. In the shortrun it is both easier and more fruitful to harness the presently existing incentives at the periphery to the centre's objectives than to attempt fundamentally to alter them. This is less a matter of ideology or philosophy than one of practical political economy.

Underlying this whole approach is the assumption that material income is positively related to utility and that its marginal utility is never zero. A rather stronger assumption is that material advantage is a necessary though not a sufficient condition for behavioural change. One can find instances where this is unrealistic; Tanzanian peasants have on occasion planted some cotton 'for Mwalimu' even though they clearly considered it unprofitable. But in most circumstances this stronger assumption is appropriate. Certainly 'unprofitability' is the most obvious blockage or source of resistance to many programmes and must be cleared out of the way if there is to be response to more fundamental penetrative effort. In this sense the instrument of incentive manipulation may be a lubricant.

Prices are crucial to the behaviour and structural evolution of economies which are based, as are those of East Africa, upon the market rather than upon physical planning. The flows of products and factors within the nation and internationally, the composition of production, the choice of techniques and location, are all determined by calculations based upon the price system. Prices serve as signals guiding behaviour not only at the periphery, where they are intended to, but even within the government's own decision-making apparatus. Centrally-planned projects are frequently evaluated either through error or through conscious intention to mislead on the basis of market prices which are (or can be) themselves in large part the product of the planners' tax and price policies. Elaborate feasibility studies purport to demonstrate the 'profitability' of government ventures in many situations where the use of unmanipulated prices in the calculations would render them clearly uneconomic. Some suggest that in the light of the shortages of facts, skills, and sophisticated techniques for planning, market prices are the only practical guide for central planners.[7] 'Special' price arrangements are also commonly created by the 'centre' on an *ad hoc* basis to render particular private (or even public) projects commercially viable. (Commercial viability is not equivalent to social profitability.) In East Africa these have typically included import tariffs, import duty rebates, concessional prices for inputs into processing activities, and protected prices for favoured rural settlement schemes.

Penetration of the rural periphery through the use of the indirect policy instrument of incentive manipulation is a subject which could be discussed at great length. Let one here confine discussion to a few of the more obvious major possible targets and instruments.[8]

In East Africa, the governments typically exert considerable influence over, if they do not always in fact control, the producer prices of the major cash crops. This is achieved through the system of compulsory deliveries to state marketing boards, which either pay government-determined and preannounced prices or deduct various taxes and levies from the producers' earnings on the local and/or central government's behalf. Where there are alternative production possibilities (this is not always the case) relative prices will obviously influence farmers' allocation of land, labour and other inputs among them. Through the centre's price controls or tax policies it can shift the composition of agricultural production in whatever is the desired direction from the point of view of its general development strategy. At present, for example, there are short-run reasons for granting special encouragement to tobacco (in order to move quickly into the former Rhodesian-supplied markets abroad), tea (so as to improve East Africa's power in the bargaining over an international tea agreement) and rice (in order to reduce the size of the import bill and ease the strain on the balance of payments). Where pricing policies are intended to elicit increased supplies it is essential to remember, though, that storage, transport, and marketing facilities be provided in advance for the increase. On the other hand, further coffee production should be discouraged if it can only be sold at unremunerative prices in the markets of those not adhering to the International Coffee Agreement.

Agricultural pricing policies obviously can affect not only the national crop-mix but also those of the constituent regions. The frequent East African practice of promulgating equal prices for particular crops at all buying stations, regardless of the area of the country in which they are located and in defiance of transport cost considerations, can have substantial impact, no doubt unintended, on local crop composition. Since the major maize market in Tanzania is in Dar es Salaam and there are substantial costs involved in moving maize from other parts of the country to that market, up-country maize producers would normally receive lower prices than those in the Dar es Salaam area. Equalization of producer prices for maize, *but not for other crops* which still have to bear the transport costs up-country, deflect up-country producers towards maize and Dar es Salaam area producers away from it (in a socially inefficient manner). Transport rates (another 'price' subject to central influence or control) also have an obvious bearing on the level and structure of local producer prices and therefore on behaviour.

Price announcements may themselves be an important means of communicating the message as to the centre's view of which crops are to be encouraged and which not. 'Announcement effects' may be forthcoming which are quite apart from the purely 'economic' responses we have been discussing heretofore.

In order not to destroy the legitimacy of the centre's authority, however, it is essential that control prices, when announced, are effective. This rule must, of course, be applied to all other government policies as well. Land taxes, for instance, are frequently advocated as a means of encouraging improvements but since they could not be applied in the rural areas their effect could be 'counter-penetrative'. Penetration is not furthered when a controlled price announcement is followed by widespread evasion. In East Africa this is common experience with smallholder-produced food crops, only a small proportion of the marketed total of which is sold legally at the centrally established prices.

Effective price announcements are also essential if the central pricing policies are to penetrate policies and practices at lower levels of the marketing chain. Local government or cooperatives may establish market regulations, levy dues or cesses, charge all manner of deductions in such ways as to alter completely the incentive structure from that which was intended by the centre. Obviously, the 'farther down' the price is promulgated, the more effective it will be; and, one might add, if it is effective, the greater will be the credibility of the centre at the periphery. If there is too wide a spread between the announced price level and the price the farmer finally receives there may arise unnecessary and unhelpful resentment against both the government and the middlemen (including the cooperatives) who perform the useful lower-level marketing and transport functions.

Price differentials can also be employed effectively to penetrate ideas and objectives relating to quality improvement and certain aspects of husbandry practices such as the timing of planting, although these price weapons obviously cannot become so sophisticated that they lose their chief attribute of cheapness. If, for instance, the administration of quality differentials requires a lot of skilled manpower or if it lends itself easily to corrupt practices, they lose their raison d'être.

Smallholder behaviour is affected not only by the returns earnable from alternative uses of available inputs but also by the risks attached to them. It is no use for the smallholder to seek to maximize his income if the variability associated with the high income is sufficient to wipe him out in a bad year.[9] If a price or prices can be guaranteed between planting and harvest and, in the case of tree crops, over several seasons, risk of at least one type is reduced. Price stabilization, by reducing risks, can therefore encourage him to employ more inputs in agriculture and to diversify to a lesser extent his crop 'portfolio', which is his principal means of protection against risk.

The manipulation of incentives can also be an instrument for pushing agricultural innovations into more widespread employment in the periphery. The most obvious instrument for this purpose is the provision of artificially low prices for the recommended new inputs and/or for credit which make their use more attractive. Subsidies on particular inputs (including credit) may at the same time be an effective means of pursuing crop priority objectives, frequently a more 'penetrating' means that the provision of subsidized output prices, in that they reward only those who are behavioural innovators. The prices at which the new inputs are sold to the farmer can be as low as zero or even negative to persuade him to adopt them. Ultimately one would hope that the smallholders would learn their value 'by doing', after which the protected prices could be withdrawn. That such a withdrawal would be unpopular goes without saying,[10] but it is unlikely to create more opposition than an unfavourable alteration of output prices; it may be necessary to time the abandonment of subsidized input prices to coincide with an increase in output prices. Risk aversion in the welfare functions of the potential adopters can, in principle, also be countered by simple insurance schemes associated with inputs' use.

Controllable incentive structures may also play a role, though not probably a predominant one, in the pursuit of central policies relating to rural-urban migration and urban unemployment. The complex of factors accounting for the relative attractiveness of living in the urban as opposed to the rural areas is not entirely understood. Still, it can confidently be said that real rural and urban incomes can be influenced by the level of minimum wages and the degree of their enforcement, the level of controlled or taxed agricultural producer prices (allowing for such local taxes as are authorized by Central Government), the structure of import and excise duties, retail price controls, income tax legislation, and so forth. These latter policy instruments are employed primarily in the pursuit of other development targets; but the control of the flow into the cities, not to speak of the whole question of rural-urban balance, can be other important objectives to consider in their use.

Incentive structures can be important for penetration policies in ways other than those which relate to the final decision-maker at the periphery, the farmer, in terms of the discussion above. The intermediate stages of communication and activation *within* 'the centre' may also be influenced through appropriate incentive mechanisms to the end of ultimately more effective 'penetration'.

Civil service traditions, practices, and structure, particularly those of a service until recently charged with the colonial task of preserving law and order, are unlikely to be well-suited to the pursuit of the new developmental objectives, to the achievement of developmental 'penetration'. The East African government employee has a relatively high and stable income and complete security of tenure (if not of specific posting). Extra exertion, experimentation and risk-taking, or other initiatives shown by local officials such as extension officers, earn them, unlike those for whom they are responsible and whom they are to advise, few rewards. Nor are they 'involved' directly in the trends or short-term fluctuations of world prices, the effects of weather or pests upon yields, declining soil fertility induced by improper cultivation practices or over-grazing, or the yield increases attainable through available innovations. It is true that generally successful performance in the bureaucratic structure is likely to lead to promotion but this is a very imperfect and weak incentive device for development purposes. It is certainly virtually inoperative at the field level. 'Success' in the service is, in any case, not typically measured in terms of imagination and skill in the penetration effort; rather, it tends to be a matter of faithful and reliable submission of reports and unquestioning loyalty to immediate superiors in the hierarchy. This is not to deny the existence of a minority of unrewarded, hard-working and dedicated government officers in the field. It is undoubtedly difficult for the majority, however, to sustain the necessary enthusiasm and initiative without rewards (or sanctions) based upon their performance. It should be possible to devise incentive systems in the public, parastatal and cooperative sectors to stimulate successful penetration of specific developmental behaviour patterns, such as, for example, fertilizer use. Commercial firms employ them as a matter of course and their employees typically perform more effectively in the rural penetration effort. Such systems might also play a role in penetrating the messages of hard work, initiative, and austerity, all of which tend to have a hollow ring to them when transmitted by secure and prosperous government officers who do not always appear to be participants in the struggle of which they speak.[11]

The activities of the extension service and other penetrating agents are also amenable to economic evaluation. From which innovations are the economic returns likely to be greatest? What are the probabilities of adoption of various innovations with varying degrees of extension and other staff concentration and how much do the latter varying degrees cost? What is the critical staff/farmer ratio below which results are negligible? What are the relative benefits and costs of various teaching methods and techniques, e.g. Farmer Training Centres, demonstration plots, traditional extension, etc.? What are the transport and other complementary input requirements of a successful extension service, what are their costs, and in what quantities should they be supplied? What sort of manpower planning and educational strategy should be pursued for the rural penetration effort? Out of the answers to such questions[12] should come an improved distribution among areas, crops, and activities of the present effort, and improved planning for the future, and upon them will depend the structure and the success of much of the penetration effort. These are all matters for investigation by the planning unit of the Ministry of Agriculture or the Ministry of Economic Planning or both. Other agencies and media of penetration can also be subjected to benefit/cost analysis of this type — settlement schemes, community development efforts, even the functioning of the political party.

Penetration policies may take many forms. It has been my chief concern here to demonstrate that they may be no less effective for being indirect. The manipulation of economic incentives, in particular, can be a powerful force for short-run change. At the very least it can also be an essential part of the infrastructure for the achievement of more fundamental change. In many circumstances it can even lead to these more radical behavioural changes as well.

NOTES

1.   A.O. Hirschman, *Development Projects Observed* (Brookings Institution, Washington, 1968).
2.   Jon Moris distinguishes between 'awareness' and 'participation' in 'Administrative Authority and the Problem of Effective Agricultural Administration in East Africa', *African Review*, II, 1 (1972).
3.   See, for instance, Raj Krishna, 'Agricultural Price Policy and Economic Development', H.M. Southworth and B.F. Johnston, *Agricultural Development and Economic Growth* (Cornell University Press, Ithaca, 1967), esp. 506-507.
4.   J.K. Maitha, 'A Supply Function for Kenyan Coffee', *Eastern Africa Economic Review*, I, 1 (June 1969), 63-72.
5.   Brian van Arkadie, 'Trends in the Output of Cotton and Coffee in Uganda' (EDRP Paper 70; Makerere, 1965, mimeo); Kenneth D. Frederick, 'The Role of Market Forces and Planning in Uganda's Economic Development, 1900-1938', *Eastern Africa Economic Review*, I, 1 (June 1969), 47-62.
6.   K. Johansen, 'Agricultural Planning in Tanzania', in G.K. Helleiner (ed), *Agricultural Planning in East Africa* (EAPH, Nairobi, 1968), 12.
7.   See Wolfgang F. Stolper, *Planning Without Facts* (Harvard University Press, Cambridge, 1966).
8.   For a more complete discussion of some of the following points, with particular reference to Tanzania, see my 'Agricultural Marketing in Tanzania – Policies and Problems' (ERB Paper 68. 14; Dar es Salaam, 1968).
9.   For a recent elaboration upon this point see Michael Lipton, 'The Theory of the Optimising Peasant', *Journal of Development Studies*, IV, 3 (April 1968).
10.   [For some of the problems of withdrawal see the experience of the fertiliser programme mentioned in the essay on the District Development Front (Editors)].
11.   [Cf Case Study by Thoden van Velzen in this volume (Editors)].
12.   [For an analysis of some of these answers see the essay on Extension in this volume (Editors)].

BELLE HARRIS

LEADERSHIP AND INSTITUTIONS
FOR RURAL DEVELOPMENT:
A CASE STUDY OF NZEGA DISTRICT

'To decolonize, at the very least is to remove obstacles preventing the autonomous development of the country [and] implies that all the resources that can
be derived from the existing economic system must be redirected towards the
creating of a new national economy.'[1]

INTRODUCTION

This paper starts from the premise that 'decolonization' in this sense lies at the
centre of the Tanzanian socialist development strategy put forward between
1967-1969; the essence of which is to be found in its concept of self-reliance.[2]
A major argument of this kind of strategy is that economic independence cannot be achieved by a former colony which continues to rely on foreign investments, foreign-based business institutions, and the export of primary products
in exchange for imported manufactured goods. It is argued that the most that
this would achieve would be 'growth', but not 'development', in either the
rural or the urban areas, or at the national or the local levels.[3] We shall further
recognize that an integral part of this national strategy consists of the policies
outlined in *Socialism and Rural Development*, and most particularly upon the
success of *ujamaa* villages. Therefore, a micro-study of leadership and institutions and their effectiveness in implementing this policy within a rural district is pertinent to the wider study of the realization of socialism in Tanzania.

The tactics of the national development strategy have been made explicit in
many of President Nyerere's statements.[4] To the President, 'Development
means the development of the people [but] people cannot be developed; they
can only develop themselves'.[5] The major role of 'Leadership' (not confined to
TANU — the ruling party) is 'to bring the *word* to the people'.[6] The specific
role delegated to TANU has not changed significantly from that outlined in
1962: to provide a 'strong political organization in every village which acts like

a two-way all-weather road along which the purpose and plans of the government can travel to the people at the same time as the desires and misunderstandings of the people can travel to the government'.[7] But whilst the party's prescribed role has not changed, the substantive content of the plans and policies has been spelt out in infinitely greater detail, thus, in fact imposing on it a much more exacting task than has been faced hitherto.

Tanzania, then, is attempting to implement a radical policy of economic transformation by political means. Moreover a clear choice as to method has been made, at least by the central leadership, in favour of the democratic policy of raising the level of the people's political understanding, as against the 'bureaucratic' approach of 'development from above'. Given the colonial heritage, choice of the latter would probably serve not only to consolidate former authoritarian practices;[8] it also would not, in President Nyerere's opinion, achieve its stated objective.

The prospects for the success of such a 'political approach', with its emphasis on politicization of the masses through participatory rather than bureaucratic agencies, will depend in large measure on the quality of the Party and State machine, both of which were formed during the colonial era. However, both the personnel and the structures required for democratic involvement are very weak compared with the personnel and organization of the state bureaucracy. This inherited imbalance in capabilities as between the two sets of structures inevitably enhances the strong tendency for the central bureaucracy to retain and preempt initiatives in both policy making and implementation — a tendency which inhibits the development of decentralized popular participation in terms both of the style of political activities and of the dominant interests. The existence of this immense gap between the rhetoric and the machinery for development has been stressed in the many micro-studies made by sympathetic observers of the Tanzanian 'method'. This leads one inescapably to ask whether Fanon's postulate of a syndrome of post-independence 'party disintegration' is confirmed; namely, whether in Tanzania as elsewhere the state absorbs the party until 'nothing is left but the shell..., the name, the emblem and the motto.'[9] Does, indeed, Genoud's depiction of the civil service of Ghana — 'they were competent; but... they could not apply political criteria in which they did not believe or which... were totally alien to them'[10] — characterize accurately a style and an outlook generic to all inherited bureaucratic systems in new states? And if so, is the objective of a participatory polity inherently unrealizable?

It is the aim of this paper to consider these and other questions through a case study of both the government and the political institutions at the grassroots level in Nzega District of Tanzania.[11] Within the context of the existing socio-economic and cultural structures at the local level we will examine the present functioning of these institutions and seek to assess the implications for implementing the policy objectives set forth in *Socialism and Rural Development*.

SOCIO-ECONOMIC STRUCTURE OF NZEGA[12]

The social and economic structure at the district level represents in microcosm the national neo-colonial economy, succinctly described by Reginald Green as 'concentrated, external economic dependence'.[13] The Nzega economy is dominated by the growth of primary crops (both for cash and subsistence). Cotton is the major cash crop of the north-east, rice and groundnuts are more important in the west, while in the south tobacco and food crops are most prominent. The industrial sector is confined to first-stage processing units (e.g. cotton-ginneries), small extractive units, and some building and construction works.

The trading sector again reflects the national pattern, namely, domination by non-indigenous persons. Those of Asian origin largely control the wholesale and retail trades in the towns, and also compete with those of Arab origin dominating trade in the minor settlements and outlying villages. As at the national level, there are few African businessmen, these operating mainly in the less profitable or less important sectors of the market places, such as eating-houses and bars and, in a few cases, in transport. Moreover, these businessmen are predominantly migrants to the District from other parts of Tanzania or neighbouring countries. However, local Africans monopolize positions in the cooperative societies and in political and bureaucratic organizations. These aspects of the district-level pattern illuminate the essentially colonial economy, namely, the separation between the holders of political power (including the civil service) and those of economic power. This in turn gives rise to a client/dependency relationship in which political activities take on the character of the bargaining and negotiations of the 'bazaar'. And obviously such a bargaining process does not guarantee that 'national interests' are always paramount.

There is no automatic progression from being a wealthy local peasant to becoming a local capitalist; on the contrary, the movement has seemed to be in the opposite direction, namely, the local capitalist becoming the wealthy farmer. It was quite common for those in the trading sector, whether African or non-African, to expand their interests into farming having, as they do, a better endowment of capital equipment. Also, they would be more likely to employ seasonal low-paid labourers (2-3 shillings per day), to acquire larger plots of land, to be in a position to make greater use of the extension services, and therefore have higher yields than those of less advantaged neighbouring peasants. Ironically, this has largely come about as a result of local leaders defining the word 'self-reliant' to mean 'self-sufficient' and insisting on traders combining business with cultivation. In areas of land shortage this has created obvious anomalies and hostility. One farmer deprived of his customary rights of 'usage' argued that the 'leaders used their position to get land for the Arabs'. Another that the land obtained for an *Ushirika* (communal) plot by a court order had been taken over by a local bar owner 'who is the brother of the magistrate'. Although this group of non-indigenous *nouveau riches* constitutes only a minute percentage of the population, and in absolute terms is not a very wealthy group, nevertheless the gap between its wealth and that of the peasants is ever widening, and is therefore a certain source of nascent class conflict and future tension in the district, as well as a clear impediment to the socializing of agriculture.

In such an economy it is not surprising that the demand and supply of skills outside of those related to traditional farming are extremely limited. This is reflected in the employment structure at the district level. The local trade union branch of the National Union of Tanganyika Workers (NUTA) has approximately 400 members on its books,[14] although the district comprises an area of 3,600 square miles with a population of 298,132 (1967 census). A rough estimate would place this 400 as representing about 50 per cent of the total non-casual labour force, mostly consisting of those affected by the check-off system — that is, the teachers, civil servants and district council employees. Small as it is, this employed group still constitutes the major elite group,[15] even though the inherited income structure has ensured wide differences of income with only a few at the district level in the higher brackets. In the early 1970s, salaries ranged from the majority at the bottom of the pyramid around the minimum of 186/- per month (including office messengers and TANU Branch Secretaries) to the few senior field administrators at the top around 2,000/- per month. Earnings of the latter are generally above those of such national politicians as members of the National Assembly and Area Commissioners who then received 1,166/- per month. But whatever the level, any recipient of a regular income would still be able to have a life-style setting him apart from the overwhelming majority of peasants, even when the peasants concerned could be classified as being relatively well-off, as are some of the cotton farmers in the north-east.

In Nzega, as in much of mainland Tanganyika, cash crop farming has from the beginning been entirely in the hands of indigenous farmers. There has been a remarkable expansion in cotton and tobacco in the post-independence period, and farmers have been quick to utilize such modern apparatus as insecticides, fertilizers, improved seeds and ploughs. This has reflected obvious growth, and the area is classified as relatively prosperous. Yet the prosperity that exists is characterized by a 'blocked' economy and represents only a modicum of true development. Partly this is caused by the perennial factors of limited supplies of capital; reliance on family labour; shortage of credit, water, storage units and, in some cases, of land.[16] Mostly, however, it arises from the aspirations of the farmers to acquire cattle.

The peasants of Nzega fall into a category described by Barnett as those 'whose major motivation for growing a cash crop is to strengthen and reinforce the traditional sector rather than the emergence of different interest groups.'[17] It is characterized by the combination of the growing of a cash crop and cattle ownership. About one-fifth of the total population of Tanzania falls in this category, including the Nyamwezi, the largest ethnic groupings in Nzega, who with the Sukuma inhabit the north-east. Referring specifically to the Sukuma it has been noted that: 'Many of the growers who had earned a lot of money from increased cotton production invested their money in cattle; the cattle merely changed ownership. As the land was put down to cotton production so there was less land for grazing. But as the income of the growers increased they purchased more cattle thus creating a completely new set of problems.'[18] Although there are marked differentials in earnings and land usage in Nzega, these differentials have not yet led to the emergence from the ranks of the local peasants of a 'Kulak' category, in the usual sense of a stratum of large farmer cum money lender, cum landlord, cum trader. What is likely to occur in the near future is a widening of differentials and exploitation by migrant trading-business elements, assisted or reinforced by the official elite group, with the peasantry remaining relatively unstratified.

This is particularly so as regards their life style. Consumption patterns are remarkably similar, whether a peasant earns 2,000/- p.a. or 200/- from his cotton, whether he has 50 head of cattle or five. Diet is basically the same: meat is eaten only if 'by bad luck cattle should die'. It is generally rare for children to go to school.[19] Among the poorer peasants, school fees are a barrier, while the children of the better-off are needed to look after the cattle. Almost the only items bought (or bartered) are essentials such as matches, salt and clothes. Expectations are narrow indeed. A prevalent attitude is that 'The Wageni [strangers] begin in the next village. No one accumulates for the building of schools, roads or dispensaries. Accumulation stops at one's kitchen door.'[20] This view has probably been enhanced by the abolition in December 1969 of the local poll tax, which to some extent has been replaced by a sales tax not significantly affecting Nzega peasants.

POLICY IMPLICATIONS

An immediate conclusion to be drawn from this brief survey of the local economy is that the existing organization of agricultural production in Nzega is an obstacle to improving the peasants' standard of living. It is a barrier to the accumulation of capital and even to raising consumer demand, except for cattle. It is, therefore, also a barrier to the broader development of the national economy because it makes it impossible for agriculture to serve as a base for 'the creation of the basic inputs for agro-industrial complexes, allowing nationally-based industrialization rather than the import assembly "paint, polish, and packaging type",' as Green has argued.[21]

The social and economic strategy put forward in *Socialism and Rural Development* aims at the redirection of all resources towards encouraging the development of ujamaa cooperative communities in which people 'will live together and work together for the good of all'. It is envisaged that in time these villages will become not only a vehicle for the development of diversified skills and activities as well as the centre for social services, but also the primary unit of marketing and retail cooperatives and local government. It is well recognized that this revolutionary development will undoubtedly involve a struggle on all fronts, with as wide as possible appeal being made to as many people as possible, and by leadership at all levels and of all types. As officially stated:

If this type of organization is to spread, every rural worker who understands the objective must play his part. The TANU cell-leader may in some cases be able to persuade the members in his cell to make a beginning; the Agricultural Officer may be able to persuade a group of farmers how much more he would be able to help them if they were living and working together; the community development officer who has won the confidence of the people in his area may be able to do it; or the TANU official at any level. The teacher in a primary school could help or any individual Tanzanian who understands (even if he is a Sheikh or a Padre) and whether or not he has an official position.[22]

The ultimate success of this 'frontal' transformative strategy for rural development will be determined by several distinct but interrelated aspects of the local scene. These include the differentials within the agricultural economy; the related question of the social composition of representative, implementing institutions; and the character of the different kinds of local leadership. Equally crucial will be the nature of the two-way communication network between the centre and the village and, in particular, how information passes from the centre to the people and the controls over what information reaches the centre. We shall consider each of these in turn.

ECONOMIC DIFFERENTIATION

Economic stratification with a local community has to be seen within the context of regional inequalities, and whether these are due to inherited imbalances from the colonial period or more fundamental ecological factors. Such inequalities are not likely to be automatically overcome by spontaneous development from below. Moreover, the central allocation of development resources on an equal basis between localities within a region can, and probably would, perpetuate existing inequalities. A prerequisite of the new development strategy, therefore, is a leadership knowledgeable about and sensitive to the local socio-economic structure so that development allocations and priorities do not have the effect of further enrichment of the local 'haves' at the expense of the 'have-nots'.

One can illustrate this point by taking as an example one ward[23] (Igunga) within Nzega District. Villages separated by less than 10 miles have widely differing standards of living. Of two specific villages studied,[24] one was characterized by being over-populated, with a standard of living well below even the local concept of the poverty line. The total acreage for 23 of the 26 households visited amounted to 65 acres, 44 of which were used for cotton, leaving less than one acre per household for growing food crops. In addition, 21 of the households possessed neither cattle nor goats, which offer the major local insurance against starvation in the event of adverse weather conditions. Such circumstances meant that many were forced to 'labour' for others. Many people were receptive to ujamaa but lacked the requisite spare land to 'pool' for any viable communal effort, as well as the confidence to give up the barely tolerable insecurity of the 'known' for the anxiety of the 'unknown'.

By contrast, in the second, neighbouring village, most farmers had sufficient acreage (the average was 10 acres, with a range from three to the largest holding of 45 acres, farmed by a local trader) to be able to employ casual labour, and use ploughs or tractors. They possessed cattle and goats, and (a fact which is connected!) they generally had more than one wife. In this village it was therefore possible for land to be made available for a communal plot.[25]

REPRESENTATIVE BODIES

Another relevant aspect of the common front strategy concerns the composition of the various representative bodies at the local level, namely, the TANU Branch Conferences and Committees, the Village Development Committees (up to December 1969) and the cooperative society committees.[26] Given the prevailing patterns of economic differentiation, the socio-economic status of the members of these bodies undoubtedly has some bearing on the zeal and effectiveness with which they promote the ujamaa strategy. However, the titular office holders in these organizations are also important in the local power base as they are often ex-officio delegates within the political hierarchy.

The membership of the TANU Branch Conference includes cell-leaders plus a few ward-based politicians, delegates from affiliated associations and co-opted members. Its importance lies in it being the primary electoral college for delegates to the District, Regional and National Conferences. The latter select the lists of candidates for Members of the National Assembly (MPs), who are ranked by the District Conference and approved by the National Executive Committee (NEC). The Regional Chairman, an ex-officio member of the NEC, is elected by the National Conference from among two candidates selected by the Regional Conference. The elected Members of the National Executive (MNE) are ex-officio members of the TANU Central Committee, which is self-nominated through the Regional Executive Committee, approved by the NEC and elected by the National Conference. The District Chairman, who is ex-officio chairman of the District Council, is elected by the District Conference. During the first National Conference, held at Mwanza following the Arusha Declaration, a resolution was passed to further democratise the Party by increasing the number of delegates allowed to each tier from two to ten. It was assumed that this would make it more difficult to lobby and manipulate results.

It is interesting to note the composition of the delegations chosen by Nzega District and Tabora Region for the TANU biannual National Conference held in mid-1969. The delegates were not primarily cell-leaders, and were not from the villages;[27] in some cases they were not even local people. One Branch conference included in its nominations of delegates to the District Conference all five of its appointed Village Executive Officers (VEOs); and six of its ten delegates were District Council employees. Another Branch Conference included in its list of nominees a Police Officer, the TANU Branch Secretary, a Teacher, a *Maendeleo* Assistant, and a Divisional Executive Officer. The Nzega delegation to the National Conference consisted of four Government employees (including the Police Assistant Superintendent), four District Councillors (including the Vice Chairman of the Council and a UWT Official), a religious leader (Sheikh), and the newly elected member of the National Assembly.

The immediate implication of the foregoing pattern is to doubt the effectiveness of the actual representatives in carrying out those important communication functions with which they are charged. An investigation in one area of Nzega revealed that the activities of one of its councillors were almost totally unknown to his constituents. The explanation for this general tendency lies in the fact that most Councillors reside in the town or minor settlements and have no means of travelling to the outlying villages, some of which are situated up to 25 miles from the centre of the ward. Thus, the present structure of conferences and representation does not in practice adequately ensure the performance of the essential democratic function of two-way communication between government and people.

Cooperative societies illuminate another aspect of the problem of representation. In a rural district economy with its low level of economic activity these societies provide perhaps the major, if not the sole, means for acquiring wealth. They are, therefore, inherently vulnerable to corruption. The watchdog mechanism is supposedly performed by the elected committee. Yet a study of all six societies in north-east Nzega revealed a turnover in membership during the last three years, due to 'financial shortages' of one kind or another. The membership of the new committees represented the more prosperous members of the community. Almost all possessed cattle and ploughs (in one case a tractor), and each had an average of over 10 acres of cotton and more than one wife. Almost all were migrant Sukuma from the north who were more knowledgeable about cooperatives than most locals. Most were elected by a show of hands at public meetings. Because of their relative economic affluence it is unlikely that these particular 'leaders' would be either sympathetic to, or help in campaigning for, *Socialism and Rural Development*.

The conclusion to be drawn, at least at the local level discussed herein, is

that the egalitarian prescriptions of the 'leadership resolutions' of the Arusha
Declaration, namely, the affirmation that leaders at the local level be 'peasants'
and 'workers', and not 'exploiters', have not been fully implemented or realized. The new procedures do not ensure the selection of leaders who are
representative, 'committed', and motivated to campaign for ujamaa villages.[28]

GOVERNMENT AND PARTY LEADERSHIP

Any assessment of prospects for realizing the goals of a socialist pattern of
rural development must take into consideration the quality and the orientation
of representatives of the centre. The nature of this particular stratum of the
elite in a neo-colonial economy and especially their potential role in development has been the focus of increased attention. Referring to the civil service
elite generally, Green has observed that 'In a majority of cases the pattern of
their education and life style... gives rise to attempts to deal with African realities in Western terms (no matter how strong the verbal reaction against
Western domination).' He adds that 'economic development cannot be regu-
lated, much less induced, primarily by means of complicated bureaucratic rule
books especially when the civil servants operating the rules are too few, too in-
experienced, too little grounded in applied political or technical economics and
possessed of too few instruments to detect and sanction avoidance of
evasion.'[29] Another indictment of the central bureaucratic elite is that it is an
'expensive instrument for change ... salary scales at the upper levels reflect the
level of affluence of the former colonial ruler ... resources lavished on the
means and resources unavailable for the end itself.' At the local level civil
service representation of central government reflects all of these weaknesses.

Before examining the nature and functioning of the local bureaucracy in
greater detail, one further feature of local officialdom also needs to be noted.
Many observers have been struck by the relative absence of corruption, and
particularly nepotism in Tanzania. The prevailing situation in Nzega confirms
this observation. Nepotism was virtually non-existent; indeed, almost no locally
employed Rural Development Assistant, Branch Secretary or Village Executive
Officer came from the same area within the Region. Corruption among officials
does exist — a judicial investigation of a NUTA official was in progress at the
time of the study — but outside of the cooperative societies it tends to be of a
petty and marginal nature and not the central feature of political and administrative life.

This phenomenon may reflect, in part, the influence of the Arusha Declaration, but most of all it would seem to be due to the extreme scarcity of
available jobs. In such a context it is obtaining and retaining a salaried position
which emerges as the greatest imperative. Very few alternative sources of income exist. Under these circumstances the distinctive quality of leadership becomes 'loyalty' rather than 'initiative' or 'agitation'.

THE NETWORK OF COMMUNICATIONS

It is important that local institutions be examined in terms of how they relate the village and the regional levels to the national centre. The key political pivot in this network, outside of Dar es Salaam, are the Regional and Area Commissioners. Through their offices they are able, when necessary, to control the major communication network linking the different levels of the periphery to both TANU Headquarters and to the important Ministry of Regional Administration and Rural Development. In addition, as de facto chairmen of the regional or district Development Committees (whose influence has been enhanced by their control over development funds independent of Ministry votes), commissioners have an influential power relationship with the civil servants from Ministries posted in their regions. Although these civil servants have greater career security than do the politicians, their chances for promotion or, alternatively, for transfers to 'punishment stations', are dependent upon their maintaining good local relationships, especially with the Commissioners.

The trend toward the bureaucratization of the role of Commissioners, as an attempt to raise their quality and efficiency, has not and probably will not affect the Commissioners' prominence as the nexus in the centre-periphery communication network. Indeed, this very trend only strengthens the bureaucratic ethos of 'development from above'. The commissioners have become what Bienen has called a 'regional and district oligarchy [who] dominate the flow of information to the centre.'[30] Although the Area Commissioner in Nzega had a reputation for being extremely hard-working and honest, his activities during a Parliamentary by-election in 1969 and at TANU conference meetings did illustrate his use of a wide measure of discretionary power which ensured that 'sensible' people and not 'troublemakers' were selected, thereby in turn reinforcing his own position. This bureaucratic and oligarchic tendency in local institutions and leadership undoubtedly constitutes a barrier between the President — the major exponent of development by the people — and the people themselves.

STRUCTURAL ANALYSIS OF POLITICAL AND GOVERNMENT INSTITUTIONS

Recent changes in Tanzania's formal political structure have been of a dual nature. On the one hand there has been a deconcentration of civil servants and a devolution of power from the centre to the regions, a process furthered by and reflected in the shift to regional planning of programmes, as well as regional financing from the Regional Development Fund.[31] On the other hand, there has been a concentration upwards from the former administrative unit of the Village to the Ward and Division.[32] This latter upward shift in the centre of gravity of development initiative could be a serious deterrent to the evaluation of the much-sought ethos of 'development from below'. The links between the ward and the established grassroots organization, i.e. the party cells, could be stretched so thin as to make it impossible for the ward to perform its 'two-way all weather communication function' or to be a useful instrument for politicization and mobilization.

What is taking place — and this is ironic in the post-Arusha period — is a reversion back to more administrative, authoritarian methods, a pattern of direction and penetration forced on officials by their having to travel down to the people rather than residing with the people. This pattern tends to be characterized by visits to the periphery by unknown itinerant officials who spend one day sloganizing and exhorting, and who then disappear.

This upward shift of the centre's presence at the periphery is probably explained by the failure of the higher echelons of the bureaucracy to distinguish between the structural requisites for planning and those for politicization. Democratic participation by the peasants in the implementation of plans is a necessary condition for development but it is not a prerequisite for the formulation of plans. Critics of the now-defunct Village Development Committees tended to concentrate on their deficiencies as planning units to the exclusion of their other functions.[33] However, the Village Development Committees in Nzega District functioned effectively as instruments for popular participation. They at least provided a structure through which there could be and was feedback of information, a forum for grievances, and a stage giving visibility to vested interests. Given the limitations of other media of communication in the rural areas it was also an effective structure for dissemination of information from the centre. In fact, perhaps the major weakness of the Village Development Committees was that they were too few in number.

Each of the administrative areas in Nzega served by a Village Development Committee contained between five and seven (natural) 'villages'. In each case 90 per cent of the delegates (cell leaders) on the VDC were drawn from the immediate vicinity in which the VDC meeting was held. No delegates attended from villages which were further distant than 15 and 20 miles. As a consequence, the people in many villages at the periphery were hardly involved in any kind of participation. This fact largely frustrated realization of the declared aim that: 'lower organs must discuss directives in detail in order to understand the meaning and decide on methods of implementation.'[34] One is here reminded of Aneurin Bevan's lament that 'bigness is the enemy of mankind',[35] as well as Schaffer's suggestion that the critical factor in community development 'is political, not administrative'.

Indeed, over-development of central administrative structures has many dysfunctional consequences. The bureaucratic hierarchy of a functionally organized Ministry of Community Development, Schaffer observes, 'is in fact a heavy user of administrative resources: an addition rather than a solution to the administrator's burdens [it is] committed not to output but to institution maintenance.'[36] Giving responsibility for implementing the policy of *ujamaa vijini* to the Ministry of Regional Administration and Rural Development, rather than to a strongly organized political party, will not only increase the cost of rural development, it may also be a major deterrent to spontaneous grass-roots activity.

For historical reasons there has been a tendency, which has persisted until today, for central government bodies with their more highly-trained personnel to seek remedies for the perceived failures of local organizations by establishing extensions of themselves at the regional and district levels. In the past this admittedly had the advantage of establishing a central presence. The legacy of this is the existence at the district level of numerous, fragmented, centrally-directed developmental agencies. These include fieldworkers of the Ministry of Rural Development, the Ministry of Agriculture — which includes its Veterinary, Forestry, Fisheries, Game and Co-operative sub-divisions as well as the *Bwana Shamba* (the agricultural field extension officer) of the Ministry of Health, and the District Council. The net developmental impact of this complex array of disparate agencies is certainly not commensurate with the costs involved. Most of the limited resources available for development tend to be spent on the maintenance of the separate administrative organizations and on relatively high salaries of civil service supervisory staff; the residue available for actual extension work is spread too thinly to be effective.

The immediate impression of the Party at the district level is that much of its supposed strength is a mirage. As Bienen has observed, TANU is not the strong monolithic structure which some observers 'misinterpreting success for strength', had supposed. Rather, 'the loose decentralized forms of Party organs inherited from the period of the anti-colonial struggle have not been overcome.[37] The impression of strength suggested by high membership figures is deceptive. In Nzega District, for example, membership subscriptions were collected at the livestock markets at which cooperative officers assisted the TANU Branch Secretary. Payment for subscriptions was demanded in the same manner as the local tax ('the handcuffs were on the table'). Given this bureaucratic and directed mode of eliciting popular participation in the party it is in point to speculate about the possible depressing effect on TANU subscriptions of abolishing local taxes and eliminating the position of Village Executive Officer.

A second striking feature of the Party at the district level is that power is not visibly in the hands of the rank and file members. Of course, whether it ever can be, or even should be, is another debate. In the discussions leading up to the Arusha Declaration one of the most controversial issues faced was whether TANU should remain a mass party or become a strongly organized 'vanguard' party. The formula finally accepted and embodied in the Declaration was that 'quality' rather than 'quantity' should be the criterion for party membership. At the subsequent Mwanza Conference the implied change to a more dynamic party was rejected as 'alien' and 'undemocratic' and a demo-

cratization of the formal representative structures of the party was adopted in
its stead. The main consequence of this decision was the enlargement of the
District, Regional and National Conferences of the Party. Henceforth, the
TANU bureaucracy of appointed secretaries was to have the passive role of
carrying out decisions and not a role of leadership. The consequence was the
loss of local party leadership per se.

In Nzega most of the 12 Branch Secretaries were relatively young, in their
early twenties. Four were women, three unmarried. The single qualification for
appointment was Standard VII education. Most were too young to have suffered directly from colonial rule or to have taken part in the nationalist
struggle. Their leadership capabilities were not unlike those of corresponding
Party officials in North Korea, described by Kim Il Sung: 'our party workers ...
execute directives from above in a mechanical way ... they do not know how to
analyse things independently in accordance with the lines laid down by the
centre and in conformity with the specific conditions of each locality.'[38] The
absence of any clear ideological unison among local party secretaries, coupled
with limited capabilities, places them in a weak and disadvantaged position
alongside the better-educated, more highly-trained and higher-paid, agents of
the central bureaucracy supposedly engaged in the same task of promoting
'socialist' villages![39] This relative weakness of local party leadership is not com-
pensated by other ostensible mobilizing agencies such as the TANU Youth
League, and the women's organization (UWT) which have a presence in Nzega.
Their activities usually amount to little more than rhetoric and often they do
no more than enable existing leaders to 'wear two hats'.[40] It is under these isolated circumstances that the party cell, the one body actually rooted in the
mass of the peasantry, could become an atomized and ineffectual unit.

Given the tremendous size and urgency of the task of rural development,
greater reliance is increasingly being placed by default on the central bureaucracy and its extensions at the periphery. The task of mobilization is de facto
being centred not upon a monolithic party but a monolithic Ministry of Regional Administration and Rural Development: the commonly-accepted concept of 'The Leader' is a bureaucrat and not a representative, or a 'cadre'.

The country of Tanzania and its President have inspired great hope in a
wider audience than that of Tanzania. It is held up as an example of how a
form of socialism, geared to local needs, can succeed in raising the quality of
life of its people without recourse to either authoritarian rule or the more in-
sidious neo-colonialism. There are many inherited problems left unresolved at
both the local and the national levels, but an overall strategy appropriate for
achieving this path has been laid down. This paper has concentrated on the
characteristics of the personnel and structures through which this strategy is to
be implemented. A concentration on their inadequacies for the task has been
intentional because of the belief that Tanzania still has the possibility for
avoiding the mistake made elsewhere of neglecting to transform its party and
governmental institutions into a more relevant form.

APPENDIX ONE
POLITICAL INFRASTRUCTURE (DECEMBER 1969)

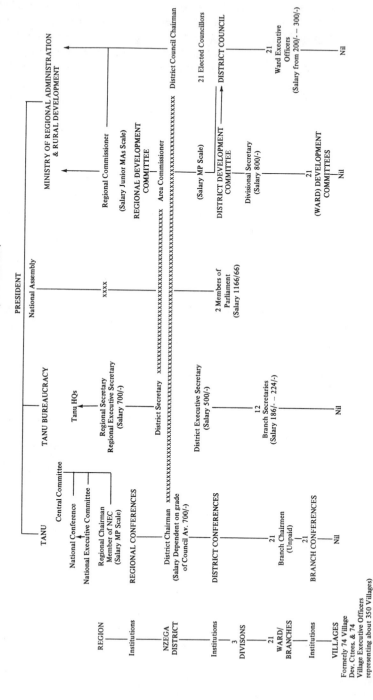

Appendix Two

INFRASTRUCTURE OF NZEGA DISTRICT

I.   Nzega District (Tabora Region) 3,600 sq. miles. Population 298,132 1967 census.

II.   *Estimated crops for sale 1969*: Cotton 310,000 Bales; Rice and Paddy 60,000 tons; Groundnuts 18,000 tons; Maize 7,000 tons; Millet 4,000 tons; Hides and Skins 1,000 tons. (Tobacco goes through the Tabora distributive network.)

III.   Revenue earned from the Council *List of Licensed Businesses* (Estimate for 1969): Trading 50,000/-; Intoxicating Liquor Licences 15,000/-; Local Liquor Licences 376,000/-; Grain Licences; Forest Licences 100/-. Also Butcher Licence Fees 18,000/-; Hide Drying fees 100/-. Bicycle discs 53,000/-.

IV.   *Hospital and Dispensaries*: There are three hospitals with resident doctors, plus 21 Dispensaries under the District Council and eight under the Missionaries without doctors. Sixteen out of the 29 Dispensaries have clinics. Also there is one Health Centre.

V.   *Roads*: There is no tarmac road within the District. The major trunk roads passing through the District are all-weather roads. All other roads are often closed in the rainy season (3-4 months of the year).

VI.   *Public Works*: The Town Council has one Garage and one Workshop – Comworks is reponsible for all main roads – and a total of 13 Government Landrovers – 2 Comworks; 3 Medical; 5 Agriculture; 1 Education, 2 Police; 2 Community Development, which have been donated to them.

VII.   *Training Centres*: Two Homecraft; One Mandeleo and Farmers Training Centre particularly for ploughing.

VIII.   *Post Offices*: One main post office – one departmental office. Three sub-post offices.

IX.   *Banks*: No permanent bank in the District. Since Nationalisation a mobile unit operates once a week.

X.   *Cooperative Societies* (which also act as agents for the National Agricultural Products Board): thirty-five Cooperative Societies were opened between 1961 and 1967. Additional collection points may be set up during the harvest season.

XI.   *Courts*: One District Court; 19 Primary Courts and approximately 11 Magistrates.

XII.   *Police*: 1 District Police Headquarters; One Class C Police Station and one Mobile Police Station. One District Prison and one Prison Farm to be opened.

XIII.   *Phone booths*: Three, two of which are in Nzega Town.

XIV.   Ten *Dams* and Water Reservoirs.

XV.   *Markets*: Eleven permanent Livestock Markets and three others in dry season only. Approximately 20 food markets.

XVI.   *Schools*: 16 Local Authority primary schools. 32 White Fathers' primary schools, One Seminary and Teacher Training College; 11 Pentecost Church primary schools; 9 Moravian Mission, 7 Muslim Schools (75 in all). Most would now come under the control of the Ministry of Education (in addition there are 4-6 TAPA schools). Only approximately 15 percent of these would have classes for standards VI and VII.

XVII.   *Taxi cabs*: None.

APPENDIX THREE

POLITICAL & EXTENSION STRUCTURE – IGUNGA WARD (HEADQUARTERS OF IGUNDA DIVISION)

Population: 29,857   622 sq. miles

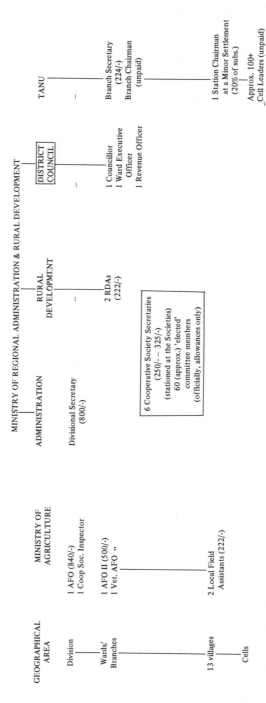

MINISTRY OF REGIONAL ADMINISTRATION & RURAL DEVELOPMENT

GEOGRAPHICAL AREA	MINISTRY OF AGRICULTURE	ADMINISTRATION	RURAL DEVELOPMENT	DISTRICT COUNCIL	TANU
Division	1 AFO (840/-) 1 Coop Soc. Inspector	Divisional Secretary (800/-)	–	–	–
Wards/Branches	1 AFO II (500/-) 1 Vet. AFO ,,		2 RDAs (222/-)	1 Councillor 1 Ward Executive Officer 1 Revenue Officer	Branch Secretary (224/-) Branch Chairman (unpaid)
13 villages	2 Local Field Assistants (222/-)	6 Cooperative Society Secretaries (250/– – 325/-) (stationed at the Societies) 60 (approx.) 'elected' committee members (officially, allowances only)			1 Station Chairman at a Minor Settlement (20% of subs.)
Cells					Approx. 100+ Cell Leaders (unpaid)

Notes: 1. The new position of Divisional Secretary will now be the main coordinator below the district level, between Regional Administration – Rural Development – (Ward) Development Committee and TANU Branch.

2. Prior to the Local Government changes of 1969-70 there were within Igunga Ward three Village Executive Officers and three Village Development Committees.

NOTES

1.   Roger Genoud, *Nationalism and Economic Development in Ghana* (Frederick A. Praeger, New York, 1969), 12.

2.   In Tanzania's first Five Year Plan (1964-69) the major anticipated source of development funds was foreign — the basic generator of rural development was to be the establishment of highly capitalized 'model' villages. Thus the subsequent failure to attract these funds — partly explained by Tanzania's independent foreign policy (see 'Principles and Development' by J.K. Nyerere; Dar es Salaam, 1966) and partly due to Nairobi being a more 'attractive' base for investment (as well as an absolute fall in sisal prices) — created a situation in which the fundamental assumptions of development and economic independence had to be re-examined.

3.   A classical statement of this distinction can be found in A. Gunder Frank, 'The Development of Underdevelopment', *Monthly Review* (New York, September 1966).

4.   These statements provide the main body of principle of the 'Tanzanian method' although often more than this is claimed for them. For example, Henry Bienen: *Tanzania Party Transformation and Economic Development* (Princeton University Press, Princeton, 1970), quotes on p. 459: 'One man is both source and articulator of the stated principles'; this would seem to be an overstatement, for the source must be the total situation of the Tanzanian society — the essence of its leadership in this case is the unique ability of President Nyerere to concretize this in the 'language of the people'.

5.   Julius K. Nyerere, 'Freedom and Development' (Dar es Salaam, 1969).

6.   Quoted from an interview in the *Daily Nation* (Nairobi, August 1968).

7.   Julius K. Nyerere, 'Independence Message to TANU' (December 1961), reprinted in his *Freedom and Unity: Uhuru na Umoja* (Oxford University Press, Dar es Salaam, 1966).

8.   J.S. Coleman and C.G. Rosberg (eds), *Political Parties and National Integration in Tropical Africa* (University of California Press, Berkeley, 1964), 659, describes the colonial period as 'bureaucratic authoritarianism'.

9.   Frantz Fanon, *The Wretched of the Earth* (Penguin Edition, Harmondsworth, 1965), 136.

10.   Genoud, *Nationalism and Economic Development in Ghana*, 218, 164.

11.   In particular reference will be made to Nzega District and one Ward within that District: Igunga Ward. This stems from field work undertaken whilst participating in an interdisciplinary project under the auspices of the Bureau of Resource Assessment and Land Use Planning, University College, Dar es Salaam from April to August 1969. Nzega is one of the Northern Districts within Tabora Region. The South and West is populated mainly by the Nyamwezi; the North-East is mixed but predominantly Sukuma.

12.   See Appendix One, The Infrastructure of Nzega District.

13.   Reginald Green, 'Political Independence and the National Economy' in Christopher Allen and R.W. Johnson (eds), *African Perspectives* (Cambridge, 1970). Many other writers have also analyzed the implications of this 'dependent' relationship. These include: Frantz Fanon, *The Wretched of the Earth*, 120; Andre Gunder Frank, *Latin America: Underdevelopment or Revolution* (Monthly Review Press, New York, 1970; e.g. Part III); Roger Genoud, *Nationalism*, 85-224 & 255; R. Dumont, *False Start in Africa* (Andre Deutsch, London, 1966), 46-52 & 276; G. Arrighi and J. Saul, 'Socialism and Economic Development in Tropical Africa', *Journal of Modern African Studies*, VI: R.H. Green and A. Seidman, *Africa Unity or Poverty?* (Penguin, Harmondsworth, 1968), e.g. pp. 91-94; H. Alavi, 'Imperialism Old and New' in R. Miliband and J. Saville (eds), *The Socialist Register 1964* (Merlin Press, London, 1964); and Gavin Williams, 'Social Stratification of a Neo-colonial Economy' in Allen & Johnson, *African Perspectives*, e.g. p. 239 (proofcopy).

14.   The construction of a dam in North-East Nzega was at that time the largest employer of labour — 300 including casual labour.

15.   As many observers have noted of Tanzania there is an absence of a traditional elite with an entrenched economic-political base. This seemed to be particularly true among the Sukuma cotton farmers — almost all of whom had moved southwards from various places in the North and were new to the area, and as a consequence seem to possess very loose 'traditional' ties.

16. In a sample of 100 farmers selected from a larger sample of 700 farmers in Igunga Ward, 9 percent only owned a radio, but 49 percent a bicyle and 55 percent a plough.

17. To the question 'If you had more money what would you buy?', 62 percent mentioned cattle, radios were only mentioned twice and school fees three times. The quotation is from D. Barnett, 'Three Types of African Peasants' (mimeographed, n.d.).

18. G.L. Cunningham, 'Problems of Mobilisation in the Rural Areas' (cyclostyled Paper, Dar es Salaam).

19. The figure given for school enrolment in Nzega is 39 out of 1,000 and it is further estimated that this represents a figure of only 19 percent of the school-age population who get to attend standard VII and thereby complete their primary education (Sam Rae, unpublished thesis). These figures would be considerably lower if confined to the rural areas.

20. See *Report on Four Villages in Igunga Ward* by the author (BRALUP, September 1969).

21. Green, 'Political Independence', p. 312 (proof copy).

22. Julius K. Nyerere, 'Socialism and Rural Development' in *Freedom and Socialism* (Oxford University Press, Dar es Salaam, 1969), 357-358.

23. The ward is the primary political constituency for local government and is coterminous with the TANU Branch. In most rural districts there is one elected councillor for each ward. See Appendix Two.

24. Harris, *Report on Four Villages*.

25. A similar pattern to the above also applied to the four ujamaa villages in the locality – three of them TANU Youth League settlements renamed as ujamaa. These have been written up in a separate report.

26. TANU Youth League and TAPA (Tanganyikan African Parents Association) have not been included as they were largely defunct in Nzega District.

27. David Abernethy (cyclostyled paper, Dar es Salaam).

28. A 'leader' is classified as anyone holding a political position from the cell-leader upwards and also any government employee in the higher and middle-level income bracket.

29. Green, 'Political Independence', 312-313.

30. Bienen, *Tanzania Party Transformation and Economic Development*.

31. This fund consists of a flat-rate of 1,000,000 shillings annually given to each of the 17 regions for developmental purposes.

32. The 'Village' (usually an artificial unit, equivalent to a 'parish') was previously the lowest administrative unit and had its own Development Committee and Executive Officer; these are now amalgamated into the slightly bigger Ward.

33. For example Stanley Dryden writes: 'Many village plans submitted to the District Development Committee were scarcely legible and were written on any scrap of paper, which came to hand', *Local Administration in Tanzania* (East African Publishing House, Nairobi 1966); or, on the same theme, an Economic Research Bureau Paper argues 'the most crucial limiting factor in the entire regional planning process is the lack of skilled manpower able to plan and evaluate programmes and projects properly most striking in the lowest organisational forms'.

34. Mao-Tse-Tung, *Selected Works*, Vol. I (Foreign Languages Publishing House, Peking, 1965), 108-109.

35. Quoted in Bernard Crick's 'Gaitskell Memorial Lecture' (19 January 1968).

36. B. Schaffer, 'The Crisis in Development Administration' in C. Leys (ed), *Politics and Planning in Developing Areas* (Cambridge University Press, Cambridge, 1969).

37. Kim il Sung, *Selected Writings*, Vol. II (Pyongnyang), 46.

38. Ibidem.

39. See Appendix Three.

40. For instance, the Member of the National Executive was also the TYL Chairman; the MP was a UWT official.

IV

DISTRICT POLITICS AND RURAL TRANSFORMATION

G.B. LAMB

PROMOTING AGRARIAN CHANGE:
PENETRATION AND RESPONSE IN MURANG'A, KENYA

Since Independence a consistent aim of Kenya Government policy has been to extend administrative capacity to control events in the countryside. In particular, offices of the Provincial Administration have been given extended power especially over 'development' activities, and the staffs of technical departments have been expanded. What this paper will do is to discuss how far this extension of administrative controls in the formal sense has actually increased governmental capacity to influence rural society. Clearly, this kind of question has policy implications, about organizational structures and bureaucratic behaviour as well as about the content of 'rural development' programmes themselves, but these are not the central concern here. What I wish to concentrate on is the social and political environment of rural development administration, and in particular on the capacity of bureaucratic institutions to receive, assess and adapt to information from that environment.

I want to do this by examining two very different areas of rural development policy in Murang'a District as they were implemented during one important phase in the recent past:[1] (a) the set of measures intended to control the output and quality of coffee, the district's and Kenya's main export crop; and (b) the promotion of self-help activities under the aegis of the Department of Community Development.

These are both 'sensitive' areas of policy in the sense that they are closely concerned with the cash income of the Murang'a peasantry (or rather of that 30 percent or so who are officially coffee growers), and with the provision of highly valued rural services. They are also very directly related, as will be seen, to questions of stratification, the distribution of political power, and the allocation of state resources — indeed, it is precisely the inter-connections between those issues which are usually designated 'administrative' and those which are clearly political which this paper will try to illumine in a way which has some relevance to debates about inducing and controlling change in rural communities.

*   *   *

Government coffee policy problems in independent Kenya have chiefly been those of careful limitation of production and of quality control. These aims were largely determined by a desire to remain in good standing with the International Coffee Organization, thereby enabling Kenya to sell the great bulk of its coffee on International Coffee Agreement 'quota markets' — i.e. the large consuming countries of Western Europe and North America whose prices, as consumer signatories of the Agreement, have historically been markedly higher than coffee prices in non-quota markets. Although Kenya only signed the Agreement in September 1966, it had adhered rigidly to ICO regulations before that date, and had in fact introduced fairly drastic measures to control coffee production — control of production being, of course, the main requirement which the ICO imposes on its producer members, with the sanction of a cut in the quota tonnage of any country which violates the Agreement. The Kenya Government sought to conform to ICO requirements (and to its own assessment of marketing possibilities) by banning new planting of coffee in 1964, about two years after the planting rush by African growers which began as Department of Agriculture control broke down with the advent of independence. Even after new planting had been prohibited, however, it was clear that controls were being circumvented by growers buying seedlings ostensibly for infilling (i.e. for filling in the gaps caused by dead or diseased trees) and in fact using them for new planting. By January 1967, therefore, Government regulations provided for an infilling allowance to individual growers of no more than 2 percent of their total tree numbers in any one year. Furthermore, illegal new planting, it was threatened, would be combatted by the appointment of coffee inspectors, with power to order the uprooting of illegally-planted trees and the prosecution of their owners.

Murang'a District's growers were severely affected by these provisions, more especially since uncertainties prompted by land consolidation problems in the district in the early 1960s had prevented Murang'a peasants from planting as much coffee at that time as they would otherwise have wished. There were a number of ways in which farmers could hope to circumvent the new limitations: by simply ignoring them, and hoping that the infringement would not be discovered, or by paying some degree of attention to the law by purchasing seedlings from cooperative society nurseries ostensibly for infilling purposes and then using them for new planting. Certainly during the rains of 1966 (when only slightly less onerous limitations on infilling had been in force), growers had planted out approximately three times as many trees as the Director of Agriculture's estimate of their legitimate allowance, his estimate being based on the district's 1964 authorised acreage of 20,661 acres. This wholesale breach of regulations had been accompanied by an intricate battle of wits between Department of Agriculture officials in the district, who were responsible for enforcing planting control, and growers' leaders. The growers were represented by the committees of individual coffee cooperative societies (16 in

Murang'a) and by the leadership of the Murang'a Farmers' Cooperative Union, the district union to which each primary society was affiliated. During 1966, the conflict had mainly taken the form of long arguments over the 'true' acreage of coffee in the district (and therefore, of course, about permissible infill levels) — arguments which were based on a Department of Agriculture tree census and a rival register of growers and trees by the cooperatives themselves.

By 1967, however, the situation had changed, with a further reduction of the infill allowance, and the threat of coffee inspectors with powers to uproot African coffee. It was at this point that the limitations on administrative action became apparent, as officers at the local level were faced with an issue which became politicized through the efforts of the most influential growers' leaders — those coming from the southern division of the district, Kandara. The Kandara leadership set out, in the early months of 1967, to mobilize the Union to take an active political part in the struggle against restrictions, and later to involve the district's KANU organization and the district's four Members of Parliament. The effect on administrative behaviour was quickly apparent: officers of the Department of Agriculture sought to withdraw from the developing conflict as much as possible, both because of the risks involved in incurring the hostility of the most powerful section of the Murang'a farming community, the coffee growers, and because it soon became apparent to local officials that they could not be certain of wholehearted support either from their departmental superiors or from the District Commissioner.[2] The reasons for the reticence of technical officers, and especially for the hesitancy of the District Commissioner when faced with quite a substantial threat to order and good government in the district, have much to do with the relationship between local peasant hierarchies and the national centres of power.

In Murang'a, the years immediately before and after independence had been a period of intense factional conflict within the district's KANU organization. Conflict revolved around the two outstanding politicians in the district, Bildad Kaggia (who had been tried and imprisoned with Kenyatta for allegedly organizing 'Mau Mau'), and Dr. Julius Kiano, a prominent member of the 'new generation' of Kenyan politicians who had emerged during the 1950s when the leaders of the nationalist movement were all in prison or detention camps. From the beginning, the competition between the two men and their followers had strong ideological overtones: where Kiano had sought, since his entry into the Legislative Council in 1958, to act as a unifier of pro- and anti-'Mau Mau' Kikuyu, Kaggia emphasized the social and economic cleavages which the Emergency had reinforced in the Kikuyu areas, and demanded strong Government action to rectify the grievances of former detainees and forest fighters.[3] In the period 1964-65, these differences widened into a bitter conflict over land, socialism and the distribution of development resources, and conflict over the control of the KANU branch: Kaggia and his group succeeded in wresting control of the executive from Kiano in August 1964, but they were unseated in May 1965 in a 'coup' which coincided with a nationwide series of KANU branch elections which resulted in the defeat of leading radicals and followers of the party's and the country's Vice-President, Oginga Odinga. During 1965, too, as the ideological conflicts developed in Nairobi between Odinga and his supporters and their conservative opponents, President Kenyatta made several trips to Murang'a to rally support for the Kiano group.

In Kandara division itself, where Kaggia had his constituency and his political base, the conflict was even more intense, and its social basis and ideological nature even more explicit. Kaggia was opposed at this level by Taddeo Mwaura, until September 1965 the Senator for Murang'a District. Mwaura, although a former detainee, had aligned himself emphatically with the conservatives at the local level, and in particular had emerged as the political representative of the larger coffee growers and the African traders. His political message was neatly summarised by the DC in his report for 1965 as being 'work hard, forget the past and buy land'; whereas Kaggia was defined as wanting 'free land and the dismissal of colonial civil servants to be replaced by forest fighters'. If Mwaura had powerful support at the local level, however, he had no claim to independent political status in the district as a whole or nationally. Kiano's relationship with Mwaura (which had been forged largely as a response to the threat of ex-detainee militants taking over KANU) possessed a degree of tension which accurately reflected the social groups from which the two men drew support: in the Kangema, Kiharu and Kigumo divisions Kiano's supporters included many poor people and ex-detainees who were for the most part hostile to the Mwaura group, which was clearly seen in the district as the political vehicle of the Home Guards[4] and the rich. Although Mwaura was defeated in his campaign for re-election to the Senate in 1965 (largely because Kiano, perhaps aware of the political ambitions of the powerful group of Kandara peasant leaders who backed Mwaura, conspicuously failed to support him), the influence of his local support in Kandara division was such that, when Kaggia finally split from KANU along with Odinga in March 1966 and was standing for re-election to Parliament as Kenya People's Union (KPU) candidate[5] for Kandara, Mwaura secured the KANU nomination over the strenuous objections of Kiano (the district branch chairman) and of the national secretary of KANU, Tom Mboya. Mwaura won the election, after a violent election campaign and KPU complaints of electoral fraud. Thus, what had become clear during the course of the political struggles in the district was that there existed in Kandara a powerful, cohesive and independent group of wealthy peasants who were capable of enforcing autonomy from the district and the national political organizations, and acting decisively to advance their interests. During 1964-66, their interests were best served by sponsoring Mwaura; it is clear that his limited political impact in subsequent years persuaded them to abandon him in favour of other politicians.[6]

But it was not only by purely political action through established political channels that the interests of the wealthier peasants were fostered. The above outline of the coffee control issue clearly demonstrated that they had gained considerable power within the cooperative movement. In fact, the wealthier growers and in particular those from Kandara (which contains over half of the total Murang'a coffee acreage, insofar as this can be accurately estimated), were soon to dominate both local primary societies and the district Union.

In the early months of 1967, Mwaura and other Kandara KANU leaders began to hold 'growers meetings', at which resolutions were passed urging that no African coffee should be uprooted, and that Government should rescind the control policy, At the same time Kandara cooperative societies' delegates to the Union management committee tried to ensure that the Union would not cooperate, whatever it felt itself obliged to say formally, in the centralization of seedling supply or in any of the other planting control measures. And, increasingly, the political campaign within the coffee societies was extended to the other divisions.

Ultimately, the KANU organization in the district outside Kandara was compelled to become involved. It had at first tried to stand aloof from the growers' discontent, since KANU participation would involve an attack on the Government of which Kiano was a Minister. But growers' leaders in Kiharu, Kangema and Kigumo exerted pressure on their political representatives to join with Mwaura and the Kandara leaders in pressing the Government to rescind the planting restrictions. The political campaign in Murang'a culminated in a KANU-convened meeting of political and cooperative leaders in the County Council chambers in May 1967, at which a series of uncompromising anti-restriction resolutions were passed. There followed a special meeting of the Union, which appointed a delegation to visit the Minister of Agriculture.

The real significance of the campaign, however, was that it succeeded in uniting the political organization of the district, and the cooperative movement as well, behind the demands of the coffee growers, demands which had been articulated most forcefully and effectively by the wealthiest coffee growers. This was the important feature of the Murang'a campaign for Government, that the control policies were faced with a militantly hostile and unanimous opposition in a politically very sensitive district. Moreover such powerful Kikuyu political figures as Kiano and the Murang'a Cooperative Union 'patron', ex-Senior Chief Ndung'u Kagori, interceded directly with the President to secure rescindment of the control measures.

It is also clear that a major danger from the Government's point of view was that the conflict would be broadened into a more general critique of rural development policy: indeed, the Murang'a campaign indicated that this is precisely what was starting to occur. The restriction issue brought into focus other, related grievances — over what the growers saw as discrimination by the Ministry of Agriculture in favour of the existing large European coffee estates, and over the levies and taxes extracted from coffee growers by Government and by the complex Kenya coffee bureaucracy.

The outcome of the campaign was a straightforward victory for the growers, with an announcement (made, significantly, at a KANU rally in Murang'a) that the President had personally ordered that all uprooting of African coffee was to cease immediately. This was, of course, tantamount to saying that control was being abandoned, since coffee inspectors were deprived of their only effective sanction against illegal planting.

Murang'a political leaders were thus able to effect a decisive change in Government development policy. The economic and social effects of their defeat of control measures have not been clear, however; if Government's assessment of Kenya's coffee production problems was right, the effects of the failure of control might have been expected to be severe indeed from 1970 onwards, as the freely planted 'illegal' trees came into bearing. At that stage, the problems of tight ICA quotas and chronic over-production would have been accentuated, forcing on growers and Government alike a new and even more costly set of political choices.

This has not been the case, however: Kenyan coffee production was seriously affected by disease in 1967 and 1968, exacerbated by extended rain in the latter half of 1967. Weather and disease accomplished what Government could not: production dropped by nearly 9,000 tons in 1967 and by a further 8,000-odd in 1968, making the total production of 39,600 tons in 1968 some 30 percent below the 1966 figure.[7] Aside from the breathing space resulting from under-production, however, the 1969 Development Plan showed evidence of a new approach to marketing possibilities in non-quota countries. In this initiative, so firmly resisted in 1967 and before, the Government's awareness of the political problems of production control can have played no small part.

*   *   *

The outcome of the coffee control issue emphasized one aspect of the problem of penetration and rural administrative control. The problem for Government officers here was largely political and external, in that the political connections between the rural groups with which they were trying to deal, and the national elite, were so direct and so strong that it was not only impossible to succeed in implementing control, but even somewhat inadvisable to try, despite the array of formal powers available to both technical and administrative officals at the local level.

In the case of the second area of policy to be discussed here, that of community development, the difficulties could again be described as political, but were of a rather different kind. They involved questions of the distribution of political power within the district itself rather than lines of influence running to the capital, and 'internal' political questions as well — that is, considerations of conflict, status and power within the administrative apparatus itself.

Community development is more directly concerned with political themes, and more susceptible to local-level political influences, than many other areas of 'development' activity. The norms of self-help are those of popular participation, of the democratic control and utilization of resources, of a conscious effort to 'modernize' attitudes and create capacities and desires which were not present before. Community development administrators hope to instil an awareness not only of 'community', but of the individual citizen's relationship to Government, and of the responsibility which both bear in the ordering of economic and social life (the fact that the picture drawn of this relationship by the development agent may be a highly idealized one brings its own problems, of course).[8] At least in the short term, however, perhaps more important than the 'social consciousness' aspect is the fact that community development programmes involve the formation of formal, localised groups with broad social objectives and some economic resources. Particularly in rural areas, where few non-government organizations exist, local self-help groups or community development committees offer both a training ground and a political arena for local political actors, and a potential constituency of organized support for local politicians.

It is clear that Kenya community development differs substantially from the 'ideal', and from some other approaches. In keeping with its origins in the colonial period in such programmes as communal terracing, it carries strong administrative overtones (i.e. less emphasis on *animation rurale* and communal goal-setting, more on administrative control and identification of desirable projects). In addition, the programmes and controls are seen as complementary to and subordinate to the requirements of economic planning.[9] The character of the programme — directed, bureaucratized and bearing an uncertain relationship to other administrative functions at the local level — implied problems of accommodation and reconciliation for the community development officers responsible.

The most important aspect of community development work in Murang'a in the late 1960s was undoubtedly the building of self-help secondary schools — the so-called Harambee schools. The enthusiasm with which the idea of communally-built secondary schools was taken up in Kenya after the idea was put forward by President Kenyatta in 1964 had quickly created problems of staffing, standards and recurrent finance — problems which, inevitably, involved pressure on Government to take over the schools, and Government determination to resist such manipulation and ensure minimum standards of planning and budgeting.[10]

If Harambee schools were quickly seen to incur economic costs, in the form of a drain on teaching resources and on the small capacity of local communities, they thus also became a liability in political terms. As well as leading to the demands for Government to take over the running and financing of the schools, the difficulties and, in many cases, outright failure of the schools had repercussions on community development programmes and on the propagation of the self-help ethic. The Government response was firstly to demand that local communities be able to show a capital of £2,000 before being permitted to register a Harambee school, and secondly to state that no self-help school building should be built without the approval of the Development Committee of the Cabinet.[11]

Again, the formal controls were comprehensive. Through the Community Development Officer, Government could exercise a Cabinet veto over the building of Harambee schools, while the County Education Officer checked on the capital requirements before registering a school. At the same time — and this was an important part of the whole process of control of self-help activities — local community development groups were dependent on the Community Development Officer, and through him on the District Commissioner, for a permit to collect money for their projects.

There were, however, gaps in the system as it actually operated. Neither the Community Development Officer nor the Education Officer had on file any circular, nor were they aware of any order, requiring them to submit Harambee school building plans to Nairobi for the approval of the Cabinet, for example. But more important than these administrative shortcomings were, once again, the political pressures on government officials. The impetus toward school building was so strong in many parts of the district, that it could not be resisted without serious damage to other community development objectives for the area. Moreover, popular pressure to start schools was often assisted and sometimes initiated by county councillors, who were in a position to exert considerable influence over the Community Development Department's allocations, since local authorities provided the recurrent budget for all departmental staff and expenses, with the exception of the CDO himself and his driver.

What emerged, then, was a mode of operation on the part of the Community Development Department which involved (a) some manipulation of local political conflicts, mainly taking the form of using financial sanctions to prevent factional competition hurting self-help programmes; (b) accommodation of the community development structure to the most powerful and aggressive political forces at work in the self-help groups — the Kandara conservatives; and (c) the adoption of brokerage and mediating roles by the Community Development Officer, as between County Council and District Commissioner.

The origin of conservative control of self-help in Kandara lay in the factional struggles of 1964-65, and particularly in the activities of the *Atiririri Bururi* Union (roughly Union of Patriots), an organization founded by the Kandara elite in this period to oppose Kaggia, who then had control of the district KANU organization. The self-help groups had offered a favourable constituency for conservative leaders, since the groups were very often built up from local school committees. During the Emergency, the committees were composed, under British control, of (mainly Christian) loyalists and Home Guards; in many cases, these committees had retained their positions in the school system, either because of missionary patronage or because of the absence of any electoral procedures for challenging them. Mwaura and his colleagues thus had a sympathetic base in the self-help structure from which to attack Kaggia — a fact of which Kaggia was very well aware.[12] But there were also broader considerations. The rhetoric of the Mwaura group emphasized the themes of patriotism, national unity and self-help; more specifically, the Atiririri Bururi Union propagated the view that the conflicts of the past, between those who had supported the colonial power during the Emergency and those who had opposed it, should be forgotten and buried in a new Kenya founded on hard work and individual initiative. The District Commissioner's summary of the group's view, quoted earlier, as 'work hard, forget the past and buy land' is precise in that the Union's propaganda, while broadly similar to the unifying themes of KANU, laid much more emphasis on the bourgeois virtues of self-achievement and private ownership. Community development and self-help, of course, did not conflict with this ethic at all; rather, it offered a vision of 'socialism' which did not include the socialization of property, but which at the same time offered some opportunity of advancement and the provision of services to the poor who might otherwise have been hostile to the Union and its wealthy supporters. Mwaura and his followers were thus assiduous in supporting self-help activities in Kandara: while this fitted in well with the group's general political outlook, they also perceived that it was essential to prevent Kaggia's supporters from extending their influence into this field.

The administrative-political style which the Community Development Officer had evolved — one which was based, incidentally, on a fairly long stay in the district — could not cope with this kind of polarization. The CDO had evolved rules which enabled him to identify the types of project which would incur political interest, and the sorts of decision which would enable political interference or conflict to be minimized. Thus his actions vis-à-vis the County Council were designed to eliminate interference from one important category of politicians and at the same time increase his own influence with them, by making himself valuable to the Council generally and to individual councillors as an advisor and as a mediator between local authority and the local representatives of the central government. As far as particular projects or parts of the district were concerned, the CDO's concern was to manage conflict engendered by the activities of his Department by distributing prestige (membership or chairmanship of committees, sharing the platform at *barazas*, and so forth) among a wide section of 'secondary' local leaders, while avoiding prominent politicians, chiefs and other civil servants.

In Kandara, however, his Department was compelled to back out of the dispute in the self-help movement between the supporters of Mwaura and those of Kaggia. After an initial attempt to bring about the personal agreement of Kaggia and Mwaura that they would refrain from politicizing community development activities had failed, the CDO had to accept the structure of self-help in Kandara as it existed, albeit with an acute appreciation of the implications of Mwaura's dominance of self-help:

It's a difficult situation there. You see, the KANU group has now got the support of the
self-help groups, or nearly all of them. Now it is difficult for us, because they are doing
good work, and also they are the supporters of *Mzee* and the call of Harambee in the
division, and Kaggia always wants to obstruct. But now we have this thing that is troubling
us: sometimes these Mwaura people have caused some trouble, and the people get a bit dissatisfied with the way things are going. And then they think we are one with them [i.e.
with the Mwaura group], so in some areas some of them have gone to the KPU people with
their complaints, and Kaggia says the Government and Community Development are discriminating, and this leads to quite a lot of bad feeling. But now there is nothing we can
do — we must work with the groups which are there, and they are the ones who want to
develop the country in the spirit of Harambee... It is always political trouble that causes
our difficulties. [13]

In the Kandara case, of course, the problem for the CDO was that he was
not faced with a number of isolated local conflicts, but with a division-wide
political dispute which had involved the self-help groups, and which by its
nature could not be dealt with by the methods he had evolved. Short of re-
making the Kandara self-help structure virtually from scratch, which would
have involved more resources than he possessed (aside from the far more crucial factor of the unacceptable *political* costs of trying to do so), he had little
alternative but to support the dominant group with money and with administrative services — at the same time being unhappily aware of the potential
future costs of that line of action.

                                    *   *   *

Governmental capacity in the rural sector thus emerged, in the Murang'a case,
as subject to severe political constraints. The structure of local politics, the distribution of local political power, exercised a decisive influence on the outcome of important administrative programmes, notwithstanding the impressive
centralization of bureaucratic authority and the array of formal powers which
administrators possessed at the district level.

The really interesting questions in this situation, however, lie less in the
ability of aggressive rural leaders to divert development resources or prevent
the implementation of policies unfavourable to them, than in the socio-
economic characteristics of the leadership groups, and the degree to which
their successes are cumulative. In Kandara, there seemed strong evidence that
the activities of the wealthier peasants represented the beginnings of self-
conscious action, on *class* lines, in a rural political situation which had hitherto
been defined in terms of location or faction: in other words, that the social
stratification which had been set in train by colonialism, and immeasurably
speeded up in the 1950s and 1960s, was leading to a redefinition of the criteria
of status and power by the dominant rich peasant group which had come to
dominate Kandara — and indeed Murang'a — politics once Kaggia had been
ejected from prominence. This tendency, it must be emphasized, is as yet uncertain and embryonic: while there are some data about landholdings and in-

comes which tend to support propositions about the growing importance of class in the Murang'a countryside,[14] there are also many countervailing pressures operating as well. Not least among them, in the Murang'a setting, has been the influence of the central government, which Murang'a politicians spent so much of their energy — often successfully — opposing, but which has nevertheless operated to paper-over processes of rural stratification. It has had some success in blurring class differences by emphasizing ethnic and factional modes of political competition but these methods could clearly not indefinitely contain the kind of conflict implied by the actions of the Kandara elite — nor, for that matter, contain the kind of class-based conflict implicit in Kaggia's programme as it stood in 1965-69.

Some of the most important questions about Government's ability to control events in the countryside, therefore, revolve around the success of rural elite groups, such as the wealthier peasantry which assumed such importance in Murang'a's economic and political life in the 1960s, in ensuring that the general peasant surplus, insofar as it returns to the countryside at all and is not devoted to underwriting the living standards of urban dwellers, is mainly diverted to their welfare and the advancement of their interests.

The emphasis in Government agricultural development policy on the upper peasantry, ironically, may therefore have the effect of increasing the economic — and thus the political — capacity of this sector of the rural population at the expense, not only of the poorer inhabitants of the rural areas, but of bureaucratic power at the local level as well, precisely because of the complex web of political relationships and obligations which have so rapidly developed between the national leadership and the local peasant elites.

NOTES

1.   The material here presented is based on field research in Murang'a District during 1967, more fully written up in *Politics and Rural Development in Murang'a District, Kenya* (D. Phil. thesis, University of Sussex, 1970).
2.   Agricultural officials often expressed the wish for the DC to 'give a lead', so that they could be confident of acting to enforce the law: in the absence of such reinforcement from the Administration, they concluded that the issue was so 'hot' (i.e. politically contentious) that the Office of the President had ensured that DCs proceeded cautiously.
3.   In particular, Kaggia was concerned with the distribution of land, and the impoverishment of many who had been in detention when the land consolidation process had been under way. For details of consolidation and its effects on the social structure of the Kikuyu, see M.P.K. Sorrenson, *Land Reform in the Kikuyu Country* (Oxford University Press, Nairobi, 1967).
4.   Home Guards were the loyalist militiamen recruited by the colonial authorities to bolster police and army control of the Kikuyu areas.
5.   Kaggia had in fact become the national Vice-President of KPU on its formation.
6.   In the KANU primary elections of 1969 (which had the status of a general election, since the KPU was by that time proscribed, and hence the KANU primary victor was un-

opposed in each constituency), Mwaura came second-last of five candidates in Kandara. Kaggia was also defeated (he had returned to KANU in August 1969), coming second to the victor, an employee of the East African Community.

7.   Standard Bank *Annual Economic Reviews of Kenya*, 1968 and 1969.

8.   For a critical discussion of the norms of the community development movement, see Bernard Schaffer, 'The Deadlock in Development Administration', in Colin Leys (ed), *Politics and Change in Developing Countries* (Cambridge University Press, 1969), esp. 203-206.

9.   See *Development Plan 1966-70* (Government Printer, Nairobi, 1966), 324-327, and Sessional Paper No. 10 of 1965, *African Socialism and its Application to Planning in Kenya* (Government Printer, Nairobi, 1965), 36.

10. See the speech by the Minister of Economic Planning and Development, *Parliamentary Reports* 5th July 1966, cols. 1388-9.

11. See Mboya's statement, Ibidem.

12. Interview with Kaggia, 25th May 1967.

13. Interview with CDO, May 1967.

13. See the *Economic Survey of Central Province 1963/64* (Statistics Division, Ministry of Economic Planning and Development, 1968).

GORAN HYDEN

POLITICAL ENGINEERING AND SOCIAL CHANGE: A CASE STUDY OF BUKOBA DISTRICT, TANZANIA

The notion that concerted government action to direct and control society is a precondition for economic development and social change is widespread in Africa. African political leaders of differing ideological orientations see the state as a chief instrument to achieve social change. The state is not expected to be concerned with maintenance of law and order only; it should be equally preoccupied with the rational pursuit of economic and social development policies. The state is there to change the economic sub-structure of society.

Social scientists in Africa have, by and large, accepted this notion, though they have started from different premises. One group, using a structural-functionalist approach, have emphasized the need for structural differentiation and cultural secularization as a way of promoting the twin objectives of 'nation-building' and 'economic development'.[1] Another, starting from Marxist premises, have argued for a strong state as a way of restructuring national society in order to tackle the problem of class formation and of dependence.[2]

These two approaches at least share a view which regards the development of an improved government capacity for the mobilization and extraction of resources as a particularly crucial aspect in the study of social change. This is what is referred to as the problem of 'penetration' — the 'pumping' of members of society by government for resources and the problem of improving the capacity to do so.[3]

Politics, however, is more than 'mobilization of resources' by central government. Politics is also a struggle within society for power and control and this is as apparent in Africa as it is elsewhere. In this chapter we will be specifically concerned with those limitations on 'political engineering' which arise from political activities that run contrary to centrally defined goals of social and economic development. This phenomenon is illustrated in this paper by two major issues in Tanzania's rural development — the abolition of the *nyarubanja* land tenure system and the introduction of *ujamaa* villages. The empirical material is exclusively drawn from Bukoba and Karagwe Districts in north-western Tanzania.

THE LOCAL SETTING

These two Districts are inhabited primarily by members of one of the larger ethnic groups in Tanzania, the *Haya*. The area is often referred to as Buhaya — the land of the Haya. It is situated immediately to the west of Lake Victoria and borders on Uganda to the north and Rwanda to the west. Bukoba, situated on the lake, with about 9,000 inhabitants, is the only real urban centre. It has regular boat connections with Mwanza at the southern end of the lake, Port Bell (Kampala) to the north, Musoma and Kisumu on the eastern side of the lake. There is no railway in the area, but a trunk road links Bukoba both to the rest of Tanzania and Uganda.

The visitor coming from the south is usually struck by the freshness of Buhaya and its apparent fertility. The fresh and green landscape is the result of a high rainfall distributed all through the year.[4] Without the rain, Buhaya would certainly never have been attractive to human settlement. Soil quality is poor and erosion is quite heavy in many areas. Without a farming system involving both banana cultivation and cattle keeping, land would have yielded little. The ecology of the area very much resembles that of southern Uganda, the main difference being the relatively poor soil quality.

The Haya have traditionally preferred to settle on the ridges, which run in a north-south direction, and in the valleys where water has been easily accessible. While Karagwe and the western parts of Bukoba District have never been very densely populated, the eastern parts near Lake Victoria have had a population density exceeded in few other places in Tanzania. An average plot of land in this area in 1965 was just 1½–2 acres. In many places some plots were too small to support an ordinary family.

Bananas are the staple food of the Haya. Many keep cattle, though the practice was even more common in the old days. Coffee, both robusta and arabica, is the main cash crop, the first type having been grown in the area long before the first Europeans came. The Germans, however, were the first to encourage it as a cash crop. Crop diversification has been promoted in the area after independence. Tea is now grown among smallholders in the area around Bukoba and cotton in the southern part of Bukoba District. Vegetables and wheat are grown extensively in the Karagwe Highlands while sugar estates are to be found in the northern part of Buhaya, north of the Kagera River. A large cattle ranch has been established just south of Kagera in the previously uninhabited areas of western Bukoba District.

LAND TENURE IN PRE-COLONIAL HAYA SOCIETY

Like the history of other Interlacustrine tribes[5] in East Africa, that of the Haya is not known in detail; much of it is still under dispute.[6] A widespread tradition in Buhaya is that a long time ago, probably at the end of the 16th or the beginning of the 17th century, nomadic herdsmen invaded the area from the north in search of new pastures. The invaders, known as *Bahinda*, after their leader Ruhinda, met little resistance from the indigenous population, agriculturalists growing millet and yams.

The area today known as Bukoba and Karagwe Districts was divided among five, eventually eight, separate petty chiefdoms mainly due to dissension within the new ruling Hinda clan. Some of these latter initially governed through the clan heads they found in the area and the heads of other cattle-keeping clans, known as *Bahima*, who invaded this area soon after the Hinda invasion. The Bahima were originally clearly distinguished in style of life from the indigenous people, referred to as *Bairu*. As time went on, however, this distinction decreased, particularly in what is now Bukoba District. The Bahinda bought loyalty from Bairu by giving them cattle, and manure from cattle made it possible to grow bananas, introduced soon after the Hinda invasion, on the otherwise poor soil in the area. The agricultural system, which has survived up to this day, based primarily on cultivation of bananas and coffee, as well as cattle-keeping, was developed at that time. Due to a general shortage of land in the eastern part of the area the originally cattle-herding Bahima settled and adopted a mixed agricultural system like the rest of the population. This pattern of development in what is now Bukoba District contrasted with the development in neighbouring areas, notably western Buhaya (Karagwe District) and Ankole in what is now Uganda. There, land was never as scarce as in Bukoba and soil was of a better quality. As a result, in these areas the Bahima remained socially and economically more isolated from the Bairu than was the case in eastern Buhaya. In the latter area the established banana plantations became permanent; in Karagwe, however, cultivation shifted from one area to another at regular intervals.

The importance of the permanent banana plantations and the mutual dependence that developed between the originally nomadic herdsmen and the agriculturists in the densely populated areas of eastern Buhaya explain why the *nyarubanja* land tenure system emerged in this area but not in others.[7] Nyarubanja means literally 'big plantation' and this particular land tenure system developed many feudal characteristics. Its historical origins, however, seem to have been diverse. It partly developed because in return for protection poorer peasants became the clients of richer patrons for whom they undertook to perform certain household duties and to whom they provided some of the food produced by them on their own banana plantations. Over time the rich patrons acquired a prescriptive ownership of the property of their poorer clients. In many instances, however, it is claimed that the clients voluntarily accepted the dependency relationship expecting some benefit from their patron.

Many nyarubanja plantations, however, were created as a result of initiatives from leaders of the ruling clan, generally referred to as *Balangira* (princes). In the course of making claims and fighting for the throne in their chiefdom they very often developed independent sources of power. In some cases, they had been given nyarubanja holdings by the *Mukama* (king). These were used by the princes as a means of collecting sufficient tribute and assembling enough men either to fight for the throne at the time of succession or to fight for indepen- dence from the king. Boundaries of the Haya chiefdoms constantly changed as a result of fighting between members of the Hinda clan, which is one reason for the persistence of several petty chiefdoms. This fragmentation and decen- tralization contrasts with the emergence of large-scale kingdoms under strong central authority, as in neighbouring Buganda. The explanation of the differ- ence is largely found in the existence of this semi-feudal nyarubanja system. Haya history is full of abortive attempts by individual kings to centralize auth- ority. These failures occurred despite the fact that the *Bakama* developed their own centrally controlled political organization, staffed by Bairu on whose loyalty they could more easily count. Many Bairu became 'big men', often being rewarded with a nyarubanja holding. This resulted in an extension of the system beyond the princes and the 'nobility' (the Bahima). But even though they had lost their social distinctiveness through intermarriage and by be- coming agriculturalists, the latter were still regarded as enjoying higher status than the Bairu.

The nyarubanja system, though it probably never involved more than 10 per cent of the total population, was clearly an important factor in pre-colonial Haya society. It was a factor, in some instances towards increased central control, and in others towards limiting central authority; it was a means to gain social power and to gain social protection. In some cases, nyarubanja tenants were no doubt treated as serfs, but in one sense the dependency relationship between land-holder and tenant was of course mutually rewarding, both socially and economically. It was a complex system with different origins and different effects.

EFFECTS OF THE COLONIAL SYSTEM

Subsequent intrusions by Arabs, Europeans and Indians into Buhaya in the latter part of the 19th century, resulted in significant changes in political relationships and the structure of authority. The Germans were the first to establish control over the Haya chiefdoms, though not without resistance. They introduced a highly centralized system, but retained the chiefs as their principal instruments of rule, appointing and removing them at will — slavish subservience being the sole qualification for office.[8] They introduced coffee cultivation on a commercial basis and made the local households pay a poll tax. The function of tax collection was assigned to parish chiefs, the lowest rank in the chiefly hierarchy. Education was started on a small scale by the German administration as well as by Roman Catholic and protestant missionaries, who

with government approval were given large areas of land by the chiefs. As time
went on, a number of Haya settled on the mission land and became still another type of nyarubanja tenants.

When the British acquired colonial authority over Tanganyika at the end of
the First World War they continued the system of 'indirect rule' through the
existing traditional authorities. Like the Germans, the British had two main objectives in colonizing Tanganyika, namely, to maintain law and order, and to
encourage production of coffee. In order to maintain the administrative system, tax rates had to be increased; in order to improve coffee production, new
regulations had to be imposed. These new extractions and coercions, however,
met with resistance from the local Haya population.

During the British colonial period chiefs came increasingly to function as
civil servants; their demands for regular and higher salaries increased. This in
turn, led to an increase in poll tax rates. As under German rule, popular criticism of chiefs was discouraged by the colonial authorities, it being interpreted
as an attack on the colonial administration as such. Hence, the British were
usually prepared to defend the chiefs and their actions. The growing dissatisfaction felt by many educated and commercially active Haya led them to organize welfare associations. The first was the Bahaya Union, started in 1924,
which became the mouthpiece of the 'new elite' in the area, and the first tribal
association in Tanganyika. It reflected both the relatively greater social and
economic advancement of the area and the growing discontent over the failure
of the colonial administration to respond to demands of the new elite for education, health and urban development in Bukoba. The Bahaya Union was the
first sign of a breach between a 'traditional' elite, closely associated with the
colonial administration, and an emergent 'new' elite depending on other resources, notably privately accumulated capital and/or education. The differences in interests and status between these two categories became progressively
deeper, as the following discussion illuminates.

In the 1930s the British administration introduced changes in the nyarubanja system. The system was regarded as offering the possibility of developing
an individual land tenure system, a prerequisite, in their view, for agricultural
development. Accordingly, steps were taken to define the relationship between
nyarubanja holders and tenants, which included the assessment of a specific
rent to be paid by each tenant. By 1936, when this process ended, 9,000 individuals had been registered as tenants, an estimated 10 per cent of all heads of
households in Buhaya at the time.[9] The result of these new regulations was a
lowering of the social status of the tenants in that it became legally explicit
that they did not own, but were only renting, the land on which they worked.
Previously, the nyarubanja holder was regarded primarily as the protector of
the tenants. As land ownership was an important criterion of status, the new
measures of legal formalisation served only to deepen consciousness of social
differences in Buhaya. This was intensified by the requirement that tenants

must pay to the landholder not only the specified rent but also poll tax. Unlike other peasants in Buhaya, therefore, nyarubanja tenants had to pay two annual exactions — and both these to the landholder.

Though the new nyarubanja system affected only a relatively small number of Haya farmers, their reactions to it inevitably found political expression. By the early 1950s it became a major political issue. In Kianja chiefdom, a political association known as the Kianja Labour Association (KLA) was formed. Its political programme was directed against the nyarubanja system, the privileges enjoyed by the Balangira and the rule by the incumbent chief, Bwogi. However, hardly more than one-third of all tenants joined the KLA,[10] due not so much to peasant apathy as to the fact that the leading KLA supporters were themselves nyarubanja holders. Moreover, attempts made in the District Council[11] to amend, if not to abolish the system, also failed, mainly because 32 of the Council's 45 members were nyarubanja holders. Elsewhere in Buhaya tenants associations were organized as pressure groups, but their activities proved ineffective due to lack of coordinated effort and the lukewarm attitude of the colonial administration, despite its realization that the changes in the nyarubanja system instituted in the 1930s had failed to achieve its original objectives. Thus, by the time of independence the whole land issue in Buhaya remained largely unsolved.

The new nyarubanja regulations of the British colonial period were not the only impositions to affect the Haya peasants. Even more politically provocative were the attempts by the colonial administration to improve banana and coffee cultivation. In 1937, for instance, people in certain parts of Buhaya rioted against new regulations regarding coffee growing. Again, in the late 1940s, official efforts to enforce the cutting down of banana stems after each harvest to prevent the spread of a damaging weevil, were interpreted as a colonial plot against peasant interests. Resistance was intensified by the fact that a fee was imposed upon them to cover the costs of the programme of improved cultivation. As the chiefs were made responsible for the enforcement of the new rules, their authority was questioned by an increasing number of Haya. Both the KLA and the Tanganyika African Association (TAA), the successor to the Bahaya Union in the area, used this issue and the discontent it engendered to build up support in the villages throughout Buhaya.

There are several explanations for the failure during the colonial period of attempts to push agricultural improvement in Buhaya. Haya peasants over the years evolved a farming system that made sense to them under existing ecological conditions; they therefore resented external advice, however well-meaning and rational it may have been. Also, developmental innovations during the British colonial period affected those areas of the lives of the villagers which had been regarded for generations as 'sacred', notably the system of cultivating coffee and bananas.[12] Thus, political reaction in Buhaya was partly the result of an expansion in the scope of government penetration in society. A third factor was the scarcity of land. Both the colonial administration and the peasants realized that agricultural innovation had to take place on the already cultivated areas of land. As the majority of the peasants in the densely populated eastern part of Buhaya had only small plots, they were unwilling to take such risks as uprooting poor coffee trees, their only significant source of cash income. These resistances were naturally strengthened by the fact that agricultural policies were introduced in an authoritarian manner by alien authorities, and were in some instances for the benefit of tenant holders or other privileged groups.

When Tanganyika became independent in 1961 Buhaya was by no means typical of the rest of the country. As a result of the introduction and spread of a monetary economy and the specific legislation enforcing standardized rent rates for nyarubanja tenants, Haya society was more deeply stratified than most others. The close link between the colonial administration and the traditional chiefs in many parts of Buhaya had undermined the authority of the latter. Political activities in the rural areas had grown since the late 1940s, TANU having effectively built upon the political consciousness already generated by the Bahaya Union, Kianja Labour Association and the Tanganyika African Association. Despite its peripheral location Buhaya was among the most socially and economically advanced areas in the country, due not only to the ambitions of the Haya themselves, but also to such factors as relatively greater educational facilities and the coffee boom in the 1950s. The latter made the Haya relatively wealthy despite their resistance to modernized coffee cultivation.

PROBLEMS AFTER INDEPENDENCE

The TANU Government came to power after general elections in 1960 and faced no formal parliamentary opposition. Local resistance to TANU did exist, however, in certain parts of the country, notably the more economically advanced areas which had also been most politically active before independence, namely, Buhaya, Kilimanjaro and Sukumaland.[13] In the following parts of this paper we shall examine more closely how the TANU Government has tried to achieve social and economic development in one such area — the Bukoba and Karagwe Districts of Buhaya, through changes in their social structures. Attempts to abolish the nyarubanja system and to introduce ujamaa villages offer good illustrations of the problems connected with political engineering in a peasant society.

The Abolition of Nyarubanja

The nyarubanja issue in Buhaya continued to be important, but took on a different light during the first three years of independence. TANU leaders in Bukoba had promised before independence that with TANU in power the nyarubanja system would be abolished. During the late 1950s nyarubanja holders, in addition to the colonial administration, were the main targets in the political rhetoric of TANU leaders. The first step of the independent TANU government to implement its pledge was the Land Tenure Amendment Act of 1962, which brought all land formally under the ownership of the state. Because of the tradition of individual ownership of land in Buhaya this action undermined much of the support that TANU leaders had previously enjoyed. The fear grew that under the new act the TANU Government was going to take land away from all sections of Bahaya society – a reaction similar to that against the colonial administration prior to independence. In the 1963 election to the District Council in Buhaya a number of independent candidates, mostly Catholic teachers, were able to exploit this fear, resulting in the defeat of half of all official TANU candidates. The land tenure amendment was not the only issue of importance; the official abolition of chieftaincies was equally provocative. The two taken together created a deep split between two groups of politically active Bahaya: those who were loyal to the central TANU Government and those who favoured more local autonomy.[14] Indeed, ironically, many who had previously been in favour of abolishing the nyarubanja system now came to its defence, claiming that the tenants were lazy and unsuccessful farmers.

It was evident that the local TANU leaders in Buhaya could not solve the nyarubanja problem by themselves.[15] The issue was therefore taken up at the national level. Throughout 1964 and 1965 political leaders from the centre – including the President – visited Bukoba and pointedly condemned the nyarubanja system. Finally, in early 1965 the National Assembly passed the Enfranchisement Act aimed at giving land to nyarubanja tenants and prohibiting the creation of any new holdings. However, the Act delegated to the Bukoba District Council the authority to pass bye-laws. Moreover, the important question of compensation to the landholders was not dealt with in any detail in the new law. Thus, despite the political backing and new legislation from the national level many problems of implementation remained.

A special commission headed by the first Regional Commissioner for West Lake, himself related to the royal family in one chiefdom,[16] was appointed to deal with the problem of interpreting the Enfranchisement Act in view of the many local variations in the tenancy that existed. From the beginning the Commission faced pressures from various individuals and groups. Moreover, it lacked firm principles on which to base its decisions. There was evidence that influential persons tended to receive preferential treatment. These and other aspects of the commission's work had persistently fought for the abolition of the nyarubanja system. Their renewed pressure eventually led in 1968 to the passing by Parliament of another act aimed, like that of 1965, at abolishing all feudal land tenure systems in Tanzania. It was a more comprehensive and detailed piece of legislation. It also clearly outlined rules for compensation of holders who had invested money in agricultural improvement of plantations which they were likely to lose as a result of the new law.

Responsibility for implementing the law was given to a judicial commission. This body was known as the Customary Land Tribunal and its members included two Haya elders, one of them a Member of Parliament and a legally trained Secretary. During the first six months of its work a relatively small percentage of tenants brought their cases before the Tribunal. The official explanation for this was that the majority of the 8,000 tenants in Bukoba District had solved the land tenure problem with their landlords on a voluntary basis. However, this explanation should be viewed in the light of the general problem of communication in the rural areas and the fact that many peasants were not aware of the procedure for resolving the issue – for the onus, under this system, was on the peasant to bring forward his case. The majority of the cases settled on a voluntary basis were those involving tenants on mission-owned land. The Tribunal counselled the missions to settle their cases on such a basis, and most of them were so resolved. Decisions in the other cases were not always in favour of the tenants. In December 1969 the Tribunal reported that far more judgments were 'going in the tenant's favour, yet a fair percentage of the landlords still win the land'.[17] This fact reflects the complexity of the land tenure situation in Bukoba, and particularly that some individuals who considered themselves nyarubanja tenants were no more than temporary occupants allowed to cultivate land at the discretionary whim of the acknowledged owner. However, one can say that the nyarubanja issue in Bukoba has been very significantly ameliorated by the new judicial commission.

Table 1. *Cases heard by the Customary Land Tribunal in Bukoba,*
September 1969 – February 1970

	Cases Settled	Cases Partly heard	Total
September – December 1969	84	24	108
January 1970	14	69	83
February 1970	31	77	108

Source: Information collected from the monthly reports of the Tribunal, available in the Regional Administration Headquarters, Bukoba.

The history of the nyarubanja issue in Bukoba, and the problems associated with the various efforts to resolve it, illuminate the more general process of centre-initiated transformational change in the social structure of rural areas in developing countries. It is in point to examine some of the constraints and impediments in this process.

The influence of the nyarubanja holders was clearly an important factor. It was significant in the government, party and the judiciary. As Mutahaba points out,[18] the Primary Court Magistrates were almost all Balangira (thus both they and their relatives were nyarubanja holders) and could not easily be considered impartial in judging land cases. However, under a directive issued in 1965 by the Regional Commissioner they were prevented from dealing with nyarubanja cases. Thus, they were never formally involved after that date in the implementation of the law. Nevertheless, informal interviews I had in Buhaya in 1965-66 suggest that those court officials who were Balangira were suspected by other villagers of indirectly undermining and frustrating changes in the land tenure system.[19]

A second circular on the nyarubanja issue issued by the Regional Commissioner prescribed that tenants who wanted to bring up their cases in the future had to seek the advice of the Area Commissioner.[20] However, the fact that the matter was now subject to the discretion of individual officers in the Regional Administration was also not satisfactory. Politicians in Buhaya who had made the nyarubanja system their main political target feared that influential Haya government and party officials would obstruct the policy. Many of the latter were also nyarubanja holders and were suspected of putting pressure on the Area Commissioner to protect their interests.[21] We can see, therefore, why it became necessary in 1969 to set up a separate land tribunal —neither local political organs nor central agencies had demonstrated themselves capable of solving the issue satisfactorily.

The issue also illustrates the limitations of a political system based on a single broad-based 'frontist' party in solving problems of a socio-economic character. Bukoba District was one of the few parts of Tanzania where there was theoretically a possibility for conflicting political groups based on social class. The nyarubanja system had acquired enough unpopularity towards the end of the colonial period to be the focus for a potentially radical initiative. However, the land issue was confused with a number of others and, moreover, the convention of showing unity within TANU at almost any cost limited its effectiveness as a catalyst of social change. It may even be argued that this kind of consensual one-party structure served to prevent the emergence of a new peasant consciousness. As I have shown elsewhere,[22] the rural Haya in general favour a one-party system. It is in line with their view of society: the most important thing in rural society is to maintain peace and harmony. The 'parental' authority of TANU is accepted by the majority of the people. This is a common attitude in all self-sufficient peasant communities, where members have not yet realized that they share their destiny not only with members of their own community, but with outside people in the same socio-economic situation. My point here is that the conditions for the creation of such a consciousness existed in the Bukoba area due to the widespread existence of the disliked nyarubanja system. Tenants' associations had been formed at an early stage and it was the main issue espoused by several Haya politicians. Because of the need to maintain unity, however, such issues which figured locally within TANU and which could create embarrassing divisions had to be papered over. In the end, therefore, the issue had to be 'taken out of politics' by giving the power to settle the issue to a judicial tribunal.

Another reason for the relative ineffectiveness of the party and the government administration in dealing with this issue was the lack of information available to the legislators when Parliament passed the Enfranchisement Act in 1965. After the defeat of the official TANU candidates in the District Council Election of 1963 and the later expulsion of the victorious independent candidates, the new council members, appointed to replace the latter, tried to gain legitimacy by attacking the nyarubanja system as a feudal remnant. They, as well as some other local TANU dignitaries, provided the central government and the national politicians with information along these lines. To judge from the provisions of the Enfranchisement Act as well as the parliamentary debate, they were both based on an over-simplified analysis. As Mutahaba emphasizes,[23] the 1965 Act did not consider the various grounds on which the system had evolved. It ignored the fact that the same principle could not be used to settle all nyarubanja cases. Thus, in 1965 when the Regional Administration and the District Council sought to implement the law, it was extremely difficult to explain the new arrangements to the people. There was confusion in all parts of Bukoba District.

Though the nyarubanja issue may for some time remain in the minds of many Haya, it seems as if the Land Tribunal has dealt relatively effectively with the remnants of this semi-feudal land tenure system. Greater social justice has been secured and the elimination of this historically divisive issue from Buhaya politics has no doubt enhanced the potential capacity of the centre to mobilize the human resources of the area. In being released from their obligations to the nyarubanja holders the former tenants are more accessible, as free and equal citizens, to central government political and administrative penetration.

The Ujamaa Village Programme

Our next case study also deals with the problem of creating greater social justice and equality in the rural areas. The ujamaa (collective) village represents the principal strategy of the Tanzanian Government in its declared policy of preventing the formation of classes in the rural areas. However, the ujamaa programme has encountered problems of similar range and magnitude as did efforts to abolish the nyarubanja system, although the social causes are not exactly identical. In Bukoba District the ujamaa programme confronted three initial difficulties: (1) the inevitable resistance generated by the superimposition of collective concepts on pre-existing village settlements based on the individual ownership of land; (2) the precipitate and frequently ill-advised nature of government action to launch the scheme; and (3) the lack of complete understanding on the part of the peasants of what the programme was intended to achieve. However, the negative reaction to the new programme is related to other more fundamental underlying factors, particularly the shortage of land in Bukoba District, and the sense of 'relative deprivation' that many Haya have felt in the years following independence.

Many farmers owned plots of land that were too small to support their families; cultivable land in many parts of eastern Buhaya had been so extensively sub-divided that most plots were economically unviable. Also, many Haya felt that independence did not bring the fruits that had been promised and expected. More generally a number of Haya were further aggrieved by the fact that most important developmental investments were made elsewhere in the country. It was not only a question of relative deprivation but of 'status reversal'. The following letter, one among many published in the local newspapers in Buhaya during 1965 and 1966, reflected quite well the prevailing opinion: [24]

Some time ago Buhaya was more highly developed than other places in Tanzania with regard to education, agriculture and local government. It is terrifying to see our Buhaya now decline and die. Poverty is our first problem. Secondly, there is hunger .... The number of people in Buhaya is increasing, while food is decreasing. We also lack schools. We have no money to make our children continue schooling. Coffee price is also very low...

The opinion expressed in this letter and by others was not unjustified; it was a fact that the rate of implementation of development programmes in various parts of Tanzania during the First Development Plan period 1964-69 was lower in West Lake Region than anywhere else.[25] The dissatisfaction with the material conditions of life among the Haya was also amply brought out in our 1965 survey.[26]

The Arusha Declaration of 1967 became a springboard for new development initiatives. The Regional Commissioner, a highly ambitious and authoritarian man, together with his technical officers, drew up a plan for the implementation in West Lake Region of the policies outlined in the Arusha Declaration.[27] The document, which was issued before the policy of ujamaa villages was conceived, contained such specific recommendations as the enlargement of farms, crop priorities, new farming techniques, improvement of the extension service, encouragement of local trade and marketing, and the general strengthening of the infrastructure of the Region. Regarding farm size, it argued that production of food and cash crops could not be adequately promoted unless farms were of a minimum size of two acres. Indeed, it was recommended that, preferably, husband and wife should have two acres each; that is, at least four acres for each family. A rough distinction was made between three categories of people in the Region:
— those with large enough farms in close proximity to their village;
— those with small farms but with no opportunity near their villages for enlargement of their holding;
— those who possess no farm nor have a job.

People belonging to the latter categories were to be considered for new settlements. These were established in the western and southern parts of Bukoba District. The idea was to give each person a farm of decent size so that they could support themselves and their families. In the initial stage of this scheme there was no question of collective production; the main purpose was to provide people with individual holdings. In January 1968 the local adminis-tration − the Village Executive Officers and members of the Village Develop-ment Committees in particular − was asked to identify all people in the re-spective areas who fell within the two categories mentioned above. Three months later the people were given notice that they should be prepared to leave for the new settlement areas.

The programme encountered immediate difficulties. Many people were not eager to leave their traditional village environment, despite the prospect of an economically better life. Ties with relatives and friends were too strong. Some recruited to the new settlement schemes were unsuccessful farmers in their original traditional villages; others had no farming experience at all; some were young men with a preference for urban employment. As party officials had not properly explained the reason for the move, some of the prospective settlers even felt that they were 'criminals'. Few were able or willing to perceive the positive aspects of the programme.

Additional serious problems occurred once the settlers arrived in the new settlement areas. The most serious was a shortage of food and the long distance to water. To obtain food many of the settlers had to go to work for farmers in neighbouring villages, with the consequent neglect of the development of their own new plot. It soon became necessary for the Government to feed the settlers in order to salvage the situation.

In April 1969, one year after the inception of the programme, the situation could be summarized as follows: 19 settlements had been established in the whole Region, approximately half of which were in Bukoba District.[28] These settlements had a total population of 3,473 individuals − 1424 men, 736 women and 1313 children − constituting 0.5 per cent of the total population in the Region. The 2,160 adults had cleared a total of 1282 acres, or 0.6 acres per head. During that period nearly half a million shillings (half of the Regional Development Fund) had been spent on the settlers, viz:[29]

Table 2.

From the Regional Development Fund	310,955.80
Food	268,355.85
Transport	24,091.75
Tools	11,359.30
Seeds	7,303.90
Manure	285.00
Water Supply	560.00
From the District Council	180,000.00
Total	491,955.80

This first experiment in the new settlement programme provoked much resentment and criticism. Some settlers alleged they had been taken to the new

villages by force, a charge taken up by two Haya MPs in a scathing attack on
the Regional Commissioner in the National Assembly. This led to a major row
within the party, which prompted the President in mid-1968 to appoint a
special commission of inquiry. Such action was made imperative by his own
firm admonition that only rational persuasion should be employed; no person
was to be forced into new settlements. The Commission presented its report to
the President in September 1968. It found that the allegations made by the
MPs in the National Assembly were false. As a result, at the next meeting of
the National Executive Committee of TANU, the two MPs were expelled from
the party and thereby automatically lost their seats in Parliament.[30]

A question could be, and among some was, raised regarding the complete-
ness of the findings of the Commission's report, which effectively exonerated
the Regional Commissioner from the charge of having acted irresponsibly. It
found that the specific allegations and the general attitude of the two MPs were
negative and destructive. Yet, even though the Commission found little evidence to support the allegation,[31] there is the possibility that none dared to
say anything against the party because leading officials had from the outset
condemned the stand taken by the two MPs. To question the authority of
TANU would be the same as being impertinent to your own parents, a serious
breach of good conduct in Tanzanian peasant societies. Indeed, some people
have suggested that the two MPs, together with seven other leading MPs, were
at that time chosen as scapegoats in an attempt by the central party institutions to reinforce party discipline. An editorial in *The Nationalist* could be
interpreted as supporting this position. It accused the MPs of being preoccupied with power. The leading article continued:

Disrespect for the People and disregard of their humanity is dangerously anti-Party action.
The National Executive Committee of the Party cannot avoid disciplining such leaders.
Those who have forgotten that they owe the Party and therefore the People their responsi-
bility and their power, must be sharply reminded.[32]

The commission of inquiry accused the two MPs of having subverted
TANU's policy in the Region. Their actions, it claimed, were aimed at keeping
the poor still poor and to make 'the poor people in the region the permanent
victims of the terror of feudalism'.[33] As a sequel, however, it is worth noting
that the Regional Commissioner who was the target of the attack by the MPs
was himself dismissed from office a few months later seemingly on the grounds
that he did not rule in the interest of the people.

When the commission of inquiry visited Bukoba in August 1968 the new
settlements had not yet developed into ujamaa villages.[34] As Rald has shown,
even a year after the inception of the programme, the settlements were nothing
but 'traditional' villages with quadrangular plantations made up of individual
plots.[35] It was not until May 1969 that a more deliberate effort was made by
the Regional Administration to promote collective production in the new

settlements. Two ujamaa ideologists from the party toured the various settlements and stayed several days in each to work together with the people. Chairmen in the new villages and progressive farmers were sent for training, some to Bukoba and some to the Ruvuma Development Association in Songea Region, which had been made responsible for setting up the first real ujamaa villages in Tanzania.[36]

By early 1970, TANU officials and the technical officers had achieved a better coordination of their efforts. Government has concentrated its extension work on these new villages, which have increasingly acquired the features of an ujamaa village, that is, some production on a collectively-owned plantation.[37] However, it is too early to say what will be the next phase in the development of ujamaa villages in Bukoba.

A brief analysis of the ujamaa policies shows that to a certain degree, the same problems of 'penetration' as were experienced in connection with the nyarubanja issue have occurred. There have been political pressures for Government to act swiftly and at the same time the need to maintain unity at the expense of criticism. On ujamaa development, it appears as though other considerations that have obscured ideological clarity, as in the nyarubanja case, have become increasingly important in the implementation of this policy. Another related problem common to both the nyarubanja and ujamaa cases, has been that of creating a peasant consciousness in support of the government action. In the case of nyarubanja, the party failed primarily because it sought to represent the incompetent interests of both landlords and tenants. In the case of ujamaa, party and government officials have zealously endeavoured to prove to their superiors, and ultimately the President, that they support the new policy of collective farming. But no effort has been made to mobilise poorer peasants on the basis of potential social cleavages that we have noted earlier; ujamaa was locally interpreted as a programme for small farmers and landless, leaving the better-off undisturbed. In many instances peasants and persons with no farming experience at all have been combined together in new ujamaa villages without explanation of the benefits of communal production. Rald reports that sometimes only 50 per cent of the village population turn out for communal works.[38] Nevertheless, many members of the villages now appear relatively satisfied with their new life. They are becoming aware that government is concentrating its resources on the development of ujamaa villages and that they therefore get benefits they would otherwise not obtain.[39] But how deep their satisfaction goes is difficult to assess. It remains to be seen to what extent their positive feelings are a function mainly of the special government favours bestowed upon them at this time.

CONCLUSIONS

This paper has endeavoured to illustrate problems of achieving social change and economic development through centrally initiated and directed change, what we have here called 'political engineering'. No farreaching conclusions can be drawn on the basis of this study, but it does illuminate certain points.

Our material suggests that when trying to identify the determinants of receptivity to political and social change it may be more fruitful to examine such variables as the character of the economic system rather than to seek explanation solely in terms of the attitudes and styles of the political leadership or to concentrate solely on the prevailing value systems.[40] Government capacity to penetrate society for the purpose of mobilising new resources will probably depend, as Martin Doornbos has pointed out elsewhere,[41] more on the ability of political and administrative leadership to anticipate and adapt to new situations than on the assumed all-pervasive values of a group whose behaviour they are endeavouring to change. Our case studies illustrate, however, that political engineering is no easy task. Both the nyarubanja and the ujamaa cases show that local power bases inexorably tend to interfere with and affect the instrumental and administrative factor. Influential political and administrative leaders can bring about modifications in the application and implementation of policies. The ordinary peasant, often seen as the 'object' and even beneficiary of such political engineering, is in fact often distinctly disadvantaged because he does not possess the same power to defend and promote his interest.

Political engineering may be rendered ineffective as a result of intentional or unintentional disregard for or insensitivity to the complexity of the local situation and what the various target groups want themselves. Both cases prove this. Even though politicians are usually better informed about local opinions than civil servants, they do at times fall victim of giving too much regard to political directives from the centre as a way of proving their ability to the top leadership.

NOTES

1.   This approach characterizes much of the literature which has sought its inspiration from the work of the Committee on Comparative Politics of the Social Science Research Council in the USA. Political development is assessed in terms of the capacity of a particular system to solve major political crises inherent in any society. The crises are generally recognized as those of identity, legitimacy, penetration, integration, participation and distribution. For further explanation of this approach, see Gabriel A. Almond and Bingham Powell Jr, *Comparative Politics: A Developmental Approach* (Little, Brown and Co., Boston, 1966). I have myself, with some modifications, tried to apply the 'crisis' model to empirical research in the very same area of Tanzania as dealt with in this essay; see *TANU Yajenga Nchi – Political Development in Rural Tanzania* (Scandinavian University Books, Lund, Sweden, 1968).

2.   See, e.g. Giovanni Arrighi and John Saul, 'Socialism and Economic Development in Tropical Africa', *Journal of Modern African Studies*, 6, 2 (1968).
3.   See Almond and Powell, *Comparative Politics* and Martin R. Doornbos, 'Political Development: The Search for Criteria', *Development and Change*, I, 1 (1969).
4.   Bukoba township gets as much as 2000 mm per year on average. The quantity of rain falling declines, however, as one gets to the south and the west.
5.   This term is used to refer to the tribes inhabiting the areas between the big lakes in Uganda, north-western Tanzania, Rwanda and Burundi.
6.   Cf. K. Ingham, *A History of East Africa* (Longmans, London, 1965).
7.   For a detailed account of the *nyarubanja* system and its development in Buhaya, see Gelase R. Mutahaba, 'The Importance of Peasant Consciousness for Effective Land Tenure Reform' (Department of Political Science, University College, Dar es Salaam; undergraduate dissertation, 1969).
8.   This was at least the opinion recorded in the *Bukoba District Book* by the first Political Officer posted by the British to Bukoba.
9.   Mutahaba, 'The Importance of Peasant Consciousness', 12.
10.   Ibidem, 18.
11.   The Council of Chiefs was turned into a District Council in the late 1940s. It retained until the end of the 1950s a majority of ex-officio members, most of them chiefs and sub-chiefs.
12.   Carl J. Hellberg in his study, *Missions on a Colonial Frontier West of Lake Victoria* (Gleerups, Lund, 1965), has information which underlines this; see also T.S. Jervis, 'A History of Robusta Coffee in Bukoba, *Tanganyika Notes and Records* (No. 8, Dar es Salaam, 1939) and Peter W. Mukurasi, 'The Problem of Transforming the Peasant Mode of Farming in Bukoba (Department of Political Science, University College, Dar es Salaam; undergraduate dissertation, 1970).
13.   Cf. Andrew Maguire, *Toward 'Uhuru' in Tanzania — The Politics of Participation* (Cambridge University Press, Cambridge, 1969).
14.   For further information, see Mutahaba, 'The Importance of Peasant Consciousness'.
15.   The politicians had at that time been told that the bye-laws of the District Council (1956) were *ultra vires*. Ibidem, 34.
16.   In 1963, as Regional Commissioner, he had had his cousin, the chief of Kyamtwara chiefdom, detained. The chief was released after six months.
17.   Customary Land Tribunal: *Monthly Report* (Bukoba, 1969).
18.   Mutahaba, 'Importance of Peasant Consciousness', 38.
19.   This was particularly underlined in the Kamachumu area of Kianja chiefdom.
20.   *Circular from the Regional Commissioner* (13th July, 1965).
21.   Mutahaba provides some evidence to suggest this, 'Importance of Peasant Consciousness', 40.
22.   *TANU Yahenga Nchi*, Ch. 9.
23.   Mutahaba, 44 ff.
24.   *Rumuli* (Bukoba Catholic Press; June 15, 1966).
25.   *Tanzania Second Five-Year Plan for Economic and Social Development*: Vol. III (Government Printer, Das es Salaam, 1970), 15.
26.   *TANU Yahenga Nchi*, Ch. 11.
27.   P.C. Walwa (ed), 'The Plan for Accomplishing the Arusha Declaration in West Lake' (Bukoba, 1968, mimeographed).
28.   Jorgen Rald, 'Ujamaa — Problems of Implementation', East African Agricultural Economics Society *Conference Paper* (Dar es Salaam, March 31—April 4, 1970), 4.
29.   These funds were set up in 1967-68, each of the 17 regions in Tanzania obtaining 1,000,000 shillings for local development purposes.
30.   *The Nationalist* (Dar es Salaam; October 19, 1968).
31.   The actual evidence (see Report of the West Lake Commission of Inquiry, TANU, Dar es Salaam, 1968, reprinted in *Sunday News*, Dar es Salaam, October 13, 1968), does indicate that some administrative pressure was used. For comments on the significance of this case see H.U.E. Thoden van Velzen and J.J. Sterkenberg, 'The Party Supreme', *Kroniek van Afrika*, 1 (1969) and L. Cliffe, 'The Policy of Ujamaa Vijijini and the Class

Struggle', both of which are reproduced in L. Cliffe and J.S. Saul (eds), *Socialism in Tanzania* (East Africa Publishing House, 1972).

32. *The Nationalist*, October 16, 1968.

33. Ibidem, October 10, 1968.

34. I visited the area at that time and some people referred to them as *Makazi mapya* (new settlements) others as ujamaa villages, though none of the settlements at the time had any collectively farmed plantation.

35. Cf. Rald, 'Ujamaa – Problems of Implementation', 9.

36. The RDA was dissolved in October 1969, following some controversy between local TANU leaders and representatives of the Association.

37. I.K.S. Musoke, 'The Establishment of Ujamaa Villages in Bukoba Rugazi (Nyerere) Village: A case study' (Department of Political Science, University of Dar es Salaam, undergraduate dissertation, 1970); also B.B. Bakula, 'The Effect of Traditionalism on Rural Development: The Case of the Omunurazi Ujamaa Village, Bukoba' (Department of Political Science, University of Dar es Salaam, undergraduate dissertation, 1970).

38. Rald, 'Ujamaa – Problems of Implementation', 13

39. Mukurasi, 'The Problem of Transforming the Peasant Mode of Farming in Bukoba'.

40. Cf. Lloyd A. Fallers, *Bantu Bureaucracy* (Heffer, Cambridge, 1956); Raymond J. Apthorpe, 'The Introduction of Bureaucracy into African Politics', *Journal of African Administration*, XII, 3 (1960); David E. Apter, *The Politics of Modernization* (University of Chicago Press, Chicago, 1965).

41. Martin R. Doornbos, 'What Determines Receptivity to Political Change?' (Institute of Social Studies, Occasional Paper, 1968, mimeographed).

ANN SHARMAN

IMPROVING NUTRITION IN BUKEDI DISTRICT, UGANDA

INTRODUCTION

Malnutrition in developing countries has considerable health and socio-economic costs and has serious long-term effects. Improving nutrition is, therefore, an important practical problem. As Scrimshaw has written:

> ...the cost of malnutrition in less developed areas is exceedingly high: it includes the waste of resources in rearing infants who die before they can become useful citizens and the reduced working capacity of malnourished adults.... Nearly all children among the less privileged population of the under-developed countries show retarded growth and development at the time they reach school age; and although they are rarely seriously malnourished during school years, they do not make up for the deficit acquired during pre-school years.... This means that the future development of a country is compromised by serious malnutrition in young children.[1]

There is increasing evidence of the relationship between nutrition, health and performance at work and at school.[2]

Certain categories of people are particularly vulnerable to malnutrition, namely, young children and pregnant or lactating women. In particular, the impairment of women's efficiency and working capacity through malnutrition is likely to have a farreaching effect on both food supply and the health of their children. Women play a vital part in the process of agricultural production, as well as in carrying out domestic activities and caring for children.

A variety of factors may contribute to a high incidence of malnutrition, as calculated by biochemical, clinical and anthropometric measurements. These include:

(i) Biological and medical factors, such as genetic characteristics and inability to adapt to a poor diet; the parasite load carried by people; and the extent and severity of infections, which may both reduce the amount of food consumed and the absorption of nutrients from those foods which are consumed.[3]

(ii) Psychological determinants of food choice, preferences and tastes. Emotional disturbance may also affect the consumption and absorption of nutrients.[4]

(iii) Economic factors, including sources, and the amount of different food-stuffs produced; the availability of cash and other resources for improvements in food production and/or purchase of foodstuffs; and the relation between economic status and the consumption of different foodstuffs.

(iv) Social factors. These include a great variety of conditions which may be closely related to economic factors; convictions of the members of the society which affect the evaluation of foodstuffs and their use, including the relation thought to exist between food and health. Finally, composition and structure of groups may affect the production, distribution and consumption of food-stuffs, as will the organization of specific activities which contribute to these general processes.[5]

Clearly, the problems involved are highly complex, so that it is difficult, when attempting to improve nutrition, to isolate the most important variables and define a limited field in which to take action. Furthermore, the variety of factors to be taken into account in combating malnutrition in the East African situation inevitably requires the participation of a number of different government departments in the planning and organization of such action. The administration of a programme for improving nutrition is thus likely to raise many problems, and is at least as important in contributing to its impact as the characteristics and responses of local people. If a project is poorly planned and implemented it has little chance of success. This can be seen from the experience of the Bukedi Food and Nutrition Project. As will be shown, its ineffectiveness can be attributed largely to inadequacies in its conception and organization. Difficulties were encountered which were related to the nature of the local social and economic life, but these were exacerbated by the way in which the project was organized. For this reason I am going to concentrate on organizational aspects of schemes to improve nutrition in this paper, although I will consider characteristics of the local community where these are relevant.

THE BUKEDI FOOD AND NUTRITION PROJECT

Malnutrition, particularly protein-calorie malnutrition, has been recognized as a serious problem in Bukedi District in general and West Budama in particular for many years. During 1953 and 1954 an experiment was carried out in which the children in certain primary schools were given dried skimmed milk, after which both their health and their school performance were considered to have improved in relation to that of children in neighbouring schools. Application was subsequently made to UNICEF for assistance in running the scheme, for which the district had inadequate financial resources. From these beginnings developed the Bukedi Food and Nutrition Project, which ran from July 1960 to the end of 1963. This project had assistance from both UNICEF and FAO. By

1965, when I first visited Bukedi, few traces remained of it, and as a result of the rapid turnover of district officials, few of those who had been involved in implementing it were still in the area. In this section I shall describe the problems which the project encountered, and discuss some of the reasons for its ineffectiveness.

Several requirements can be suggested for the successful organization of such a project:

1. detailed background information on the condition to be improved and the suitability of different types of organization for this purpose;

2. definition of specific and limited aims, based on the background information available;

3. careful consideration of the scale of the project in the light of existing conditions, and possibly very limited pilot projects, where the main project is to be a composite and complex one;

4. means of evaluating the results, which will in part be dependent on a clear definition of the project;

5. selection of suitable types of worker and forms of organization and coordination of the work done by different agencies;

6. organization which facilitates continuation of activities after the termination of the project, through the involvement of local people and institutionalization of new activities, and forms of cooperation within and between government departments.

In the early planning of the Bukedi Food and Nutrition Project, apart from a lack of systematic background information, the second and third of these requirements were not met. Specific aims to be achieved by a limited number of courses of action were not clearly outlined, and the project was implemented in a large area without there having been any small-scale piloting. The large and amorphous scheme itself was seen as a pilot project and a test of possible means of improving nutrition in all districts in Uganda. These shortcomings also prevented the fourth, fifth and sixth requirements from being met, and contributed to the aggravation of other difficulties which it could have been anticipated would be encountered in the area.

The Expansion of Aims and Proliferation of Courses of Action

The original aims of the project were specifically to improve the health and performance of school children by adding milk to their midday meal. Later these aims were generalized and became

... to improve the nutritional status of the population, principally the children, by increasing the production and consumption of the right kinds of food needed to balance the diet, through school feeding programmes, nutrition and health education, and promotion of food production in the schools and the community.[6]

This led to a multiplication of the actual programmes of action to be taken. In its final form the project consisted of schemes for the improvement of the existing primary school feeding programme, an environmental sanitation programme, the development of school gardens (this alone involved a number of activities, protecting springs and water courses, improving home hygiene, improving cattle stands, marketing sites and so) and fish ponds, and the intensification of nutrition and health education. Nutrition and health education was related to work already being done by government departments, but was nevertheless planned as a major activity to be developed through a number of different channels. In addition to these schemes it was suggested that there should be a special one for pre-school children, but this was rejected.

Vagueness of the relation between the aims of the project as a whole and the specific plans for action was reflected in plans for evaluation. Baseline information was collected on the health and nutritional status of children of all ages in one out of six counties in the district, namely West Budama. This county was thought to be more or less representative of the district as a whole, although it was not made clear why. It is doubtful whether any one county could be representative of the district since there are five major tribes in the area with different patterns of food production and consumption. Altogether about 2,000 children were examined at different centres, but they were not randomly selected and were not necessarily representative of the children in the county. No indicators were chosen by which to measure the improvements it was hoped to achieve.[7]

Again, poor formulation of how to achieve the aims of the project led to confused thinking about how to ensure the continuation of activities initiated by it. At the beginning it had been hoped to enlist the interest of the local people in continuing the school milk scheme. The idea was that during the course of the scheme the value of giving the children additional protein foods with their midday meal would be demonstrated. It was not clear, however, how this could be done, nor that this would be sufficient to persuade the parents to continue paying for the milk, or to provide a supplement after the end of the project. No such support was, in fact, obtained, and at least up until 1967 no supplements were generally provided for school meals.

No other means of obtaining or measuring local involvement in the project seems to have been suggested. Nor does there seem to have been any attempt to ensure that increased cooperation within and between government departments at a local level would be developed and continue after the termination of the project.

The Scale of the Project

Both the way in which government personnel were organized and certain characteristics of the local social and economic organization were likely to make implementation of a large-scale project difficult. Bukedi District is about 1,770 square miles in area and at the time that the project was in operation had a population of between 400,000 and 500,000.

Government departments were characterized by rapid turnover and frequent shortage of staff.

Each new incumbent of an appointment either knew nothing of the project or its objectives, or held different views from that of his predecessor. Similar changes took place in the schools, hospitals, dispensaries and other institutes...[8]

The difficulty of maintaining continuity and of coordinating activities on such a large scale led to poor teaching by ill-informed government personnel. Though particular emphasis was to be put on the production and consumption of protein-rich foods,

very few of the officers engaged in the project seemed to be aware of this or even of its meaning. To many of them the terms 'proteins' and 'calories' were synonymous, and the general view was that greater production and consumption of bananas and other fruits and vegetables, particularly 'exotic' ones, was the primary objective of the project.[9]

Furthermore, instruction given by different teachers on short-term nutrition education courses, for people who were working in the local areas, was sometimes contradictory

... while one instructor urged more schools and free education, together with greater medical services supported by 1/- per head contributions by the population, to a UNICEF-supported nutrition training course of primary school teachers, another urged that infants be weaned from their mothers' breasts at six-weeks old and then be bottle-fed on proprietary foods thereafter.[10]

In Bukedi as in most extension programmes local level workers were directly responsible for communicating information to the people whose behaviour was to be changed. It was assumed that if they were given an academic training in their subject they would be able to translate it into a readily comprehensible local idiom, but they seldom had the training or the experience to do this. Earlier studies have shown the confusion and lack of response resulting from inadequate training of local workers.[11] It is often at this level that communication breaks down.

Other setbacks resulted from religious conflicts. As elsewhere in Uganda, Bukedi has a long history of conflict between Protestants and Catholics, and while the majority of the population was Catholic many of the chiefs were Protestant. Towards the end of the 1950s there were many complaints that the chiefs were abusing their power, by calling on adult males to do other than community work and by unfair assessment of tax. Dissatisfaction with the chiefs reached a climax in January 1960 with riots throughout Bukedi District.

These riots were ostensibly against the tax assessments, but in West Budama they were also an expression of the resentment felt by the Catholic population against the Protestant chiefs, whom they felt were favouring the Protestant minority.[12] Following these riots district finances were low, since many people refused to pay taxes. Relations between chiefs, councillors and villagers seriously deteriorated, so that the work of government departments was hindered, because they often depended on the assistance of the chiefs for calling meetings and communicating with the villagers. In addition there was often hostility towards extension workers of a different denomination from that of the villagers with whom they were working.

The financial situation of the district and the ability of the local people to cooperate was further impeded by serious floods which severely damaged the cotton harvest of 1961-62.

Many people had to sell their food crops instead of the usual cotton production in order to pay their taxes and education fees. The consequence of these disasters was that local material support for the project was out of the question during 1961 and 1962.[13]

In fact at no time during its effective life were political and economic conditions favourable to the reception of the project in the district.

The Project's Achievements

My assessment that the Bukedi Food and Nutrition Project failed to achieve lasting effects is based on reports of the project, and on informal discussions with district officials and local people in West Budama. However, the organizers of the project did see it as having some achievements to its credit. These refer largely to equipment provided and other assistance given to schools, the training of local personnel, and suggestions for improvements to be made in the schools. On the basis of the experience of the project a number of recommendations were made, including the establishment of a national food and nutrition organization, and for a training programme in nutrition at higher levels and of agricultural education for boys and homecraft for girls at post-primary level.

Eradication of any major, preventable, endemic disease and the introduction of clean water supply and sanitary latrines in all homes were seen as prerequisites of any nutrition project. However, a regular consumption of adequate protein foods by the provision of by-laws, in addition to education, is not discussed either in the body of the report or in the minutes of the meeting held during the operation of the project. Nor is the value of the health centres dealt with. As regards the question of concentrating educational effort in the primary schools, there is no explanation of why this is considered to be the most effective means of promoting nutrition education.

Research was recommended into the storage of grains, oil seeds and pulses, so that a statutory 'protein-famine reserve' can be required by every house-holder. Establishment of health centres at every dispensary was also recom-mended, as was the use of primary schools as the main centres for nutrition education.

These recommendations refer to organization at a national level, which I am not concerned with here. Three recommendations are concerned with the im-plementation of government policies at the local level (although they do not seem to derive from the experience of the project). Other difficulties were also associated with the use of school gardens as educational aids and sources of food in primary schools.

The net result is that school gardens usually contain a varied assortment of vegetables, fruits and cash crops, and sometimes even trees, but the foods produced seldom have any value in helping to balance the local diet.[14]

The experience of the Bukedi Food and Nutrition Project thus suggests that large-scale projects with varied aims and running for limited periods of time are likely to encounter considerable difficulties and are thus not the most effective means of improving nutrition. It is necessary then to consider alternative strat-egies.

ALTERNATIVE STRATEGIES FOR IMPROVING NUTRITION[15]

In introducing possible alternative approaches, the organization of the perma-nent government departments is of primary importance, particularly local educational establishments and the extension services, which provide a continu-ing means of communication with the villagers. If it is necessary to intensify or reinforce work being done, then this inevitably implies modification of these services. However, any such strategy must be based on a proper understanding of the practices and their social determinants of food consumption in the society concerned.

In West Budama there are a variety of staples and relishes, some with a high protein content. Staples include finger millets, plantains, cassava, sweet potatoes, maize and rice, and the main relishes are groundnuts, sesame, cow peas, animal products and greens. High-grade proteins such as soya beans are also known. Thus, although the standard of living is low, the components of a good diet are available in the area.

The quality of the diets of consumption units of low economic status[16] ap-pears to be poorer than that of consumption units of high economic status, indicating unequal distribution of foodstuffs between consumption units. But this does not account for the distribution of infant malnutrition. In my study, no statistically significant relationship was found between economic status and the nutritional status of the children.

Thus, it is necessary to look for other possible reasons for variation between consumption units, or for reasons for maldistribution within the consumption unit. Since the Adhola, who occupy West Budama, see no link between general nutrition (except in the sense of starvation) and health, choice of foodstuffs for their children is based on other considerations. Although lack of a particular food is not recognized as a cause of illness, diarrhoea and some other illnesses are considered to be caused by eating certain foodstuffs. Among these are mutton, fish, sesame and legumes, all good sources of protein. Other taboos on high protein foods are associated with the subordinate roles of children, and also of women. Furthermore, men take precedence over both women and children in the distribution of foodstuffs. It is not thought that children have different requirements from adults, and no special foods are prepared for them. There is little variation, even in the contemporary, changing situation, in the care of children and the foods considered appropriate to them.

It can be seen that where the standard of living is generally low, and infant nutrition has a low priority, education may be an important means of bringing about changes in the relatively short term.[17] An increase in the standard of living, sufficient to bring about a general improvement in the nutritional level of all members of the community, is likely to be effective only in the long term. Nevertheless, bringing about changes in patterns of behaviour through education is still a slow process. There must be frequent repetition and reinforcement of what is taught, and it may only be through passing on information to the younger generation that behaviour will change. But the older members of the community without formal education must not be neglected since, although they may be unlikely to change, they may be the ones who determine whether or not the younger generation is free to follow new patterns of behaviour. Against this background, we can now consider the role of the various government agencies touching on the issue of malnutrition.

Government Services

A number of government departments are involved in activities related to the improvement of malnutrition in West Budama, particularly the departments of Health, Agriculture, Veterinary Services and Animal Industry, Community Development and Education.

The Health Department is divided into two sections, the medical staff who run the hospitals and dispensaries and first aid posts;[18] and the health inspection staff who work in the villages. On the medical side the work is almost exclusively curative, although some group talks and advice to individuals on public health are given, and special child welfare clinics are held at the local hospitals and dispensaries. There is no follow-up work in the villages, except where dispensaries or maternity centres are converted into health centres.[19] In health centres the work of the medical staff is linked more closely with that of the inspection staff, both types of personnel being attached to the centre. Within a selected area near the health centre all medical cases should be followed up by the inspection staff and some intensive home improvement work is carried out there. The work of the health inspection staff is essentially preventive. They are generally responsible for issuing trading licences, and inspecting trading premises, water supplies and so on, as well as for home improvement. For home improvement, even when they are attached to a health centre, they have a choice between concentrating on a few better homesteads as examples to other people, and spending more time at the worst homesteads which are those needing help most urgently. The former alternative is generally chosen.

Extension work is also carried out by the personnel of the Agricultural Department and the Department of Veterinary Services and Animal Industry. The work of the latter department is concerned with the increase and proper care of livestock, and the enforcement of the relevant by-laws. There is a tendency for the staff to concentrate on those farmers who are already well-advanced in the care of their livestock and who can afford the cost of fencing, the training of oxen for farm work, and so on. There is sometimes competition between the personnel of the two departments for the allegiance of wealthy and industrious farmers. Each may attempt to make the farmer concentrate on his particular sphere of production, since the farmer's success will rebound to the credit of the local worker concerned. The personnel of the Agricultural Department also have to enforce by-laws, as well as advise and encourage farmers, and carry out the directives of the Agricultural Department. In general work, the Agricultural Assistants used to concentrate their efforts on the progressive or emergent farmers[20] in order to build them up as an example it was hoped others would follow. In theory, policy has changed and more attention is to be paid to those farmers who make little progress in their methods of farming, but Agricultural Assistants still visit mainly the 'progressive' and emergent farmers. Educational courses for both men and women are held by the Agricultural Department at the District Farm Institute in Tororo, where nutrition is one of the subjects taught. Young Farmers' Clubs have also been formed in some areas.

Community Development workers aim to reduce the gap between the educated younger people and the people who have no formal education. They represent the only government department concentrating on extension work without the enforcement of by-laws. They work through clubs, rather than house-to-house visiting. In these clubs literacy is taught, together with a variety of other subjects, such as health, home improvement, and crafts. It was planned that the members of other departments would also use these clubs as channels of communication with the villagers, but more frequently they work on their own. The clubs are largely attended by women and are regarded locally as women's clubs, although there are Community Development workers concerned respectively with men's and women's work. Voluntary leaders of the clubs and other influential women may attend courses at the District Farm Institute run by the Community Development Department. There is also provision for the teaching of nutrition in primary schools though its impact has been low. There is class room instruction and school gardens are meant to be used for educational purposes, though work on them may be used as a punishment.

Social Differentiation and the Effect of Extension Services

There are three problems in the organization of the extension services to which the results of my study are relevant, namely, the questions of who should be approached (particularly consideration of the roles of 'progressives' and women); how they should be approached; and selection of the unit with which to work.

Progressives

In West Budama the obligations of the wealthy to the rest of the community cannot be expected to lead to an automatic and general redistribution of wealth. The obligation is to keep people alive, not to raise their standard of living, nor to distribute all types of wealth more evenly through the community. Concentration on those with a higher standard of living will therefore tend to increase wealth differentials. Furthermore, though the wealthy person may be more willing and able to implement the advice of the different extension workers, he is not necessarily the one who is listened to and taken as an example in the community.

In the field of agriculture and animal industry, the government personnel might suppose that the farmers want to raise their incomes, and will thus copy the farming methods used by those who can be seen to be profiting from their farming and to have a higher standard of living. But from the villagers' point of view other activities, such as trading and employment, may continue to seem preferable and more rapidly beneficial than farming. Their point of reference may often be someone in employment or successful trading. Such people frequently do not follow the recommendations of the extension workers. Also even when farming is a man's sole activity and he would ideally like to increase his income, he may not see the work of the extension services as being relevant to him. Few farmers of low and intermediate economic status have any regular contact with extension workers. Most farmers in the intensive survey saw them as working with wealthy people who could afford to spend more money on their farming activities. In some cases they would still have liked to be visited and advised on better farming methods, but others did not think that such advice was relevant to them. As one farmer said

I do not want them [veterinary and agricultural extension workers] to advise me because I do not have cattle or the means for farming which they require. But I do not mind if they just come to visit me. I like people.

The fact that many farmers would not even see these methods as being relevant or open to them, because of their low standard of living, may also limit the effect that any select category of farmers within the community could have on farming methods. For example, there is one senior man and progressive farmer, who is both a clan and village chief (selected by the villagers as their representative), and much respected in the area in which he lives. But I could find no evidence of any particular influence he had had on the farming methods of the other farmers. This is not to say that the Adhola are loth to emulate others. There are plenty of examples to the contrary. Nor is it an indication of a low value being placed on individual innovation. Many young people try out what are for them new activities, such as trading, in an attempt to advance themselves.[21]

There are also other reasons why a selected category of farmers may have a limited influence. Selection may not follow the specified procedures. There are examples of so-called 'progressive farmers' being chosen and visited by extension workers not because they seek and follow advice, but because they are powerful men who have had official positions and consider that the attention of extension workers is their due and a recognition of their status.

Similarly, 'the demonstration effect' is unlikely to lead poor people to improve their homes by emulating those who have attracted the attention and become the show pieces of the health inspection staff. They lack the means, and sometimes the inclination. There has in the past been resistance to digging latrines and other activities that are promoted by the chiefs and enforceable by law.

When a farmer does look for an example to follow in the community he will turn to someone with whom he has an amicable relationship and whose advice he respects, not just someone whom he can see to be farming profitably. A variety of factors will determine those in the community who are liked and respected and by whom. Factors to take into account are a person's economic and social position, individual life history and personal characteristics. These factors are also likely to affect reactions to the extension workers themselves and the success of their work.[22] Determinants of a person's structural position in the community which are relevant in West Budama are membership of religious groups and political parties,[23] position in the status hierarchy and position in the domestic unit. Religious and political conflict may be the reason for disruption of any relationship in the community, even that between husbands and wives or parents and children. It can hinder the work of extension staff and has particularly impaired the work of chiefs in the area, as will be discussed below.

Seniority does not necessarily ensure attention. Conversely, a senior position is not necessarily required for a person's opinion to receive consideration. Influence is often related to age and seniority where these are related to wealth and expanding networks through marriage and other forms of cooperation; but how wealth is used, as well as its possession, affects the influence of a person in the community. There is one example of a senior man and a rich progressive farmer who is harsh and ungenerous. Although in the past he has had a powerful position and is considered important, he is treated with caution and would not be turned to for advice. In this case the personality of the person involved, as described by others, is important. So is his past career, since he was a chief in the area at the time of the riots. Hostility may result from a variety of other conflicts and past events in a person's life, such as disputes over land, and will affect the range of his influence.

Central to the idea of a 'big' man, a man of influence, is the idea of a person who can converse well, bring people together and, most important, is generous in feeding people at his home and giving feasts and gifts. It is good to be generous and sociable, so much so that some people say that a man may be 'big' even if he is not rich, if he has these qualities. But in specifying who is a 'big' man it is generally found that he also has considerable resources to distribute.

Chiefs and by-laws

The chiefs have an important role in facilitating communication between extension workers and villagers, and their work overlaps with that of other government personnel. All meetings to be addressed by government officials have to be organized by the chiefs, and they are also responsible for enforcing by-laws. They are expected to ensure that the requisite amounts of cassava and sweet potatoes are grown as a famine reserve, that latrines are dug and kitchens built, and that licences are obtained for brewing beer and spirits. Conflict between Protestant chiefs and Catholic villagers over favouritism towards the Protestant minority (between 10 and 30 percent of the population)[24] has already been mentioned. This conflict in the past also affected the work of other government departments. For example, from 1957 to 1959 it was the policy of the health department to hold competitions between sub-parishes for the cleanest and best kept area, so that everyone would be involved and encouraged to improve their homes. But there was resentment, because the chiefs were said to concentrate on sub-parishes which had a majority of people of their own religion, and to take people from other sub-parishes to do communal work in the chosen area.

This situation has been reflected in people's attitudes to extension workers, and sometimes in the behaviour of the extension workers themselves, since they do not always succeed in remaining aloof from local political and religious involvements. It puts in question the value of trying to combine educational work with that of the enforcement of by-laws, which promotes conflict between these two approaches. This is even more the case where the chiefs and extension workers themselves fail to comply with the by-laws, or do not attempt to improve their homes and living conditions. Some chiefs made a poor showing in a survey carried out by the Health Department in 1964.

Women, decision making and nutrition policy

One basic dimension of differentiation is sex, which affects a person's status, influence and freedom to follow new patterns of behaviour. There are some cases of women becoming progressive farmers, competing with the men for the attention of extension personnel and recognition as the best farmer in the District. In their case it is necessary to know not only what influence they have as farmers but again also what influence they would have in getting other women to assert themselves and promote their interests. The position of women and the question of which women can be used as spokesmen is extremely important when considering the improvement of nutrition.

Care of children is the responsibility of women, and control and use of subsistence crops is largely left to them. Few men have granaries of their own; decisions about consumption are mostly left to women and almost all transactions involving exchange or gifts of food are carried out by the women. But men are likely to oppose consumption patterns which contravene prohibitions, and they are the ones who largely control the marketing of cash crops and who administer the cash income received. Opportunities for women to acquire a cash income of their own comprise only a small section of the budget. Any attempt on their part to obtain a larger independent income is usually opposed by their husbands, since such activities are seen as threatening the husbands' authority. Thus a group of women who once attended Community Development classes and started to cultivate their own groundnuts for sale were forced to stop by their husbands.

Regular attendance of women at the Community Development Clubs is low. In a random sample I made, of 188 women with children under five, only twelve participated in the Community Development Clubs. Only five of them had any formal education and none of them were organizers. Lack of participation may be due to a number of factors. The women themselves most frequently say that they have no time, that participation in these groups and fulfilment of wifely obligations are incompatible. 'If I go to the meeting who will cook for my husband?' The time element is of significance. Six of the twelve lived in the two villages which were further away. However, it is perhaps more than simply lack of time since women can leave home for days on end to mourn, to participate in funerals or other ceremonies, and where the husband and children are left behind there are always those in the neighbourhood who will look after them. Religious affiliation may be significant in some cases, although few women actually left or stayed away from their club as a result of these conflicts. Many other women however, are hardly aware of the existence of the clubs, or say that they do not see how they can help them. The clubs do not provide a reference point to which these women look in order to advance their position and improve their style of life. Again, they are seen as being relevant to other types of people in the community, to women who are rich, and have others to help them with their work; or women in polygamous domestic units who may be better able to spare the time to attend. Still, probably the most important factor of all is opposition by the husbands.

Information not only on the position of women, but also on the process of decision making within the domestic unit, is important for a number of reasons. Decision making within the domestic unit can influence the effectiveness of any general policy chosen. For example, in West Budama there seem to be two general policies from which to choose, although they are not necessarily mutually exclusive. Protein supplies may be increased either through farm production or through the introduction of new manufactured protein products which have to be bought.[25] In the Bukedi Food and Nutrition Project the purchase of dried skimmed milk was an important part of the scheme for improving the diet of primary school children. But decisions as to consumption and distribution of food are primarily made by women, whereas most cash expenditure is in the hands of men, who may not give the purchase of new protein foods a high priority, judging from patterns of expenditure found in the area. However, even a neglected wife who has little cash income has some scope for growing small amounts of additional protein foods for her children. Thus in relation to decision making within the domestic unit, increased production of foodstuffs is likely to be more effective in improving nutrition than introducing new, commercial protein foods.[26]

The domestic unit

Such considerations as these, the relation between men and women and the different activities performed by husband and wife within the domestic unit, must also be taken into account when considering the unit with which the extension services work. No one department deals with the domestic unit as a single unit. Community Development Clubs are largely attended by women. The Agricultural and Veterinary workers and even Health Inspectors deal largely with men. This separation of extension activities directed towards men and women is congruent with the separation of their social activities outside the domestic unit, agricultural activities are not exclusively the concern of the men, nor allocation of resources for consumption and the care of children exclusively the concern of women. Women carry out a large part of the cultivation of all crops, and thus also need training in farming. Again, any innovations which women may wish to make in carrying out domestic activities, particularly where these involve the use of cash, immediately affect and become a concern of the men. Thus it is crucial to try and coordinate the nutrition improvement activities of different government departments more fully and focus them on the domestic unit as such, rather than on any of its components. There could, for example, be considerable advantage in educational work being concentrated in the hands of the Community Development Department, whose members have no obligations to enforce by-laws. And a single channel of communication might facilitate the treatment of the domestic unit as a single unit for educational purposes.

Coordination and Follow-up

Except in the work of the Health Centres, there is little coordination of the work of the two sections of the Health Department, nor between them and the other government services. For example, there are no institutionalized arrangements for following-up malnutrition cases. However, in the past this has been done to a limited extent through the interest and initiative of individual medical staff concerned with the prevention of malnutrition. A scheme which was devised in 1963 by two doctors in Tororo, where the main hospital serving West Budama was situated, provides a concluding example of the way in which the work being done by different institutions and government departments might be institutionally coordinated and reinforced at relatively little expense.[27] This scheme was not primarily to follow up cases of malnutrition, but to promote nutrition education. It is by no means presented as an ideal scheme. There was no satisfactory evaluation, no systematic means of measuring its success, although changes in the behaviour of some individuals were noted. But it did contain a limited and feasible idea: to demonstrate precisely the connection between consumption of particular foodstuffs and health. In previous projects the mechanism by which demonstration would show the effect of food on health had not been so clear. The recovery of a child from protein-calorie malnutrition by correct feeding is very dramatic, if successfully achieved.

The original plan was to carry out more systematic educational work within the hospital, particularly for those parents and other attendants who brought malnourished children into the children's ward. The idea was to have a 'protein garden' attached to the ward in which high-grade protein food would be grown, with the help of those villagers attending the malnourished children. These foodstuffs would be cooked and fed to the children while they were recovering. This would enable the attendants to appreciate their crucial importance for their children, as well as to see how the plants could be grown and to learn how to cook them when, as with soya beans, they were known but not widely used.

There are two words to describe protein-calorie malnutrition in West Budama, *ther* and *kidimbiya*.[28] Kidimbiya is said to be an ordinary illness, often associated with diarrhoea, which can either be treated with local herbs or by European medicine. The term more generally used is ther. Ther is said not to be an ordinary illness but a condition which develops when the mother becomes pregnant again while the child is still breast-feeding, the situation which often does exist when a child is malnourished. European medicine is thought to be ineffective in treating ther. The child, after all, often goes to the hospital and receives treatment, only to fall ill again soon after returning home. It continues to live under the same conditions and to receive the same food. Thus, it is important to make a connection in people's minds between treatment and food, rather than between treatment and medicine, which is that normally made by the local people.

It was also thought that this education in the children's ward might reinforce and in turn be reinforced by teaching done in other institutions. Thus, periodically, attendants from the children's ward were taken to the District Farm Institute and shown the work being done there, among other things the demonstration vegetable gardens and a small animal project in which rabbits and guinea pigs were being reared.[29] Similarly, people attending courses at the District Farm Institute were brought to the children's ward.

Any such scheme is clearly limited by lack of follow-up in the villages. People come into the children's ward from many different areas, and general shortage of personnel, together with lack of staff specifically responsible for follow-up work, makes further encouragement difficult. If such a scheme was to be developed more fully, systematic coordination with Community Development and other workers might lead to reinforcement.

CONCLUSIONS

Large-scale schemes tend to appeal to government personnel. They provide an illusion of a final solution to apparently intractable problems, and they appear prestige-full; however, they are unlikely to be the most effective means of improving nutrition. Instead, small-scale but long-term schemes, closely bound-in with the existing government organization in an area, are preferable. These should be combined with an emphasis on increased production and use of existing local foodstuffs, rather than manufactured foodstuffs which have to be bought. Such schemes are not dependent on a large financial outlay, and have a greater chance of a cumulative effect. Should greater financial resources be available they might be used more beneficially for appointing additional staff to perform neglected tasks. Thus, for example, an extra person might be put on a children's ward, responsible for health education, or more staff deployed to carry out follow-up work in the villages.

Apart from organizational factors, we have also seen that there are characteristics of the local community which make rapid change in the field of nutrition unlikely. Shortcomings in programmes can derive both from intrinsic deficiencies in the structure for implementation of schemes and failure to take into account the characteristics of the local community.

Another issue raised in this paper is the role of by-laws in inducing changes in behaviour. Discussion of the relative virtues of force and persuasion in extension work has a long history. It has frequently been pointed out that forced changes in behaviour may be abandoned as soon as the sanctions forcing compliance are removed. In West Budama, the use of by-laws for the improvement of infant malnutrition has had even more severe limitations, due to conflict for other reasons between the local people and the enforcement agencies. In addition, the spheres in which behaviour can be altered by the application of by-laws are very limited. It may be possible to ensure that famine reserves of cassava and sweet potatoes are kept, possibly together with stores of protein foods, as recommended in the report of the Bukedi Food and Nutrition Project.[30] But allocation of these foodstuffs to children cannot be enforced, and can only be brought about by parents accepting the value of these foodstuffs for maintaining the health of their children. In West Budama a high priority is placed on the health and welfare of children, and large amounts of money may be spent on things which are thought to ensure their well-being.

Finally, to be effective, a demonstration has to be limited and show precisely what the relationship is between the recommended activities and the goals to be achieved.

NOTES

I wish to thank Dr. Caroline Hutton and Mr. Graham Fennell for reading and commenting on earlier drafts of this paper.
1.   N.S. Scrimshaw, 'Food: World Problems', in D.L. Sills (ed), *International Encyclopaedia of the Social Sciences*, Vol. 5 (MacMillan, New York, 1966), 503-504.
2.   See, for example, K. L. Howard, *Diet and Achievement Among Schoolchildren in a Depressed Community* (Unpublished M.Sc. Thesis, University of Hawaii, 1966); F. Lowenstein, 'Nutrition and Working Efficiency (with special reference to the tropics)', *Food and Nutrition in Africa* (The news bulletin of the joint FAO/WHO/OAUSTRU Regional Food and Nutrition Commission for Africa, Ghana; 6, 1968); E. Pollitt, 'Poverty and Malnutrition: Cumulative Effect on Intellectual Development', *Les Carnets de l'Enfance* (Assignment Children, 14, UNICEF, 1971).
3.   For example, P.L. Pathak, 'Nutritional Adaptation to Low Dietary Intakes of Calories; Proteins; Vitamins and Minerals in the Tropics', *American Journal of Clinical Nutrition*, 6 (1958); J.C. Waterlow, 'Observations on the mechanism of adaptation to low protein intakes', *The Lancet* (November 23, 1968); G.W.E. Wolstenholme and M. O'Connor (eds), *Nutrition and Infection* (Ciba Foundation Study Group, 31, Churchill, London, 1967).
4.   For example, A. Burgess and R.F.A. Dean (eds), *Malnutrition and Food Habits* (Tavistock Publications, London, 1962); M. Gober, 'The Psychological Changes Accompanying Kwashiorkor', *Courier*, 6 (1956), and 'The Psycho-Motor Development of African Children in the First Year and the Influence of Maternal Behaviour', *Journal of Social Psychology*, 47 (1958); M. Gober and R.F.A. Dean, 'Psychological Factors in the Etiology of Kwashiorkor', *Bulletin of the World Health Organization*, 12 (1955); C.W. Golby, 'The Role of the Experimental Psychologist', in J. Yudkin and J.C. McKenzie (eds), *Changing Food Habits* (McGibbon and Kee, London, 1964); N.S. Scrimshaw and J.E. Gordon (eds), *Malnutrition, Learning and Behaviour* (M.I.T. Press, 1968); World Health Organization,

'Deprivation of Maternal Care: a Reassessment of its Effects', *Public Health Papers 14* (World Health Organization, Geneva, 1962).

5.   See, for instance, M.Read, 'The Role of the Anthropologist' in Judkin and McKenzie, *Changing Food Habits* and A.I. Richards, *Land, Labour and Diet* (Oxford University Press, London, 1939).

6.   Baker Jones, 'Food and Nutrition Projects in the Bukedi District of Uganda' (Expanded Programme of Technical Assistance Report, 1825; FAO, Rome, 1964).

7.   Ibidem, 15.

8.   Ibidem, 11.

9.   Ibidem, 11.

10.   Ibidem, 14.

11.   For example, M. McArtheur, 'Assignment Report on Malaya' (WHO, 1950, mimeographed); S. Wallman, 'The Communication of Measurement in Basutoland', *Human Organization*, 24, 3 (1965).

12.   See F.G. Burke, *Local Government and Politics in Uganda* (Syracuse University Press, Syracuse, 1964); C. Leys, *Politicians and Policies* (East African Publishing House, Nairobi, 1966); Uganda Protectorate, *Report of the Commission of Enquiry into Disturbances in the Eastern Province* (Government Printer, Entebbe, 1960).

13.   Baker Jones, 'Food and Nutrition Projects', 11.

14.   Ibidem, 12.

15.   The study on which this discussion is based was carried out from 1965 to 1967 in West Budama county, and it is the organization of government departments during this time which is described. A fuller presentation of data collected is to be found in the author's 'Social and Economic Aspects of Nutrition, in Padhola, Bukedi District, Uganda' (Unpublished Ph.D. thesis, University of London, 1969); 'Nutrition and Social Planning', in R. Apthorpe (ed), *People, Planning and Development Studies* (Frank Cass, London, 1970), and 'Food Consumption Patterns in Padhola', D.G.R. Belshaw and J.P. Stanfield (eds), *Nutrition and Food Supply in an African Economy* (Makerere Institute for Social Research, Kampala, 1972).

16.   For the purpose of this study economic status is defined in terms of cash income. As cotton is the major source of farm cash incomes, income from cotton was taken as indicative of total farm incomes. The only non-farm income taken into account was that earned by regular employment or by shopkeeping or trading in fish. Economic status refers to the status of a man who is head of a cash-budgeting unit. A single cash-budgeting unit included a man and his wives and dependents, and may consist of a number of consumption units. A consumption unit consists of all those who feed from a single kitchen.

17.   It has been shown in a number of other studies that there is a relationship between malnutrition of children and the education of their mothers; see, e.g. Scrimshaw and Gordon, *Malnutrition, Learning and Behaviour*. However, in my study no statistically significant relationship was found between the nutritional status of the children and the educational history of their mothers. There are a number of possible explanations for this lack of correlation. One important consideration is that very few of the women had any education. 81 percent of the women in my sample had no education at all.

18.   Many villagers are never reached by the medical staff, since for a great variety of reasons they do not go to the various medical centres. See Sharman, 'Social and Economic Aspects of Nutrition in Padhola'.

19.   A maternity centre was completed at one of the local dispensaries in 1966 and later acquired the status of a health centre. Prior to this there were no health centres in West Budama.

20.   A 'progressive' farmer has been defined as one 'who actively follows the advice and puts into practice the instructions given to him by the Department of Agriculture, or the Department of Veterinary Services and Animal Industry, for the proper management of his farm.' In practice these are all farmers who have made some success of their farming and are thus wealthier men. 'Emergent' farmers are those who are becoming progressive farmers!

21.   These findings are relevant to discussions which have been going on for about 50 years among economists, and latterly among sociologists and social anthropologists on the

nature of 'dual economies' and the means whereby economic development and improvement in living conditions may be brought about in the areas concerned. For a short resumé of the history of the discussion and reference to some specific studies, see W.F. Wertheim, 'Economy, Dual', in D.L. Sills (ed), *International Encyclopaedia of the Social Sciences*, Vol. 4 (Macmillan, New York, 1968).

22.   For a general discussion of the material relevant to this question, see B. Brock, 'The Sociology of the Innovator' (paper presented to the East African Agricultural Economics Society Conference, 1969, mimeographed).

23.   Until recently religious and political affiliations were almost completely coincident at the local level in this area. While I was there the situation was becoming more complex and the banning of the Democratic Party and later upheavals will, of course, have altered the situation further. For the development and organization of political parties at a national level, see D.A. Low, *Political Parties in Uganda, 1949-1962* (Institute of Commonwealth Studies, Commonwealth Papers 8; Athlone Press, London, 1962).

24.   Estimates of the number of Protestants and Catholics in West Budama tend to vary depending on the religious affiliations of those making the estimate. Also, the proportion of Catholics to Protestants varies within the county, so that no accurate estimates can be made from a survey in one parish.

25.   This is an important consideration in Uganda. See, for example, D.M.S. Coles, *The Vegetable Oil Crushing Industry in East Africa* (Makerere Institute for Social Research, Occasional Paper 4; Oxford University Press, Nairobi, 1968).

26.   There are many other factors to take into account when assessing these respective policies. See Sharman, 'Social and Economic Aspects of Nutrition in Padhola'.

27.   See P.S.E.G. Harland, 'Mulanda Project Report', mimeo, 1963 and 'Mulanda Project Report', *Journal of Tropical Paediatrics and African Child Health*, 12, 1966.

28.   Harland, ibidem, gave only the name *ther*. *Kidimbiya* is generally translated as anaemia, but children who are severely malnourished but are not followed by another child are also said to have kidimbiya.

29.   It should be mentioned that these animals were not previously reared in the area, and it was uncertain how palatable the local inhabitants found them.

30.   Baker Jones, 'Food and Nutrition Projects'.

V

THE DYNAMICS OF RURAL SOCIETIES

H.U.E. THODEN VAN VELZEN

STAFF, KULAKS AND PEASANTS:
A STUDY OF A POLITICAL FIELD

POWER AND PENETRATION

The Penetration Model

This paper is concerned with the complex reality of penetration at 'grass-roots' level, presenting a picture of penetration in a particular corner of the periphery. The study is based on case material from the Rungwe District in Southwestern Tanzania.[1] In particular, the consequences of penetration for emerging power relationships among the peasantry will be explored.

The fieldworker operating at the local level has the use of at least three concepts for studying penetration problems, i.e. penetrators, penetration goals, and penetrative efforts. The *penetrators* are entrusted with implementing the policies designed to achieve the penetration goals. The *penetration goals* are defined by the authorities of a polity. They can be divided into (a) goals pertaining to administrative penetration, and (b) goals related to the transformation of social and economic relationships in a country. The first type includes (a) the creation and maintenance of law and order (e.g. the establishment of a unified legal system and the combatting of physical aggression); (b) the provision of social services such as schools, health and agricultural extension facilities to the peasantry; and (c) the extraction of resources, e.g. local rate collection, beer taxes and other revenues. The second, the transformation type of goals, is more specific to Tanzania. It includes (a) the abolition of the traditional political organization as an officially recognized authority structure, (b) the establishment of a formal micro-political structure — TANU's cell system and Village and Ward Development Committees, and (c) the establishment of a new pattern of economic relationships among peasants. The latter, known as *ujamaa*, is clearly the most ambitious goal as it tries to influence the distribution of the means of production among the peasants.

The distinction between administrative and transformation penetration goals is analytical; in real life they are frequently conjoined. For example, the levying of taxes stimulated the cultivation of cash crops by African small-holders because they needed money to pay their local rates. Administrative penetration thus caused — and very probably was aimed at — the transform-ation of rural society. This is also true of schools and other services provided by the Government. As Saul has rightly stressed, an analytical model built on these concepts cannot deal adequately with 'the complex sorts of interaction which take place between *social forces*, mature and emergent, in a country like Tanzania...'[2]

Penetrative efforts are conscious attempts by penetrators 'to reach down to the village level and touch the daily lives of the people', as Pye formulates it.[3] The situation is far more complex than a mere enumeration of types of efforts; the changes wrought by government in rural communities run much deeper and have far wider ramifications than the results of specific penetrative efforts would suggest. For example, TANU Cell leaders (*Barozi*) have almost overnight acquired an important judicial function, which greatly exceeds the instructions received from Dar es Salaam, local government officials and TANU leaders. Cell leaders settle cases, impose fines and charge fees for arbitration. They also act as a 'court of appeal' for people dissatisfied with the judgement of another cell leader. During the period of my fieldwork one primary court magistrate at least had objected to these practices, although with little success. Thus, if the analy-sis were to be focused too narrowly on separate penetrative efforts, some of the more important changes which are triggered off by the penetration situ-ation might escape our attention. Similarly, an approach which concentrated on entire institutions would be an extension of the study of penetrative efforts. One might then study the problems which arise from the scarcity of skilled manpower as this affects particular government agencies, or deficiencies of strategy in regard to the allocation of necessary funds, or the blocking of clogged and overloaded communication channels.

Such studies have shortcomings, not least because they divert attention away from the total situation in which the penetrators operate. Conclusions drawn from such 'partial' investigations would in many cases be irrelevant to the understanding of rural society in East Africa because they would overlook the complex nature of the interaction among the various political actors and the close weave of interest between penetrators and wealthy peasants. More-over, this approach would fail to recognize that the 'modernizing elite' is itself being influenced by the very forces which it tries to control and give direction to. Above all, it does not offer an analytical framework which enables us to interpret all the detailed findings which a study of institutions may produce. Instead, what is needed is a theoretical framework which can generate relevant analyses and integrate the findings of research of more limited scope into a larger and more meaningful context. An attempt to outline such a framework might start with some notions from political anthropology.

The Power Struggle

All human societies experience conflict over scarce resources and social honour, though the struggle may assume different forms depending on the society concerned and its particular point in history. At times it can be between classes; in other cases it is difficult to recognize any pattern among a multitude of antagonistic actions. Nonetheless, the central theme of this paper is that *penetration alters the struggle by adding a new dimension to it*, acting as a ferment on some emergent forces while stifling others, and giving rise to un-planned and often unexpected forms of power concentration and political alignment. Penetration may halt some forms of competition while exacerbating other conflicts into higher levels of intensity. Thus, the struggle over scarce re-sources and social honour is taken as a variable and its interrelationships with processes of penetration are explored.

There seem to be three general ways in which these two variables relate. First, processes of penetration create a class of penetrators, 'the people who ride the "penetrative" machine and therefore have a vested interest in it'.[4] They act as gatekeepers[5] in the sense that the resources that accompany the penetrative efforts flow into the community through channels which they con-trol. To some extent they are in a position to re-direct this stream and shift its projected course, thereby providing privileges to certain sectors of the peasantry. The gatekeepers may also take their toll as the resources pass them, and often do so. Thus, the penetrators are contestants in the struggle for two reasons. They play a minor but increasingly important role in shaping the dis-tribution of resources. More important, the penetrators cannot be indifferent towards developments in rural areas because they use their advantageous pos-ition to develop mutually profitable exchange relationships with the wealthier peasants. They thus acquire a stake in the distribution of wealth.

Second, once the resources arrive at their destination, a new factor is intro-duced into the power equation. They may bolster the establishment, but they may also disturb the status quo by giving the unprivileged a chance to improve their position. In whatever direction these consequences point, the 'external' resources alter the power profile of a rural community. Fundamental to the analysis, therefore, is a study of the power distribution in the recipient com-munity and the way in which it 'digests' the incoming resources.

Third, penetration means changing the rules of political competition. Physi-cal aggression in many communities is no longer feasible. In many areas of Tanzania the traditional village meeting can no longer proscribe a person, as effective intervention by the administration and party officials has curtailed this traditional means of social control. The primary court now occupies a more prominent place in the settlement of disputes. Also, the establishment of the 'ten house group' or TANU cell system introduced new sets of rules by which to regulate competition. A change in the rules of political competition meant a change in the power equation.

For all these reasons, it is necessary to explore the relationship between penetrators and rural communities, differentiated in terms of wealth, honour and power. We shall distinguish between two categories in the rural community: the wealthy farmers who own most of the land, and the poor peasants. There is no clear-cut demarcation line between the two groups. The wealthier peasants are here referred to as *kulaks*,[6] a concept stripped of most of the emotional connotations of oppression, repression and exploitation which it acquired in Soviet history. By 'kulaks' I simply mean the better-off farmers whose position in rural areas has become controversial since Tanzania committed itself to socialism. 'Better-off' is a relative concept and therefore has to be operationally defined anew for each rural community.

The basic concept for our analysis is that of a 'political field': *the totality of relations among actors oriented towards the same political prizes and/or ideology*.[7] Our political field comprises the relationships between three main sets of actors: penetrators, kulaks, and peasants. These political actors are oriented towards the scarce resources which are significant for all agrarian communities: land in the first place, but also 'external' resources, i.e. the expertise, financial support and other forms of assistance which the penetrators, government personnel and party functionaries, can make available.

Rural communities in Tanzania are encapsulated in larger wholes. Following Bailey,[8] a distinction between the internal political structure of the rural community (Field A) and the structure of the encapsulating system (Field B) will be useful. In fact, various 'B' fields encapsulate the rural community: those of the administration and the political party (TANU) are the most important. However, as these fields overlap to a considerable extent and as our analysis will be mainly focused on Field A, we shall not discriminate between 'B' fields.[9]

The penetrators are participants in both field A and field B; the kulaks on some occasions are participants in field B, the peasants as yet seldom participate in the encapsulating field. To give these abstract statements more concrete form, a member of the penetrator 'class' such as an agricultural extension officer may be at pains to establish good relationships with the District Chairman of TANU, while at the same time he may defend a kulak who fights to retain a valuable garden. This extension officer is then a participant in the field of district politics (a 'B' field) as well as that of the local community (the 'A' field).

In the following sections a descriptive account will be given of the composition, power base and operations of the two elite groups and their relationships with the peasants, while the final section will analyze the balancing of power among these various groups in the political field. Thus, while the earlier parts examine mainly structural aspects, the later ones focus on the dynamics of power in the field.

'STAFF PEOPLE': A RURAL ELITE

This analysis of the elite position and role of government personnel is based mainly on fieldwork in Bulambia Division in Rungwe District. The administrative centre of Bulambia is Itumba (see map), which is first and foremost a peasant community. Of the 230 households comprising approximately 1000 people, nearly 200 households depend exclusively on agriculture for their livelihood; the remainder are households of government personnel.

General Characteristics

The agents of penetration in Rungwe District — and probably also in other rural areas of Tanzania — are almost exclusively civil servants. The role of TANU leaders at village or ward level is generally of less consequence than that of the administrative officers. All civil servants, whether paid by local or central government, are called 'staff people' (*WaSitafu*) by the peasants. Resident staff in Itumba comprises the Divisional Executive Officer (DEO), his treasurer and messengers; the Village Executive Officer (VEO); the teachers of Itumba Extended Primary School; the agricultural extension officers; a veterinary assistant; the magistrate of the primary court with his clerk and messengers; the medical dispenser (Rural Medical Aid) and his sweeper; a community development officer; a midwife; and a police officer with his constables. In other parts of Bulambia there are two medical dispensers, teachers of a few primary schools, three VEO's and three extension officers. Forty-three of the 58 wage-earners in Bulambia Division were resident in Itumba.[10]

The staff people play a major role in the development of Tanzania. Actively propagating the values of self-reliance and egalitarianism at village meetings, they transmit the national ideology to the peasants and organize communal efforts to build the political and social apparatus necessary for the transformation of rural society. They have thus been engaged in the extension and consolidation of TANU's grass roots cell system and claim a major share in the success of many local government councils, particularly the Village Development Committees.

At the same time, the presence of staff people introduces a not insignificant element of inequality in rural areas, although they personally are not responsible for each and every aspect of their lives which differentiates them from the peasants. The single most important factor that sets this group apart from the peasants as a highly envied elite is the fact that they draw salaries. Their regular and guaranteed income is in almost all cases higher than the income of the richest peasants. Tea, coffee and pyrethrum farmers, who are the most successful in Rungwe District, can manage to net a cash income ranging from Shillings 1,000 to 2,500 per annum.[11] But these are exceptions. Average income among cash crop farmers in coffee and pyrethrum does not exceed Shillings 750 and

500, respectively, per annum. The annual income of the most lowly paid staff category, the messengers, averages Shillings 2,000. The field assistant, the lowest functionary among extension personnel, often receives more than Shillings 2,500 per annum. Furthermore, government personnel enjoy substantial fringe benefits.[12]

The elite position of the staff people is demonstrated by their attitudes and symbolic behaviour. The staff form a social grouping with distinctive prestige symbols, enjoying a higher living standard, as evidenced in their clothing, housing, food and recreation. After working hours they associate more with each other than with the peasants. Almost all staff people, with the exception of some messengers, are members of the Moravian Church, whereas most peasants are adherents of traditional religions.

The staff people consider themselves an elite entitled to social esteem. They seek to project an image of honesty and devotion. A staff person may be heard to remark in a village or in a court case: 'But X [another staff person] has come to serve all the people; how can he possibly have cheated Mr. so-and-so?'

Staff have messengers, but many functions of the messenger serve merely to underscore the hierarchical pattern of relations within the staff superstructure and the privileged position of the staff in general. Regarding the relations between messengers and other staff within the cooperative, an institution so often depicted as the bulwark of rural democracy, Sterkenburg[13] has observed that 'the messenger is a legacy of colonial times, automatically appointed wherever an office is opened. In addition to his usual duties he is ordered to carry out all sorts of activities considered by the secretary as not in agreement with his [the secretary's] position, such as opening windows and removing typewriters and even personal services to the secretary.' Sterkenburg's observation equally applies to other organizations, such as the primary court or the council of the division, the Divisional Executive Officer, and his treasurer and assistants.

Staff people manifest a mild distaste for manual work. Although some till their own fields, their absence from nation-building projects and other communal manual work is conspicuous. They may not even join in the traditional collective digging of a grave. At meetings of the Village Development Committee (VDC) and on similar occasions, they tend to adopt a paternalistic posture. Thus, at one VDC meeting an extension officer remarked: 'Remember, you farmers are the chickens and we are the mother hens. If you follow our example you will survive, but if you are not attentive you will perish.'

Staff people have tended to assume certain prerogatives which are widely resented. For example, when a limited ujamaa programme was introduced in Itumba in November 1967 the peasants were told to perform all future agricultural activities – from tilling to harvesting – collectively within their TANU cell. It soon became apparent, however, that staff who had fields to cultivate did not participate in the new socialist agriculture. In fact, they were the only

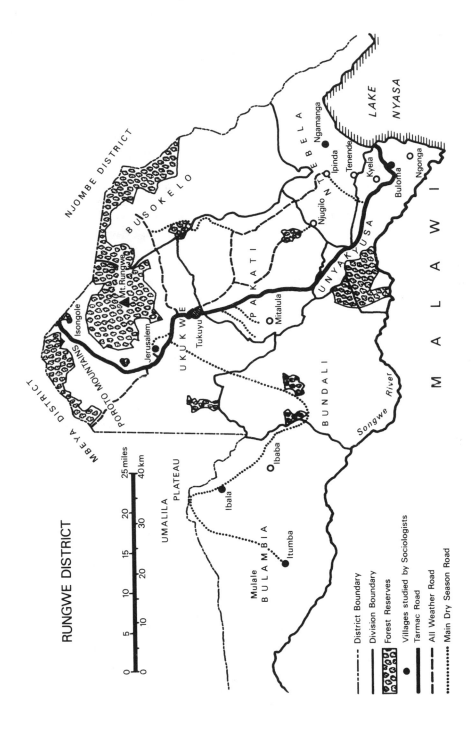

people in Itumba who managed to escape the obligations implicit in this programme.

Although staff people do not usually themselves participate in nation building projects, they admonish the people to undertake such works. A community development officer commented on his technique to keep a road construction project going: 'It is my aim to make the peasants enthusiastic by helping them for a short period, say ten minutes. A longer period is not necessary; they will not even like to see us, their leaders, work like common men.' Furthermore, the peasants are expected, without compensation, to build and repair the houses of staff people. Neither the staff nor their wives join them, let alone help them, in these activities, not even if it concerns their own houses.

Meetings are the order of the day in Tanzania and Bulambia is no exception. A fair estimate is that one-third to a half of the total available time of functionaries like the Divisional and Village Executive Officers, extension officers and community development workers is spent at meetings. Meetings of the VDC are convened at about ten places in Bulambia, the intervals varying from two weeks to three months. Attending meetings and giving speeches constitute an important part of a staff member's task in a rural area.

A paternalistic tone characterizes the speeches of staff members at such meetings. The staff operate as a group of specialists, relying on exhortation rather than discussion regarding a wide range of subjects from the buying of a TANU membership card to the wearing of clean clothes. A report of a meeting which took place in May 1967 in the area of the Mulale Village Development Committee might illustrate some of these characteristics.[14]

The chairman of the VDC opened the meeting with a short prayer and expressed his gratitude that so many important people had come to show the people the true path to a better life. He asked the people of Mulale to listen carefully so that none of the lessons taught would be lost on them. He castigated the cell leaders (about half of the total number) who had not come to the meeting.

After the chairman's introduction, a series of officials then spoke. The Village Executive Officer of Itumba Ward: 'Mulale is one of these areas which makes us ashamed because of the laziness and foolish activities of its people.' As examples of the latter complaint he mentioned: 'Backward tribal customs', 'witchcraft'. The VEO admonished them to 'buy TANU membership cards and pay your taxes'; without these things, he warned, they would be in serious trouble. He also took strong exception to the fact that so many of the cell leaders were not present: 'they will be punished without mercy'. He wound up his speech with a joke: 'a lorry will come very soon, loaded to the top with blankets. All of you will get one and afterwards you will not be disturbed by any more meetings because you will sleep soundly.'

The TANU chairman of Itumba ward:

I have heard that many of you are very big witches. Why don't you weed out your fields or construct good roads with your witchcraft? That is much better than killing the children of your neighbours. You people here are wasting your time, instead of working hard for progress. You are thinking all day of making one big medicine which when it is completed will kill one man. But what is the use of this? On the same day many people are born in this world, there will always be more and more. This must make it clear to you that your work is without good sense. I am happy today because I see that your wives have put on clean clothes; that is how we want it to be. But we know there are still many women in this area who do not want to work hard. In this way they cannot sell anything and the result will be that they will have no money to buy new clothes. Furthermore, I know that many women around here do not wash regularly; at night they sleep on the hides of cattle. All this will have to change.

The Community Development Officer:

I am new to this area, so it will be useful if I tell you something about my character. I am not a kind and polite man: I am cruel. If I see that government orders are not obeyed, I will know where to find you and how to punish you. I do not care if you hate me. The only important thing to me is that the orders of the government are fulfilled. I know you are truly blind otherwise you would have appreciated more the progress that staff have brought to Bulambia. Now we are going to make you rise from a long sleep. I have a strong medicine for this job, we will give it to all lazy people. It is better than the poison which you use when you want to kill somebody. The old people should lead the younger ones, but instead of giving guidance they are engaged in bewitching others and they only select good citizens and victims for their heinous crimes.

He then announced that every Saturday from then onwards, the people would have to work on a road construction project.

The representative on the District Council, the *diwani*, then exhorted them to work harder and pay more tax. He was followed by a traditional headman who urged them to pay tax and buy a TANU membership card:

Tax receipt and TANU card always go hand in hand; without these two you are in trouble. If you want to make a trip to a relative in Mbeya, the TANU Youth Leagues will stop the bus and check if you have got these two papers. The same might happen if you go to a hospital to ask for medicine. If you cannot produce the documents people will know: this is a man who opposes our beloved government.

The Divisional Executive Officer urged the audience to start the road construction work announced by the DCO and to continue with the building of a permanent school building. He pointed out the dangers of drinking ('laziness is the result') and dancing ('your daughters will get syphilis'). He advised the women to buy TANU cards, because without these cards they could never hope to get a divorce from the courts.[15] He then turned to the men: 'I will never employ a man as a messenger if he cannot show me his TANU card.'

Following the speeches and one or two questions from the peasants, the chairman closed the meeting with a short prayer.

A second, 'joint staff'[16] meeting of interest was held in Itumba from August till December 1967. The committee dealt with two main problems: (a) licenses

and regulations concerning the consumption of home-brewed beer, and
(b) nation-building projects. As regards the first, desirous of preventing tax
evasion and curbing fighting, government officials announced that everybody
who wished to drink beer at home should inform the Village Executive Officer.
When some staff in the meeting protested, they were assured that this only pertained to people of low rank because 'we all know that people of high rank will
not tolerate fighting in their houses.'

Most of the time was spent discussing nation-building activity. The TANU
Branch Chairman of Itumba warned the staff that the Arusha Declaration made
it extremely difficult for them to avoid direct involvement in such activity.
There could be no legitimate excuse for shirking such involvement, particularly
because it would not entail more than a few hours of work per week. This
point of view was backed by the DEO. While paying homage to the Arusha
Declaration, most other staff people nonetheless argued that they and some of
their colleagues should be exempted from such work. As one put it, 'We staff
are already working for the Government, why should one work twice for the
same employer?' Another remarked that some staff people, e.g. the rural medical aid personnel, the midwife, and the police officer must always be at their
posts: 'If these people are to participate in nation-building projects, all progress
in Bulambia will stop.' Still other staff submitted that the best way for them to
help the nation would be to work harder and to increase the quality of work in
their assigned roles: 'It would be useless for a staff person to waste his education and training on road construction.' In the end, little headway was made
in resolving this issue at the joint staff meeting. It was clearly the *manual* work
which nation-building projects involved that degraded them in the eyes of the
staff. As a result, only the DEO continued to work regularly with the peasants
on self-help schemes; the majority of the staff never participated.

The Position of the Staff in the Political Field

The staff are salaried and thus not dependent on agriculture, although many
have acquired land. Few have relatives in the area, a fact which debars peasants
from communicating their grievances via the staff member's kin and putting
pressure on him in this roundabout way. Moreover, many staff people are regularly transferred,[17] a factor which makes for even less dependence on the
peasants. A transfer also makes it easier to leave one's debts unpaid, or even
escape prosecution or disciplinary action, as the following specific example illuminates: Protests were piling up against X, a community development officer,
who among other things had said on at least two public occasions that 'all
peasants should come and work on self-help schemes, the half-witted ones not
excluded.' This statement was extensively discussed in the local beer clubs and
was generally interpreted as implying that 'many of us are half-wits'. Two

TANU cell leaders finally decided to bring the matter before the next VDC meeting. At the meeting X was absent, ostensibly due to illness. When one of the cell leaders raised the issue he was cut short by the chairman who ruled that as the community development officer was not present to defend himself the matter could not be discussed. Before the next VDC meeting took place X had requested and obtained his transfer and had left the area.

The policy of frequent transfer for civil servants was common practice in the colonial administration. One reason advanced for it is that it prevents the establishment of patronage relationships which take some time to cultivate. True as this may be, the above indicates that there are also disadvantages. Moreover, as we shall subsequently note, the close cooperation among staff often entails the inheritance of the network of clients developed by a particular staff member.

In addition to their close contact during the working day, staff of a rural centre meet daily in local beer clubs or, on a rotating basis, in the houses of colleagues. These after-work gatherings usually start late in the afternoon and continue until the beer is finished around nine or ten o'clock in the evening. They listen to music over the radio, drink, play cards and discuss local and district events. In Itumba during 1966 and 1967 there were two such groups, one composed of teachers, the other of staff like the DEO, magistrate, police officer and treasurer of the council. The main function of these 'recreational clubs' was to kill time. As one member of staff explained: 'In these remote areas we suffer many deprivations. That is why we need these clubs. They help the time to pass more quickly.' Staff who have been resident in an area for an extended period, may invite one or two peasants to their parties; however, peasants are not usually present at the gatherings.

The majority of the staff in the Rungwe District are territorially concentrated in one or two and sometimes three places in a division. This physical concentration facilitates contact and regular visiting, thereby reinforcing the tendency towards in-group solidarity. During weekends the staff in places such as Itumba are visited by their friends from more outlying posts who come to share their beer and exchange news. Many of the staff pay regular visits to Tukuyu, the administrative centre of the district, some staying there as long as one week every month, waiting to draw their salaries.[18] That news travels so quickly is obviously a result of this high degree of interaction and the mutual dependence it creates among staff members.

In circumstances where most of the staff circulate among a limited number of posts — for the majority within the district, for a smaller group within the region — there is a high degree of mutual awareness of each other's experiences. They provide their colleagues with social information on the places where they will be posted: who are the troublemakers among the peasants, where to buy the best beer, and who are persons of consequence from whom certain services and gifts can be expected. For instance, the day after magistrate Y arrived at his new station in Itumba he sent a message to Chomo, a kulak, to come immediately to the court building. Upon Chomo's arrival the magistrate asked him if it was true that he was a bad man, noting that he was impressed by the number of cases in which Chomo had been involved, either as the one who brought action or the one who was himself prosecuted or sued. Chomo gave many excuses, after which the magistrate assured him that for the moment he would let the matter rest. Chomo hurried home and the evening of the same day his children brought cabbages, onions and sugarcane to the house of the magistrate.

The implementation of government programmes often involves the combined approach of all staff. At meetings with peasants, the majority of staff in the division are present and a wide variety of topics are discussed. As we have seen, staff support each other's views, often advocating programmes which lie outside the scope of their immediate competence. Though the community development officer is a natural jack-of-all-trades, a magistrate may be found advising peasants on measures needed for ujamaa farming or an extension officer giving technical advice on road construction. Meetings for more specific purposes may also be attended by a large number of staff. Thus, a meeting organized by the CDO to start a road construction may be attended by the DEO, VEO and the extension officer. Again, at the meeting to introduce ujamaa, all staff were present.

A salaried job in the local or central government is highly coveted. To keep their job, staff may use irrational as well as rational means. Some may consult diviners to know which persons intend to use sorcery to make them ill so as to be able to take over their jobs; others buy charms and medicines to protect themselves. All realise that to keep a job, good relations with colleagues and superiors in the department and in the local authority or TANU hierarchy are essential. At some future day one might need the intercession of a colleague with his superiors so as to keep a job, to get a transfer or a promotion, or to be employed elsewhere. The latter is especially important wherever staff have been forced to resign after irregularities. Sterkenburg reports, for example, that of the 16 former secretaries of primary societies of the Rungwe District who occupied posts in TANU or in the local or central government services, eight had earlier been dismissed from their secretarial posts for irregularities.[19] This suggests the maintenance of fairly effective contacts on the part of these secretaries.

A further reason inducing staff members to close ranks is to maintain their powerful position vis-à-vis the peasants. If staff members cooperate they can control most of the legitimate political and juridical arenas — the council of the division[20] the primary court, the joint staff meeting, the parents' committee of the local primary school, and particularly the Ward (previously, Village) Development Committee. Although not formally members of the latter, staff have usually always been present during their meetings and have influenced their decisions.

The presence of the staff ensures, for example, that the Ward Development Committee does not turn into a platform for discussing issues which are — in the eyes of the staff — harmful to their interests or to what they regard as the interests of the nation.

Only in exceptional cases is it possible for the peasants to develop a common front against a staff member who has aroused their displeasure. A peasant may on occasion impulsively castigate a staff member at a meeting, but before it is over he is likely to make an about-turn and lavish praise on the man he had just finished criticizing. Good relationships with the staff are coveted for the favours they will bring; the last thing to do is to remain *openly* hostile to one of its members. In the Development Committees, which are the scene of much infighting between kulaks, the aim of many skirmishes is to curry favour with staff members and to discredit other kulaks.

A peasant who gets involved in a dispute with a staff member expects to have to fight the whole of the staff because of the network of intra-staff support and cooperation which exists. A staff member who openly sides with a peasant undermines his social position. Thus, in one instance in which a police signaller and a corporal thrashed a man from Itumba, one of the constables (who came from Itumba) wrote a letter of protest to the officer in charge of the district. Shortly thereafter the police signaller and the corporal were arrested, but the complaining constable was dismissed two months later after his colleagues had complained to their superiors about 'his unwillingness to cooperate'.

The staff take care that disputes within their ranks remain behind scenes. The controversy that erupted in the joint staff meeting over nation-building projects, for example, was shrouded in a veil of secrecy. TANU chairmen are explicitly requested by the staff not to report to the peasants what is discussed in meetings.

The staff people form the first and most powerful elite in rural areas. We now turn to the second elite — the kulaks. First, we will examine the existing forms of stratification based on disparities in the ownership of land. We will then consider the interplay between the kulaks and the penetrators, the participants of the encapsulating field B.

THE KULAKS

Unequal Distribution of Land

In *Socialism and Rural Development* President Nyerere draws attention to the emergence of classes in Tanzania's rural areas resulting from the introduction and spread of a cash crop economy. The increasing scarcity of land in the Rungwe District has been shown to be a factor moulding social and political relations in that area. Wilson points to the influence of 'land scarcity' on political leadership and mentions that class distinctions are developing in the Lake Plain of the Rungwe District.[21] For the same area Gulliver discusses the relationship between 'land shortage', 'labour migration' and 'social conflict'.[22] Elsewhere we have argued that the most important factor determining social inequality in agrarian communities is an unequal distribution of land.[23] This we found to be the case for areas with strong economic differentiation — where part of the agrarian population has no land at all (Buloma on the Lake Shore of Rungwe District) — as well as for areas with less marked differentiation. Bulambia division belongs to this latter category. Two facts have to be noted as regards economic differentiation in Itumba: (a) each peasant possesses enough land to provide for his own subsistence needs; (b) the higher quality fields — the river gardens or river plots — belong to a minority among the peasants.

Three distinct agricultural zones can be distinguished in the area:[24]

(i)   *The zone of ash cultivation.* Here, slash-and-burn agriculture is practised on so-called *chitemene* fields in the hills and on the high plateau. Millet is the main crop. The two other agricultural zones are found in the wide river valley where most of Itumba's inhabitants live.

(ii)   *The zone of the intermediate fields.* These fields are situated a little higher on the valley floor. Maize, sweet potatoes, ground nuts and cassava are grown in this zone. Apart from places close to the house where manure and sweepings are deposited, yields from this type of field tend to be considerably lower than those from chitemene fields and river gardens. Fields in the intermediate zone are tilled from four to six years continuously under a system of crop rotation. After this period the land is left fallow for two or three years.

(iii)   *The river zone.* During the long dry season stretching from the end of April until the middle of November only a narrow belt of low-lying river plots remains cultivable, the other fields becoming withered and barren. During those months the green ribbon of river plots forms a luxuriant contrast against the brown and yellow setting of fields where nothing grows.

River plots offer three advantages to their owners: (1) they consist of fertile alluvial soils with yields on the average three times higher than in the intermediate zone; (2) river gardens are either irrigated or retain enough moisture to yield a second crop during the dry season; (3) crops different from those cultivated in the other zones can grow in the river gardens, viz. sugarcane, tobacco and vegetables. The most important crops in the river zone, however, are maize and beans.

None of these different types of zone produces a cash crop of any importance. Both chitemene fields and river gardens form closed resources, whereas the less valuable fields in the intermediate zone are still an open resource. As the river gardens are the most important of the closed resources, it will be useful to look more closely into the ownership of river land.

The river belt within the area of Itumba village comprises 125 acres (ap-

Table 1. *Distribution of River land between Peasant Households in Itumba*

Acreage	N	%of households
- 0	70	34
0 - ½	56	27
½ - 1	40	20
1 - 1½	25	12
1½- 2	6	3
2 - 2½	2	1
2½ or more	6	3
Total	205	100%

proximately 50 hectares). It is intensely fragmented: the rather small river zone is divided into 650 parcels. Notwithstanding this extreme fragmentation, marked disparities in the ownership of river gardens occur. Most striking, 34 per cent of Itumba's peasants have not been able to obtain any land here. On the other hand, twenty households, that is 10 per cent of the total number, own 45 per cent of the total acreage of river land. Table 1 shows the distribution of these discrepancies.

The Dominant Coalition

The wealthy peasants and the penetrators cooperate in many spheres. Reciprocal forms of assistance between the two groups are so numerous by comparison with the rest of the peasantry that the kulaks and the staff may confidently be regarded as constituting a coalition. In Caplow's terms: 'A coalition is a combination of two or more actors who adopt a common strategy in contention with other actors in the same system.'[25] It is called here the 'dominant coalition' because it is the prevailing, most powerful coalition on the rural scene, although other forms also exist.

Evidence of preferential treatment being accorded to kulaks by government staff illuminates the existence of this 'dominant coalition'.

When I first arrived in Bulambia, the then Divisional Executive Officer took me on a tour to some peasants who were 'worth knowing', as he put it; he added: 'these men are willing to develop'. We first visited Chomo who, with 13 acres of riverine land, is by far the biggest landowner in Itumba. On a subsequent trip to the surrounding plateau where slash-and-burn cultivation is practised, we visited peasants X and Y who, together with four others, are immigrants of the Ndali tribe. They use irrigation techniques to water small plots along creeks. However, the original inhabitants of this area, the Nyiha, are only slowly starting to adopt these new forms of cultivation. The Divisional Executive Officer described our Ndali hosts as 'active' and 'willing to develop', while the local indigenous peasants were characterized as 'backward' and 'superstitious', prone to use witchcraft to harm the Ndali innovators. One of our Ndali hosts had been elected chairman of the Village Development Committee, despite the fact that he was only a few years resident in the area and not a member of the majority tribe among the population. Significantly, he had been proposed as a candidate by the Village Executive Officer and was elected by the raising of hands.

Visiting government and party officials to Bulambia also tend to call upon the same peasants — the richest in the community — for meals and lodging. 'M', another peasant from the Ndali tribe, has settled in an area mainly inhabited by the Malila tribe. M is known to be a rich man: he has four wives, many head of cattle, and large and fertile plots. When the agricultural extension officer visits this area once every two or three months, he always spends the night at the house of M and seldom visits other farmers.[26] Again, in Ngamanga, a village in the Lake Plain, Japhet owns between one-quarter and one-third of all paddy fields. All other peasants of the village are much smaller landowners. Japhet is the only peasant in this village who is regularly invited to join the informal meetings of the staff in Ipinda, the headquarters of Ntebela division.[27]

Government policy at times has been and is explicit in favouring the wealthy peasant. During the latter phase of colonial rule considerable pressure was exerted by the District Council on the Parish Councils to make sure that only 'progressive farmers' stood as candidates.[28] This emphasis has continued to some extent since independence. Thus, in 1968, a crop production committee (*Kamati ya chakula*) was formed in every ward, the territorial unit of the Ward Development Committee. These committees were charged with regular stocktaking of the acreage planted in various crops and with reporting their findings to the crop production committee of the district. The chairman of the ward crop production committee in Itumba received explicit instructions to select two progressive farmers for this committee; the two selected were kulaks.[29]

Although the officials of the VDC, TANU Cell and Branch are elected by the people, the authorities can influence their choice in a variety of ways. Sometimes the persuasion is indirect and subtle; on other occasions quite explicit instructions are given. Outright praise and other forms of verbal support, as well as repeated visits, are among the indirect techniques indicating favourites. If these clues are not effective, more direct measures are taken, such as demands for re-election, or allowing only one man from a certain village in the ward to stand as a candidate while no restrictions are placed on candidates from other villages within the ward.

The foregoing observations on the cooperation of staff members and kulaks as a dominant coalition are based on impressionistic and circumstantial evidence. However, there is a more objective and quantitative index with which to measure the extent of staff-kulak cooperation, namely, the representation of kulaks in official positions. The latter are here defined as Government or Party posts or functions which have been established under some kind of official

Table 2. *Official positions occupied by the wealthiest 20% of peasant households in five villages (Itumba, Ibala, Ngamanga, Buloma and Jerusalem) of Rungwe District*

Village	Total official positions available	Occupied by the wealthiest 20%
Itumba	39	26
Ibala	11	5
Ngamanga	28	17
Buloma	50	17
Jerusalem	15	7
Total	143	72 (50.3%)

sponsorship. Thus, peasants elected to local authorities, Party organizations (such as ten-house groups) and Development Committees hold official positions, but so do low-echelon personnel recruited locally, e.g. the messengers. Over-representation of kulaks in these positions is an important dimension of the dominant coalition. Kulaks recruited to fill such posts as sweepers, messengers and constables, for example, play a vital role as intermediaries between the peasants and the penetrators. Because the latter are frequently transferred and may lack adequate local information, they inevitably have to rely significantly upon the advice and initiative of these kulak intermediaries.

Over-representation is, of course, a relative matter, depending on which farmers one includes in the kulak category. Arbitrarily, the line is here drawn at the richest 20 per cent of the peasant population. The question then arises as to how many official functions are occupied by the richest 20 per cent of the population. The data for five villages are given in Table 2,[30] which shows that kulaks occupy just over half of the total official positions, thus confirming the hypothesis about their over-representation.

An additional measure of over-representation of richer peasants in 'official' elite positions would be to look at their distribution *within* the ten house groups. In the case of Ngamanga, for example, this was ascertained for 11 ten house groups. Out of a total of 22 positions, only four were occupied by peasants from the poorer half, while half of all positions were filled by peasants from the richest quarter of the population. This situation is illustrated in Table 3, the data suggesting that richer people stand a much better chance of being elected as chairman or assistant than poorer peasants.

Elite positions in the Village Development Committees (until 1967) and TANU Branch Executive Committees (after 1967) carry more weight than positions of chairman and assistant in the TANU cells, and thus provide an even better indicator for the measurement of kulak influence.

On the basis of the data given in Table 4 it appears that the tendency towards over-representation is strongest for the more important functions: kulaks occupy more than 60 per cent of all these positions. The three tables together (2, 3 and 4) show that kulaks have been more successful than other sectors of

Table 3. *Positions of chairman and assistant occupied by the richest 25% and 50% of each 'ten house group' in four villages*

Villages	Total positions	Richest 25%	Richest 50%
Itumba	24	15	20
Ibala	7	5	6
Ngamanga	22	11	19
Buloma	62	23	43
Total	115	54	88

the peasantry in occuping political and 'intermediary' functions. This fact is of no small significance in their drive to control the local political arenas.

Table 4. *Positions in Village Development Committees (until 1967) and Branch Executive Committees (after 1967) occupied by the wealthiest 20% of peasant households*

Village	Total number available	Occupied by wealthiest 20%
Itumba	10	6
Ibala	1	1
Ngamanga	5	5
Buloma	19	10
Jerusalem	7	4
Total	42	26

Forces Sustaining the Coalition

The government relies heavily on local initiative for the realization of many national goals. Self-help schemes, in particular, play a crucial part in the transformation of rural Tanzania. The central idea behind these development programmes is to have local leaders among the peasants take the initiative in the improvement of living conditions in their areas. Responsibility for the day-to-day organization is in their hands, and does not rest with government personnel. The underlying rationale is that nation building will lose momentum if local leaders do not assume this responsibility. The agencies of central government lack the means and the manpower to take over these projects. Moreover, the government has no intention of doing so because this would contradict Tanzania's participating self-reliant ideology.

Kulaks tend to emerge as leaders in self-help programmes. They stand a better chance of being elected to official posts partly because they are influential, as their powers of persuasion are greater. They can nudge their clients into nation building projects; indeed, they can even threaten them with sanctions if they do not respond. Though the influence can be exaggerated, it is clear that the wealthier peasant, generally speaking, is in a better position to exercise persuasion than are the others.

Other reasons why the staff would select their coalition partners from the richer sector of the peasantry include the fact that the wealthy peasant enjoys a higher standard of living and therefore, in the eyes of the authorities and peasants alike, exemplifies development. The following are illustrative of remarks commonly made by government officials: 'Look at the house of so-and-so. It is well built and has a corrugated iron roof. The owner is a man who knows what development is.' Or: 'Farmer X is growing cabbages. X is a man who wants his country to develop.' Authorities who voice such opinions, however, fail to make allowance for the fact that cabbages cannot be grown outside the belt of river gardens and that a sizeable minority in Itumba does not possess any river land, while the majority of peasants own so little that they need every square yard for more essential food crops such as beans and maize.

Although staff people are not dependent on agriculture for their livelihood, all staff resident in Itumba for a period longer than two years have acquired gardens from wealthy peasants. These plots are in effect a perquisite that constitutes a valuable addition to staff salary, and incidentally fortifies the ordinary peasant belief that the staff are beholden to the big landowner.

The economic position of the kulaks upholds the dominant coalition. Their power base and its attendant patronage relationship give them preferential access to official positions.[31] Kulaks are in a position to act as patrons because they have enough land to loan to other peasants. A threat to withold plots can force these clients into supporting them in elections, as well as in votes in the Village Development Committee or on other occasions. These patron-client relationships are strongest where the dependent peasant population possesses no land at all. But even in agrarian communities such as Itumba where all peasants have sufficient land to cover their subsistence needs, the unequal distribution of the river gardens gives rise to a pattern of patron-client relationships.[32]

Another reason why staff members cannot afford to ignore the kulaks is that, paradoxically, the poorer peasants are instrumental in electing kulaks to positions of chairmen of the ten house group or as members of TANU's Branch Executive Committee. A triangular set of expectations may help to explain this. Government officials make it abundantly clear whom they regard as the best citizens, i.e. the kulaks. This in itself may suffice to legitimate the latter as middlemen in the eyes of ordinary peasants, for people reckon that a favourite of the government may more easily obtain funds and other forms of assistance for the ward or village. This argument became plain when the peasants of Ibala were discussing why they had voted for J as their representative on the board of their cooperative primary society. They argued that 'J is subservient to the authorities.[33] He is afraid to stand up to them and defend our interests. But we also know that he will not anger them or irritate them and in that way spoil the reputation of our area. The government seems to like him.'

THE BALANCING OF POWER

It was argued earlier that the concept of 'field' is useful in the analysis of the interrelationships between penetrators and other social categories in rural areas. Having delineated the various actors in the field, their power base, ideology and links with the encapsulating unit, we now turn to the dynamics of power. The balancing of power has been defined by Lasswell and Kaplan as 'the power process among the participants in a field.'[34] For this purpose it will be useful to introduce some relevant concepts from political anthropology, namely: (a) *power base* — that part of a person's resources which gives him the potential to exercise power; (b) *arena*[35] — a smaller enclave within the political field in which part of the power process takes place, which has an institutional framework for restricting and channelling antagonistic interaction; (c) the *arena map* of each participant — this comprises the perceptions of a participant concerning the power position of others in an arena or political field; (d) the *strategy* of each participant — a general plan of action for the allocation of resources, determining the scope for manoeuvre to consolidate one's gains and to inflict losses on one's rivals; and (e) a *political drama* — a series of antagonistic interactions precipitated by a crisis situation, i.e. by a state of marked or extreme insecurity among actors in the political field.

The political drama described below unfolded between 1962 and 1968 in Itumba and involved a fight over the control of resources. The danger as perceived by the mass of the peasants came from the dominant coalition of kulaks and staff people. Following this account, we shall discuss the power base, arena map and strategy of the dominant coalition and of the peasants.

A Political Drama

Mwakalinga, an agricultural extension officer (a Nyakyusa from east Rungwe District) came to live in the village of Itumba with his wife and children seven years before social tensions broke out against him. His predecessor, a native of Itumba, had prosecuted many people and left the area under fear of being bewitched by his clientele. Mwakalinga had been more lenient, but eventually he began to have similar troubles. His youngest son fell ill and died two days later; soon after, his first-born son, Simon, was attacked by bees. A sickbed visitor warned Simon that people were taking revenge actions against the family. Mwakalinga's wife was also told that witchcraft had been involved in both cases. Village talk mounted, and one name mentioned as a possible antagonist was Metson Kajinga, son of a church elder, who had several complaints against the Mwakalingas.

Metson and Simon had once vied for the hand of the same girl. When it appeared Simon would win, Metson attempted to rape the girl, and rumour had it he was prepared to use sorcery against Simon. Soon Simon fell ill and left the area temporarily. He eventually recovered and went to work for a time in Dar es Salaam. Meanwhile the girl was seduced by someone else, became pregnant, and was finally married off. The girl's father vented his anger on Metson, calling him a misfit and a parasite on others. Mwakalinga corroborated this sentiment, adding that the Kajinga's were ignorant peasants who grew arrogant when some of their number became church officials.

The Mwakalingas and the Kajingas had had a falling-out over another issue involving a man called Chomo, who had married Metson's mother, and with whom Metson did not get along. Chomo came into possession of two plots of sugarcane after the owners died, and allowed his friends, Mwakalinga and the medical dispenser, to work part of the land. Metson attempted to annex some of the land onto his own adjacent plot, and was taken to court by Chomo. In defence, Metson claimed the land did not belong to Chomo but to the sons of the former owners, who now joined Metson in pleading his case. The sons claimed they had loaned the land of their fathers to Metson, and that Chomo now claimed it because he happened to have married Metson's mother. Villagers rallied to Metson's support, and the magistrate, under considerable pressure, conceded the case to him. Feeling he had wronged Chomo, the magistrate confided through Mwakalinga that Chomo should appeal to a higher court, and gave particular instructions. Chomo borrowed money from Mwakalinga to make the appeal, and ultimately the decision was reversed. Metson continued to be rankled about the loss, telling one of the sons to beware of witchcraft by the Mwakalinga family. The son enlisted police help; eventually the matter was dropped, but not before more seeds of discontent had been sown against the Mwakalingas.

It becomes clear that villagers in general are predisposed against 'staff', such as agricultural extension officers. It is widely believed, for instance, that staff get superior medical treatment from the local dispensary. When Metson's mother falls ill and dies, the blame is first placed on the medical dispenser. Then it is noted that the medical dispenser had been loaned land by Chomo in the same way as Mwakalinga. Metson fans the flame by telling the villagers that Mwakalinga had urged the medical dispenser not to give medicine to his dying mother.

Thus events in Itumba begin to mesh to reveal a political drama which can be analyzed with the help of the concepts introduced above: power base, arena map and strategy.

Power Base of the Penetrators

The peasants have an exaggerated view of the extent to which staff members and kulaks cooperate and collude to further their interests and safeguard their privileges. Nonetheless, an objective basis for at least part of their feelings exists in the power base of the penetrators. This includes at least three considerations.

(a) The fact that staff directly control a number of legitimate arenas (the Primary Court, the investigations of the local police commander, the enquiries set up by the Divisional Executive Officer as 'Justice of the Peace'), and indirectly have insignificant influence in a number of other arenas, the most important of which is the Village (or Ward) Development Committee.

(b) The fact that staff controls access to certain material resources and benefits such as medicine and medical treatment, employment as messenger or other forms of unskilled labour, farm implements, seed and transport.

(c) The operating alliance of staff and kulaks previously analyzed and illuminated by the political drama.

Arena Map of Penetrators

A basic tenet of the penetrators is the equation of success and wealth with what are presumed to be superior innate capacities and higher ideological motivation for furthering the interests of the country. Unsuccessful or poor peasants are accordingly regarded as lazy, ignorant and conservative, and prone to practice witchcraft.

Strategy of the Penetrators

The penetrators follow two basic strategies namely, (a) 'betting on the strong' and (b) concentrating their attacks on weak spots. A 'betting on the strong' strategy accounts for the selective and preferential approach which penetrators use to bring about innovations. As Wertheim has shown, this is the strategy used by the Indian and Indonesian governments in introducing innovations:

> It is they who show a greater responsiveness to all kinds of innovations and technical improvements and who are much easier to approach for government agencies or special services. Such an approach starts implicitly from the assumption that the advanced farmers will set an example to the poorer sections, who are expected to follow the model which they are able to observe from close by. The innovation is intended to spread, like an oil-stain, to other layers of rural society. It is this approach which could be called: *betting on the strong*.

Wertheim argues, however, that the oilstain does not spread beyond a certain level and that the gains will accrue — especially when cheap agricultural labour is abundant — to a small landowning group. The same tendency has been observed by sociologists in Tanzania; it has been called the progressive, or model farmer approach. Instructions from above ensure that progressive farmers represent the peasant population on government committees. Other than that, however, there is no clear-cut government policy. 'The extension officer works in a climate of *laissez-faire* which permits him to select his audience according to his own inclinations and interests', and the same appears to hold true for personnel of other government departments. The Tanzanian paradox is that the tendency to give preferential treatment to a restricted segment of the total peasantry definitely goes against the grain of the post-Arusha national ideology.

A complementary strategy of the penetrators is to concentrate attacks on weak spots and only demand compliance with unpopular measures by those peasants who may be expected to put up the minimum of resistance. The following case illuminates this point. The fields in Itumba's intermediate zone are often cultivated for periods of four to six years continuously before the field is left to lie fallow for a period of three years. A widow Namatanga let one of her fields in this zone lie fallow in 1965. In November 1967 — at the beginning of the new agricultural season — Kalinga, a kulak, visited the Divisional Executive Officer and asked his permission to take over the widow's plot. The official called Namatanga to his office and urged her to start tilling the field immediately. The Divisional Executive Officer warned her that if she did not comply with his suggestion he would regrettably be forced to confiscate her plot and hand it over to others. He remarked: 'There are too many people around here who have not enough land.' In vain Namatanga pleaded that the plot had not sufficiently recovered its fertility. The same day Namatanga went to her daughter who received a small money income from the maternity clinic. She borrowed 15 shs and hired a neighbour to till the field for her. Work started the following day. In the same year, however, Chomo left unused several acres of river land, which need no regeneration cycles. These plots could have satisfied the immediate needs of a number of poorer peasants if they had been taken from Chomo and been given to them.

Another example relates to Ibala, in the pyrethrum growing area in the northern part of Bulambia. There, it was explained to me that one of the tasks of a representative of the farmers on the board of the cooperative is to make sure that members pay the necessary attention to the quality of their crops, to admonish the neglectful cultivator, and to report him to the board of the cooperative. Many peasants, however, neglected the weeding of their pyrethrum plots. But when two of the representatives were asked whether they had ever reprimanded farmers for improper weeding, they could give only two examples. The first was an old man without any relatives in the area, the other a widow.

Arena Map of the Peasants

Peasants may be inclined to dramatize the collusion of staff, and of staff and kulaks. Although the peasants' suspicions may lack any factual basis they are nevertheless important as they mould their strategy and influence their actions and therefore form an integral part of their arena map. Thus the following accusations and suspicions came to light in the political drama related above.

The medical dispenser was alleged to have kept a stock of medicines reserved for his colleagues and kulak friends in times of scarcity. This, according to the peasants, had resulted in a lower mortality rate among children of this group than among peasant children. Furthermore, the medical dispenser was accused of withholding medicine from the divorced wife of Chomo and thus, indirectly, to have caused her death.

The Primary Court magistrate was believed to have come to an impartial judgement only after pressure had been brought to bear on him. In the eyes of the peasants he had relinquished his impartiality by advising Chomo, via Mwakalinga, to appeal.

Chomo was reported to have supplied the medical dispenser, the Primary Court magistrate, Mwakalinga and two teachers with vegetables, onions and sugarcane. It was well known that staff were often among the guests at his beer parties.

Finally there was the stock reaction of peasants to a civil case decision, namely, to accuse the magistrate of having been bribed by the winning party.

Thus, the arena map of the peasants is largely based on the perception that
(a) all legitimate arenas are dominated wholly or largely by staff,
(b) staff control access to vital resources,
(c) in case of conflict staff will close ranks,
(d) in case of conflict the richer peasants are supported by staff.

Strategy of the Peasants

On the basis of this arena map, peasant strategy includes the following elements.

(1) In a case of conflict with a member of staff it is extremely difficult to press a charge against him although a possible course is to enlist the backing of another member of staff when taking action. This was what one of the young men in the case study did when he succeeded in getting the police officer to escort him to the house of Mwakalinga in order to protest about the alleged sorcery of his son.

(2) In a case of conflict the 'legitimate arenas' should not be entered but other battlegrounds in which more effective manoeuvres can be performed ought to be explored.

Thus, the medical dispenser at X was alleged to have had affairs with married women in the community, a charge which would have resulted in a civil case if the seducer were a peasant. But on the basis of the above stratagem peasants reacted differently; for two years no action was taken, then in the middle of a night in October 1968, people set fire to his house. The dispenser escaped just in time from the blazing house. Alternatively, peasants have recourse to threats which are equally as effective as arson. In 1967 some villagers of Itumba bore grudges against the magistrate. His wife was accordingly advised by a 'helpful' neighbour to leave because 'people' intended to set fire to the thatched roof of her house. Two weeks later they left the village on transfer. Similarly, the magistrate who resided in Itumba in 1965 was told by people to pass a judgement favourable to Metson; if not, 'things would happen to him'.

A war of nerves is also a way of inflicting harm on an opponent. Mwakalinga was assailed in this way, which involved numerous threats ('this is only the start of people's revenge actions'), accusations, and possibly more important, indications of unpopularity ('we have killed your child'). This particular war of nerves was quite effective because it led Mwakalinga to consider leaving Itumba, even at the risk of substantial loss because no-one was prepared to give him a penny for his two houses with corrugated iron roofs. Not least, it meant giving up the fertile river plots which he had on loan from Chomo and another kulak.

CONCLUSIONS

This paper has been concerned with the composition, power base and operations of two elites and their relations with the poorer peasants. At a higher level of abstraction this contribution represents a study of a political field interlocked with and encapsulated by other political fields. The field which forms the focus of our interest is then analyzed in its basic triadic structure consisting of three political actors: the penetrators or staff people, the kulaks or wealthy peasants, and the mass of the peasantry. This study of Bulambia division of Rungwe district suggests that the staff members and the kulaks form a dominant coalition, excluding the mass of the peasantry from a variety of privileges and power positions. Thus, to paraphrase Simmel, the peasantry plays the role of the 'suffering third' (*tertius patlens*). However, there is no Iron law which dictates that the peasantry will always be excluded from coalitions. During meetings of the Village Development Committee in Itumba, poor and wealthy peasants occasionally form a united front against staff members, even though this is shortlived and does not result in a major shift in the power profile. Another possibility in the foreseeable future might be a coalition between the penetrators and the mass of the peasantry; that is, if sufficient pressure is brought to bear on government personnel by their superiors in the party and administration. It is by no means certain that this will happen, but in view of the present ideological climate in Tanzania it seems at least a possibility. Evidence of such coalitions, with accompanying strategies of 'betting on the weak and the many' has been found elsewhere. Baks[36] for instance, has described a case in India where penetrators struggled with the local powerholders to improve the lot of the poorer peasants.

In sum, therefore, this study of penetration in a particular corner of Tanzania has been based on the following steps and assumptions.
(a) In every community a power process takes place, which consists of antagonistic interaction and supportive coalition processes.

(b) The penetrators are deeply involved in this power process. This does not mean that they are party to every conflict, but as controllers of external resources they are drawn into the major political dramas.

(c) All participants — staff members, kulaks and peasants — are guided in their antagonistic interaction and coalition selection by an arena map and strategy.

(d) Participants operate from a status quo conception, a basic set of ideas on the existing distribution of resources, goods and privileges. This does not imply that all participants are in basic support of the status quo. In our case study, for example, they clearly were not. But people in a rural community to a large extent share a cognitive map which indicates how everybody stands in relation to the resources.

(e) Participants watch and interpret each other's moves. They weigh these moves with a view to the threat they might pose to their control of the material and symbolic environment. At the same time, they scan the whole complicated pattern of movements for any advantages which it might offer.

(f) If a move affects the command of an individual or a group over assets, whether favourable or unfavourable, that move tends to be seen as a *disturbance of the status quo*.

(g) Such disturbances create reaction, i.e. they are either combatted or supported by the antagonists within a field. Disturbances of major proportions may prompt a crisis situation.

(h) Penetrative efforts are among the most important disturbances of the status quo in a modernizing nation such as Tanzania. New assets channeled through the penetrators into the community continually disrupt the status quo.

(i) Most of the penetrative efforts in the areas under study have strengthened the position of kulaks and of the penetrators themselves.

NOTES

1.   This contribution is based on field work conducted in the Rungwe District of the Mbeya Region in the southwestern corner of Tanzania, from August 1966 until December 1968. The first half of this period was spent in Itumba, the administrative centre of Bulambia division (see map). In 1968 I moved to Ibala, a village in the northern part of Bulambia. I was a member of an interdisciplinary team from the Afrika-Studiecentrum at Leiden (Netherlands), engaged in investigating factors which hamper or stimulate the development of the rural economy. My colleagues on this project have generously allowed me to make use of their fieldwork data. The responsibility for the conclusions, however, is solely mine.

     Another version of this paper has been published in Lionel Cliffe and John Saul (eds), *Socialism in Tanzania* (Nairobi, 1973), Vol. II, 153-79.

2.   John S. Saul, 'Class and Penetration in Tanzania', in Lionel Cliffe and John Saul (eds), *Socialism in Tanzania*, Vol. I, 118-126.

3.   Lucian Pye, *Aspects of Political Development* (Boston, 1966), 64.

4.   Quotation from Saul, 'Class and Penetration'. I have been greatly influenced by Saul's analysis of the fabric of socio-political relationships in the rural areas of Tanzania.

5.   David Easton, *A Systems Analysis of Political Life* (New York, 1965), 86-96.

6.   The word 'kulak' has been borrowed from recent Russian history and introduced as a useful social category in agricultural research by Rene Dumont, *Types of Rural Economy* (London, 1957).

7.   The notion of a 'political field' has been given a central place in the conceptual framework of political anthropology; cf. the introductory chapter to Marc J. Swartz (ed), *Local-Level Politics* (Chicago, 1968). As my definition of 'political field' is somewhat different to his, a few clarifying remarks seem necessary. Orientation denotes 'interest and involvement' (Ibidem, 9) in the processes in which the actors are the participants. Orientation could mean a competition for scarce resources among these actors, or a shared interest to safeguard a particular distribution of resources; a willingness to uphold a particular normative order among some and intentions to destroy it among others in that field. It would not necessarily imply that the participants are always in competition, or that such rivalry is an essential part of relations in a political field. Harmonious fields are equally conceivable. During my field work I did not come across anyone who doubted the legitimacy of the present political order in Tanzania. Therefore, we could call the relationships among the actors oriented towards 'the political prize or value of legitimacy' as 'harmonious' or 'supportive'.

8.   F.G. Bailey, *Stratagems and Spoils* (Oxford, 1969), 144-186.

9.   A penetrating analysis of the relationships and tensions among the various 'B' fields is given in Lionel Cliffe and John S. Saul, 'The District Development Front in Tanzania' (1970).

10.   Oral communication from J.J. Sterkenburg.

11.   H.A. Luning, 'Cash Crops and Money Income in Rungwe District, 1955-1967' in *Some Preliminary Results of the Rungwe Agro-Socio-Economic Research Project* (Afrika-Studiecentrum, Leiden, 1968, mimeographed).

12.   H.A. Luning and L.B. Venema, 'An Evaluation of the Agricultural Extension Service' (Technical Paper No. 1; Afrika-Studiecentrum, Leiden, 1969), 13.

13.   J.J. Sterkenburg, 'The Size of Coffee Primary Societies in Rungwe District' in *Some Preliminary Results of the Rungwe Agro-Socio-Economic Research Project*, 27.

14.   The area of Mulala VDC borders on Itumba to the west (see map). It is an area of slash-and-burn cultivators; and is considered underdeveloped by the staff of Bulambia division. Irrigation of small plots alongside creeks is a technique introduced and used predominantly by six immigrants of the Ndali tribe. There was no school until recently. Almost all of Mulale's inhabitants are pagans (of the Nyiha tribe) but the Ndali chairman of the VDC is a christian.

15.   The area has a high divorce rate and women often take the initiative.

16.   Joint staff meetings are meetings of all staff in the division together with the TANU Branch Chairmen (three in Bulambia). The first of such meetings to be held in some years was convened in August 1967 in Itumba.

17.   'On average, staff occupied posts for 2 years and 7 months in their working area, according to the survey' (Luning and Venema, 'An Evaluation of the Agricultural Extension Service'.

18.   Extension workers spend on average three days every month in Tukuyu, the administrative centre of the district (Ibidem).

19.   Oral communication.

20.   The people of Rungwe sometimes refer to the Divisional Executive Officer and his staff of collaborators as 'the council of the division'. In other contexts, when using this term they refer to the building where the DEO and his staff perform their official functions.

21.   Monica Wilson, 'Effects on the Xhosa and Nyakyusa of Scarcity of Land', in Daniel Biebuyck (ed), *African Agrarian Systems* (London, 1963), 386-387.

22.   P.H. Gulliver, 'Land Shortage, Social Change and Social Conflict in East Africa', *The Journal of Conflict Resolution*, V, 1 (1961).

23.   P.M. van Hekken and H.U.E. Thoden van Velzen, *Land Scarcity and Rural Inequality* (The Hague, 1972).

24. For more information on farming patterns in Bulambia see H.A. Luning, 'Farm Economic Survey' (Technical Paper No. 3; Afrika-Studiecentrum, Leiden, 1970, mimeographed).

25. Theodore Caplow, *Two Against One* (Englewood Cliffs, 1968).

26. Oral communication, J. de Jonge.

27. Oral communication, Nel van Hekken.

28. Oral communication, Mr. Gordon Mwansasu. The 'Parish Council' was the predecessor of the Village Development Committee in Rungwe District. This experiment took place in the late 1940s and early 1950s. Z.E. Kingdon, 'The Initiation of a System of Local Government by African Rural Councils in the Rungwe District Tanganyika', *Journal of African Administration*, III, 4.

29. The two peasants did not live in Itumba village itself but in another village of Itumba ward.

30. The data on the occupation of official roles in Buloma and Jerusalem were kindly made available by Mr. J.H. Konter. Nel van Hekken generously provided me with similar information for Ngamanga.

31. Van Hekken and Thoden van Velzen, *Land Scarcity and Rural Inequality*, chapter III.

32. Ibidem, chapter III.

33. The staff of the cooperative is called 'Serikali', a Swahili word meaning 'government'. This identification of the cooperative, often depicted as 'a people's organization', with the administration gives a telling insight into rural elections.

34. Harold D. Lasswell and Abraham Kaplan, *Power and Society* (New Haven, 1950), 250.

35. Note that my use of the term 'arena' differs considerably to the definition used by Swartz, *Local-Level Politics*, 9.

36. C. Baks, *Afschaffing van Pacht* (Abolition of Leasehold Tenancies; doctoral thesis, Amsterdam, 1969, mimeographed) 82-94.

DAVID K. LEONARD

THE SOCIAL STRUCTURE OF THE AGRICULTURAL EXTENSION SERVICES IN THE WESTERN PROVINCE OF KENYA

In his study of Bulambia Division in the Rungwe District of Tanzania, Thoden van Velzen found that the social structure of administration was itself a constraint on socialist and economic development. Government employees were seen by peasants and by themselves as a highly cohesive, mutually interdependent elite group. They had very frequent social contact with one another, apparently without regard for rank or speciality, but interacted much less often with the local peasants. Maintaining a relatively high standard of living and speaking Swahili among themselves, they had a paternalistic attitude toward peasants and were disdainful of doing any manual work. Those locals with whom government staff did have social contact were almost invariably rich farmers. Staff built up a symbiotic relationship with these rich peasants, which involved the latter providing land, food, and assistance on government projects to the staff. They in their turn helped the well-off farmers with access to government aid, supported their dominance of local political institutions, and assisted in their conflicts with other peasants. The consequences of this social system were such that staff were themselves prime examples of inegalitarian behaviour and, in their support for the rich peasants, were reinforcing and accentuating inequality within the rural society. Their isolation from poorer peasants was such that they seemed to learn little from them and to provide them with relatively little in the way of direct positive benefits. The tension between rich and poorer peasants was such that we may infer that diffusion of innovations from the first to the second was limited.[1]

For convenience we can summarize Thoden van Velzen's argument in three propositions: (1) The distribution of extension benefits is skewed in favour of the wealthier farmers; (2) part of the reason for the inegalitarian administration of these programmes is that the civil servants responsible for agricultural extension are part of an isolated, cohesive, social elite and that this involves them in a social class alliance and exchange of benefits with the richer farmers; (3) this favouritism accentuates rural inequality and may prevent the maximum possible economic growth.

Thoden van Velzen's work seems to us to be provocative and important. For this reason we propose to examine his propositions as they might apply to the administration of the extension services of the Ministry of Agriculture in the Western Province of Kenya. The data analyzed here are drawn from two sources. The first is 213 interviews we conducted with junior extension staff and 25 interviews with senior staff of the Ministry in all of Western Province.[2] The former represent a 40 per cent random sample of all junior staff in the Province.[3] The latter comprise 85 per cent of all senior staff in the Province, other than those assigned to the Provincial headquarters of the Ministry. The excluded senior staff were either in the Mechanization Division, which is not examined here, or were very new to the Province at the time of interviewing. The second set of data examined here is drawn from a large survey of small farmers which the Agricultural Statistics Section of the Ministry of Finance and Economic Planning conducted during the 1970 long rains.[4] The survey gives us detailed information on 637 randomly selected farmers in Western Province.[5]

THE DISTRIBUTION OF EXTENSION BENEFITS

From an analysis of the Agricultural Statistics data we can gain an accurate picture of the distribution of various easily identified farm characteristics. The growing of hybrid maize is one of these. Maize is the basic food for the great majority of people in Western Province, and hybrid maize is a relatively recent but well-established agricultural innovation in the area. The package of hybrid seed and fertilizers was introduced in the Province in 1963, and hybrid maize (with or without chemical fertilizers) is now grown by 48 per cent of the farmers there. The return on the use of the hybrid and fertilizer package varies, but it is not likely to be less than a 100 per cent net profit over a farmer's extra cash investment. Thus, a farmer is likely to have accepted hybrid maize if he has been innovative over the last few years. Nonetheless, the use of hybrid seed varies from an estimated high of 80 per cent of the farms in Kimilili (Bungoma) and Lurambi (Kakamega) Divisions, where land holdings are large and maize is a major market crop, to a low of 4 per cent in the Central and Southern Divisions of Busia, where soil and climate are less favourable and where cassava competes with maize as a food staple.

Different cash producing farm enterprises are appropriate to each of the ecological zones in the Province, and the profitability of these enterprises varies considerably. Grade dairy cows have a very high return on investment, whereas the profitability of cotton is relatively low. Prices of the robusta type of coffee (but not the arabica) are so low now that many owners of these trees do not consider it profitable to care for them or to harvest the berries. Nonetheless, ownership of one of these farm enterprises does indicate that the farmer has

Table 1. *Distribution of agricultural enterprises among farms in Western Province*

	Have cash farm enterprise %	No cash farm enterprise %	Total %
Have Hybrid Maize	10	38	48
Have No Hybrid Maize	5	47	52
Total	15	85	

Based on a weighted sample of 637 farms. Excludes Northern Division, Busia and the settlement schemes in Bungoma and Kakamega Districts. Data collected by the Agricultural Statistics Section of the Ministry of Finance and Economic Planning during the 1970 long rains.
A cash farm enterprise is defined as one of the following: grade cattle, coffee, cotton or tea.

had investment funds available at some point in the past and that he is now or was once deriving a cash income from his produce. This marks him as being of above average wealth in what is still a predominately subsistence economy. Farmers with such cash producing farm enterprises constitute 15 per cent of the total in Western Province.

We can define a progressive farmer as one who both uses hybrid maize and has one or more cash producing farm enterprises. Only 10 per cent of the farmers in Western Province meet these two criteria. Our impression is that this definition approximates the minimum behaviour that Agricultural staff in Western Province expect of what they call a progressive farmer. Such a farmer probably has been innovative over a fair period of time, has access to small amounts of capital, and is well-to-do relative to his neighbours. Conversely, we define a man who has neither hybrid maize nor a cash enterprise as a non-innovator. In Western Province, 47 per cent of the farmers fall into this category. For these farmers the adoption of new farming methods is not a habit and access to investment capital is often a problem.

Of course, it does not follow automatically from a farmer's being progressive that he is relatively rich. For this reason the Agricultural Statistics Section's survey data on cattle holdings is particularly interesting. In the past cattle were overwhelmingly the symbol and substance of wealth in rural Kenya. Although this traditional attachment to cattle has diminished in Western Province, a Luhya's wealth is still likely to be reflected in his livestock holdings. Thus, it is interesting to note that those who grow hybrid maize in Western Province are twice as likely to have five or more cattle as those who do not grow it. (For the purposes of this exercise one grade cow is counted as equal to two local cattle, the difference in their market value.) Furthermore, those whom we have defined as progressive farmers are one-eighth as likely to have no cattle as those whom we have labeled non-innovative (see Table 2).

Thus we see a fairly clear relationship between progressiveness and wealth. The only exception is that small category of farmers who have adopted a cash

Table 2. *Cattle-holdings of non-innovative, middle and progressive farmers in Western Province*

No. of cattle	Non-innovative Farmers Neither cash crop nor hybrid maize	Middle Farmers Cash crop but no hybrid maize	Hybrid maize but no cash crop	Progressive Farmers Hybrid maize and cash crop	All Farmers
0	198 (63%)	32 (67%)	77 (35%)	4 (8%)	311 (49%)
1-4	56 (18%)	7 (14%)	54 (24%)	19 (37%)	136 (21%)
5 or more	58 (19%)	9 (19%)	91 (41%)	29 (56%)	187 (30%)
TOTAL	312 (100%)	48 (100%)	222 (100%)	52 (100%)	634 (100%)

crop but not hybrid maize. These are very much like the poor farmers in their livestock wealth. The bulk of farmers in this category raise cotton in Busia. Southern Busia is almost devoid of livestock because of tsetse fly. Furthermore, as cotton seed was provided free to the grower, until recently it was the one cash crop which did not require a capital investment to plant and hence was accessible to the poor. Unfortunately, cash investment was required for insecticides if the plant was to produce good yields, so many farmers in this category were disappointed by their harvest and remained poor.[6]

Having identified the proportions of farmers who can be called progressive and non-innovative, we now have a base line against which to compare the actual distribution of agricultural extension services. The basic technique of extension in Western Province is visits to individual farmers. On average, 2.9 days in an agent's five-day week will be spent on this activity.[7] In our interviews we asked each staff member who works in direct contact with farmers to name for us all the farmers to whom he had paid extension visits in the previous week. For each of these farmers we then inquired as to whether he grew hybrid maize and as to whether he had a cash farm enterprise. In the Province as a whole, the average extension agent spends 57 per cent of his visits with progressive farmers (who are 10 per cent of all farmers) and 6 per cent of his visits with non-innovative ones (47 per cent of the total). Thus extension attention is very greatly skewed in favour of the more progressive and wealthier farmers, exactly as Thoden van Velzen found in Rungwe, Tanzania. Furthermore, the concentration on progressive farmers is achieved at the expense of the non-innovative ones. Farmers who have either hybrid maize or a cash crop but not both are 43 per cent of the total and extension agents devote an average of 37 per cent of their visits to them. A farmer in this middle category, who has shown some innovative drive, has about one-seventh the chance that a progressive farmer has of receiving an extension visit. But his odds are still 6.5 times those of a non-innovative farmer, who has 1/44th the chance of a progressive farmer (see Fig. 1).

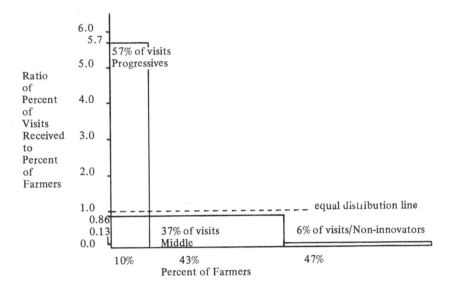

Figure 1. *Distribution of agricultural extension visits between progressive, middle, and non-innovative farmers*

THE SOCIAL SYSTEMS OF THE AGRICULTURAL STAFF

We have accepted Thoden van Velzen's proposition that the distribution of extension benefits is skewed in favour of the more progressive and wealthier farmers. We now need to examine his proposition that this inegalitarian behaviour is partly caused by the fact that agricultural extension agents are part of an isolated, cohesive social elite. This requires that we begin with a detailed analysis of the social structure of the Ministry of Agriculture in Western Province.

Let us start with an outline of the formal structure of agricultural administration (see Fig. 1). At the district level, the Ministry is headed by a District Agricultural Officer (DAO). He is supported at the headquarters by several specialist personnel of both degree (Agricultural or Veterinary Officer) and diploma levels (Assistant Agricultural or Livestock Officer). In charge of each division is an Assistant Agricultural Officer (AAO), who is sometimes joined by a Livestock Officer (LO). At the divisional headquarters there are usually a few holders of certificates in agriculture (Agricultural Assistants —AAs) or veterinary medicine (Animal Health Assistants - AHAs). These AAs and AHAs will be performing specialist duties, such as processing IDA loans, farm planning, and organizing 4-K Clubs. Very occasionally these AAs and AHAs may be assisted by a Junior Agricultural Assistant or Junior Animal Health Assistant, who lack any formally recognized training in agriculture. Each location will have a team of extension workers, varying in size from seven to twenty-one. The agricultural part of this team will be headed by a Location Agricultural Assistant (LAA) and will be comprised of AAs and JAAs. In addition the Veterinary Division will be represented by one to seven AHAs and JAHAs. Most of this team will be assigned to specific sub-locations for general extension work, although the Animal Health personnel and one or two Agricultural ones may work on a speciality, such as coffee or cotton, over the entire location.

The Animal Health personnel used to have an autonomous organization from that of the Agriculture staff, although the basic characteristics of the two groups are quite similar. Rather than further complicate the following presentation with two parallel sets of statistics, we shall exclude the junior veterinary staff from our analysis from here forward.

Following the generally accepted convention, we shall term those staff who have degrees or diplomas *senior staff* and those who have certificates or no formal training *junior staff*. To state it another way, those whose title includes the word 'Officer' are senior staff and those whose designation involves the word 'Assistant' are junior staff. As a rule junior staff work in or near their home area, while senior staff work outside it. In order to more easily discuss the AAs who are in charge of locations or are on divisional duties (and who enjoy superior status and responsibility to the other junior staff), we shall label them *senior AAs*.

So much for formal hierarchies. What then are the characteristics of the informal social system of the agricultural administration? Our main data for studying this question are the friendship choices of staff. At the end of each interview, which was very much work oriented, we asked, 'Now finally, we find that an extension agent's work is often helped or hindered by his personal relations with those around him. For this reason we would be grateful if you would name for us your friends whom you see regularly.' Where the respondent was unclear, we stated that we were interested in his friends in this general geographical area and that our question included all types of friends. After this first query was answered, we probed with 'Now, in addition, what (other) friends do you have in the Ministry of Agriculture?' In total we recorded up to 15 friendship choices of which no more than 10 were from outside the Ministry of Agriculture. In only a very few cases were these upper limits reached. In addition we ascertained the nature of each friend's occupation and where he lived. Cooperation in answering all these questions was generally very good. In using this sociometric data to describe the informal social system of the Ministry of Agriculture, we do not want to imply that social structure consists only of friendship patterns. This is obviously not the case. When one claims another as his friend, he is not saying either that he sees this person often, or that he does not interact frequently with others. A friendship choice only indicates those whom one likes or would like to have contact with. But this information is extremely useful in locating the boundaries of people's affections, which in turn is helpful in identifying status and other barriers between people.

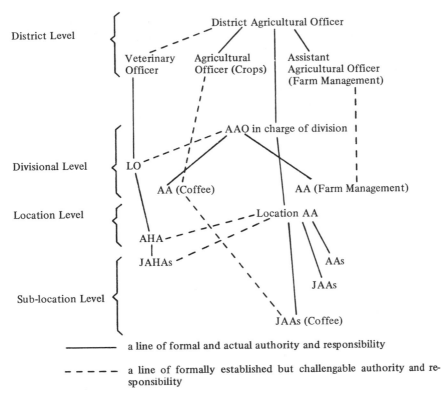

District Level

Divisional Level

Location Level

Sub-location Level

─────────── a line of formal and actual authority and responsibility

─ ─ ─ ─ ─ a line of formally established but challengable authority and responsibility

Figure 2. *A 'Typical' organization chart for the Ministry of Agriculture in Western Province*

Our first problem is to establish the social units we are to analyse. If we define a socially salient group as one within which friendships are formed, it is clear that we can take the Ministry of Agriculture as a meaningful unit to its staff. An average of 51 per cent of the friends named by senior staff are from within Agriculture, prior to any probing by us in this direction. Junior staff name an average of 24 per cent, which indicates a less intense but still significant social involvement in the Ministry. For senior staff an average of 37 per cent of their friends are in other Government employment and only 12 per cent are not civil servants. Junior staff name an average of 35 per cent in other Government employment and 41 per cent outside the civil service. Thoden van Velzen's proposition that Government employees are enmeshed in an almost exclusively civil servant social circuit is verified for the senior staff. Junior staff in Kakamega are only predominately involved in Government circles, however, and retain a significant number of contacts outside. One explanation for the difference between junior and senior staff in this regard is that the latter are more distant from their places of birth, and, more importantly, live in Government staff compounds.

The Ministry of Agriculture itself is not a single social unit. Senior staff at district headquarters tend to be a socially cohesive group, and this social system reaches out in a weak but distinct manner to include the senior staff in the divisions. Kerlinger suggests that we measure the cohesiveness of a group by the proportion of reciprocal friendship choices made out of the number possible.[8] On this measure the ratio among the headquarters staffs of the three districts are .30, .33, and .17. The figures for the whole senior staff in these districts are .19, .13, and .06. Another way to measure the same phenomenon is to give the average proportion of other group members who individuals name as their friends. Here the headquarters' figures are .42, .50, and .30, while those for the full districts are .36, .30, and .16. The involvement of the divisional AAOs and LOs in a district-wide senior staff social system is clearly weak, although existent. This is not surprising as they would need transportation to reach their counterparts, and this is a notoriously scarce resource in the Ministry. Although the cohesiveness for two of the three headquarters teams is moderately good, it does seem low for groups who share common offices, a common speciality, and common problems. The high rates of transfer in the Kenyan senior civil service doubtless depress the levels of group cohesion.

The junior staff at location level are very weak in their cohesiveness. The average proportion of other group members named as friends is .26 (with a range of .06 to .46). The proportion of reciprocal friendship choices averages only .06 (with a range from .00 to .25). Despite these low figures, 46 per cent of the Ministry friends whom an individual names are working in the same location with him, and we estimate that an additional 27 per cent are in another part of the same division. Furthermore, no less than 85 per cent of the junior staff are named as friends by at least one other junior member.[9] These statistics indicate to us that the level of junior staff interaction is by no means as great as Thoden van Velzen's work would have suggested. Nonetheless, there does appear to be some kind of weak informal social system among junior staff, focused on the location and even more weakly including the division, but not reaching beyond it.

But do the senior and junior staff social systems overlap? If they do, they are certainly not cohesive, for only one officer (an AAO) makes a reciprocal friendship choice with a junior staff member. If we include all the senior staff in our analysis, the statistics show clearly that they do not belong to the junior staff social systems and vice versa. But we wish to argue that the Luhya, i.e. local, members of senior staff are involved in the junior staff systems, weak as they are, and that the others are isolated from them. In order to make the point, let us compare the two groups of senior staff with the senior AAs, who are the junior staff with any comparable status and visibility. Table 3 shows how the Luhya senior staff are seen in ways very similar to the senior AAs while both are quite different from the non-Luhya senior staff. Table 4 takes the point further by demonstrating that Luhya senior staff relate socially to

Table 3. *Frequency with which one is named a friend by junior staff*

	Average times chosen	Number in category
Non-Luhya Senior Staff	1.79	14
Luhya Senior Staff	4.48	11
Senior AAs	4.21	34
Other AAs	3.82	45
JAAs	2.16	89

Table 4. *Frequency with which non-senior AAs and JAAs are named as friends*

	Average number of choices	Number in category
Non-Luhya Senior Staff	.21	14
Luhya Senior Staff	1.27	11
Senior AAs	2.41	31

their juniors much more than do their non-local colleagues. All this means that Luhya members of senior staff, especially if they are stationed in a division, are often part of the divisional informal social system of the junior staff (although not quite as much as their senior AAs). Other senior staff are isolated from their subordinates' informal networks. Thus for any one area there are two distinct social systems, a junior and a senior, and usually only the Luhya senior staff enjoy the possibility of overlapping membership. On a divisional basis it is clear that Thoden van Velzen's suggestion that the staff social system is strongly cohesive and undivided is not applicable to Western Province.

Having established their distinctness, let us now proceed to analyse the senior and junior staff systems separately. We might begin by asking what is the social status of the people with whom senior staff associate? The pattern is quite different between those stationed at the district headquarters and those in the divisions. Table 5 analyses the friends chosen outside of Agriculture and presents the average percentage chosen at each status level. We see that district senior staff draw 83 per cent of their friends from people of equivalent status to themselves, in effect the highest status group in the area. Socially speaking, this makes them very isolated from the realities of their areas. The divisional staff name friends in this high level group only 49 per cent of the time. Nonetheless, this is far in excess of the 14 per cent or less named in this category by senior AAs, and supports the hypothesis that when divisional senior staff interact with farmers, the farmers are almost certainly rich.

Turning again to the junior staff social systems, we have already established that these groups are not very cohesive or intense, drawing only 24 per cent of their members' friendship choices. The social units seem concentrated on the location although they also involve divisional level interaction. Approximately 73 per cent of the friends that junior staff name in the Ministry live within their home division and 46 per cent are members of their location work group.

Table 5. *Average percentage of friends chosen from each status category*

Position or Status Equivalent of Friends	Respondent		
	District Senior Staff %	Divisional Senior Staff %	All Senior Staff %
District head of department	61	13	37
Divisional head of department or district aide	22	36	29
Chiefs, Teachers	10	20	15
Lesser employees, traders, farmers	7	30	19

Junior staff friendships with non-Ministry people are even less cosmopolitan. Forty-five per cent of these live in the extension agent's home sub-location, and 30 per cent more are from within his location.

What is the social status of the friends with whom the junior staff interact socially and, by inference, what social status do they assign to themselves? We asked respondents to tell us what kind of work each friend does. On this basis each non-Ministry friend was assigned to one of four predetermined status categories and the percentage of friends in these categories was calculated for each respondent.[10] Table 6 defines the four categories and gives the average per cent of friends in each one. From these figures it seems clear that junior staff see themselves as part of the rural elite, but in the lower or middle part of that group. The data confirm our impression that junior staff belong to a status a little lower than that of a primary school teacher. As the Western Province progressive farmer fits more into the middle status group, the agricultural extension agent is probably more often his social equal than his status superior, contrary to what is suggested by Thoden van Velzen's analysis. Nonetheless, these data support his assertion that staff associate very largely with the richer peasants in their social contacts with farmers. The approximately 90 per cent of the rural population which falls into the Low Status category receives only 20 per cent of the friendship choices.

Is it then true that agricultural extension staff visit progressive farmers because these are their acquaintances or are the people most like themselves socially? Our limited evidence indicates that the answer is no. There is no positive correlation between the percentage of an agent's high and upper middle status friends and the proportion of his visits which he devotes to progressive farmers ($r = -.12$, Sig. $= .08$). If anything, there is a slight tendency for those who name the smallest percentage of friends in the high and upper middle groups to give a larger proportion of their time to progressive farmers than do the staff who identify more with the elite. Nor does it seem credible to argue, as Thoden van Velzen does, that extension services are being provided to progressive farmers in Western Province as a reward for their help in official

Table 6. *Average percentage of non-ministry friends named by junior staff in various status categories.*

Percentage	Category	Exemplary Definition
7	High	Chiefs, headmasters, County Councillors, big businessmen, other relatively well-to-do people
39	Upper Middle	School teachers, sub-chiefs, moderate businessmen, big farmers, middle salaried group
33	Middle	Small businessmen, traders, moderate farmers, lesser employed
20	Low	Average farmers

and private affairs. This exchange of benefits does occur in Kenya, but it will not serve as a dominant explanatory variable.[11] As can be seen in Table 7, those services that are most desirable to progressive farmers — loans and veterinary medicine — are better distributed among the classes of farmers than are the other types of extension visits. The distribution of veterinary services will be discussed later in greater detail. It is sufficient to note here that although progressives receive an average of 57 per cent of all extension visits, only 39 per cent of the loan investigations are made on their farms. If the coveted extension services were basically given to those who would 'pay' for them, the distribution of items such as loan investigations would show an even greater skew in favour of the wealthier farmers than do the less desired services. Since the opposite is the case, we conclude that 'pay-offs' do not exert a major influence on the total pattern of extension visits. Other and more powerful factors appear to be at work.

Table 7. *Average percentage of extension visits to progressive and poor farmers by agents with differing functions*

	Average % to progressive farmers	Average % to non-innovative farmers
Function:		
General (88)	60	3
Coffee (10)	91	0
Animal Husbandry (7)	57	0
Supervisory (13)	52	4
IDA Loans (19)	39	5
Cotton (9)	57	19
Veterinary (32)	51	17
All (178)	57	6

THE PROGRESSIVE FARMER STRATEGY

What then are the causes of the emphasis that is placed on progressive farmers in extension work? The most important factor is the strategy which agents have consciously and openly adopted for their work. In a Tanzania-wide opinion survey of farmer contact extension agents, R.G. Saylor found that 87 per cent agree with the statement, 'If I worked most of the time with a few of the better farmers, I would get better results.' This opinion was expressed despite the fact that it runs contrary to the official policy of the Tanzanian Ministry of Agriculture, Food and Cooperatives.[12] That junior staff should support a hierarchically disapproved strategy so openly indicates that they believe there are strong, legitimate arguments behind it. The progressive farmer strategy enjoys deep support among extension professionals at all levels in East Africa and is an important determinant of their behaviour.[13]

Nonetheless, it may be that the strategy is mistaken. To investigate this possibility, we need to examine the major justifications for the progressive farmer approach. There are two major sets of supporting arguments. The first arises out of the diffusion of innovations school. Progressive farmers are not only the most receptive to agricultural change, they also represent the informal leadership of their communities on technological matters. Innovations proved on their farms will diffuse to the other farmers in the area through a natural process of social communication. Therefore, extension agent concentration upon progressive farmers simply represents a highly efficient technique for eventually reaching all farmers.[14] The members of this school of thought see the progressive farmer strategy as achieving a wide distribution of benefits to the entire farming community.

The second set of arguments is most frequently offered by economists. Here, extension services are seen as only one of a number of agricultural inputs and the focus of concern is upon their most economic use. Progressive farmers have a number of characteristics which make them the most efficient target of agricultural extension: they are psychologically predisposed to change and so require less persuasion; they have access to the other inputs necessary for innovation (especially capital) and thus are quicker to change once they are convinced; in East Africa they typically own larger farms and the adopted innovation will therefore be applied to a larger acreage. For all these reasons, more agricultural output will be achieved for the average visit to a progressive than will be gained per visit to other farmers. Thus the economic arguments for the progressive farmer strategy do not depend upon its achieving a wide distribution of benefits. Extension is conceived of as a tool for economic growth, not social welfare.[15]

The wide distribution of benefits promised by the diffusion of innovations argument depends upon two conditions that often are not met in Western Kenya: (1) all or most farmers will eventually be able to adopt the proposed innovation; and (2) there are no significant social barriers to the communication of agricultural practices from progressives to others. Hybrid maize has been the model for most diffusion of innovations thinking.[16] As maize is the staple food crop in East Africa, it is likely that hybrid varieties will ultimately be grown on most small farms in the region. But this wide potential spread is not a common characteristic of agricultural innovations. Coffee and tea are more typical of the new crops offered to farmers in Africa, only a small proportion of whom will ever grow either. When African growers in Kenya were finally permitted to raise coffee, the innovation began to spread rapidly, the market became saturated, and new plantings were prohibited. Hence, progressives were not just the first to adopt this innovation; they were the only farmers to do so. Tea illustrates a slightly different pattern. When the crop was first introduced to small holders in Kenya, the price of cuttings was subsidized and the minimum area to be planted was one-quarter acre. Smallholder tea is still being expanded, but since the innovation is established, cuttings are now being sold at their full cost and the minimum planting is one acre.[17] Thus the investment was made easy and subsidized for the relatively well-to-do progressives; it is not for the poorer mass of farmers. The conclusion is that access to extension services and the early adoption of an innovation is not simply a temporary advantage; it often represents a permanent gain in the basic profitability of the progressive's farm relative to that of his neighbour.[18]

The second condition upon which the diffusion of innovations depends is a free flow of agricultural information in the farming community. We have reason to suspect that this condition is often unfulfilled in Western Kenya, although our data base here is too weak for our discussion to be conclusive. Early in our research we interviewed a small random sample of farmers in the Vihiga Division of Western Province. We found that at least some farmers who have no personal contact with extension workers are getting new agricultural information from other farmers who do have such contacts. Thus diffusion of new information does occur. Nonetheless, it seems to us that this second-hand information often loses something vital in the process of transmission. The several farmers whom we interviewed who had heard of a hybrid maize innovation only through other farmers had no idea if the change would increase yields. Without yield information, an innovation discussed with others carries little conviction and is unlikely to be adopted.[19] Yet it is uncommon for farmers in Western Province to reveal freely the amount of profit they have made from an innovation. Publicized income differentials may give rise to a higher tax assessment, increased social obligations, jealousies, or even rare accusations of witchcraft. Thus, most Luhya farmers probably require a new institutional context in which discussions on profitability are expected in order to talk readily about yields.[20] Visits from professional agricultural change agents and meetings organized by them are the main social settings in which the crucial question of returns will be treated in many parts of Western Province. The informal channels for the dissemination of agricultural information are therefore not so strong as the diffusion of innovations theory presupposes. Of course, a good new agricultural practice will still spread despite the weakness of the informal information system, but general acceptance will be slower than would otherwise be the case.

If there are barriers to the free, informal communication of agricultural information, it would seem undesirable to apply a strategy of working almost exclusively with progressives. When a broadly applicable innovation, such as hybrid maize, is first being introduced, it might be thought wise to begin with the progressive farmers as those most able and willing to take the associated risks. Once the new practice has gained a foothold, however, it would seem rational to shift attention toward the less innovative farmers so as to speed the spread of adoption. It can be inferred from Table 7 that such a strategic change in focus does not occur. General extension agents, who carry the burden of work on hybrid maize, give only a tiny proportion of their time to the half of the Province's farmers who do not grow it. Further, they devote at least as many visits to progressives as do their specialist colleagues, who would have much more justification for working with an advanced clientele. Presumably the general agents are trying to achieve improvements in the technical standard of cultivation on the farms of the adopters rather than spreading hybrid maize to the present non-adopters. This set of priorities is difficult to justify by any criteria, as the marginal increase in output is usually greater with adoption of the new variety than it is from improvements in the quality of cultivation.

From the foregoing, it should be clear that the progressive farmer strategy does not provide the extensive distribution of benefits that its diffusion advocates have claimed. A broader range of extension contacts would probably lead to profitable innovations achieving widespread acceptance more rapidly. Further, that the bulk of these services is being provided to the progressive and wealthier farmers means that they also are helping to increase the gap between the rich and the poor. We do not mean here that rural inequality is caused by the agricultural extension services. The farmers who are already somewhat better off than their neighbours are in the best position to invest in new and profitable farm enterprises, and we must expect that they will do so and hence increase their wealth. If the farm economy is based on land, labour, capital and knowledge, those who have more of these will make more money from their farming. But it does not follow that those who have the most of the first three should also be provided with a disproportionate advantage by extension workers with respect to technical knowledge.

We believe that the middle group of farmers may be a more appropriate focus for extension than the progressives, for reasons of both equity and maximum diffusion. There is good reason to believe that poorer farmers will be quicker to adopt agricultural innovations from farmers who are basically like themselves than they will from the socially elite progressives. Although evidence is lacking, it also seems likely that profitable innovations will spread faster from less innovative to progressive farmers than they do in the other direction.[21] A highly innovative farmer with access to reasonable amounts of capital (and this is the definition of a progressive) will be quick to hear of profitable new products and techniques and will seek them out for himself from a neighbour. This self-drive does not characterize the middle or non-innovative farmers to anything like the same extent. In dealing with agricultural changes that are capable of general acceptance, we suggest that adoption will be maximized in the long run by avoiding those farmers who are most anxious to innovate and concentrating on those who would normally be considered marginal.

But we have already pointed out that most agricultural innovations can only be adopted by a small proportion of the farming population. Furthermore, many new products and techniques require access to above average amounts of land and capital if they are to be adopted. Wide acceptance is not a relevant criterion for assessing extension strategy on such innovations. Nonetheless, we believe that middle farmers are still the appropriate focus of attention for many of these change programmes. There seem to be a significant number of middle farmers who have *sufficient* land and capital for certain innovations and who are passed over in the rush to their progressive neighbours, who have the *most* of these resources.[22] Both a better distribution of wealth and a more specialized small farm economy will be gained if farmers who already have a major cash crop are bypassed in the extension of new ones.

We have shown serious deficiencies in the diffusion of innovations justifications offered for the progressive farmer strategy as currently practiced in Kenya. This strategy is based upon certain assumptions which are often invalid in Western Province. As a consequence, the wide distribution of benefits aimed at by the diffusion strategy could probably be better achieved through a focus on the middle farmers rather than on the progressive farmers.

The economic arguments for the progressive farmer strategy now must be faced. It is much more difficult to find logical fault with this set of justifications, for the inegalitarianism of the approach is openly accepted. 'Betting on the strong' maximizes economic growth. Since the Kenya Government acknowledges that its first concern is with growth,[23] it is legitimate to challenge its agricultural extension employees only if their distribution of services goes beyond that which growth alone would justify.

It may be useful here to examine a part of the extension services where the economic argument can be divorced from the diffusion one. Such a case is offered by the veterinary services. Visits by Animal Health personnel to individual farms are made almost exclusively for the treatment of cattle disease. As less than half a per cent of the cattle in Western Province in 1970 were of the economically highly prized grade variety, the cattle needing treatment may be considered as broadly equal in terms of their innovation demonstration effect. The Ministry of Finance and Economic Planning survey which we quoted earlier indicates that the progressive ten per cent of the Western Province farmers own approximately 16 per cent of the cattle. Yet their farms receive 51 per cent of the veterinary calls. On the other hand, non-innovative farmers own about 33 per cent of all cattle and receive only 17 per cent of the attention of the Animal Health personnel. As can be seen from Figure 3, veterinary services

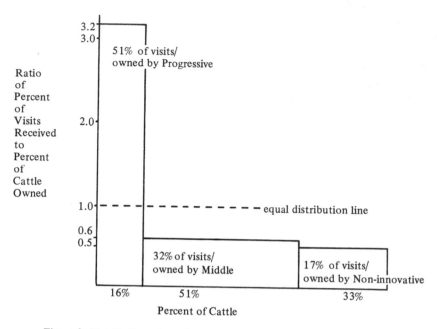

Figure 3. *Distribution of veterinary extension visits between cattle owned by progressive, middle, and non-innovative farmers*

are distributed relatively equally between middle and non-innovative cattle owners. Progressive farmers, however, receive over five times better service than these other two categories do. The top to bottom ratio of 6:1 would seem a vast improvement on the 44:1 observed for strictly agricultural services. But the latter had the diffusion of innovations theory as a rationale while the former does not.

Are there grounds of economic efficiency which might support this unequal distribution of veterinary services? A first response may be that progressives have larger herds and that a visit to one of their farms will be more efficient because of the greater number of cattle treated at one time. But this argument would be invalid for there is actually very little difference in herd size between the categories of farmers *for those actually owning cattle*. Non-innovative cattle owners have an average of 5.9 head; middle farmers, 6.4; and progressive farmers, 6.6. The overall inequalities in cattle wealth between these groups, discussed earlier in conjunction with Table 2, were largely caused by the differing proportions of those with no cattle in each category.

Further justifications for the skewed distribution of veterinary calls might be as follows. The progressive farmers probably take better care of their cattle, so that their cows will generally be producing more milk and have greater economic value. They also will be more likely to dispose of the economically relatively unproductive males, so that their herds will frequently be more valuable on these grounds as well. Finally, the better-off farmers are more likely to be willing to pay the small amounts of money necessary for medicines. Each of these arguments is basically valid and between them we can doubtless account for a substantial proportion of the differences in veterinary services provided to the three categories of farmers. Nonetheless, the distribution in Figure 3 has one feature which makes one reluctant to accept these economic explanations as adequate: whereas there is a substantial gap between the services provided to progressives and the other farmers, there is very little inequality in the distribution of visits between middle and non-innovative farmers. As middle farmers are situated between progressives and non-innovators in the modernity of their agricultural practices, it seems reasonable to expect that they would also be somewhere mid-way in their animal husbandry. If this is so, however, it would be *economically* efficient for them to receive less services than the progressives but they should also be getting more than the non-innovators. But this is not the case. Thus we are led to suspect that there are additional, non-economic grounds which lead to a special emphasis upon progressives. Our belief is that although economic efficiency criteria can be used to justify a substantial stress on progressive farmers in the distribution of both *agricultural* and *veterinary* services, the actual favourable allocation goes beyond that which is 'economically rational'.

THE CAUSES OF EXTENSION BIAS

What factors other than extension strategy might lead to a skew in services toward the progressives? The most important reason is probably that progressive farmers are the ones most likely to complain to a senior officer if extension is not provided to them. Junior staff do only a small amount of work and seem to sometimes organize themselves informally to reduce the amount of effort they put into their jobs.[24] As the work of visiting farmers is carried out in a very wide area, the junior staff are largely free of any supervision. Complaints are one of the very few ways which an Assistant Agricultural Officer has of judging whether or not his subordinates are on the job. Thus the rational extension strategy for the agent who wishes to minimize his effort is to see the complainers and forget the rest. By virtue of their relative wealth and their past innovativeness, the progressive farmers are among the few who will have the self-confidence actually to complain to an officer. Thus the progressives do have a power advantage. But it is not one born of a social class alliance, exchange of benefits, or political influence. Their power often derives quite simply from their presumption that Government should provide them with services and that they can tell an officer if it does not.

Our hypothesis that extension services are skewed toward potential complainers is strengthened by two facts. One is the slight tendency, reported earlier, for the lower status agents to give a greater proportion of their visits to progressives. These junior staff are less secure in their positions and so must devote more care to preventing complaints. Similarly, the best educated extension workers make the smallest number of visits altogether.[25] They are more secure and better able to survive unfavourable reports to their superiors.

Extension for the complainers is buttressed by the distorted picture which Government often has of the small agriculture world. Senior staff, in particular, are likely to have an optimistic view of the degree of acceptance of modern farming. Joseph Ascroft was told by agricultural officers in Nyeri that Tetu Division had 100 per cent acceptance of hybrid maize, but his random survey of 354 farmers found only 31 per cent growing the crop.[26] The social isolation of senior staff from the areas in which they are working helps sustain these distorted perceptions. Even junior staff, who largely are drawn from the communities in which they work, have an optimistically biased view of their areas. This is well illustrated by the reactions of the AAs who conducted the preliminary survey of farmers for the current Vihiga Division extension experiment. Confronted with a genuinely random sample, they confessed that they had never realized that such poor people even existed in the areas in which they were working.[27] It is much easier to ignore the non-progressives if one is unaware of their proportionate importance.

Attention to the complainers and the invisibility of the rural poor probably account for a substantial part of the inequality in the distribution of extension. Nonetheless, the dominant explanatory variable must be the progressive farmer strategy and its supporting ideas of the diffusion of innovations and the maximization of economic efficiency and growth. We have accepted that the economic growth arguments are logically sound (even though I doubt their political wisdom). Certainly an emphasis on growth rather than equality needs no special explanation in Kenya's political system. More interesting is the acceptance of the 'diffusion of innovations' idea when its assumptions do not seem to fit Kenya's economic and social realities. The strength of this belief system must be due in good part to the fact that it has been dominant in almost all of the agricultural education institutions (in Kenya and abroad) in which extension personnel have been trained and socialized. In addition there is probably an unconscious mechanism supporting the belief system — a visit to a progressive farmer is simply more satisfying. One can expect to encounter less resistance to new or difficult farming practices, and one is more likely to see a change on that particular farm. Therefore, the agent feels he is getting better results, as did the extension workers polled in Tanzania by Saylor. It is emotionally difficult to accept that a better long-run, total impact may be achieved in one's area by working with somewhat less receptive farmers. Net effects are hard to see whereas the contacted farmer is immediate and real.

CONCLUSIONS

In summary, then, Thoden van Velzen is correct that the distribution of extension is skewed in favour of the wealthier farmers and that this favouritism accentuates rural inequality and probably prevents the maximum possible distribution of agricultural innovations. In fact, this phenomenon is probably general to all agricultural extension systems and only the degree of the problem varies.[28] Our data from Western Province also confirm that the senior agricultural staff are part of an isolated, relatively cohesive elite group. We found, however, that the junior staff, who are in contact with farmers, form groups distinct from their seniors' and that they are local in their orientation, part of the middle, not the upper, rural elite, and are not very cohesive. Consequently, they are only partially isolated from their communities. Furthermore, neither their middle elite social status nor any private exchange of benefits seems to account for their stress on work with progressive farmers. Thus, this proposition of Thoden van Velzen is not sustained in Western Kenya. The bias of junior staff toward progressive farmers seems to be best explained by the progressive farmer strategy, even though part of its 'diffusion of innovations' if not its 'economic growth' ideological underpinnings are deficient. The other factors explaining the skew are a weak commitment of junior staff to their work, the pattern of farmer demand for extension services, and a somewhat distorted perception by agents of the proportion of rural societies made up of progressive farmers. An even more optimistic view of their areas is held by the senior staff and is doubtless sustained by the isolation of all except the officers of local origin from their subordinates and the local community. The explanations which we have advanced for the progressive farmer bias leave us somewhat more hopeful than would the exchange and social class alliance proposition of Thoden van Velzen. The factors we have advanced as leading to the disadvantage of the less wealthy farmers may be organizationally manipulable. The skew might well be lessened by Ministry of Agriculture programmes that carefully redefined extension strategy, developed very specific guidelines for working with the middle or even bottom rungs of farmers, and gave the agent some solid basis for resisting progressive farmer demands. It is not clear, however, that the Ministry would want to follow a more egalitarian programme. As with many cases of inequality, the first step is to realize that a problem exists. Out of consciousness can come debate and a deliberate political decision rather than an unwitting drift dictated by past beliefs and domestic pressures.

NOTES

1.   H.U.E. Thoden van Velzen, 'Staff, Kulaks and Peasants', chapter in this volume.
2.   These data were collected during 1970 and early 1971 while I was a Junior Research Fellow of the Institute for Development Studies of the University of Nairobi. The research project out of which these data are drawn has been supported generously by the Institute. I also would like to express my appreciation for the invaluable research assistance of Bernard Chahilu, Edwin A. Luchemo, Jack K. Tumwa, and Humphries W'Opindi. Thanks are also due to Niels Roling and Peter Hopcraft for comments on earlier drafts of this paper.
3.   Details of the sampling strategy followed may be found in David K. Leonard, Humphries W'Opindi, Edwin A. Luchemo and Jack K. Tumwa, 'The Work Performance of Junior Agricultural Extension Staff in Western Province: Basic Tables' (Nairobi, Institute for Development Studies, University of Nairobi, 1971), 1. Note too that the settlement schemes in Kakamega and Bungoma were not studied and that on the basis of random selection, the Northern Division of Busia District did not fall in the sample.
4.   We are extremely grateful to the Ministry for making these data available to us. The analysis and interpretation of these data are our complete responsibility, and the views expressed should not be interpreted as reflecting those of the Agricultural Statistics Section nor of the Kenya Government.
5.   This number of 637 excludes interviews conducted on settlement schemes and in the Northern Division of Busia District. Neither of these had been included in our initial study of extension workers, and they were excluded here so as to give us comparable information between the two sets of material.
6.   I am grateful to my colleague W. Ouma Oyugi for this insight, which he gained during research in South Nyanza.
7.   D.K. Leonard, 'Organizational Structures for Productivity in Agricultural Extension', in D.K. Leonard (ed), *Rural Administration in Kenya* (Nairobi, East African Literature Bureau, 1973).
8.   Fred N. Kerlinger, *Foundations of Behavioural Research* (New York, Holt, Rinehart and Winston, 1964), 559.
9.   As our sampling unit was the location and not the division we rarely interviewed all the staff in a division. This means that some staff may have had friends who would have named them but whom we missed.
10.   My Luhya research assistants and I established these categories on the basis of our perceptions of status differentia in Western Province. They are judgmental only and are open to criticism, even though we believe them to be basically accurate. The main problem with the classification system concerns the placement of farmers who are not running large commercial enterprises. Generally, what we have here termed the progressive farmers would have been put in the Middle category and all others in the Low one. Unfortunately, there were doubtless errors of judgment here when the coding was done in the interview. We believe that this problem was not serious enough to invalidate the results.
11.   Mr. J.D.N. Olewe, now of the Institute for Development Studies, University of Nairobi, has information on such trading of favours in the cooperatives in the Kisumu area.
12.   R.G. Saylor, 'An Opinion Survey of Bwana Shambas in Tanzania' (Economic Research Bureau, University of Dar Es Salaam, 1970), 12, 17.
13.   That what we have reported of extension behaviour in Western Province is consistent with intended action was firmly driven home in a discussion we had with Mr. Kimani, the Provincial Director of Agriculture, and Mr. Gatheru, the Provincial Farm Management Officer. Both men are in positions too high for them to be influenced in this policy decision by the social persuasions or favours of local farmers.
14.   Cf. F.E. Emery and O.A. Oeser, *Information, Decision and Action* (Melbourne University Press, 1958).
15.   The greater part of my insights into these two sets of justifications have come from frequent discussions and occasional arguments with those who offer them. I am particu-

larly grateful for the intellectual stimulation offered by the economists and communication specialists in the Institute for Development Studies of the University of Nairobi.

16. Cf. E.M. Rogers, *The Diffusion of Innovations* (New York, The Free Press, 1962).

17. Private communication from Jeffrey Steeves, who has been doing research on the Kenya Tea Development Authority.

18. Similar conclusions on permanent income disadvantages to late, less well-off adopters have been reached in investigations on the diffusion of miracle rice in India. See E.M. Rogers, J.R. Ascroft and N.E. Roling, *Diffusion of Innovations in Brazil, Nigeria and India* (Department of Communications, Michigan State University, 1970), 4-53 to 4-55.

19. David K. Leonard with Bernard Chahilu and Jack Tumwa, 'Some Hypotheses Concerning the Impact of Kenya Government Agricultural Extension on Small Farmers' (Institute for Development Studies, University of Nairobi, 1970), 6, 7, 10-12, 13.

20. I am indebted to former chief Mathew Mwenesi for this particular point and to him and former locational clerk Benjamin Kapitain for confirming my intuition on this general problem.

21. Some of the extension experiments being conducted by Joseph Ascroft and his colleagues in the current Kenyan Special Rural Development Programme should cast light on these two propositions.

22. The argument here for a focus on the middle farmer leaves the poor farmer, who lacks adequate capital, out in the cold. In view of the permanent and cumulative additions to rural equality caused by the constant repetition of this innovation process, it at least needs to be investigated whether subsidized credit now may not be preferable to public welfare later.

23. Cf. Tom Mboya, 'Sessional Paper No. 10 – It is African and it is Socialism', *East African Journal*, VI, 5 (May 1969), 15, 16.

24. Leonard, 'Organizational Structures for Productivity in Agricultural Extension'.

25. Ibidem.

26. Joseph Ascroft, 'The Tetu Extension Pilot Project' (paper read at the Workshop on Strategies for Improving Rural Welfare, University of Nairobi, 1971), 17.

27. Private communication from Peter Moock, Institute for Development Studies evaluater of the Special Rural Development Programme in Vihiga.

28. Cf. Robers, Ascroft and Roling, *Diffusion of Innovations in Brazil, Nigeria and India*, 4-53 to 4-55.

MARC J. SWARTZ

LEGITIMACY AND COERCION IN BENA POLITICS AND DEVELOPMENT*

INTRODUCTION

The most striking effort for rural development among the Highland Bena[1] is the cooperative work party or *mugove*. Bena villagers give one day a week to this cooperative activity, and their joint work is devoted either to public building or to cultivating crops which are used as source of funds for public activities. This collective work is by no means new. Through the century of remembered history the inhabitants of Bena villages have worked as a group on the fields of their political officials, whether these were the Bena *vatwa* ('kings') or the local rulers put over them by the two conquering neighbouring tribes, the Sangu and the Hehe. Collective work often in the form of porterage but also in roadwork was also done under the German and English colonial regimes. All these collective labours were at the instigation of political officials and under their supervision, as is the present work. There has also been collective work on fields, also called mugove, originated and supervised by private individuals for their own benefit. This latter type of work, which is entirely voluntary, has also been characteristic of the Bena throughout their remembered history and is still found.

Some of the basic problems raised by the political mugoves are also found in trying to understand the private ones. Because of this, I shall consider both types of collective work parties for the light they throw on each other, despite the fact that the private mugove is not a political activity in any sense.

These problems all centre around the question of why people participate in the mugoves. The two obvious answers are that they have to in the sense that they will otherwise suffer some consequence that is more undesirable than participation, or that participation is directly rewarding in some way to a degree that is greater than would result from non-participation. These are not mutually exclusive; in fact, both direct reward and direct punishment are importantly similar in that they entail highly specific expectations on the part of actors. Of course, the expectations are of opposite kinds, but focusing on their specificity I shall group them together as 'coercion'. Compliance to political directives where there are either clear and direct rewards or clear and direct punishments will be considered compliance arising from political coercion. When compliance arises from expectations that are general and indirect rather than specific and direct, it will be said that compliance is based on 'legitimacy'; this will be so whether the general and indirect expectations are of a positive nature (i.e. rewards) or of a negative nature (i.e. punishments).[2]

I shall try to show that both legitimacy and coercion, as understood here, are involved in the Bena mugove and that neither alone provides the basis for understanding villagers' participation in these collective work activities. In attempting to demonstrate the basis for this view some examination of Bena society and culture and of some motives commonly found in Bena individuals will have to be undertaken.

REWARDS AND PUNISHMENTS IN COLLECTIVE WORK

The indirect nature of the incentives in cooperative work becomes perhaps most obvious if we first consider the private mugove. If a man, more rarely a woman, wants to accomplish a large-scale agricultural task such as bringing a new field into cultivation with the substantial hoe work that that involves, a common procedure is to let it be known that the work will be done on a particular day and then to brew beer as refreshment for those who help in the work. It might be thought that the work is done to 'earn' the beer, but this is shown not to be the case by the observation that some of those who drink the beer are merely passers-by who have not participated in the work, and the further observation that those Protestants of the Lutheran and other denominations who follow the teaching of their church closely will not drink any of the beer even though they have worked on the beermaker's project.

If the beer is not the answer, perhaps the basis for participation in a private mugove is direct reciprocity. That is, A works in B's mugove because he knows that he too will sponsor a mugove, and he wants to assure B's participation in it. Informants specifically deny that this is a motive for participating in a private mugove, and a check of the small number of mugoves about which I have relatively complete information indicates that although individuals *may* participate in the mugove of those who have participated in theirs, they also may well not do so. The probability that an individual will participate in a given mugove does not seem to be materially affected by whether or not the other individual has participated in his, and this is true in both a negative and a positive sense. That is, if A has participated in B's mugove, B may still not participate in A's, and if A has not participated in B's mugove, B may still participate in A's.

This should not be taken to mean there is no reciprocity, however. People who never participate in a mugove and whose wives and unmarried children do not participate are said to be unlikely to give a mugove of their own because they know it would be doubtful that many people would come to help them. This is part of the explanation of why a few relatively wealthy villagers sometimes hire people for wages to do cultivation that other villagers might have done through a mugove. The few relatively wealthy individuals I observed were storekeepers who were unwilling or unable to take time from their businesses and livestock (or to allow their wives or children to do so) to participate in any private mugoves and who gave none of their own.

Reciprocity, then, does play a role in participation in private mugoves but it is an indirect role. Gaining the general reputation of being a person who never participates in a mugove seems to be part of a conscious wish to stay out of the mugove giving-participating pattern, but if one participates in mugoves at all, one's own mugove will attract at least a sufficient number of people to accomplish the work at hand. (In my 20 months in Benaland I neither observed nor heard about a mugove which did not attract enough help to accomplish its purpose during the time set aside for it.) The nature of the social ties between mugove goers and givers will be considered below, but for the moment the important point is that participation in a particular mugove keeps alive one's right to give a mugove of one's own and in that sense there is a reciprocal return for the work done. The claim established by work in an individual's mugove (if 'reciprocity' means the establishment of claims), it must be stressed, is against the village as a whole rather than against the individual who gives a particular mugove.

To assess the practical significance of establishing the general claim for mugove help, it must be noted that the number of private mugoves given each year is relatively small. I do not know exactly how many mugoves were given during the agricultural year in the village where I lived for 13 months (this is because I am fairly sure that there were some I did not hear about), but I think 20 would be a fair maximum. It could be that other Bena villages have a drastically different number, but survey work throughout Benaland provides no basis for thinking this is so. In the mugoves which I observed there were as few as eight people in one and as many as 37 in another, but the average is nearer twenty. (The difficulty in giving exact figures is due to the fact that participants come and go during the work and an exact count is nearly impossible.) Participation in a private mugove is entirely voluntary and the people who participate in one are not particularly likely to participate in another. Few villagers participate in more than one or two mugoves in a given year. This means that in the year I observed mugoves in the village where I lived there were roughly 300 individuals out of the population of 950 who participated in them during that year, so that most participants do not give a mugove of their own in a year when they have participated in other people's mugoves. If my figures are even approximately correct, many mugove participants never give a mugove of their own. This inference is supported by many participants' statements that they never have given mugoves of their own and do not plan to in the foresee-able future. This does not mean that none will ever get a direct return for his work in the mugove, but rather that the return is often distant and contingent upon presently unforeseen needs and for many there will never be a direct return.

It is essential to point out that the participants in a particular mugove are not necessarily those with close kinship or neighbourhood ties to the giver. There are always a few neighbours and/or kin in a mugove, but there are usually more people present without any obvious close tie to the giver. A characteristic response to my question as to why a particular person was par-ticipating in a mugove was 'I heard about it and I thought it would be good if I came'. The important point, of course, is that most participation in any private mugove cannot be explained on the basis of any particularly close ties between the participants and the giver. It might also be noted that those who participate in a mugove do not have any claim to the produce of the field on which they are working nor do any of them share in its ownership, since field ownership is either strictly private among the Bena or shared by husband and wife or parent and unmarried child.

Considering the question only in the light of work given and work which might be received in return, both the rewards and the punishments connected with private mugoves are both indirect and distant. On a pragmatic basis the individual usually stands to gain little of immediate benefit through his mugove work and to lose little of pressing consequence if he never participates. The situation regarding village-wide mugoves under the direction of political of-ficials is in some ways similar, especially with respect to rewards. The projects sponsored by the modern government – through its village officials – provide indirect and rather indefinite benefits for the participants in the work con-nected with those projects. Better roads provide better transportation of people and goods, of course, but this is only immediately useful to those who are in a position to benefit from the improved service and this by no means in-cludes all villagers in equal degree. The situation may have changed since 1965 (when I studied it) but at that time, at least, the majority of villagers I talked to were extremely dubious about receiving any personal benefit in the foresee-able future from the 'self-help' roads and bridges they were building in their day per week village mugove. Somewhat more direct benefit was seen from the building of schools and dispensaries, when the work turned to these projects, but even here there was some doubt about the immediacy and value of the results of these projects. It is not that villagers fail to see good coming from the roads, schools and dispensaries, but rather that they did not see that it would come to each of them particularly. They thought that having a dispensary in the village would be a very useful thing, but many commented that the mission hospital was only a few miles away and that, except in rare emergencies, having a dispensary in the village itself would not be likely to be useful to them as individuals. These projects were viewed as a more or less good idea, but for the village as a whole rather than individually for each participant in the work involved in building them.

The general feeling with respect to the public work projects was that although they were not particularly likely to be personally beneficial, they were 'good for the village'. This is the sort of general feeling which it is easy to disregard and take as simply rhetoric, but this paper will argue that, in fact, this concern is a very real one and has very substantial social, cultural and psychological foundations. The idea that the welfare of the village is a real concern for individuals appears in the statements people make about the advantages of having children. One of the most commonly given reasons for wanting as many children as possible (and this is a universal desire) is 'to make the village grow'. Although this statement has a number of possible meanings attached to it, one of them is that people are genuinely interested in seeing their village flourish. It is not the contention here that that is the sole interest that people have in doing public work, but rather that it is a real interest and the main one as far as the usefulness of the results of public work are concerned.

The part played by this general interest in the overall welfare of the village is hard to weigh in determining why people work in the village-wide, politically organized mugoves, but it almost certainly has some role. Still, the possibility of punishment for refusing to participate probably has a more direct and more palpable role. The old Bena 'kings' are said to have destroyed the livestock of villagers who did not participate in the work on the kings' fields and this is thought by informants to have been a main basis for participation in that work. This may have been the case under the conditions prevailing in the mid-19th century, but there are some difficulties in the use of these punishments under modern circumstances. In the village where I spent the longest period of time, one of the headmen was a particularly vigorous proponent of public work. There were a number of households in his ward whose members were participating in public work in only a desultory way and after a group of officials from the TANU headquarters in the nearby town visited the village and praised the methods of the old rulers, the headman followed ancient precedent and killed some chickens belonging to the reluctant workers in public mugoves. This move by the headman was probably effective in renewing the vigour of the chickens' owners, but it brought a storm of unfavourable comment throughout the village. Although this headman subsequently became Village Executive Officer (VEO) and served quite effectively in that position, the chicken-killing incident was never forgotten and was used against the official in an unsuccessful attempt to block his becoming VEO. Most significantly, the official did not again use direct sanctions against those who were uncooperative in collective work.

The point is that quite direct sanctions can be used against those who do not cooperate in village-wide mugoves, but the village official who uses them risks serious harm to his general position in doing so. In fact, the incident just related is the only direct coercive action connected with public work I have been able to discover in modern Benaland. However, coercion of a less direct nature is available to village officials in the form of the *baraza*, or village dispute settlement sessions. In these sessions, which I have described in detail elsewhere (Swartz 1964, 1966),[3] there is always an accuser and a defendant (usually both are individuals but occasionally one or both can be two or three people usually closely related through kinship or marriage) who are questioned by those who participate in the baraza. The first part of the questioning is carried out until the facts of the case at issue are no longer disputed; then a second round of questioning begins which continues until a settlement is agreed to by both litigants. Barazas can be under the charge of any prestigious man, but the more important and/or difficult disputes are taken to village political officials. Regardless of who runs the baraza its decisions cannot be enforced since there is no established procedure for doing so. Enforcement depends upon the loser accepting the baraza's decision. In this sense the baraza is coercive, but indirectly so since its force is mediated through the acceptance of that force by the object of the force.

When the 'case' (all things brought before a baraza are called *kesi* in Swahili and Kibena) concerns a public event such as failure to join in a village-wide mugove, the accuser is the village official directly in charge of the event at issue, and the person or persons he believes not to have followed his authority are the defendants. In all other respects such cases are handled by the same procedure as all others save when — should it be heard before the baraza of the official concerned — someone else takes his place as leader of questioning while he stands before the baraza as the accuser. Thus, the most a person who does not participate in public work is likely to suffer is a fine or extra public work to which *he himself agrees*. If he refuses to agree, there will be no official punishment and his general social relations will not suffer immediate or drastic disruption. In fact, should a person refuse to accept the punishment arrived at by the baraza, it is unlikely that any observable change in his social relations would take place.

I have to say it is 'unlikely that any observable change' would occur in his social relations, because I have never observed anyone refusing the findings of the baraza in a case of this nature. Informants say that no one could be so stubborn as to refuse the findings of what might be called 'the baraza of last appeal'. Cases can be appealed if either litigant is dissatisfied with the decision of the first baraza involved (for cases involving public works this means appealing from the headman to the VEO), but such appeals are almost always carried out when the facts of the case cannot be agreed upon. Such disagreement did not occur in any of the cases (three cases involving eight defendants) I observed regarding participation in public work. Here the facts as presented by the official in charge of the work were not disputed by the defendants.

The important point here, so far, is that the type of coercion easily available to public officials for use in gaining participation in public mugoves depends upon acceptance of the coercion by the object of the coercion and although this acceptance is universal, the coercion does not take us far in answering the question posed in this paper: Why do Bena villagers participate in public work projects? Even if baraza punishments were frequently invoked against non-participants, we would only have moved our explanatory task back a step to the question: Why do people accept punishments which make it impractical for them to avoid public mugoves? In fact, barazas are only rarely called for cases of non-participation because such non-participation is very infrequent. That there should be little need to use barazas to bring about participation in public work is a key fact for the argument to be advanced here in that it will be contended that very much the same forces which make the baraza effective lead to participation in public mugoves.

To sum up the argument to this point we have seen that private mugoves provide only indirect rewards for their participants as regards work exchange in that they establish a claim against the community for some of its members to come to a mugove should a participant give one in the future. It strongly appears that most people never give private mugoves but that they participate in those of their fellow villagers anyway and this participation is not on the basis of special kinship or neighbourhood ties.

Those who do not participate in private mugoves at all appear to be barred from giving their own, but few people do this and they seem to be wealthy individuals who have the same work done for wages. The rewards for participation in private mugoves are distant and uncertain, and the punishment for never participating has very little effect on the few who refrain from participating completely. In other words, the economically coercive aspect of participation of private mugoves is rather slight either with respect to direct punishment or with respect to direct rewards. Public mugoves have the same status as private ones inasfar as material rewards are concerned. These rewards are indirect and indefinite in that villagers do not see that they, as individuals, will necessarily benefit from the products of their collective labour. They do see the results of the projects as improving the village as a whole, but this is also an indirect sort of benefit. The negative aspects of coercion regarding public work are rather more palpable. Political officials can take direct action against those who refuse to engage in public work, but it was seen that it is costly for these officials to do so and that, in fact, it is practically never done. Less drastic negative coercion is available in the form of the baraza, but this is a highly indirect form of coercion in that it can only work when the object of the coercion agrees to accept his punishment. At a minimum, it has been established that direct and specific expectations of either material reward or punishment do not explain participation in mugoves completely and that other factors have to be considered if this participation is to be understood. The remainder of this paper will be devoted to analyzing the forces which contribute to some indirect and non-specific expectations of a non-economic sort vital to the understanding of participation in public work. These forces are divided into three categories: motivational, cultural, and social.

SOME COMMON BENA MOTIVES

I have attempted to show in an earlier paper (Swartz, 1966) that many Bena individuals can be correctly characterized as having three central psychological constellations based on drives which I called distrust, dependency, and hostility. There is no need to recapitulate the evidence for this characterization here, but some of the behavioural consequences which are associated with it need to be mentioned. Most importantly, many Bena feel that they need the help of others in a variety of ways if they are to manage to live in what they view as a harsh and unfruitful environment, but at the same time they have little confidence that these others will provide the needed assistance even when they 'ought' to do so for reasons of connection through kinship, marriage, neighbourhood, or as a matter of direct reciprocity. In other words, the felt necessity to be able to get help is complicated and its success perceived as uncertain because there are grave misgivings about other people's dependability. Dependency and distrust are closely connected with the third constellation, that based on hostility, and this further complicates the attainment of such goals as feeling that help will be available when needed. One of the main manifestations of the Bena hostility drive[4] is seen in the classical mechanism of projection whereby the individual experiences fear of retaliatory action from those against whom he harbours hostile feelings (based, for example, on resentment deriving from unmet dependency needs).

There are many consequences of these broad psychological constellations, but the three which are of the most concern in understanding participation in mugoves are the wish to cause other people to be willing to help one, the fear that they may not be willing to do so, and a dread of hostile action against oneself in retaliation for any hostile feelings one may oneself harbour. Each of these leads to a variety of observable behaviours and often more than one constellation can be seen as a motivating force in particular actions and types of actions. Thus, to take a readily observable and very common sort of behaviour, most Bena individuals are extremely polite and amiable in their relations with others. A ready smile, a pleasant word, and a careful avoidance of giving offence are commonly found in Bena interactions.

By this characteristic sort of behaviour (which helps to make living among the Bena very pleasant for an outsider) all three drives are served. Amiability shows no hostile feelings exist, and at the same time its ingratiating effect increases the likelihood that its object will be willing to be helpful if needed.

Should the partner in interaction be brought by the actors' behaviour to respond with similarly polite and agreeable behaviour, the basis for distrusting
and fearing him is thereby lessened, to some extent at least. None of this is to
suggest that the three drives always work together, or that they are operative
only in producing politeness and amiability, or that their goals can be fully
achieved by this type of behaviour alone. In fact, the limitations of politeness
are clearly recognized by the Bena, and other expressions of these drives will be
shown to be crucially important in understanding the willingness of most Bena
individuals to participate in public work. The main concern with these drives
here will be to show how they motivate both widespread acceptance of certain
commonly held values and beliefs and how they lead to participation in certain
patterns of social relations. Both the acceptance and the participation will be
shown to be at the basis of actors' expectations of indirect benefits deriving
from participation in both public and private mugoves.

SOME ASPECTS OF BENA CULTURE

I take it as axiomatic that there is always a close but complex relationship between the values and beliefs which are shared in a community and the motives
which are found in the personalities of the members of that community. I am
particularly concerned here with aspects of Bena culture which provide most
Bena individuals with ready-made means of managing the three psychological
constellations which have just been discussed. If these constellations are as important in shaping the behaviour of Bena individuals as I believe them to be,
the culturally provided means for dealing with the problems and achieving the
goals arising from these constellations can only fail to be highly important if
individually devised, idiosyncratic means of managing the forces within the
constellations are generally more widely used than those which are culturally
provided. Idiosyncratic behaviour is no less common among the Bena than in
many other groups; but as in most groups which maintain their cohesiveness,
this sort of behaviour is less common than is behaviour which takes advantage
of the culturally provided and approved forms of action. The usefulness of
politeness and amiability has already been noted, and it hardly needs to be said
that these two related forms of behaviour are highly valued by the Bena. It was
also noted that amiability and politeness alone fall far short of exhausting the
types of behaviour which arise from the dependency, hostility, and distrust
drives.

Another value which is closely related to all three drives concerns sociability. The good man likes to be with other people and is isolated from them
for long periods only when the necessities of making a living require that he be
by himself. He builds his house as near to the houses of others as is practical
given the availability of appropriate space and the requirements the terrain

places upon him regarding the juxtaposition of his home and his fields.[5] This is a key determinant of the compact nature of the Bena village. More than just building near other people, the good man visits the homes of other people as often as possible, and he asks all those who come near his house to come in and visit him.

The value on sociability needs to be looked at together with the values on amiability and politeness since the first deals with the constitution of social settings (i.e. there should be a number of people together whenever possible) and the second deals with the content of social interaction holding that it be amiable and polite. The Bena say that a good man is one who 'walks around a lot' (i.e. visits other people) and who talks of pleasant things and is quick to laugh.

There is a negative side to the value on sociability which also needs to be considered in that it has the effect of strengthening the values on sociability and politeness-amiability. This negative side is the belief that those who are by themselves a great deal, who do not live near other people, are not hospitable and who do not 'walk around' are highly suspect. Witchcraft[6] is done in private and although not all witches shun the company of others (some are guileful and appear to be virtuous men), all those who are not sociable are likely to be witches. Similarly, those who are not amiable and polite — especially if this takes the form of quarrelsomeness and aggressive deportment — are likely to be thought witches. There are practical consequences to being thought a witch — these include being ostracized, having one's house burned down and even being killed by someone who thinks himself your victim — and this serves as a very present basis for carrying out valued behaviour even if that behaviour does not directly satisfy drives. It has been argued that politeness and amiability do contribute to the psychological welfare of most Bena, but it should be noted that there was no claim that the constellations discussed were characteristic of every Bena. Those who differ substantially from their fellows regarding the dependency-distrust-hostility constellation are still brought toward behaving in the valued ways provided only that they desire the consequences of being thought a witch less than the consequences of behaving in ways which are not socially approved however personally rewarding they may be. For the majority, for whom sociability and politeness are rewarding, the belief in witchcraft simply adds further inducement to manifest behaviour which is generally desirable and rewarding to them in any event.[7]

A further belief which affects the pattern of values so far considered is that 'no one can know another's heart'. The Bena believe that long-term predictions of individuals' behaviour are not likely to prove correct, and they claim not to be surprised by rather sharp deviations in the behaviour of a given individual from his usual pattern. That people who are so filled with distrust of others should hold this view is not surprising, but it should be noted that this is not an idiosyncratic judgment made by separate individuals. It is a shared belief, often repeated publicly, and having the status of a social 'given'. One of the main consequences of this is that goodness must be constantly demonstrated. The value on sociability which brings people into contact with each other constantly provides the opportunity for individuals to allay the fears inherent in the belief that their hearts cannot be known by allowing them to constantly demonstrate their virtue in public.

Thus, the values on sociability, politeness and amiability combine with the belief concerning the indeterminate nature of character to form a pattern in which behaviour satisfying one component can also satisfy another and, conversely, failure to meet one of the values will hinder being viewed as behaving in accordance with the others. Obviously, the pattern is not perfectly integrated in that it is possible, for example, to be polite and amiable without being as gregarious as the sociability value requires. However, one's general standing in the community cannot be very high as far as being a moral person is concerned if one is *only* polite and amiable. This is so not merely because a major value, sociability, is not observed, but also because by being relatively isolated such politeness and amiability as is manifested cannot allay suspicions that one is not *really* polite and amiable, given the view that basic character must be constantly demonstrated.

A final value needs to be considered before turning to a brief examination of village social structure. This is the view that a good man helps others whenever they need it and that he does so without regard to the likelihood that he will be repaid in any direct way — or, for that matter, that he will gain any material return for his efforts at all. The fact that this value is closely connected with the dependency drive will be obvious, but the nature of the connection and the value's relation to the hostility drive and other values and beliefs requires some exploration.

In many ways the value attached to help is an extension of the values on sociability and amiability-politeness. People are expected to help only those in their nuclear families (with this 'family' constituted of own father, own mother, own spouse and spouse's parents, own children, and/or other kin who have assumed these roles through adoption or inheritance) on a regular, daily basis. The value on help applies to extraordinary situations in the lives of the individuals who require the help. Informants mention such things as attacks by wild animals (a rare but real danger), sudden illness, unusual sorts of work, and quarrels which cannot be easily settled, as sorts of situations which require the valued help. When someone gives the distinctive call which means there is an emergency, all those who hear it are to run to its source to determine what is wrong and do what they can to remedy the situation. When people have disputes they cannot settle themselves, others should help them — usually through the previously mentioned baraza — to settle those quarrels and return their relations to normal amity. If someone needs an unusual type of work done (clearing a new field, for example), those who have time and are available should help him in the private mugoves already discussed. These occasions for help are hardly more than extensions of sociability-amiability-politeness in that the help is expected from those who are present rather than from specific individuals or occupants of particular statuses, and the help does not require commitments which interfere with an individual's pursuit of his own interests in any consequential way. Being around people, as the sociability value requires, and being agreeable toward them, takes one most of the way toward helping them in the limited ways called for by the value on help.

The connection of the value on help to the dependency drive may be somewhat obscured by the inclusion as part of the value of the stipulation that help should be forthcoming without regard to any return. This means that there is no particular pressure for someone you have helped to help you. If one cannot depend upon those whom one has helped to provide assistance when needed, who can be depended upon? The answer is that all people who are both virtuous and available can be depended upon and that, given Bena distrust, this is in many ways more satisfactory than any other arrangement since it shifts the locus of dependency from particular individuals to the community of moral persons at large. Informants report that it makes them happy to see people working together and helping each other because it 'shows the village is good'. They explain this to mean that there are not many unsettled quarrels in the village and that there are many 'good-hearted' people there. It is surely justified to infer further that seeing people help someone brings happiness because it shows that help really is available, and that if others get it there is a reasonable chance you will too. As long as there are some 'good people' in the community, the prospects are favourable that help will be available without having to depend on the virtue and availability of those particular individuals who have specifically benefited by your assistance.

We need to stress another aspect of informants' statements about why it should bring happiness to see people working together and giving help. This is that such work shows that there are few outstanding quarrels in the community. Joint work is not only a way of showing willingness to follow the value on help, it is also a way of showing that one harbours no hostile feelings against those with whom one works. This, of course, is similar to the fact that in being sociable and amiable a lack of hostility is demonstrated. In fact, in joint work such as mugoves the singing, chatting and laughing involved are unmistakable evidence that help and sociability-amiability are by no means mutually exclusive. In helping someone, however, your non-hostile feelings toward him and toward your fellow helpers are demonstrated in a different and perhaps more potent way by the expenditure of work for which there is no material return. Greeting people, entertaining them, and being with them shows a lack of enmity but the cost involved in the demonstration is low. Being willing to do work for no gain is a powerful indication of goodness of heart, i.e. of the absence of hostility, and being without hostility helps protect you from the hostility of others. The fear of retaliation for hostile feelings is not the sole and direct cause of participation in helping, but it plays a part together with the wish to be in a position to believe that the members of the community help one another so that, as a member of the community, it is likely that you too will be helped when that is called for.

SOCIAL GROUPINGS IN BENA VILLAGES

Nothing has been said so far about the composition of the groups which come together in accordance with the values just discussed. In order to understand how these values and the psychological forces which make them effective contribute to participation in public work it is necessary to consider some basic facts about the composition of Bena villages.

The Bena are ideally virilocal and my census figures show that 85 per cent of all married men have their homes in the villages of their fathers. However, this does not mean that fathers and sons usually have their houses close together. The Bena believe that it is better for close kin to live in houses separated by the houses of non-relatives because they maintain that people who see each other all day and every day are likely to quarrel, and it is better to quarrel with strangers than with close kin. The explicit reason for avoiding constant close contact with immediate kin is that 'they cannot be replaced' should the relationship be ruptured by quarrels. It has already been seen that assistance with the ongoing business of getting a living is not part of the value on help and that if such assistance is needed only close relatives can be called on. If a man is out of food, needs money, or requires long-term support because of illness or age, he is expected to go to his father, his brothers, or his sons and their wives for these things and not to 'strangers'. In the hypothetical case in which a man did not go to the close kin just mentioned (or more distant kin who have taken their place[8]), those whom he approached would say, informants report, 'have you no brothers?' The Bena say that if you quarrel with a neighbour who is a 'stranger' (i.e. not a close relative), you or he can move away to another part of the village and little will be lost because you can always get new neighbours. One needs both neighbours and close kin, but the first can be easily replaced by others while the second cannot. It is therefore vital that ruptures in relations with close kin be made as unlikely as possible.

The fact that an individual has the right to claim continuing support only from his close kin, and the further fact that the continuation of ties with those kin depends upon the maintenance of reasonably friendly relations with them, has observable effects on Bena social groupings and alignments. It has already been seen that the Bena believe that it is necessary for fathers and sons and for brothers to live separated by strangers and, from the discussion of the private mugove, it will be clear that the responsibility to help others in emergencies and unusual situations falls at least as heavily on 'strangers' as it does on close kin. Similarly, gregariousness requires association with everyone and not just with fathers and brothers, and amiability, though vital within the crucial kin relationships, is also highly important in relations with others. This leads to most social groupings — at beer drinks, informal assemblies in people's houses, mugoves, and barazas — being made up of a cross-section of the village or, in large villages, of the neighbourhood, and by no means of close kin alone. Thus, although the Bena put great stress on the relationship between a man and his sons and among those sons, social groups gathering on most occasions are usually composed of 'strangers' as well as kin.

It is worth taking a moment to note that 'strangers' are vital to the peaceful continuation of the most important kin relations not only through serving as buffers between the kin in living arrangements. The only way that family disputes can be settled if the disputants cannot make peace by themselves is through barazas. Close relatives of disputants do not attend these, so they are carried out wholly by strangers. Strangers are also vital as witnesses who will help prevent future conflict in such family matters as the distribution of a dead man's goods, the transfer of bridewealth, and the ritual by which an errant son apologizes to his father (who may or may not be alive) for having struck or cursed him.

Clearly, although social relationships with brothers and fathers are vital to the Bena, these are part of wider community relationships among nonrelatives which make the close kin relations less likely to rupture and which offer the main possibility to mend them if they should rupture. As noted, fathers and sons and brothers usually live in the same village but not next to one another. They depend upon one another for continuing aid with maintaining life when that is needed, but it needs to be made clear that they do not often act together and that they do not own property in common after the sons marry. In short, the scope of vital activities which a group of close kinsmen can carry out in isolation from other villagers is severely limited. The most important gatherings of people in a Bena village from many points of view — barazas, mugoves, beer drinks, and informal gatherings — are not restricted to groups of agnates or any other sort of near relatives. On the contrary, they all require a fairly wide representation from the community at large.

INDIRECT AND GENERAL EXPECTATIONS CONCERNING MUGOVES

All the foregoing has been intended to show that Bena psychological constellations, Bena beliefs and values, and Bena social arrangements, all militate toward the manifestation of polite, amiable, and helpful behaviour in social relationships which are necessarily spread throughout the village. Giving help was said to be not only a way of behaving in accord with particular, isolated values and/or the direct result of several separate psychological constellations, but rather the product of a complex interaction of factors. To help to display one's virtue and to see help given shows that one lives in a virtuous community from which help can be expected when it is needed and whose members have their hostilities under control. It was also argued that the cultural and social factors which lead to the diffusing of expectations of help to the whole village helped to lessen the social and psychological difficulties engendered by widespread distrust. The application of all this to the private mugove will be clear enough. As long as you participate in some of the private mugoves sometimes, you can at once satisfy some important shared values and the psychological needs commonly associated with them, and reassure yourself that there really are people throughout the village who do help and get along with one another and some of whom will get along with you and help you should you need it.

The private mugoves are entirely voluntary and no one has any particular obligation to participate in a given one. Having to do your own work is a perfectly acceptable reason not to participate in any particular private mugove, and if you are not around when word is passed informally that there will be one, there is nothing to require that you should be there. However, if you do hear of a private mugove and do not have work of your own to do, you should be there; in the course of time this is sure to occur so that everyone participates in some mugoves (with the exception of the very few rich individuals who stay out of the mugove system altogether). This participation, it will now be understood, is not on the basis of the specific expectations of immediate reward or punishment which I called 'coercion' at the beginning of this paper.

Participation in the public mugove is fundamentally similar to the private except that refusal to participate does not have such an acceptable foundation as it has for a particular private mugove. A day is set aside for public mugoves each week; everyone is told by the Village Executive Officer what day it is and that they are expected to arrange their affairs so as to be available on that day. Having your own work to do is not acceptable as a reason for absence as it is in the private mugove, and there is no possibility of your not knowing about it as you might in the case of a private mugove. All the psychological, cultural and structural forces which lead to the relatively general and indirect expectations of benefit, which lead to participation in the private mugove apply also to the public one; however, the basis for missing a private mugove is absent and the maintenance of these expectations without attending each public mugove is made difficult.

We have seen, but not dwelt upon, a coercive element in attending a private mugove. This was the view that anyone who was not sociable-amiable-helpful was likely to be a witch and witches are dealt with rather sternly. Missing private mugoves does not make one a witch anymore than failure to be sociable on a particular occasion, but never attending a private mugove is rather suspicious and might contribute to the perception of a general pattern of behaviour leading to witch-suspicion.[9] This may not be very coercive in the sense in which that term is used here, but it surely tends more in that direction than in the direction of legitimacy.

In the public mugove this also applies, but more directly coercive is the possibility of being accused of non-participation by the headman or the Village Executive Officer in a baraza. At the beginning I said that the forces which make the baraza work are the same as those which make the public mugove work, and it is now possible to show how that is so. Being internally and externally driven to be helpful and amiable, a person cannot easily withstand the questioning of the baraza and its suggested settlements, and his wish to maintain ties throughout the community makes this all the more so since the sessions are attended by people from all parts of the village. The important difference between the general requirement to attend the weekly public mugove and the ability of the baraza to get recalcitrant individuals to accept a penalty for not doing so, is that in the baraza the forces that have been examined here are potently focused on the accused individual rather than spread throughout the whole community.

Should he fail to go to a public mugove a person can blunt the force of the values involved as they apply to his psychological needs and the values and beliefs he shares with fellow villagers by telling himself that the appeal for participation was not directed specifically at him in his circumstances but at the group in general. This view is not easy to maintain — and, as noted, few individuals fail to come to the public mugove in the first place — but for those few who try to hold it, there is the strong possibility that they will have to stand alone with their accuser (litigants stand in the midst of the seated group which questions them) and defend their actions and/or refuse to accept suggested penalties. It will be clear from all that has been said that this is not something most Bena can easily or comfortably do. The focusing of all the psychological, cultural and social pressures on the isolated individual is not qualitatively different from the general requirement to participate in public work, but it is surely quantitatively different. The coercion which is applied in the form of fines or extra work imposed by the baraza is one which works, rather paradoxically, on the basis of legitimacy in that it depends on the individual's acceptance of the general and non-specific benefits which come from adherence to the values and social ties characteristic of Bena villages.

The general issues concerning the relationship between legitimacy and coercion, as these concepts are defined here, focus around the fact that analytically the two forces are not really different in kind but are, rather, ends of a single continuum. This is true both from an analytic point of view and from the point of view of actors. The general expectations that people will help, that they will not harm you, and that there can be some assurance that these desired things will come to pass, shade easily into specific expectations about particular numbers of people helping on specific occasions, specific expectations about how particular situations will affect behaviour, and about how these situations will occur in specific circumstances.

The baraza provides an excellent example of the interplay between specific and general expectations. It has already been noted that the baraza's ability to coerce depends upon the general expectations of the coerced in order to be effective since the baraza is not equipped to enforce its decisions and depends upon the consent of those appearing before it for the enforcement of its decisions. At the same time, the fact that an individual is summoned to the baraza (e.g. in the case of a political official bringing charges for missing a public mugove, a messenger would inform the individual that the official had a complaint against him and would present it at the baraza to be held at a particular time and place) raises highly specific expectations and is, by definition, coercive. The individual can ignore the summons and the only thing that is likely to happen is that he will receive another summons; or he can heed it and face the close questioning of the most prestigious men in the village before a participating audience of his fellows. In the first case the individual is faced with the prospect of being thought a difficult person (*mkatagi* in Swahili; *mnyangng'ani* in KiBena), and in the second case with the close and unrelenting questioning of representatives of the community. That these alternatives affect the behaviour of many who might consider not participating in one or more public mugoves can hardly be doubted, so that there is a coercive basis for the participation of at least some people, and however important the more general expectations may be they are not isolated from the operation of much more specific expectations.

Both with respect to the baraza and to the possibility of being thought a witch it is important to note that people are affected not only by what happens to them but also by what happens to other people. Obviously, a person who is called before the baraza feels the force of specific expectations of the sort just discussed and a person who is deemed a witch the same, but it is worth making explicit that people learn from the experiences of others and that barazas and witchcraft accusations serve to modify the behaviour of individuals who are not themselves the direct object of them but only observers. The baraza is the most obvious manifestation of this, since many people come to see and participate in the questioning of anyone who has failed to meet the requirements of political officials or anyone else who feels affronted.

The baraza is a sort of bridge which serves to bring highly specific expectations to bear in areas of life where general expectations are extremely important for most people most of the time. The Bena may well depend upon general expectations to a greater extent than some other groups and their specific expectations of punishment and reward are less drastic and dramatic than in some other societies, but the two kinds of expectations surely both operate in political and other areas of life in all societies. This might seem nothing more than a tautology since some expectations cannot but be more general than others, but as a matter of empirical fact it appears useful to examine the effect and relative roles of quite general expectations (e.g. that there will be 'peace', 'a good life', 'progress', 'happiness' on the one hand, or 'oppression', 'bad times', 'trouble' and so on on the other) and highly specific expectations (e.g. 'people who do not obey are beaten', 'if you help your neighbour with his field today, he helps you with yours tomorrow', etc.) in people's responses to political authority and in other areas of life.

This paper has tried to show how the particular nature of Bena culture and social structure and some common Bena psychological characteristics and the interaction of these are related to Bena participation in public works, and in occasional cooperation in private agricultural tasks — both of them activities which figure prominently among the aims of the Tanzanian government. It is not the view taken here that legitimacy is always as prominent in political processes in all groups as it is among the Bena or that coercion always has a lesser role. Rather, the general position here is that the part played by general expectations and that played by specific expectations and the interplay of the two need to be examined if reaction to political attempts to gain public compliance are to be understood, and that this can best be done by an examination of spheres of life which go well beyond political activity as that is commonly understood.

NOTES

* An earlier version of this paper was read at a conference on 'Changes in Tanzanian Rural Society and Their Relevance for Development Planning' in December 1970, and was entitled 'Conflicting Forces in Bena Local Politics' (Afrika-Studiecentrum, Leiden).

I am grateful to my colleagues Melford Spiro, Roy D'Andrade, and David Jordan for their helpful comments on this paper.
1. By 'Highland Bena' I mean the people of the Bena tribe who live on the plateau around Njombe, especially to the north and to the south. The Bena living to the east of Njombe in the Ulanga valley have developed separately from the Highland people for more than 80 years and live in a quite different ecological zone. Having worked only six weeks in the Ulanga valley, I am not confident that what is said in this paper applies to the people in that area although I suspect it does.
2. The view of legitimacy and coercion used here is based on the work of Talcott Parsons (especially 1960) and is discussed at length in the introduction to *Political Anthropology*, pp. 14-19.
3. In my article on political compliance (1966) I examine the same interplay of psychological, social and cultural forces considered here, but the focus in that essay is on how these forces help explain the effectiveness of the baraza and the related support for village political officials.
4. Separating the hostility drive from distrust is a heuristic device which takes one of the main forms of hostility, distrust, and gives it separate standing for clarity of exposition. Psycho-dynamically, I believe it could be successfully maintained that the Bena can be adequately characterized as sharing two, rather than three, psychological states: hostility and dependence.

5. In some parts of Benaland, especially the northwest, the hilly terrain forces people, as they see it, to live at some remove from one another. However, even in these areas it is considered preferable to live as near to others as possible and those who live beyond the distance of travel of a shout are viewed as strange even though topographical considerations would appear to make the separation necessary. Sociability in general and visiting in particular are as valued in the northwest as elsewhere in Benaland.

6. The distinction between 'witchcraft' and 'sorcery' is not useful among the Bena who believe that medicines are essential for harming others by supernatural means, but that the children of those who have practised occult aggression are far more likely to be practitioners than are others. I follow English-speaking Bena in referring to all practitioners as 'witches' and all means of harming others supernaturally as 'witchcraft'.

7. I strongly suspect that all societies have culturally constituted means for winning the conformity of individuals who are different from the majority in their psychological constitution. Witchcraft beliefs serve as an important device for doing this among the Bena.

8. The replacement of kinsmen is important only with regard to father and brothers, especially older brothers. When a father dies, his eldest son assumes his authority in a limited way if all sons are adults. If the sons are children, the dead father is replaced by his oldest living seminal brother who functions in the dead man's role without restriction vis-à-vis the children. The elder brother role is particularly important for religious purposes but is also important in the settlement of disputes among siblings and their children. Succession to this role is according to seniority among seminal brothers. This issue is discussed further in another article (Swartz, 1970).

9. Not all the relatively rich men who do not participate in private mugoves were suspected of being witches, as far as I could determine, but several of them were. I do not believe, in the case of the suspected rich men, that there is a simple link between non-participation in mugoves and witch-suspicion but rather that non-participation is another indication of the rich men's unacceptable and witch-like behaviour.

REFERENCES

Parsons, Talcott
    1960   'On the Concept of Power'. *Proceedings of the American Philosophical Society*, 107, 232-262.

Swartz, M., V. Turner and A. Tuden (eds)
    1966   *Political Anthropology* (Chicago, Aldine).

Swartz, Marc
    1964   'Continuities in the Bena Political System', *Southwestern Journal of Anthropology*, 20, 241-253.
    1966   'Bases for Political Compliance in Bena Villages', in Swartz, Turner and Tuden (eds), *Political Anthropology*, 89-108.
    1970   'The Bilingual Kin Terminology of the Bena', *The Journal of African Languages*.

G. C. MUTISO

A LOW STATUS GROUP IN CENTRE-PERIPHERY RELATIONS: MBAI SYA EITU

INTRODUCTION

How we deal with the issue of penetration and the way in which we define it, depends upon our theoretical approach to the study of African political processes. Bienen[1] has considered various approaches to the study of African politics in his critique of classification systems used by political scientists, and suggests that the African one-party states 'contain party-machines at their political core'.[2] These are mainly located in the rural areas since there are few urban centres. He cites studies in Tanzania, Congo, Ivory Coast, Ghana (under Nkrumah) and Uganda (under Obote).[3] Bienen's argument carried to its extreme would suggest (1) that the process of politics evolves around the exercise of patronage by political bosses; (2) that the centre is the source of patronage and that 'tribal nationalists' (an old category in the study of African politics) act as intermediary bosses who through the decentralized party handle the patronage; and (3) that the 'machine model' will tell us something about intra-tribal exercise of patronage since the grass-root locale of the party is presumably tribal and rural.

Such assumptions about African politics are not the most fruitful if one wants to understand local level (intra-tribal) political processes. Perhaps the problem is one of level of analysis. Bienen basically seems to accept a 'tribal boss' model, which suggests that national political distribution is done on the basis of tribe and in this process the 'tribal boss' at the centre is the pivot. The data on the role of women discussed in this chapter suggest that local level (intra-tribal) political distribution is a phenomenon not related to the actors at the centre, be they tribal bosses or otherwise. The 'machine' model does not adequately account for the groups which take part in local level politics.

These questions can be better dealt with if we study the rural areas in terms of historical context and mobility of status groups and postulate that low status groups take part in the rural political process as a *means of gaining status in society*. They are organizationally independent of the parties but are used from time to time by tribal nationalists in their efforts to build intra-tribal bases of support to get access to the national distributive system (party, parliament, government). Furthermore, low status groups modify traditional organizational structures and techniques and utilize them to fulfil very modern functions. They suffer in this respect from those in high status who denigrate anything traditional. Through the modification and manipulation of traditional structures and techniques a very large proportion of the rural population is swayed away from national politics; they thus *perceive* the party and other national organizations and programmes as alien institutions.

The concept of penetration is problematic but we assume that in the African situation it means greater utilization by the political centre of available organizational skills in the society for developmental tasks. The concept assumes control from the centre. Our analysis of *Mbai Sya Eitu* as an example of low status groups suggests non-penetration, mainly because the government's perception of these groups is that they are irrelevant in the process of development. There is no evidence of their utilization by government. Yet the activities of the Mbai Sya Eitu have been of critical importance in the extractive process; though they were started for electioneering purposes we shall see that they have acquired an institutional life of their own. This paper, which will describe the organizational features of Mbai Sya Eitu in some detail, is part of wider research whose thesis is that through studying these low status extra-party organizations we can get a better picture of rural politics and, by extension, of the nature of the national political process. This study shows that in a particular area of Kenya the rural political organizations are not linked directly to the national party processes, whether the party process or the activities of the so-called administrative state. To clarify the point we discuss the historical political context below.

The Mbai Sya Eitu (literally translated as 'clans of girls') are a recent phenomena in Ukamba. They were not 'formed' until 1961. Since then their contributions to the 1963 and 1969 elections as well as that to the Harambee phenomena have made them a significant force. By October 1970, however, Government had claimed that serious complaints had been raised against them by the people. Following this they were banned by Government. Their activities were concentrated in the Northern Division of Machakos District, but between 1965 and 1969 (the years of peak activity in raising revenue for Harambee projects) they also embraced most of Machakos District and occasional meetings were even held in Kitui District. In Ukamba the Mbai Sya Eitu were able to rival all other political and social organizations through their activities. That they had developed a strongly controlled organization gave them a significant influence, particularly considering the limited number of their activities.

SOCIO-HISTORICAL BACKGROUND

Since the activities of the Mbai Sya Eitu originated and were concentrated in the Northern Division of Machakos District it is important to sketch the socio-historical background of the district and the division (the latter includes Kangundo, Matungulu, Mwala and Mbiuni Locations). Three cleavages in the society in the 1950s had a bearing on later developments. The first relates to the establishment of the Protestant African Inland Church at Muisuni in Kangundo Location in 1901 and the Catholic Church at Kabaa in Mbiuni in 1924. After the First World War the Catholic Church established a major centre at Misyani in Kangundo. This was perceived as an incursion into the African Inland Mission (AIM) area and for that reason the AIM established the rural centre at Matungulu, to hem in the Catholics. Dissidents in the AIM broke away in the late 1940s and established the African Brotherhood Church (ABC) at Kalimani in Kangundo. Those who were actively involved in the Churches were referred to as *Asomi* (the readers of the Bible), who stood opposed to non-Asomi. While this represents the first cleavage, there was also a significant division among the Asomi. This was one of Catholics versus Protestants, which became prominent in the 1961 election for the Colonial Legislative Council between Henry Mulli (Protestant) and Martin Makilya (Catholic). The Protestants were themselves split into two groups, the African Inland Mission Asomi and the African Brotherhood Church Asomi. The latter included many radicals, who were more involved in colonial 'nationalism' than the AIM Asomi. Though this cleavage did not become a major factor in the elections to the Legislative Council, nor subsequently to Parliament, most traditional clan leaders in the 1950s belonged to ABC.

An additional important background factor of the Mbai Sya Eitu was provided by the traditional clan organizations, of which there were twenty. They were patrilocal. Women were not allowed to participate in organizational activities of the clan other than sacrifices for which grandmothers were entitled to have representatives. In the early 1950s the clans concerned themselves with the traditional activity of paying *Maambo* (paying fines for a clansman who had been involved in manslaughter, etc.); they do not appear to have been involved in 'nationalist' activities. By the mid-1950s the clans began to collect money to send clansmen to school (e.g. in the 1940s the Mulli Brothers, Josiah and Henry, had with clan help gone to England and South Africa respectively). But providing this kind of support was not a general clan activity until the mid-1950s, and it was only after 1957 that all 20 clans actively sponsored students to high schools, Makerere College, and universities overseas. The clans did not go into commerce nor into politics as groups. Neither did they, as clans, join in 'terracing', but they continued to act in traditional roles.

'Terracing', however, is important as a background to the rise of the Mbai Sya Eitu. Terracing the land was a communal labour programme which needed to be done before the introduction of coffee, and was forced on the Northern Division by the colonial administration. The point to note here is not the merit or demerit of terracing agricultural land or whether coercion was used, but the fact that terracing was organized on a village basis, as a result of which the clan organizations were not utilized. Instead it was done under the aegis of the chief and his subchiefs, who were non-traditional leaders. All these chiefs were identified with the Asomi. All villages were organized into 'public *Mwethya*', communal labour groups which went terracing from farm to farm. Where they began was decided by the administration, and the penalty for not sending a family representative was one goat or 40 shillings. It is in these terracing *myethya* (plural for mwethya) as they are popularly called, that we begin to see women playing significant socio-historical roles. There were more women than men in the terracing myethya: most of the men had regular jobs within or outside the area. Some had gone to work in the urban centres or in the White Highlands. Hence most of the informal leaders of the myethya and the *Ngui* (the rhythm leaders) were women. But they were younger women — not the grandmothers who traditionally were the only women occupying public roles — and most of them later turned up in the Mbai Sya Eitu.

Soldiers returning from World War II also influenced the origin of the Mbai Sya Eitu. Especially significant was the Burma Group. In Burma this group had organized a Kamba organization — *Mbaa Lili* — which performed cultural, trade union and political roles. Since Kambas were dominant in the army it was mainly this organization which agitated for better working conditions and against discrimination. It also sought to get better demobilization conditions for soldiers; but after the war their demands were by and large ignored by the colonial government. Informants claim that as a result of rapid demobilization they could not force their grievances onto the colonial government and that they could not maintain a strong organization because of lack of close and continuing contact. After the war the soldiers were absorbed into clan organizations and clan activities. The only general organization they formed was the *Ikundo ya Mbaa Lili*, a short-lived trading company in Tala.

When the Burma soldiers were demobilized in 1948 they did not on the whole join the Kenya African Union (KAU), but were absorbed into traditional clan organizations. They argued that KAU was restricted to the educated. My informants argue further that they did not want to cooperate with the Mzungus communal work and terracing — presumably because it was beneath the dignity of a soldier. This, then, left only the women to go into the terracing activities. The women had been left without men during the war and therefore had become accustomed to accepting roles normally played by men. But earlier, as several clan leaders have argued, some clans had allowed women to sit in their councils because all the men were away in the war. Perhaps even more important is the fact that the women most active in Mbai Sya Eitu were of marriageable age (16-20) during the war and the demobilization years. Their lives were less controlled at this point than had been true for previous generations. It was these women, rather than the already politicized returning soldiers, who became the mainstay of colonial communal forced labour. This experience was important training for the day when women would have their own organizations outside the structures of the traditional clans and the party.

Another significant factor in the rise of the Mbai Sya Eitu is the history of electoral politics. Both Kamba districts were represented in the Legislative Council from 1958 to 1960 by J. Muimi from Kitui. In 1960 the Ukamba Constituency was delimited into two constituencies, namely, Machakos and Kitui Districts. It was for the Machakos constituency that Henry Mulli and Martin Makilya competed and split the Asomi. Voting was mainly along religious lines and the Protestants, who were in a majority, elected Mulli, their candidate. A new situation was created, however, when Paul Ngei came out of prison in late 1961, as he had been 'accepted' in Ukamba as the leader of the Kamba.

It is important to explain — by tracing the organizational politics of the Kamba — how Ngei became accepted and how he has continued to lead one of the minimum winning coalitions in Machakos. Probably the significant year was 1954. It was during that year that the colonial administration sought to organize the Kamba people to keep them out of Mau Mau. The formula was simple: get the chiefs to head a tribal association. Thus the Akamba Association was created under the auspices of the then Provincial Commissioner.

Almost from the start the Nairobi Branch, which was led by young and more educated bureaucrats, deviated from the policy of the national office bearers, the chiefs in Machakos and Kitui Districts. The former were more collaborative in anti-Mau Mau activity whereas the latter were more interested in acquiring businesses which had been vacated by the Kikuyu. However, Kamba unity — in terms of united action by the Akamba Association — had been achieved between the Machakos Kamba and the Kitui Kamba.

After 1958 leadership of the Nairobi Branch shifted from the young bureaucrats, most of whom departed for further education outside Kenya, to Kamba businessmen who had benefited from the policy of the Akamba Association. The latter were less educated than the bureaucrats, but more educated than the chiefs who continued to dominate the national offices. They were, however, bidding for political leadership of the tribe. It was the businessmen, potential politicians, who in 1960 and 1961 became involved in raising funds for an attorney to defend the Kambas in the Kamba/Masai intertribal clashes of the period. They used, and thereby changed, the direction of the Akamba Association.

By 1961 the chiefs who had dominated the Akamba Association were convinced that there was a need to start a purely tribal party as most of the other tribes had done. This may have been acceptance of the primacy of the businessmen who were involved in the Kamba/Masai affair and had moved away from the city to the rural Kamba areas, which they organized effectively. Whatever the reason, the Akamba Association finally gave way formally to the New Akamba Union whose organizational strength was located in the urban areas of East Africa from 1961 to 1963.

Paul Ngei came out of prison after the establishment of the New Akamba Union and through it and the agitational and organizational genius of Gideon Mutiso, the then General Secretary, sought to impose himself on Kamba politics. He was not immediately absorbed into the Kenya African National Union (KANU) national politics but through the New Akamba Union he was able to travel widely in Ukamba and the towns in Kenya where there were Kamba. As the Kitui Constituencies had already been created by the time of his release from prison he concentrated his efforts to obtain a parliamentary seat in Machakos District, and left Kitui District to Ngala Mwendwa. Thus, after 1961 the activities of the New Akamba Union became concentrated in Machakos District, from which Ngei made his bid for leadership.

Initially (1961-62), Ngei's strategy was to recruit the traditionalists by directing his attacks on the Asomi, who were represented by Mulli in the Legislative Council. He found ready support. After all, it was argued, had he not been with Kenyatta in jail and did not this mean that he should become the MP for Kangundo? Though considerable pressure was brought on Mulli to relinquish his seat to Ngei, surprisingly he did not do so. Thus, from the time of his release until November 1962, when the African Peoples Party (APP) — a purely tribal (Kamba) party — was formally launched, Ngei campaigned very hard against Mulli. He sought to identify Mulli with the Asomi (the Christian and the educated). This same technique was even more widely used in Machakos during the campaign for the 1963 election, which Mulli lost. The reason given for the Ngei split from KANU in November 1962 was that KANU leaders had refused to acknowledge him as the Kamba spokesman, both locally and nationally. Indeed, they had allowed Henry Mulli not only to remain as Assistant Minister but also to campaign on the KANU ticket. Organizationally speaking, then, Ngei concentrated on undercutting Mulli not only as a Kamba spokesman but also by mobilizing those who were less educated and non-Asomi against Mulli. Even though Ngei was himself well-educated (an ex-Makererean), he stressed the importance of traditional groups, especially the dance groups which were composed of non-Asomi. The logic of local politics in the early sixties was to clothe those groups which had been denied status in the stratification system of the rural areas — a system which had favoured the missionary-oriented Asomi — with the mantle of nationalism.

Political activities during this period were significantly influenced by a status inversion that had occurred or was in progress, particularly among the women. During the earlier period of their involvement in terracing the women had learned of the status to be earned in public matters. Many went to Ngei, and for a short period before the formation of APP they were referred to as the women's wing of KANU.[4]

After his victory in the 1963 election Ngei was ultimately absorbed into KANU national politics, but he continued to seek an organizational formula to establish himself as the controller of the Party organization, then led by Mallu. This was finally achieved in 1968. By then, however, the utility of the Mbai Sya Eitu for electoral purposes at the district level had already declined; their demise occurred as the APP collapsed.

S. Kioko, a prominent member of the APP and the major inheritor of the New Akamba Union's organizational activities in his own constituency, decimated the Mbai Sya Eitu organization and replaced it with Mwethya groups. Kioko, under the umbrella of the New Akamba Union, is the leader of the third minimum winning coalition in the District. In Western Division (Mallu's old Constituency) traditional clan organizations are more important for electoral purposes than they are in Southern Division. In Yatta Division although there is a Mbai Sya Eitu organization, the MP from the area, G. Mutiso, broke with Ngei before the 1963 elections and has not utilized the traditional clan organizations, which have been an effective opposition to him. In Central division, which has two constituencies, the Mbai Sya Eitu organization seems to have only been important in the Iveti North Constituency from where one of the clan Presidents comes.

The 'acceptance' of Ngei as tribal leader probably was highest in 1962-63 following his release from prison. During that period he used the popularity he had gained from having been in prison to organize against Mulli, the incumbent MP for the Machakos District constituency. After the creation of six constituencies the interests of the MPs led to the formation of two other proto-coalitions which systematically sought to accentuate other organizational techniques for mobilizing low status groups so as not to allow the Mbai Sya Eitu to penetrate their areas. Nevertheless, the Mbai Sya Eitu continued as a significant organizational base for elections in Ngei's own constituency. His claims for leadership of all the Kamba, however, is not backed up by analysis of the organized groups and factions in Machakos, and his effectiveness in Kitui has been minimal since his reabsorption into KANU.

MBAI SYA EITU 1961-1963

The women in Mbai Sya Eitu do not specify a particular date for its founding. They state that informal contacts developed after Ngei came out of prison when many delegations would spend days celebrating at his home. Although there was a coherent group of women ready for political mobilization, the organizational formula for their activation was not provided until 1961. Credit for this must go to Ngei's electoral strategy. As voting was still rigorously supervised by the last colonial officers, his strategy was simply to control the votes of the biggest clans and thereby assure his return. We have already pointed out that the traditional clan organizations stayed out of politics and were interested only in paying maambo and in education. The Ngei camp therefore devised the strategy of utilizing women to organize different clans. The women organized their clans of origin into matrilocal clan organizations led by the women. In this way two of the biggest clans, the *Aiini* and the *Aombe*, could be controlled. The first was controlled by Paul Ngei's mother and the other (Ngei's clan) by Mutuli Mbuluu. As these clans were close to the family, control over them cost little. It was this strategy which ultimately gave rise to the phenomena of Mbai Sya Eitu. In other words, the traditionally-based Mbai Sya Eitu were created to play a modern political role.

The Mbai Sya Eitu were organizationally responsible for the expansion of the APP. In fact, before the formal inauguration of the APP in November 1962, the Mbai Sya Eitu had already spread outside the Northern Division of Machakos and had established branches in each location in Eastern Division, Central Division, Western Division, Yatta Division and parts of Southern Division. When APP was launched, Mbai Sya Eitu became the mainstay of the party. In competing for the six lower house seats, the party gained 104,548 votes, as compared to 6,935 for KANU and 12,090 for independents, which was in part a reflection of the organizational effectiveness of the Mbai Sya Eitu under Ngei's leadership. The basic strategy was to recruit women leaders from all locations, bring them to Matungulu, and explain to them how to run the organization. They would return to their locations to organize the other women. Their political activities included not only voting for their particular candidates and mobilizing their husbands to follow suit, but also intimidating other women who were not followers to do the same. One fundamental consequence of this significant intrusion of women into the political life of the Akamba has been the withdrawal of men from the political arena – an area which was traditionally male dominated. Many men tended to feel that politics had become such a women's affair that no self-respecting man should continue to be involved. It was in this sense that the women acquired great political influence, which they also used in the 1969 election in Ngei's constituency. It is also *suggested* here that more women voted for Ngei than for his opponent in the last election (1969).

MEMBERS OF THE MBAI SYA EITU

The women who join the Mbai Sya Eitu are relatively old. All twenty Presidents are over 55 years of age, eight of them being over sixty. (Since most of the women are illiterate these data must be handled with caution.) Most of the other leaders in the organization are also relatively old. Mrs Ngei and the other Presidents reiterated to me that no woman was allowed to have any rank in the organization if she was still bearing children or had any children in school. It is therefore inconceivable that women under 35 years of age would be allowed to hold office. Most of them were therefore born before the early 1930s. This has meant that most of the officers and members have not had any formal education. Younger educated clanswomen are co-opted whenever any writing is required. As we shall see later, this lack of formal education among the officers gave rise to serious problems in the keeping of accounts.

Few of the women leaders of Mbai Sya Eitu had sons old enough to go to war in 1939. Indeed most of them talk about their husbands having served in World War II, leaving them with young children. Other than those who were married to soldiers, most of their husbands have never been anything but rural peasants earning their living from farming and/or keeping cattle. Most of the women have always traded in rural markets. Indeed, for the 20 presidents, the Tala market is a favourite meeting place where they trade in vegetables and other commodities produced at home. This marks them from the Asomi women who during the 1950s never went to trade in the rural markets and who still do not favour rural market petty trading.

STRUCTURE OF MBAI SYA EITU

There are no men in the Mbai Sya Eitu in any position. The overall President, who was not elected, is the mother of Paul Ngei. The women say that it was only natural that she became the President since her son was the leader of the Kamba. She is also President of her father's clan — the Aiini. Under her are 19 presidents: nine each from Kangundo and Matungulu Locations, and one each from Donyo Sabuk and Mitabobi Locations. Thus 90 percent of the Presidents are from two locations which form the core of the Northern Division, and of these, 12 live within 4 miles of the home of Mrs Ngei. These constitute the inner cabinet, so to speak, as they meet more often than any other group within the organization. They claim that they see each other at least twice a week at the market. This facilitates planning and coordination.

In each location in Machakos District and for each clan there was, until 1965, a vice-president responsible for that clan's organization; since 1965, clan organizations have existed only in Northern, Yatta, Central and Eastern Divisions. Under the locational clan vice-presidents are group leaders responsible for organizing the clanswomen in the sublocation. Under the group leaders are the *ngui* (master of ceremonies), the sergeant, the soldiers (sometimes called corporals) and other ordinary active members. The latter, however, represent a very small proportion of the clanswomen; organizationally, indeed, it is likely that the active women and those in formal positions represent less than 5 percent of the total clanswomen in any village or location. Why then, does the organization survive, and how has it been able to perform the extractive role we shall describe later? The explanation is in ritual control and forced extraction.

ENMISIVIZATION AND INTERNAL CONTROL

Ritual is extremely important in creating coherent and rigid control over both officials and followers. It is said that the 20 Presidents have taken an oath not to reveal to any others the details of their organization. In interviews they refused to confirm this, but the fact that they always scrupulously avoid coming into contact with anyone who has touched any pig product confirms that they have taken an oath. Pig products are the most potent cleansing instrumentalities for an oath. Indeed, contact with any pig product would erase the oath automatically. The Presidents were probably handpicked and were probably oathed to keep the aims of the Mbai Sya Eitu among themselves.

The Vice-Presidents and lower ranks have to petition for appointment. This is called *Kukavula Musivi* (enmisivization).[5] However, before petitioning for enmisivization those who aspire to become Vice-Presidents or to hold other lesser ranks, campaign among their clanswomen. In one location in what was regarded as a typical campaign a woman aspiring to the Vice-Presidency of her clan had held feasts for all women in the location in three subsequent month-ends at a cost to her of 3,000 shillings. As we shall see later, this investment is recoverable!

The petitioning for enmisivization has been regularized. An aspiring Vice-President in a location has to send a delegate to the President of her clan. The delegate informs the President of the desire of the aspiring Vice-President and leaves a bull, donated to the President by the aspirant, to keep as a personal possession. Bulls cost 350 shillings (1970 price). If the President wants the aspiring Vice-President ultimately to be initiated, she so informs the delegate, who in turn informs the aspirant. The second step is for the latter to send 40 shillings to her clan President in Kangundo. This 40 shillings is shared among the 20 clan-Presidents. Informants argue that this is traditional *kukula*, namely, the concept that to be initiated traditionally one had to send something to the elders to eat while they discussed one's merits. What we should note here is that the 20 clan presidents are brought in on deciding whether one of them should initiate a new Vice-President. This maintains coordination and control at the top as well as providing a share of wealth to all the Presidents. If the 20 Presidents agree that the aspiring Vice-President should be initiated then they send a soldier to inform her that, in consultation with the President of her clan, she must pick a date for petitioning her husband to surrender her to the Mbai Sya Eitu.

Vice-Presidents are not the only ones who petition for enmisivization; below them in the hierarchy are aspiring group leaders, ngui, sergeants and soldiers. The numbers of these vary with the number of sublocations in a district but ordinarily in a location there are 5-10 group leaders, 5-10 ngui, 10-20 sergeants and 20-40 soldiers. Each lower aspirant sends six shillings to the aspiring Vice-President; she therefore collects between 240-480 shillings from those whom she would ultimately bring into the organization under her. Depending on the cost of her own petition for enmisivization she can either make or lose money; informants claim that Vice-Presidents usually do not lose.

After the petition of enmisivization has been accepted the husband is then petitioned to let his wife return to her clanswomen. The informants call this the women 'marrying into the Mbai Sya Eitu'. Behind this is the assumption that by marrying her husband the woman effectively left her clan and in terms of social activities became a member of her husband's clan. Thus, her return to her own clan involves a switch from patrilocally to matrilocally-based socio-political activities. In terms of the effective functioning of the organization as a whole this requirement of the husband's assent is the only weak link: men can refuse to surrender their wives to marriage into the Mbai Sya Eitu. Apart from the Asomi, however, there has not been much resistance from the men. Of significance in this regard is that most of the families involved are poor and there are economic opportunities in the Mbai Sya Eitu.

The Vice-Presidents' 'marriage' to the clan is organized by the Presidents. The women argue that they do this so as to free them from the responsibilities of home and husband. Since most of the women are old this is feasible. What is the process? The President of the particular clan leads a delegation to the husband of the woman and explains that they (the clanswomen) want the husband to release the woman for 'marriage' to the Mbai Sya Eitu. The husband invariably points out to the President and her delegation that when he married he had paid bride wealth consisting of (1) a bull or heifer, (2) native beer, (3) a ram, (4) beddings, (5) unleavened bread (*Kimutu*), for all of which he must be reimbursed as a condition of his assent. They in turn agree to pay the husband 'bride wealth', which payment is usually made on the first day of the two-day initiation. It covers the items specified by the man, which are bought out of the treasury of the clan.

At the initiation itself, the Vice-President to be initiated contributes a bull to slaughter for the clanswomen and the latter contribute food for the two days. All the other 19 Presidents accompany the one who is going to initiate the new Vice-President. On the evening of the first day of initiation the husband is asked by the President whether he is affirmative; if so, he is then oathed and given gifts by all those who come. These gifts are in addition to the formal 'bride wealth' payment. Since aspirants at the lower levels are in the majority, such money is usually given; indeed, all the informants argue that initiation never leads to a loss to the particular family. The women remain overnight celebrating the granting of permission for 'betrothal' of their sister.

During the second day of the initiation the Vice-President and her retinue of Group leaders, ngui, sergeants and soldiers, pay the President an initiation fee. The Vice-President pays 20 shillings and all others six shillings each. The President therefore collects between 260-520 shillings. That evening is then spent feasting and the Vice-President is then formally initiated. She is brought indoors next to the hearth, stripped of all clothing and ornaments, and then, much as a child is dressed, she is clothed by the President in the clan uniform. If she attempts to touch the dress or the belt (musivi) she is fined 150 shillings. She is then given a ring (Western token of marriage!) and oathed. The details of this oath, like the others, nobody will discuss. She is then given the following items: umbrella, torch, overcoat, thermos flask and overnight bag. These are functional items because she must travel on the business of the clanswomen, that is, organizing. Her husband is required to give her a flywhisk — that favourite symbol of African politicians — as a symbol of her new status. This also is nontraditional: the flywhisk was carried by men only. All those present including the 20 presidents or their representatives then give her monetary gifts to pay for expenses incurred, and also 1,000 shillings — which comes out of the clan treasury — for future travel and other expenses. As a fully initiated Vice-President she is then formally authorized to start the enmisivization of the group leaders, ngui, sergeants and soldiers, in conjunction with the other Vice-Presidents in a location. To be enmisivized is to get a licence to organize and to raise revenue. Obviously since the Vice-President enmisivizes more people than the President there must somehow be an intraclan revenue sharing scheme. We shall return to this problem when discussing extraction.

What is important to note is that the enmisivization process provides for rigid control over who is to be allowed into the organization. The other 19 Presidents are consulted by the one seeking to initiate a new Vice-President in a location. Since they also have contacts with their clanswomen in the same location and, further, since the Vice-Presidents will have to work jointly to enmisivize the lower ranks, there is effective coordination. Related to this is the fact that enmisivization in one clan has some benefits for the other clans — the revenue raised in petitioning gets shared at both the Presidential and Vice-Presidential levels, which constitutes interclan revenue sharing. Also important is the oathing of both the new initiates and their husbands. It is through the oathing that the Mbai Sya Eitu have managed to build the organization and maintain its cohesiveness.

The question may be asked why the men, especially, agree to the whole process, which manifestly undercuts traditionally accepted relationships. I would argue that there are very good economic returns for the family which cannot be ignored when we remember that these are poor rural peasants whose annual per capita incomes are not above 500 shillings. They gain quite a bit from the enmisivization process but even more important is the economic opportunity of fund-raising given to the wives. It is to their economic advantage to accept the new organization even though it violates tradition. Further research is needed to discover the effect on the family of the woman becoming the major economic force.

HARAMBEE:
EXTRACTION FOR INDIVIDUAL AND PUBLIC PURPOSES

Etymologically the word Harambee simply means let us pull together. However, the word has acquired many socio-political meanings since it was popularized by President Mzee Jomo Kenyatta in the early 1960s. It is conceivable that the Europeans, who had pushed the idea of multi-racialism in the last days of the colonial period, saw it as an opportunity for their incorporation into the emergent society. This is true of most of those who were in the New Kenya Group and who by and large remained in Kenya. It is conceivable that to the Asians it also offered an umbrella under which they could stay. This aspect of Harambee is important since colonial politics in Kenya were racial with respect both to the structure of organization and to ideology.

The idea of Harambee initially also addressed itself to the African population at many levels. Probably the most obvious was the fact that it sought to create a 'national' pulling together in politics which had not existed earlier. Kenya African politics before the formation of KANU in 1959 could only be legally conducted at the district level. Hence there were many organizations which only covered tribes, or portions of them, in the districts. The only significant deviations from this were the Nairobi 'Parties' which embraced a multiplicity of tribes in the colonial capital. The idea of Harambee at this level addressed itself to the problem of attempting to shift the point of conducting politics away from the district level to the 'national' level. Even though KANU had been formed in 1959 the district 'parties' survived. Particularly important for the concept of Harambee was the idea that it was targeted against the regionalist Kenya African Democratic Union (KADU). The political argument had been made by KANU that the Africans who were in KADU and who represented minority tribes sought to delay independence — perhaps unwittingly — by pushing for a regional form of government. This, KANU argued, would only benefit the Wazungu foreigners, who wanted a weak Kenya. This should be understood in the historical perspective whereby after Mzee Kenyatta was released from detention there were attempts to merge KADU and KANU under his leadership. This, of course, failed initially, but the concept of pulling together — understood as applying to the African element in politics — undercut those not identified with him. Thus, when KADU ultimately joined KANU, a widely popularized symbol of unity was available and had gained acceptance.

All the foregoing aspects are less significant than the function of Harambee as a device for rural extraction without government involvement. It could be argued that the concept was intended to help cope with the excessive promises of what benefits independence would bring. Characteristic of the rhetoric of the pre-independence nationalist period everywhere were the many promises which politicians made to the Kenyan population. All land was to be taken from the Wazungu settlers! Asian businesses were to be given to Africans and jobs were to be given to all! Thus, a psychology of imminent deliverance was created. Any government coming into power had to scale down these fantastic expectations if it was to conduct the day-to-day activities of the state. Hence the concept of Harambee, in which the accent was to be on *what people can do together in their communities without waiting for government to do it for them*. It was this aspect of Harambee which released energies most people did not even know existed in the rural areas.

The fundamental national response to the Harambee call has been oriented towards producing infrastructural services (schools, dispensaries, roads, etc.), and economic goods (tea factories, pre-cooperative societies of many types, etc.). Most of those who have analysed the phenomenon have worn cost-benefit economic blinkers and have basically addressed themselves to its dysfunctional impact, particularly the cost of Harambee schools which allegedly give poor training to people who cannot be absorbed into the economy. Other dysfunctions are dispensaries without medicine. The critics of Harambee have stressed the need for central planning so as to bring about rational controlled change. All of these evaluations miss the central contribution of Harambee. *This is the ability of the rural population to decide what new programmes, projects or institutions they need in their area and then to create the requisite social organizations, without some distant expert or bureaucrat deciding what the needs are and what institutions will best service those needs*. Harambee leads to institutional innovation which must be the central concern of change in the rural areas.

Sometimes collectivities get together in the name of Harambee and reap enormous benefit individually. This I would argue is the case of the Mbai Sya Eitu. But moral and ideological concerns about extracting for private gain should not blind us to the wider organizational and systematic effects of low status groups which can be used for the development process.

Harambee projects have not only become politicized but also have been mechanisms for rural socio-political distribution. Politicians (MPs) have utilized Harambee meetings as campaign platforms – since they have to be licensed to meet with their followers in their constituencies. Provincial administrators have attempted to deny MPs this contact in attempts to enforce President Kenyatta's mandate of 1964, prescribing that Provincial administration was to be the major transmission belt of rulership. It is in this light that the activities of Mbai Sya Eitu must be seen. At one level they are politically manipulated, providing a public forum and organizational continuity to the local MP who had initially organized them for electioneering purposes. This is why the Mbai Sya Eitu did not participate in the biggest Harambee project in 1970, namely, the extension of Kangundo Hospital, which was seen as a project backed by the then Provincial Commissioner who was opposed to the local MP (Ngei). However, this was the only occasion on which the MP vetoed a decision of the Mbai Sya Eitu, and therefore should not be understood as a refutation of my thesis that they are functionally independent.

With the foregoing background we can now turn to a discussion of how Mbai Sya Eitu organized the raising of funds for a particular project. At the outset it should be noted that for the Mbai Sya Eitu to consider support for a particular project they must be petitioned by some clanswoman who is either a group leader, a vice-president or a president of a particular clan. The allocation of resources by the Mbai Sya Eitu is conditional upon support by the local Mbai Sya Eitu leadership. In interviews the leaders also emphasized the importance of local Mbai Sya Eitu leaders' requests to other organizations to come to help them build (*kwakya*). There is personal economic benefit for the group leader who asks the other organizations to come and help her build: she gets 100 shillings!

However, the concept of asking others for assistance in a project was operative in traditional society. If one had a big task, one asked non-clan neighbours to help. This is the traditional *vuli* — i.e. group activity which is functionally specific and lasts for one day, in contrast to a *Mwilaso* which is traditional group activity, functionally non-specific and rotating over many days.

The requirement that an official of a particular clan must ask the other clans to help build a project in her area makes the decision of where to build a significant intra-Mbai Sya Eitu trade-off issue. Indeed, there are cases of very serious competition among the various clan group leaders at both the locational and sub-locational levels. There have been attempts to avail or resolve conflicts resulting from such competition such as requiring that leaders at the various levels of a clan meet and agree on who is to initiate the request. However, these have not proved very effective; generally it is the group leader or vice-president who can most effectively convince or bully the others who ends up collecting the 100 shillings.

Before detailing the organization and process of helping a group leader with her particular *Mwako* (project), it is important that we first describe the revenue-raising activities of the sergeants and soldiers. Once a decision has been made regarding a particular project, the sergeants and soldiers are charged to visit all the homes of their clanswomen and to collect money. The organization is very efficient in this respect since the sergeants and soldiers operate at the village level and know *all* their clanswomen. In a detailed examination of one village it was found that each woman had been visited twice over a particular three-month period. It is during this money collecting phase that the coercion of the Mbai Sya Eitu comes to the fore. The sergeants and soldiers work in groups of two or three and usually visit the homes of the clanswomen in the evening. They *demand* a contribution in the name of a particular project. They ask for anything, but in the village examined the women informants claimed that they were asked to contribute at least 5 shillings. If this is refused the sergeants and soldiers walk out with a chicken, banana bunches or anything else which could be sold to raise the money. Reportedly, the sergeants and soldiers are especially vicious towards the Asomi. They do not keep collection records, but this is functional in certain respects because they are thus able to take a cut of the revenue collected before handing the money over to the group leader of their clan, who also takes her cut.

The 20 presidents interviewed maintained that sergeants and soldiers collect only between 50 cents and one shilling per clanswoman. However, this would constitute only between 10 and 20 per cent of what the village sample claim they had donated. It is therefore logical to suggest that 90 per cent of the funds collected from the clanswomen is private extraction which goes into the pockets of those active in the Mbai Sya Eitu. This is in addition to the fees paid to various office bearers as discussed elsewhere. If this money were channeled into public activity it would speed up rural development.

After the sergeants and soldiers hand over the money to the group leaders, the latter are supposed to forward it to the clan vice-president. She and the other vice-presidents then travel to see the various Presidents and hand over the money to them. All the Presidents meet and decide how much money is going to be given to a particular project. Here there is (1) presidential coordination and (2) trade-off. It is the trade-off which merits discussion. How much money gets taken to a particular project depends on whether the area is politically reliable as far as the Mbai Sya Eitu are concerned. If women in the area have not actively participated in the Mbai Sya Eitu (i.e. an area of heavy Asomi influence like Muisuni sublocation in Kangundo location), the money extracted from that area is assigned elsewhere even if much was collected. This was the case with Muisuni School in 1970, and it is significant that Muisuni is the only sublocation which up to 1970 had not received funds from Mbai Sya Eitu.

After the Presidents decide upon a project in a particular area they inform the petitioning group leader concerned, through the Vice-President of her clan. A day is picked when representatives of all the clans of the district are to assemble at the Mwako (project) to Kwakya (build) the following day. It is at these *myako* (plural of mwako) that the various organizations meet, compare notes and exchange information. Thus, the projects serve a dual function, namely, a means of raising revenue, and even more important, an opportunity for contact, coordination and exchange of ideas. The myako are occasions for forging organizational solidarity.

All the clanswomen participating in a project assemble at the site a day early and sleep there that night. Temporary structures to accommodate them are built by the clan organizations of the area, and are usually made of dry banana leaves. The necessary bedding, cooking utensils, and food are commandeered from the clanswomen of the particular area clans. Usually these are commandeered from non-Mbai Sya Eitu activists since those who are activists contribute through their organizational labour! The arrangement of sleeping and eating quarters reflects the organizational hierarchy. The food of the Presidents is always inspected before cooking and it is cooked under their supervision by soldiers from their home areas. Informants claim that this is a precautionary measure in the event of a cook wanting to erase all oaths by introducing some pig-derived product into the cooking. Presidents tend to be paranoid about this erasing of oaths. In fact, if any person enters the Presidential site of the enclosure, he or she is fined 150 shillings which is then shared among the Presidents. The other members of the Mbai Sya Eitu eat ordinary food cooked by the clans from the environs of the project.

The second day begins with breakfast followed by the public meeting for raising revenue for the project. Here we must discuss the role of the Ngui. The Ngui can be loosely understood as the master of ceremonies. Traditionally she was the singer of praises for the clan, the age group or the dance group. She is in this case featured on the platform with the President of the clan whose group leader is being helped with her project. The Ngui is paid 100 shillings for her labours on the platform! The Ngui at a project is always the local Ngui under the Group Leader who asked for the help.

Around noon the meeting begins. All the Presidents present are introduced. If they have sent representatives, these, followed by officials, are introduced. The introductions are made by the President. Then the local Vice-President who had petitioned for help in the mwako calls upon the clans to contribute. If the visiting clans who came with money to contribute have either been instructed to penalize the area for political reasons, or if they are not satisfied with the hospitality of the local organization the night before, the Presidents caucus and instruct the Ngui to sing the *Ngenda* song which is a signal that the monies raised by other clan organizations elsewhere are not to be contributed. This means that any revenue to be raised in this particular meeting is to come from the wider public since the Mbai Sya Eitu funds are going to be taken. If on the other hand the Presidents want the maximum contribution to be made to the project then they ask the Ngui to sing the *Nyololo* song which is the clue that they should contribute the targeted sum of money.

It is only during mass contributions that men are allowed to take part in the process of the Mbai Sya Eitu. There are two reasons for this. Firstly, Harambee projects are usually registered with the District Commissioner. To collect money for a particular project, a licence must be issued in the name of the project committee. These project committees, whose members are predominantly male, have found that if they do not invite the Mbai Sya Eitu to raise revenue for them they raise very little in Northern Division. They therefore surrender the whole process to the women, but they are present to count the money.[6] The second reason for men being allowed in the process is as contributing supporters of the various clans of the Mbai Sya Eitu. Once Clan X is called from the platform to bring forward its contribution, the men married to women from that clan are asked to increase (*kwikiisya*) the contribution. If contributions are low, insults are heaped on the men until they increase the contribution. Inter-clan rivalry is the basic socio-psychological technique for raising revenue. At numerous meetings I have watched insults force men to contribute cows, goats and cattle because their self-esteem has been questioned.

Usually the Presidents of the Mbai Sya Eitu do not put out all the money when the clan is first called upon for its contribution. They may just put out a quarter of the money and wait to increase the contribution during the fourth or fifth time the clan is called upon. The names are repeated time and time again until the local Group Leader establishes that nothing is being contributed as four o'clock approaches. The meeting usually disperses around this time and the project committee goes to bank the money.

How significant are the Mbai Sya Eitu in the development of the rural areas? Our efforts to answer this and other questions are based on divisional data regarding direct contributions to public Harambee projects — defined as projects for public use — by the Mbai Sya Eitu. This is not the complete picture since, as suggested above, money raised in the division is sometimes taken to projects out of the division. The statistical information which follows on the public Harambee projects was initially collected from the Divisional Community Development Assistant. It is the Community Development Department in the Ministry of Cooperatives and Social Services which is charged with 'monitoring' the Harambee projects, even though most of the projects are directly related to other ministries like education, agriculture and works (transport). The data collected by the CDAs is sometimes incomplete and as a result very extensive visits to projects to cost them were undertaken. Chiefs and subchiefs were asked to verify the number of projects in their areas. Project cost data was verified by the author who ended-up costing most of the projects.

Data on public Harambee was collected for the years 1965-1970. The year 1965 was chosen since it is generally accepted that this was when the phenomenon of Harambee began to snowball as a result of Government propaganda. During the five years, projects worth 3,197,966 shillings were carried out in the division. Of this sum, the Central Government contribution was only 44,081 shillings and Local Government (Machakos County Council) contribution was 8,301 shillings. Therefore, the people contributed 3,145,685 shillings during the period in question. The contribution by the people can be broken down into two broad categories, namely, labour and material/cash contribution. Of the 3,145,685 shillings 2,023,989 was in form of labour. It is possible that this is an over-estimate as it is based on the manhours spent at a project. Nobody keeps a register for unskilled labour which works on a project and I found the best information one could get was usually the number of people who were listed as participants in the particular project and how many days in a week they worked on the project. Unskilled labour was costed at the rate of 35 cents per hour and skilled labour at 1.25 shillings an hour, in keeping with general practice in the District. Figures for skilled labour were not so problematic as those for unskilled labour since most of the projects kept rather good records about the people they hired directly.

How much of the labour contribution came from the Mbai Sya Eitu organization? It is surprising that as an organization they do not go to projects to do the labour. However, there is no doubt in my mind that they are instrumental in getting women to contribute their labour in the projects individually. The administrators in the Division point out that on any project at any time women constitute between 80-90 per cent of the unskilled labour. My formal counting at twenty project meetings over a period of three months revealed that there were consistently between 75-80 per cent women working at projects. The manual jobs range all the way from making bricks to whitewashing completed classrooms. Thus, even though the Mbai Sya Eitu do not work on a particular project as a group, the high turnout of women can be partially explained by their agitational activities.

The Mbai Sya Eitu are more significant on the material/cash input into projects. The material/cash contribution to Harambee projects in the Division for the five years was 1,121,696 shillings.[7] These can be broken down into locational figures of 359,782 shillings for Matungulu Location and 127,178 shillings for Mwala Location. The locational material/cash contribution correlates very well with the strength of the Mbai Sya Eitu organization. It is in Kangundo and Mbiuni where the Mbai Sya Eitu material contribution is 65 per cent of the total. In Matungulu this drops to about 57 per cent and in Mwala to 49 per cent. These percentages are derived from the project records which report the sources of contributions.

It has been pointed out earlier that Presidents claim that they receive only about 10 per cent of the revenue raised by the sergeants and soldiers, and that this is the money they send to projects. It was further pointed out that those who are married to clansmen help the clanswomen when money is being raised at public meetings by the Mbai Sya Eitu. This help is about a quarter of the money ultimately contributed by the Mbai Sya Eitu and is listed as their contribution since it is their organizational mechanism which raises the money. Thus the 65 per cent of the material/cash contribution for Kangundo and Mbiuni Location, the 57 per cent for Matungulu and the 49 per cent for Mwala do not represent the 10 per cent of total revenue extracted by the Mbai Sya Eitu utilizing sergeants and soldiers, but only about 7.5 per cent of their estimated total revenue extraction.

What is remarkable is the fact that the members of the Mbai Sya Eitu do not seem to resent this accumulation by their leaders. This is quite clear in the *Munoti* song which they sing for their leaders. The Munoti song (Money tree song) specifically states that the women would build a money tree in the home of the leader so that she may get rich. In this sense it is clear that there is acceptance of the idea that public leadership is conterminous with becoming wealthy. Thus even when the leaders become wealthy they do not forfeit leadership since this is expected of them; furthermore, as the interviews reveal time and time again, the followers hope ultimately to rise in the organization and get into positions where they can accumulate wealth themselves. Another factor which helps to maintain the leadership even after it objectively passes the high status threshold is the clan solidarity induced by the oath. Given the historical significance of the oath the women who are initiated are able to define themselves as a fairly coherent group in opposition to the non-initiated. Clearly the fact that they are non-Asomi (non-educated) helps them establish their distinctive identity as felt by themselves and as categorized by others.

CONCLUSION

It is clear that the Mbai Sya Eitu have the potential to organize and extract for more purposes than they have done so far. They could be turned to other specified jobs which would help in the development of the area. To achieve this, however, the Mbai Sya Eitu would have to get governmental recognition as significant groups for rural development. This applies to many more low status groups. In the rest of Machakos District similar groups — in function rather than organization — are the *Mwethya* groups, which include a preponderance of women but also a good number of men. In most of Central Province there are the *Nyakenywa* and *Ahonoki* groups which could be used for other developmental ends. I have to emphasize that the basic constraint in terms of utilizing these groups is governmental conservatism in viewing low-status groups, and the allied view that these groups are always manipulated by the politicians. This attitude leads to under-utilization of their extractive capabilities for development purposes.

What seems to be crucial is to find alternative programmes to the building of schools and health centres and to direct groups like Mbai Sya Eitu to other types of work. There are not many activities which are closed to the women. Arguing *post facto* perhaps, the fact that the women have moved into the political arena openly is an indication of their release from whatever historical constraints have barred them from public activities. What is being argued here is that the idea that low status (and poor) groups are inflexible does not seem to hold true. At least the Mbai Sya Eitu have attempted to improve their socio-economic lot by coming up with a formula. Perhaps other institutions can be attached to this to play an economic role. Some of those could be para-cooperatives. Institutions like these could be predicated on quasi-traditional organizational ideas found among the people and not on borrowed ideas of how technically one runs a cooperative.

NOTES

1.   Henry Bienen, 'One Party Systems in Africa' in Samuel P. Huntington and Clement H. Moore (eds), *Authoritarian Politics in Modern Society* (New York, Basic Books, 1970), 99-127.
2.   Ibidem, 119.
3.   Ibidem, 113-120.

4.   APP organizationally was more important in Machakos District than in Kitui District where Ngala Mwendwa stayed in KANU. Of course, in Machakos, Mallu as an MP also stayed in KANU. He was the leader of the other minimum winning coalition.

5.   Literally, to break the belt — the connotation is that one breaks it from the President. The belt refers to the distinctive colours which each rank wears. Each clan has distinctive coloured dresses and belts.

6.   Incidentally, the Mbai Sya Eitu have forced all Harambee project committees to co-opt one local Group Leader into the assorted project committees in the whole of Northern Division.

7.   This does not include the 103,000 shillings raised by the Provincial Commissioner for extension of Kangundo Hospital towards the end of 1970, since it has not been used. All figures in the paragraph are rounded off.

VI

CONCLUSION

MARTIN R. DOORNBOS

RECURRING PENETRATION STRATEGIES IN EAST AFRICA

The essays in this volume have all been concerned with the relationship between government and rural development in East Africa. Issues of rural mobilization and bureaucracy-peasant contacts have been explored from a variety of
perspectives, on the basis of case materials from different levels of socio-
political reality in Kenya, Tanzania and Uganda. The resultant diversity is considerable, but this has been our intention from the start.

In searching for points of common interest or debate, the sources of this
diversity have to be borne in mind. They reflect the complexity of substantive
issues and the controversial nature of current strategies and choices in rural
development in the East African countries; the different disciplinary backgrounds − sociology, political science, anthropology and economics − and
methodological priorities from which the various analyses have been constructed; and the divergence, in some cases conflict, among the theoretical
positions of the authors regarding the central problems.

Such diverse points of departure inevitably limit the extent to which different analyses will converge into a neatly cumulative and comprehensive set of
conclusions. While all papers examine various rural development experiences of
Kenya, Tanzania and Uganda, they focus on particular issues which have been
interpreted, through various methodologies, on the basis of specific, mostly
local and thus by definition 'different' materials. With one exception − the
Leonard-Thoden van Velzen dialogue − this symposium is thus hardly the kind
of collective exercise in which the next contribution reconsiders the same
evidence from a new angle, or tests the same hypothesis with a fresh set of
data. *Prima facie*, each of the preceding papers has endeavoured to make its
own points, on its own terms, and with its own materials.

There are different perspectives on what are key issues in political mobilization for rural development. For example, concern with suitable institutional
mechanisms and coordination is complemented and qualified by analyses
which highlight the dynamics of grassroots conflict and increasing social inequality in situations 'reached' by mobilization policies. Not surprisingly, ques-

tions about the 'how' of institutionalization invariably lead to other questions that have first to be answered, about the 'what for' of institutionalized coordination and control. Not all of these differences are carried to the point where they could be finally thrashed out or in some way 'resolved'.

The diversity has been augmented rather than lessened by the use of the controversial concept of 'political penetration'. However, this has stimulated a good deal of debate about the nature of socio-political processes and relationships in the context of rural development policies in East Africa. The critique and discussion of government strategies have gained greater explicitness and thus greater focus. 'Penetration', in other words, has not reduced the complexities and contradictions with which we are concerned, but has brought them to more vivid exposure.

How, then, do these papers contribute to our understanding of the role of government in rural development in East Africa? They illustrate that certain aspects of this relationship have become increasingly salient. These convey a renewed, if sobering, sense of historical continuity, and underscore our awareness of patterns and dynamics of structural inequality. Key factors include the critical importance of political choice — and of political will — in any attempt towards rural and rural-urban transformation; the weight of local complexities in the realization of alternative strategies; the increasing bureaucratic encroachment upon grassroots organization and leadership; the recurrent lack of organizational sensitivity in the design and implementation of policies and, not least, the need to come to grips with the nature and configuration of the power structures in the East African states and their relation with the wider international context. In a broader sense, a shared concern has emerged with the various manifestations of neo-colonial styles and structures in East African development.

PENETRATION STRATEGIES IN DIFFERENT PERSPECTIVES

If we are to extrapolate on the basis of these papers, we might look at some of the problems of government involvement in rural development in East Africa and see how the analyses relate to issues and concerns in a wider context. We can start from two angles: firstly, with a fairly direct focus and secondly, with a more distant one directed towards broader aspects.

In a close focus, we encounter a range of issues centered on the role of the bureaucracy in field activities. Examples include the attempt to restrict coffee growing in Murang'a, Kenya (Lamb), the handling of land tenure issues in Bukoba, Tanzania (Hyden), the introduction of nutrition measures in Bukedi, Uganda (Sharman), the operation of agricultural extension services in Tanzania and Kenya (Thoden van Velzen and Leonard). In all instances, the key issue was the nature of contact between government agencies and agents and local groups and institutions.

Other essays illustrated a similar juxtaposition: with an emphasis on institutional complexity, as in those by Harris and Chambers; with a focus on socio-cultural interactions, as adopted by Rigby for Ugogo, by Swartz for Bena and by Mutiso for Machakos; or from a historical-political perspective, as in Vincent's paper on the creation of Teso and, at another level, in Mafeje's paper on the dislocation of Buganda. Central to the 'field' situations covered was the tendency of central government agencies to extend their administrative control over widening areas of social, economic and political involvement. Viewed in this light, political penetration in rural development refers to the strategies and means by which an organizing state asserts its power in rural societies, and seeks to incorporate and direct political and production processes on its own terms and premises. These tendencies of bureaucratic encroachment, however, seem to occur within, and to a certain extent notwithstanding, divergent political strategies in each of the East African countries. In a sense, they may well need to be considered as relatively autonomous processes, dictated by forces other than choice of strategy alone.

The focus on contact between officialdom and peasantry is related to a considerable body of writing on 'reaching strategies'. This includes J.S. Furnivall's discussion of the logic and merits of direct and indirect rule for different economic objectives — such as plantation economy versus peasant cultivation[1] — as well as Everett Rogers' prescriptions for stepping-up diffusion of innovations in agriculture.[2] Variants of contact theory have often outlined socio-economic, cultural or administrative dichotomies — with a 'frontier' hypothesized along a dividing line of 'original difference'.

East African societies are not dual societies in the usual conception.[3] They show profound internal and external contradictions; pluralist notions such as 'two worlds in one' or equivalent models are inadequate for an understanding of their structural conditions or basic dynamics, let alone their probable course of further development. Transformed and deformed through colonial order and export-oriented peasant production, no presumed 'traditionality' can provide the intellectual rationale for their transmutation into 'modernity'. This is stressed by various contributors: Vincent, Harris, Thoden van Velzen and Mafeje, for example. Modern-traditional based 'pattern-variables', so long emphasized in the mainstream of modernization theory, hinder rather than help the understanding of reality. It would be a different matter, perhaps, if 'dual sectors' referred to 'created' or 'recreated' differences, as sometimes they are intended to do.[4] But conceptual confusion is bound to result if the same terminology is used in the obverse, and it is therefore better avoided.

Another juxtaposition appears more relevant and relates to a key aspect of the mechanisms referred to above. The confrontation between the organized and the unorganized, in Myrdal's analysis,[5] is a major one among a complex of basic cleavages — and it is within that context that 'penetration strategies' assume their role and special significance. In that sense, too, the analyses developed in this volume are of relevance. 'Penetration' refers to issues which have long been prominent in the colonial and post-colonial discussion on Africa and Asia; which were basic to the colonial enterprise and are now to the role of the post-colonial state. Stripped of any dualist connotation, the heuristic utility of 'penetration' is that it directly indicates the strengthening of the centre's 'capacity' in matters of organization, production and control.

What further questions should be raised? Basically there are two positions. In one perspective, the key 'problem' is essentially a question of how to muster sufficient organizational strength and tactical sensitivity to 'overcome' obstacles, constraints or resistance in the delivery of development goods. The overriding concern here, as Hutton and Cohen have argued, tends to be with 'obstacle man'.[6] Obstacle man, however, is an obstinate creature — not surprisingly, in view of all the psychological, cultural, socio-economic and other attributes which have been bestowed upon him over time. Time and again the conclusion has been reached that increasing ingenuity has to be used in approaching him.

In the other view, the 'problem' is virtually the opposite; here the concern is with 'organization man' of a sort. In this perspective 'penetration' is associated mainly with the increased burden of demands, directives and extractions to which peasants are subjected at the hands of 'planistrators', in Apthorpe's term.[7] Planistrators have become responsible for an entirely new folklore in which technical shortsightedness and material self-interest alternate as central themes and stereotypes. In view of the purposes and benefits they are assumed to serve, their involvement is largely seen to reaffirm and reinforce, rather than to minimize, distance, inequality and dependency.

But the difference is compounded and poses profound dilemmas in the relatively few situations in which there is a political will to combat poverty and inequality. To be effective, the centre is likely to need increased powers; in fact, 'penetration' was first talked about in this sense. But if the centre is given extra powers, what is to ensure that these will not lead to renewed inequalities, a fresh class of 'dirigistes'? How can a concern for 'below' be validated through an approach from 'above'? Or indeed, how else? Although social analysis has achieved sobering gains in realism, the scope and content of 'betting on the weak' policies are still far from clear. Some of these queries are pursued in the papers on Tanzania, by Thoden van Velzen, Harris and Hyden, for example, and we now have some idea as to what is *not* the answer and why. Again, discrepancies between declared goals and the extent of their fulfilment draws attention to the role of intermediate cadres — and to the admonitions of Michels[8] and Fanon.[9]

THE CONTEXT OF CONTACT

Concern with penetration strategies usually implies particular interest in the connecting elements. In these essays we have seen how, in the relationship between an organizing state and rural society, government invariably seeks channels of contact at the end of the line so that its policies, instructions and controls may be passed down and enforced. Such linkage roles are performed by a number of key factors in the local field: chiefs and headmen, ward chairmen and party officials, tax collectors, policemen, certain project personnel, extension workers, and also progressive farmers. Many have been objects of longstanding interest on the part of anthropologists and administrators. Following on the coordination and compromise between departmental policies, it is at their level that government presents itself to the rural population. All are designated as channels for contact, mobilization and command. Most of them are appointed officials 'posted' to rural areas, but some are auxiliary members enlisted from 'below', e.g. certain types of client chiefs, locally elected incumbents of linkage roles, and also progressive or model farmers whose function is to transmit innovations propagated by agricultural or veterinary departments. Clearly, at this level of encounter the confrontation between bureaucracy and peasantry will find one of its most explicit expressions.

Opposite perspectives on 'penetration' are inevitably reflected in the treatment of linkage figures. Since in colonial Africa contact was frequently established through chiefs of various descriptions, it follows that they should have drawn more than usual attention in the literature. Chiefs indeed were often singled out for special interest. From a cultural perspective, concern might be with presumed role conflicts or with crises of loyalty and identity, all of which apparently added up to 'the predicament of the modern African chief', as Fallers first defined it.[10] Administrative interests were focused, quite pragmatically, on the operational utility of chiefs within bureaucratic frameworks: i.e. as 'brokers', negotiating between two worlds, systems or orientations, each with its own demands, sensitivities and expectations.

Examinations along cultural and administrative-structural lines were strongly interconnected: based on notions of dualism, and directed towards overcoming the constraints between different socio-cultural realities. What pertained to chiefs applied equally to other actors in the rural field. Model farmers, for example, selected as favoured clients of departments of agriculture, were typically seen as pioneering modern technologies amid traditional, parochial or apathetic environments. That premise is still widely held today. In support of these contact roles, diffusion theory has leant strongly on social psychology, communications techniques and other applied social sciences in developing improved methodologies for the neutralization of constraints.

If the issue of penetration is viewed from the opposite angle, chiefs and other contact agents themselves emerge as being part of the problem. Due to their relative visibility they may still get special attention, but they are more likely to be seen as the frontline of an oppressive and exploitative system whose purpose is to extract and control. Recruitment from below, through cooptation of client chiefs or progressive farmers, will do little to change this picture. In fact, it may be viewed as a way of buttressing the 'system' at the expense of grassroots interests if only because it syphons-off the latter's potential leaders. It should be borne in mind that material incentives and status expectations are powerful instruments with which to ensure the loyalty of coopted agents and their identification with the declared purposes and interests of government. Therefore, although the individuals concerned are exposed to demands and pressures by both sides, they are not likely to be subjected to chronic personal dilemmas. Such dilemmas, logical results of dualist theory, are hardly likely to emerge from variants of dependency theory.

Yet as we have seen, reality at this level can be both complex and subtle, obscuring some of the structural basis of the confrontation. Tactical consider-ations for safeguarding long-term political survival, for example, may well prompt a contact agent to play things both ways as long as he sees fit, or even at moments to favour the 'opposite' interest. Several examples of such subtle micro-politics are given by Lamb, Swartz, Mutiso and Harris. Again, as the eyes and ears of government on the rural development front, linkage figures may occasionally warn their superiors if they consider that the tribute or com-pliance demanded will exceed the tolerable or feasible. Therefore, when local people have some say in who will be recruited into contact positions, one criterion likely to be used in the assessment of a candidate is his willingness to stick his neck out. But this rarely becomes an exclusive criterion, since patron-age and prospective gain are commonly decisive factors. Intimately linked to this, structural relationships are often obscured by the capacity of contact agents to manipulate both sides to their own advantage. In all penetration strategies the middle-man's own interest is a crucial factor.

Clearly, then, penetrative contacts are not enacted in a vacuum, nor should they be treated as such. The reality of contact situations on the rural develop-ment front is determined strongly by social inequality and local class differen-tiation; by stagnation and impoverishment; and by the emergence and consoli-dation of new kulak categories. The local context is further conditioned by a complex of conflicting aspirations and ambitions, frustrations and demands; by an ambivalent mixture of old and new forms of patronage; and by the articu-lation of new and fluctuating political affinities and coalitions – chiefs with wealthy farmers, politicians with businessmen, central bureaucrats with local notables, for example. Other conflicting tendencies are exemplified within such contexts: the experimental nature of many programmes which imperil the security necessary in terms of farming routines; the gradual push towards institutionalization, substituting bureaucratic for representative roles and, again, the tendency to cream-off potential grassroots leadership by co-opting them into the state system.

The shifting power positions into which these processes are translated, with varying degrees of subtlety, form the core of the penetrative situation. These dynamics are the chief concern of many of the foregoing analyses and have provided the context in which various penetration strategies are implemented — policies and programmes officially declared to promote rural development. But here, too, local variations are significant. In some situations the dominant coalition is between kulaks and staff, as Thoden van Velzen and Leonard demonstrate — the staff favouring, and counting on, collaborative kulak farmers who assist them in the discharge of their penetrative functions. The emphasis is then on distributive benefits, situations of 'unequal access to public services', in Bernard Schaffer's term.[11]

In other cases there has tended to be more direct conflict of purpose between these categories, i.e. when wealthy farmers pre-empt government's capacity to implement particular programmes, or prevent government field officers from executing policies that would be unfavourable to themselves. Hyden and Lamb discuss such efforts to circumvent central policies aimed at more generalized objectives. In the Bukoba case, the landlords were fairly well connected with the party, the bureaucracy and the judiciary. In Murang'a, the dominant coalition was between better-off farmers and political representatives who helped to neutralize administrative policies through intervention at the centre. In the 'semi-underground' situation described by Mutiso this political connection was even stronger: the extractive bureaucracy was avoided and self-help projects were sponsored in lieu of those of the administration. Mafeje gives yet another variation. Different categories of Baganda farmers could expect different kinds of treatment from the central government and the Buganda government administration; they entered into alliances accordingly so long as political conditions seemed to make this a prudent strategy, but no longer than that.

The pattern of alliances is never identical, nor should this be expected. Lasswell's shorthand for politics, 'who gets what, when and how' might well be reformulated into 'who gets what, how, from whom', thus stressing varying opportunities, channels and coalitions without presupposing a single source of benefits and sanctions. Generalization is necessarily difficult at the micro level as its constellation is mostly determined elsewhere. Hence, a narrow search here for the 'single enemy' may prove illusory. But there is no doubt that the grassroots experiences in rural Kenya, Tanzania and Uganda provide variations on a theme, that of differently mediated confrontations between an organizing state and the peasantry. In all cases there has been a fair amount of carry-over and extrapolation from the colonial set-up — of penetration strategies, organizational forms and encounters, as well as corresponding 'contact' theories. And in all strategy choices, the bureaucracy is the principal implementing and initiating body. But this again raises the question of whether strategies have been, or actually can be, a matter of choice.

STRATEGY AS 'CHOICE' OR 'GIVEN'

Whether or not 'choice' of strategy refers to more than a figure of speech depends largely on the level of abstraction at which the question is explored. This is immediately evident if we turn from a micro to a more macro focus on the role of bureaucracy in East African rural development. At one level, several significant differences of strategy may be noted. Kenya's neo-colonialist pattern of capitalist development, Tanzania's attempts to move towards socialism, and Uganda's current military adventures, are strategic 'choices' of a sort. Again, in the rural context, these different strategies imply variations. It makes a difference, for example, whether in rural areas the bureaucracy is involved in matters like the development of *ujamaa* policy, as in Tanzania (irrespective of how that involvement has turned out); whether the rural scene is dominated by an assortment of corporals and privates turned chiefs, district officers or self-styled constables, as in Uganda; or whether, as in Kenya, a heavy provincial administration puts its colonially-derived mark and conception on any issue of 'rural development'. There is also a difference of norms. Though rural class differentiation is visible in all three countries, it is ultimately of significance whether that process is actively promoted through policy, as in the Kenyan case; whether it seems to occur despite declared objectives, as in Tanzania; or whether in the process a special bonus is reserved for particular groups, as for Uganda's military.

All these differences, then, have been a matter of 'choice' — at least if that notion is stretched to include the 'option' of a military takeover and the distinctive philosophies and styles of different ruling groups — which, if Arrighi and Saul are right, enjoy a certain autonomy and 'plastic' quality.[12] Beyond this, however, choice of strategy has been severely restricted by several basic 'givens', and in the end has often been rationalized accordingly. Notwithstanding the variations in style and approach to which we have referred, each of the East African countries has developed a rural development strategy which largely rests on, emanates from, and is implemented by the bureaucracy. In each case the state operates as a kind of 'macro' entrepreneur, in a sense that far exceeds the running of public enterprises or other specific economic ventures. The East African countries have of course become increasingly involved with foreign capital, in tourism, arms, selected manufacturing, agribusiness and other activities, each signifying additional economic roles for the state and bureaucracy. But for the vast majority of the East African population, the dominant politico-economic relationship continues to be that of an extractive bureaucracy vis-à-vis peasant production. It is that relationship with which we are concerned here, and for which Furnivall's term of a 'business concern' is perhaps still the most appropriate.

We should guard against the implication that the bureaucracy, even with regard to this more limited field, is a single-purpose monolith. In all situations, various levels of difference and conflict can be found within the bureaucracy: among departments, policy orientations, or membership categories such as 'comprador' generalists versus technocrats. Significantly, when transposed into the context of a strongly externally-oriented underdeveloped country, some of these differences acquire additional depth due to the manner in which staff/line, generalist/specialist categories relate to outside counterparts, contractors, and foreign business generally. Yet for various purposes we must and can abstract from internal differences and treat the role of bureaucracy vis-à-vis rural development as an analytic 'whole'. In regard to each of the East African cases it is evident that the bureaucracy seeks to stimulate and control peasant production, mainly in order to reach an optimal level of exportable produce. Aside from specific issues and confrontations in the local context, there does not seem to be an *a priori* opposition of interests between technical departments and the general administration. Much of the evidence in this volume underscores the extractive functions to which these various branches contribute. Helleiner demonstrates that price manipulation can be a crucial part of the incentive structure. At the end of the cycle, government intervenes again in the production process through marketing boards or equivalent arrangements and enjoys a controlled monopoly in selling the product on the international market.

Essentially, then, these mechanisms ensure that the surplus produced through peasant farming will be levelled-off, re-channelled and indirectly utilized to meet the main item on the national budget: maintenance of the government apparatus. Thus, if we consider the externally-oriented nature of peasant-based economies on the one hand, and the pivotal position of the bureaucracy within the 'formal' employment sector on the other, there appears to be a hard core of empirical validity to affirm an operative principle of 'the greatest surplus to the greatest usurper'. In this respect, the uses made of Tanzania's *ujamaa* policies have not been essentially different to those of Kenya and Uganda. Political strategies towards mutual readjustment of agricultural and industrial production processes, and thus towards generation of internal and popular-oriented development have basically been lacking. Instead, policies remain by and large oriented towards the same, outward-directed processes, differing only in approach, style, or mode of extraction.

Given this central role of the bureaucracy, 'strategy' appears discretional in only a very limited sense. In each option the bureaucracy takes on the role of planner, executor and controller. In each case, too, the expanding bureaucracy is virtually dependent for its own upkeep on the way in which it is inserted into the production process. Any fundamental redirection of that process towards internally-linked production relations, might easily imply a threat to the bureaucracy's basis of existence. Presumably this is why *ujamaa* policies are now geared towards stepping-up export production just as much as Kenya's measures towards rural 'mobilization'. The erratic interference by Uganda's military, both locally and nationally, probably constitutes the most serious disturbance of these patterns of extraction. Nonetheless, that involvement signifies no more than the military's increasingly competitive demands for a share of the surplus; it does not alter the basic trend towards bureaucratic dominance and further bureaucratization.

No wonder, then, that Michels' 'iron law' remains pertinent to an understanding of the contemporary East African scene, or that 'grassroots' comparisons between East African states continue to be made as plausible propositions — without too many complications due to divergent political strategies. It is not merely that any rural development policy is translated into bureaucratic terms and categories, posing comparable issues of 'contact' in the field. Bureaucratic interest is added to bureaucratic style, and together they define the reality of 'penetration'.

Accordingly, these dimensions have to be borne in mind when linking macro and micro perspectives and evidence. For example, we have noted the occurrence of different configurations in relationships between better-off farmers and the bureaucracy in the field. In various contexts the bureaucracy figures as the dominant element in this reciprocity, while in other situations local kulaks emerge as the stronger party of the two. But if the symbiosis is often uneasy, it is nonetheless there, based on connections of mutual benefit and dependency. Again, on the macro plane, convergence of interests must be placed next to any apparent opposition. If kulaks figure as 'compradors' in the local context, it is the bureaucracy that assumes comprador qualities at the national level. This is not necessarily contradictory, but reflects the different ways in which these elements are linked into a single process. It is also largely due to the central role of the bureaucracy in rural development that many of the *kinds* of issues reviewed in this volume have emerged: the discussion of receptivity to government programmes, questions of proper organizational linkages and organizational sensitivity — indeed, the very notion of penetration. A wider connection suggests itself, namely, that East Africa has long appeared to provide a fertile ground for policy-oriented 'applied' social science. Certainly for much of the 1960s and thereafter, many sociologists, economists, political scientists and anthropologists tended to be concerned with the operations of government in the field, trying to identify the sort of bottlenecks, gaps and dislocations on the one hand, and appropriate modifications and reforms on the other, which were derived from a vision of optimal functioning of the system as it was constituted.

Yet the bureaucracy, while having its own interest and enjoying a fair degree of autonomy, is not the sole determinant of politico-economic mechanisms. Various external and internal forces have a bearing on current tendencies and on the position of the bureaucracy. They include international market forces and quota arrangements, organizational plan requirements stipulated by donor agencies, the demands of multinationals engaged in agribusiness, and the increasing pressures for land saleability and related local forces for change that are associated with the spread of capitalist commodity production. To a certain extent these pressures have been slowed down in Tanzania by political forces favouring a socialist direction of change, but in Kenya and Uganda such countering has not been evident, not even during Uganda's abortive experimentation with the 'Move to the Left' in Obote's final year. While generalization is hazardous, there is little to indicate that the bureaucracies have *not* been receptive to these external and internal influences. Circumstantial evidence rather appears to corroborate a coincidence of interests in this regard, and a more ready inclination to oppose 'socialist' experiments which threaten bureaucratic privilege.

Still, 'given' is not synonymous with 'constant'. Continuity of bureaucratic forms and the bureaucracy's continuing involvement in policy-making do not define bureaucratic power, interest or orientation. They may give the bureaucracy a certain 'access' advantage to political resources. But its political base is primarily contextually determined, and of crucial importance is the particular way in which the bureaucracy is inserted within the general class structure and relates to the major socio-political conflicts within that context. Over time, new pressures on the bureaucracy constantly lead to redefinition and renewal of its political position, and its 'given' position must be understood against the background of changing political configurations. Thus, fluctuations have no doubt occurred in the power position of the Uganda bureaucracy between the Baganda-dominated 1960s and the present day. Likewise, orientations in the Tanzanian bureaucracy have evolved into new — though no more facilitative — givens as a result of a mixture of austerity and conscientization efforts on the one hand, and of a strengthened command position in rural mobilization on the other. In Kenya, reorientations that have reshaped the givens refer in particular to the increasingly central role which is officially accorded to the cash nexus in agricultural production relationships.

By implication it follows that the political role and position of the bureaucracy varies significantly from one context to another. In contrast to the various East African configurations, for example, several Latin American and other settings offer considerably less scope for the political involvement of the bureaucracy: with fewer policy processes channelled through the bureaucracy and its general size and manpower budget more limited, there is less chance that bureaucratic interest and power will figure independently as a variable. Besides, a less entrenched and less powerful bureaucracy appears to be in principle more easily manoeuverable and more responsive to new directives.

The costs may then lie elsewhere, but at least the contrast underscores the implications of a centrally placed bureaucracy that politically is its own constituency.

The dominant role of the bureaucracy inevitably raises questions and dilemmas, one of the most crucial of which is the question of control, a variant to 'who rules the rulers', which here is necessarily focused on the bureaucracy. The weakness of political control and the lack of effective party organization only enhance the dominance of the bureaucracy. Closely linked are questions about participation and popular involvement, recurrent themes in socio-political discussion. After noting the empirical fact that this involvement has not become effective, and that the dominant trend in all three East African countries has been one of increased bureaucratization and centralization, it must be asked whether *a priori* the frequent concern with participation is not really a non-issue. The logic of an organizing state whose centrality is vital to its own existence ultimately appears to leave very little room for participatory politics. Indeed, much of what existed by way of popular representation has been eroded away in recent years. The question appears to be whether the requirements of export-oriented economies based on peasant production are not likely to induce a progressive tightening-up of organizational forms in order to approximate these given strategies, thus further reducing the scope for any attempt at alternative policies such as those of Tanzania.

Finally, the role of the state as entrepreneur. Under the characteristic East African circumstances of vast income differentials and a largely consumption-oriented bureaucratic establishment, the question is who or what will ensure surplus reinvestment for productive purposes. This issue is extremely pertinent for although there are relatively few historical examples of successful state capitalism, mainly East European, it is doubtful whether the conditions of the East African states are even remotely comparable. In situations where there can be no question of bypassing, let alone of bringing down the predominant bureaucracy, prospects are rather of bureaucratic politics with involution as a main characteristic.

If the long-term chances for genuine development along the lines of the present trajectory are far from reassuring, the scope for alternative strategies seems small indeed. The very nature of the 'chosen' strategies and their powerful traditions make any shift towards a truly peasant-oriented route of development extremely unlikely if not inconceivable. The pull of bureaucratization processes, notwithstanding *declared* policies to the contrary, is a cardinal factor. The lack of realistic conceptions of processes and structures for development from below is another. Meanwhile, the spell of rapid social mobility for some has largely expired, and further consolidation of newly-gained rural class positions must be anticipated. Any concluding note on the prospects for progressive rural development in East Africa is thus bound to be pessimistic. In the absence of processes or potential for the social mobilization that is a prerequisite to ongoing transformation, the prospect is one of a bureaucracy-dominated pattern of relative rural stagnation, in which the question of strategic 'choice' is illusory.

'PENETRATION' IN RETROSPECT

Looking back to the beginnings of the exercise presented in this volume, i.e. the late 1960s when the project was first conceived, it is somewhat surprising if not ironic that the *concern* then should have been with the 'penetration' of government into society. No matter how 'incomplete' that process might still have been, one awareness which is brought home by the analyses presented here is precisely *how* established the central presence is, and has been. The 'centre' may have been weak in an absolute sense, as Zolberg argues,[13] but in a relative sense it has proven to be extremely powerful within the East African context. Many structures were carried over and have been expanded since colonial times, and very few groups have escaped the influence of the central presence. In retrospect, one cannot but wonder why various structural continuities — at least as far as the centre's presence is concerned — were so insufficiently recognized and under-estimated. While it was partly through involvement in these empirical studies that we began to appreciate the importance of wider contextual constraints, future research should be largely devoted to the systematic analysis of these dimensions, to a testing of the mechanisms at work, and to the exploration of the scope for manoeuvre.

NOTES

1.   J.S. Furnivall, *Colonial Policy and Practice: a comparative study of Burma and Netherlands India* (Cambridge, 1948), Chs. 8 and 11.
2.   Everett Rogers, *Modernization Among Peasants* (New York, 1969).
3.   A.B. Mafeje, 'The Fallacy of Dual Economies Revisited', in *Dualism and Rural Development in East Africa* (Institute for Development Research, Denmark, 1973).
4.   E.A. Brett, *Colonialism and Underdevelopment in East Africa* (London, 1973).
5.   Gunnar Myrdal, *The Challenge of World Poverty* (Harmondsworth, 1970).
6.   Caroline Hutton and Robin Cohen, 'African Peasants and Resistance to Change: a Reconsideration of Sociological Approaches', in Ivar Oxaal et al (eds), *Beyond the Sociology of Development* (London, 1975).
7.   This concept is developed in Raymond Apthorpe: 'Peasants and Planistrators', *Institute of Development Studies Bulletin*, Vol. I, No. 3 (1969), and further elaborated in 'Peasants and Planistrators in Eastern Africa 1960-1970', in D. Pitt (ed): *Development from Below* (The Hague, Mouton, 1976), 21-55.
8.   Roberto Michels, *Political Parties* (Glencoe, Ill, 1949).
9.   Frantz Fanon, *The Wretched of the Earth* (Harmondsworth, 1967).
10.   L. Fallers, 'The Predicament of the Modern African Chief', *American Anthropologist*, 57, 2 (1955).
11.   Bernard Schaffer and Huang Wen-hsien, 'Distribution and the Theory of Access', *Development and Change*, 6, 2 (1975).

12. Giovanni Arrighi and John Saul, *Essays on the Political Economy of Africa* (New York, 1973), Ch. 1.
13. Aristide Zolberg, *Creating Political Order* (Chicago, 1966).